Out of Bedlam

Out of Bedlam

The Truth About Deinstitutionalization

ANN BRADEN JOHNSON

BasicBooks
A Division of HarperCollins*Publishers*

Library of Congress Catalog-in-Publication Data
Johnson, Ann Braden, 1945–
   Out of bedlam: myths of deinstitutionalization/Ann
Braden Johnson.
      p.   cm.
   Includes bibliographical references (p.).
   ISBN 0–465–05427–7 (cloth)
   ISBN 0–465–05428–5 (paper)
   1. Mentally ill—Deinstitutionalization—United States.
I. Title.
RC439.5.J64   1990   90–80253
362.2'0422—dc20   CIP

For Christopher

CONTENTS

PREFACE

———◆———

I HAVE BEEN working as a "mental health professional"—in my case, a social worker—for more than fifteen years, chiefly with the chronically mentally ill. Because I got my first job as a professional in 1974, all of my work has taken place in the era of deinstitutionalization, and as it happens, all of my jobs have been part of programs designed specifically to fulfill some part of the goals implicit in the notion of community-based care for the seriously mentally ill.

My career, therefore, has been shaped by the events and ideas and fantasies that we refer to whenever we speak of "deinstitutionalization." I have worked for state mental hospitals, both on inpatient wards and in day hospitals based in "the community;" and I have worked in outpatient clinics so hidden away in residential neighborhoods that they were located, unmarked, in churches. I have worked for a freestanding vocational program for "higher-functioning" chronic mental patients; and I have worked for a child welfare agency that had diversified to include a program for chronically mentally ill adults. I have even worked for a private hospital that provided medical and psychiatric care to people in jail.

In some of these jobs, I was a line worker, a "primary therapist," which meant that I had a caseload of people to take care of in various ways. In others, I supervised staff and managed programs of differing sizes and kinds, all of which, I realize now, were related in that each of them had been created by "the system" to fill a gap caused by the removal of crazy people from state mental hospitals to the real world. As a line worker, I naturally focused on my patients and their needs, which was a relatively straightforward task, if sometimes difficult to achieve; but as a program manager, I quickly found that the fundamental goal of most treatment facilities is not to treat patients but to control deviants on behalf of an outside authority. Nothing in my clinical training had prepared me for this shift in perspective.

Next, I learned—the hard way—that a program's client is *never* the patient but *always* the funding source, no matter what the program's mission statement says. As a worker, I had concentrated on getting my patients what they needed, but as an administrator, I had to master a whole new approach: I had to learn how to do with, not for, the patients what it was the state or the city or Medicaid required. These aims were not always compatible with patients' needs, and sometimes seemed entirely contradictory. Here is an example—the very incident that taught me the facts of life in the world of mental health, as it happens.

I used to direct a community-based program intended to get mental health services to the residents of adult homes, most of whom were elderly, all of whom were quite deranged, and some of whom were physically handicapped to boot. My program and the homes were separately funded, separately monitored, and only very loosely interrelated, chiefly through a rather tenuous network of city, state, and federal agencies stuck with bureaucratic responsibility for the chronically mentally ill. My job was to see that our program took care of the mental health needs of the residents of the homes, all of them ex–state hospital patients, which meant we were supposed to keep them out of the hospital.

One day I happened to see a very frail, elderly, blind woman purchase a cup of coffee from the informal snack bar run in the home by an enterprising resident. It is hard to communicate the value of this purchase, except to say that the price—fifty cents—represented one-half her daily allowance. I saw the woman put her coffee down while she resumed her seat in the lobby. The second she took her hand off the cup, a particularly nasty old man grabbed it and took it to another room, where he quickly drank the coffee in one greedy gulp. The woman felt around for her cup, failed to find it, and sat back in mute resignation: clearly, this had happened before. Horrified, I turned to the home's front desk, where the staff on duty had watched the whole thing. "Oh, he always does that," said one in a tired voice. "We can't get him to stop; he just spits and swears if you try to talk to him." Knowing this to be true, I went to find the home's owner-manager to see if he had any ideas about how we could prevent the old man from taking advantage of his fellow resident. The owner seemed uninterested and muttered something about needing "proof," although he did point out that I could always call the state regulators if I was really concerned: "They're the only ones who can really do anything." I was too naive in those days to realize that when one authority defers to another, it's probably because he doesn't want to be bothered with the problem, so I called one of the regulators. He, in turn, made it clear that he was bored to tears by such a trivial complaint and suggested that his office, like the home's management, had no right to meddle in the residents' private affairs.

What I learned from this experience is that it is hard to get anyone in charge of programs to address the needs of an individual. As long as the home did its job, which was to house the chronically mentally ill at a cheap rate, the regulators were happy and wouldn't look too closely at how they did things. As long as the homes ran smoothly and stayed out of the newspapers, the regulators looked good and no one asked too many questions about how they functioned. And as long as my program kept its patients out of hospitals, our sponsors were satisfied and didn't get overly concerned about how we achieved their aim. No one, except bleeding hearts like me, got too worked up about a little thing like the theft of a cup of coffee from one psycho by another, even if the victim was blind. "So what? What's fifty cents? For God's sake! We're talking about a $50 million program here, and you're worried about fifty lousy cents!"

A friend and colleague considers this dilemma an example of the irony that statistics have neither meaning nor relevance when applied to individuals or single cases. Our mental health system, however, is based entirely on big numbers and is run by people whose job it is to manipulate them, people who don't much care about single individuals and their needs, which they dismiss as "anecdotal" and "unscientific data." To them, it matters if 100,000 people, say, can be shown conclusively to share a problem, because then you can *address* this demonstrated *need* with a *program initiative*.

So you can, but program initiatives do not necessarily take care of *people*, and that is what we have been seeing, thanks to deinstitutionalization. The people who left the hospitals had, and have, very real needs, but they are often singular and even idiosyncratic needs. I, for one, have yet to encounter the publicly funded program initiative that could adapt to singularity, much less idiosyncrasy. Our programs are so narrowly defined and so closely targeted to so specialized a group of populations that far too many people—often the neediest cases—"fall through the cracks."

Once I figured out that many programs implemented as part of deinstitutionalization didn't fit real patients, I started to see the problem everywhere. Convinced that there had to be a rational explanation that I simply hadn't spotted yet, I determined to study the precipitants to deinstitutionalization in a scholarly way. I did this by talking to people who had been in on the ground floor of community mental health development, reading the theory on which their work was based, and plowing through all kinds of reports and memos and budget documents of the sort that emerge in a steady stream from bureaucracies. What I found was puzzling.

Deinstitutionalization, that rational-sounding process, was never planned, nor was it even named until twenty years after it happened. What's more, it had *nothing* to do with what patients did or didn't need, and everything to do with money. Even the wonder drugs like Thorazine, which to this day we assume made deinstitutionalization possible, turned out to have become available only after the patients began their exodus and were in fact exploited by the states to speed up the process. Also exploited, at the same time, was a genuine desire on the part of many people to spare untold thousands of mental patients the horrors of the snakepit. The irony of deinstitutionalization, I decided, was that even as it represented a self-serving, politically motivated, fiscally oriented move on the part of government to rid itself of an unrewarding and expensive public burden, so too it reflected a high-minded, idealistic, happy faith in our society's willingness to tolerate the presence of the bizarre and the deviant. Deinstitutionalization was a movement at once cynical and idealistic, political and utopian, fiscally conservative and therapeutically daring. It was a great social experiment, and we are still trying to figure out if it worked.

That is how I, as a scholar, assessed deinstitutionalization. As a clinician, I see it as more dysfunctional. The patients I see don't fit readily into most existing programs, and programs they might fit in simply don't exist. Bureaucrats who dream up programs often have never seen a patient, much less treated one. Clinicians are taught to distort records of their activities in order to make regulators happy. Diagnosis is made by formula, nearly everyone is on medication, no one can get into a hospital, and we're still waiting for promised community-based alternatives to long-term hospitalization to materialize. We struggle along from day to day, doing the best we can in a huge, impersonal, fragmented, expensive system that meets no needs but its own.

I wrote this book to try to make sense out of my own disparate and paradoxical findings. I have decided that a lot of our assumptions about deinstitutionalization, like our assumptions about crazy people, are faulty in the extreme and have propelled us into making truly stupid policies; and I have tried to pin down just where it is we went off the track, where we made our mistakes, where we went a little crazy ourselves.

One of the reasons I like working with chronic mental patients is that they realize they are unrewarding cases for most professionals and are faintly apologetic about the fact. For that matter, chronic mental patients are both more realistic about their condition and more graceful in failure than the rest of us are, for their forced detachment from the normal world the rest of us inhabit has given them the wisdom that comes with tolerance of the inevitable: they know their condition is hopeless and are prepared to cope with it on that basis. We, however, are grandiose and ambitious and driven to find a cure, a foolproof method of treatment, the perfect modality, the one true solution. In our haste to do so, we have grasped at straws, dressed our emperors in invisible clothes, and based our technology on the fantastic—and that is why we have made so many mistakes. Unable or unwilling to face the fact of our own failures, we have made things worse for everybody by blaming the patients and their illness, as if they didn't have enough problems already.

ACKNOWLEDGMENTS

I WROTE THIS book because I got tired of listening to the following question from well-meaning but insensitive colleagues: "But you're so *good!* Why would you want to work with chronic schizophrenics? Why waste your talents on *them?*" My colleagues are for the most part nice, intelligent people who are devoted to righting society's wrongs and rooting out social injustice whenever and wherever they can; they recycle, wear fake furs, avoid red meat, and give money to the homeless. Nevertheless, they take a dim view of work with chronic mental patients and seem unable to understand why I would choose to do it.

The truth is, I didn't choose the work; it chose me. Chronically mentally ill people have showed me things I never would have known; they have told me things most people never hear; and they continually amaze me with their generosity and kindness toward each other and to an outside world that treats them like lepers. They have forced me to acknowledge parts of myself I'd rather not even look at, and I am deeply grateful. They have given me so much over the years that I want to do anything I can to pay them back by showing others what I have learned. This book is partial repayment to Willie B., Paul M., Robert G., Robert N., Steve O., Philip B., Diane M., John, Joe, Leslie, Albert, Lionel, Mary, Carmen, Howard, Eileen, Kathy G., and hundreds more whose names I have forgotten. I wish I could have done more.

Naturally, I had a lot of help from people who are not chronically mentally ill. I owe particular debts to Aaron Esman, M.D., who helped me see that I could write and had something to say; to John Oldham, M.D., for suggesting the device of myths as a way to look at deinstitutionalization (and for other things); to Heather Brandon, Ph.D., for shoring up my flagging spirits at a *very* low point; to my brother, William Braden, Esq., for finding, delivering, and installing my computer so I could write on it; and to Jo Ann Miller of Basic Books for believing in my material even when it was in rather primitive form. At East Facility, Susan Seidman, Ph.D., and Willie Martin, Jr., made generous gifts of their knowledge and time; and Peter Stastny, M.D., read the chapter on psychotropic medication at an early stage and made enormously useful suggestions. I received lots of free assistance from librarians, a group of which I am a great admirer in general; one librarian in particular stands out—Vernon Bruette, formerly of Montefiore Hospital Medical Library, now director of Harlem Hospital Medical Library.

Then there are my friends and my family, all of whom put up with my absentmindedness, impatience, inattention, and, in the case of my family, absence on Saturdays and evenings. Of this group, my husband deserves particular credit, for he is the one who listened to my anxious doubts, read all the drafts of the parts I had trouble writing, and kept our household intact throughout. I thank you all and I hope it was worth it.

News from the Front
in the War Against Mental Illness

*A*IDA SANCHEZ* was twenty-nine *years old, single, and Hispanic, with a lifetime history of what appeared to be mental illness, although the source of her symptoms was not entirely clear. She had a history of cocaine abuse, mental retardation, severe head injuries sustained in childhood, and many chronic symptoms generally associated with schizophrenia; these included constant visual and auditory hallucinations of the devil, who reportedly commanded her to do bad things or "got inside" and commanded her to swallow inedible objects. Thanks to this last directive, Aida had had most of her large bowel surgically removed, and she had recently been told by our medical staff that should she continue to swallow foreign objects, she would probably have to wear a colostomy bag for the rest of her life. Aida's problems did not stop here: she was also homeless, spoke very poor English, and was actively psychotic most of the time. What's more, she had an intimidating criminal record stemming from several episodes of assaultive behavior of a particularly dramatic sort: she had once pushed a stranger in front of a subway train and had on another occasion been stopped by hospital attendants as she was about to cut open the abdomen of a fellow mental patient "to see what was inside."*

In 1988, Aida Sanchez was in jail on New York City's Rikers Island, serving

---

*Although this is a true story, identifying information has been altered.

time for an assault charge stemming from an incident that had occurred during her escape from a large state mental hospital where she had lived for the past ten years. The criminal justice system being what it is, on the day that Aida "topped out," or completed her sentence, she was free to go, period. This meant she would go back to the streets of New York City, with two subway tokens and the clothes on her back.

Aida Sanchez the inmate was also Aida Sanchez the patient, treated while in jail by a large New York City hospital that provides medical and psychiatric care to the inmate population. As the mental health staff responsible for her jail-based care, we wanted to ensure a reasonable disposition for her after she left jail. Our options, unhappily, were extraordinarily limited. Had we wanted to arrange for her to live in a shelter for the homeless, for example, which was not our first choice, she would have had to go to the appropriate welfare office first, and we had no reason to think she would, or maybe even could, do so on her own. We knew that her family was fed up with her, and in fact Aida herself was so angry at her mother that she had long since changed both her first and last names—this, by the way, meant that much of her institutional history was unavailable to anyone who did not know all her names, and the only reason we did was that one of our staff had recognized her from the state mental hospital. No psychiatric day program, supervised apartment program, or halfway house would ever consider a referral like this one, if only because of the patient's criminal record; but even if the details of Aida's history were not so daunting, such programs enjoy a seller's market, so what few beds there are available invariably go to more compliant, more appealing patients with better prognoses. Any way you look at it, Aida had absolutely nothing going for her.

We had particular worries about this case. For one thing, the eight or nine months in jail had not seen much of an improvement in her symptoms or her behavior. For another, as mentioned, her history included several incidents of serious assaults on others, two of which had led to periods of incarceration. The current incarceration had come about because Aida had run away from the mental hospital and had wandered the streets for about ten days, cadging money any way she could in order to buy cocaine to get high; and we had no reason to think this release was likely to end any differently, except maybe worse. From our work with her, we knew the patient to be impulsive, self-destructive, given to episodes of violent aggressiveness, incapable of insight, and hampered by exceptionally poor judgment. We could see the headline: "Psycho Slays Mom in Subway Horror."

Stuck for a disposition, we decided to take a long shot: we would try to convince the state hospital where Aida had lived for the last decade to take her back, on the grounds that first, she had been arrested within thirty days of her leaving the hospital, and thus should be readmitted automatically; and second, we argued, the hospital should take her back because she should not have been discharged in the first place but should have been placed on something called "escape status," since she had wandered away from their custody. Technically, we figured, she was still their responsibility.

We decided that a psychiatrist should make the actual calls to the hospital to try to arrange readmission, partly to lend maximum authority to our communication and partly because the doctor in question had extensive and recent experience working within the state hospital system. We hoped to capitalize on his intimate knowledge of their vulnerabilities, and we secretly hoped he might come across a colleague he knew personally; because in a case like this, the slightest edge can make the difference, no matter how irrelevant it may seem to the patient's treatment. However, we didn't get lucky: the state hospital proved unresponsive and more than capable of outmaneuvering us on the technical points we made about the timing and nature of the patient's discharge. At no point did anyone we talked to acknowledge or take any interest in even a single detail of the patient's clinical picture—not her symptoms, nor her behavior, nor the life-threatening nature of her object swallowing, nor even the very great risk she posed to others when assaultive. Instead, the entire conversation turned on the details of her status as a case, a number, an institutional being; the faceless hospital administrators could not have been less interested in the patient herself. In fact, although the psychiatrist at our end had specifically asked to speak to the psychiatrist at the hospital in charge of clinical services, the call never even got there but was handled by a woman in charge of the admissions office, someone who was clearly very skilled at her job but who was a clerk, not a clinician. What was at stake, obviously, was not some mentally ill person's need for services but a technical question of liability and accountability. In the end, we had the body, so we had the case. Period.

As it worked out, we had to settle for a complicated arrangement with the city hospital nearest the jail, one they weren't too happy with, which involved their admitting Aida to the forensic ward until her sentence ended, whereupon they would transfer her to their "civil ward," whose entirely separate staff was supposed to transfer her to yet another state hospital. There were no guarantees that this would work and plenty of opportunities for failure implicit in the arrangement, but it was the best we could come up with and had cost us only about ten hours of meetings with various oversight agencies, which is not too bad, we kept telling ourselves. Aida got as far as the forensic ward, only to be returned to jail unexpectedly at the eleventh hour, because the probation department had discovered some outstanding warrants that would keep her in the state prison for another several months. As far as I know, that is where she is today, waiting to be discharged to the street with two subway tokens and the clothes on her back.

This is a book about deinstitutionalization, the name given after the fact to a process generally assumed to have taken place in the 1960s, when all our state mental hospitals are supposed to have opened their doors so that legions of mental patients could stream forth to take their rightful place in "the community," wherever that is. Depending on how one looks at it, this was either a very good thing, in that a large group of people whose choices in life had been very limited suddenly had other options, or a very bad thing, in that deranged and even dangerous people were let loose to do God only knew what in the streets of decent neighborhoods. The mentally ill had apparently acquired the freedom to live normal lives outside institutions, places that historically had proven to be less than therapeutic and not even safe. Implicit in our newfound regard for the rights of the mentally ill to exercise some control over their lives was the assumption that society at large had grown more tolerant of deviance—enough, anyway, to be able to stand the presence of chemically controlled former patients in the neighborhoods they had grown up in. All in all, deinstitutionalization represented an enlightened view of what is, after all, a terrible condition some people have or get, certainly not by choice—it's not their *fault* they're crazy, so why lock them up?

Of course, it didn't work out quite that way. Depopulation of the state mental hospitals did indeed take place, but not really because more enlightened public attitudes toward the mentally ill made it possible to relocate them to more suitable settings within the community—it took place because the states couldn't afford to provide lifetime care for a huge and growing chronic caseload inside enormous, crumbling hospitals built in the nineteenth century, which proved to be extremely expensive to run at twentieth-century prices. Once free of their time-honored burden of chronic patients, the state hospitals turned out to be very good at keeping it that way. The medical technology that had been heralded as newly available to make the chronically mentally ill manageable, if not well—technology that really only amounted to medication that had to be taken two or three times a day—turned out to be less than perfect in and of itself: long-term use was shown to cause irreversible side effects in an unsettling number of cases; and inconveniently, patients didn't necessarily like taking it, and often stopped, once free of the controls of the hospital. And then there was the problem of where to house the mentally ill after they got out: the earliest discharges returned to their families, but over the years it took to empty out the back wards, hospitals gradually lowered their standards for acceptable sites to transfer their patients to, so that what had begun as the enthusiastic return of the successfully treated to their family homes wound up looking more like the cynical dumping of the unwanted and untreatable in someone else's backyard.

As its failures surfaced, sometime in the 1970s, deinstitutionalization got its name and acquired its bad reputation. Until it proved to be less than a success, the movement to resettle the mentally ill in more normal settings had attracted little attention outside the mental health and public policy fields, because as a general rule mental illness is one of those things that most people would rather not think about. As long as the mentally ill were locked up in state hospitals, the public hadn't had to think about them very much, if at all. Once the patients were out, though, all this changed, probably forever. Mental illness became a regular feature of daily life, whether in the heartrending form of the homeless mentally ill living desperate, miserable lives in public, or in the terrifying form of the unpredictable "psycho" who suddenly appears with a machete and slices up innocent travelers trapped with him on a ferryboat.

Just as the previously unconcerned general public was getting accustomed to the idea of living with ex–mental patients in the community, the weaknesses in the system of care supposedly in place to cope with them were exposed by its failures. Not only was the much-touted medication less than efficacious over the long term, but so was the community mental health center network heralded in 1962 by President John Kennedy as a "bold new approach" to the age-old problem of mental disorder. When we looked to the network to cope with the chronic caseload, it wasn't built yet or it wasn't interested in treating psychotic patients, or it was out of federal money even as its services were most desperately needed. The expense to the public of caring for the chronic caseload in state hospitals was not, as it turned out, eliminated by deinstitutionalization, because the bulk of the former patients by far were simply transferred from one expensive form of institutional care to another—the nursing home, paid for chiefly by federal money, courtesy of Medicare and Medicaid.

The fact of the matter is that some people do not function very well on their own in society. This is not news, nor should it ever have been news to psychiatric caregivers that people as poorly equipped for public life as the chronically mentally ill often fail in their genuine, if sometimes inscrutable, attempts to live independent lives in a world they do not understand and cannot negotiate effectively. Nevertheless, years of research efforts have failed to turn up any evidence to suggest that living in a mental institution can impart the knowledge and skills necessary to function anywhere *but* in a mental institution, the true purpose of which has always been to protect the rest of us from its caseload of deviants. What the mentally ill used to do behind the closed doors of the state hospital, they are now able to do in full view of the rest of us, in the streets or in public buildings; and as a consequence, we are all learning what state hospital workers have always known: mental illness is not a pretty sight. Ignoring this reality for the fact that it is, we have chosen instead to blame its visibility on deinstitutionalization.

No term with so elastic an application nor so fuzzy a meaning as *deinstitutionalization* can possibly convey very much in the way of reliable information; even more, the term *sounds* so rational and technical that it is easy to miss the fact that its greatest contribution to the language has been as a symbol for our shared anxiety and fear in the face of that which is least logical and rational—psychotic behavior. The truth is that what we have since come to call deinstitutionalization was never a policy, nor was it planned and deliberate, nor is it a cause of much of anything it has since come to be blamed for. We are only fooling ourselves when we use the term to try to explain why a universal human problem won't simply go away.

This brings me back to Aida Sanchez. Surely, if there were ever a patient in need of some form of controlled environment, whether for her own protection or for ours, it is poor, homeless, retarded, psychotic, addicted, impulsive, deluded Aida Sanchez, yet in 1988, we felt as if we stood a better chance of getting her into Harvard Medical School than we did the state mental hospital that had been her home for ten years. Whatever deinstitutionalization had been supposed to accomplish, it cannot have been this—a staff of competent, experienced, and sophisticated mental health professionals totally unable to arrange the only appropriate level of treatment for a potentially dangerous and self-destructive mental patient with a seventeen-year history of mental illness and a ten-year history of treatment for that illness, with the mental health professionals rescued at the last second by the ultimate in total institutions: state prison. What makes this story even worse is that it is only a particularly dramatic instance of something that happens in the mental health business every day, over and over again: the system doesn't work the way it is supposed to, and whole parts of it use the twin slogans of deinstitutionalization and community-based care as excuses to avoid doing their jobs, for fear they'll get caught with too many long-term cases again. Deinstitutionalization, which is something that began in hope and optimism some thirty-five years ago, when we really did think we were about to cure mental illness, is foundering on the rocks of opportunism and a cumulative overreliance on the short-term political solution for social problems that are in fact eternal and universal.

What exactly did go wrong? Was deinstitutionalization a failure by design, the wrong thing to do, or was it a failure in execution, a good idea misapplied?

Was it an idea whose time had not yet come, or an idea whose time has come and already gone? In order to answer questions about the origin of the phenomenon, it is helpful to look at three admittedly complicated things: the history of deinstitutionalization, the nature of mental illness, and the nature of the mental health system. Further, to understand the failure of deinstitutionalization as currently implemented, it is necessary to appreciate the fact that the people who treat mental illness probably understand the condition but almost certainly don't understand the system or how it got to be the way it is, even as the people who run the bureaucracy have a clear picture of the nature of the system and not one clue as to what mental illness is really like. Because of this pointless split between those who know how to do the work and those who control how it gets done, we have seen a gradual proliferation of myths, legends, and faulty assumptions on both sides, fond beliefs that the bureaucracy uses to design huge, expensive policy initiatives that are doomed to failure because they don't fit the population, and by practitioners to justify doing things the way they always have done them, whether that fits into the grand design of public policy or not.

Sadly, it is not just the uninformed general public who have misapplied the term *deinstitutionalization* not only to cover its roots in public policy but also to explain its disastrous fallout in prominent social failures like homelessness. What we understand as deinstitutionalization is a phenomenon with its basis chiefly in untested assumptions, magical thinking, and anecdotes and legends; moreover, it appears that those responsible for making what mental health policy we do have are among the most faithful believers in those myths. For just as the debate over whether Aida Sanchez should be readmitted to the state hospital never focused on her illness or her needs for care, so our mental health policy has long since ceased to have very much to do with patients, their problems, or their care in any real way. Like *deinstitutionalization*, a term created after the fact but now variously used to describe and explain events that occurred at very different times, our view of the treatment of the chronically mentally ill is so haphazard and so defensive that we have lost track of what it is all about and who it is for. Somewhere along the line, a lot of hospitals and clinics and specialized programs seem to have lost interest in the problems of people who don't have the skills to function on their own; instead, those institutions have gotten themselves caught up in a spiraling effort to protect themselves through defensive maneuvers designed to ward off the blame for failing to control the behavior of people who can't function on their own, mostly by avoiding working with them at all. How this happened is an interesting phenomenon, as are the myths and legends on which it was, and still is, based.

I have divided this study of deinstitutionalization into three parts. The first looks at the history of this massive shift in public policy—its origins, the thinking behind it, how it came about, and what it was expected to accomplish. This part examines five myths that made up the practical and theoretical basis for the wholesale depopulation of much of the country's long-term mental hospital system: that deinstitutionalization was a planned phenomenon; that psychotropic medication could cure mental illness; that mental illness was itself a myth; that the mentally ill would be better off in the community; and that deinstitutionalization would save the taxpayers money. The second part shows the reality of deinstitutionalization—what really happened to all those patients once they left the hospital, and what they looked like outside its walls—and looks at another set of assumptions that confuse the idea of deinstitutionalization with related social problems: that the bulk of the mentally ill have, in fact, made it out of institutions; that most of the homeless are deinstitutionalized mental patients; that jails and prisons are full of them; and that we don't know what to do with the chronically mentally ill. The third part focuses on the mental health system itself and particularly on the curious split our mental health bureaucracy has made between the practitioners who actually care for the patients and the professional administrators who plan and oversee that work. This section explains how the administrators and bureaucrats, with little knowledge of patients' problems and needs, have come to rely on the foregoing myths and assumptions. It also shows their propensity for turning messy, unscientific social problems into neat, tidy empirical surveys and data sets, thereby transforming an ever-growing population of identified deviants into a manageable abstraction, with predictable lack of success.

I know a lot of chronic mental patients who think that it's the mental health professionals who are the crazy ones: "You're not being rational!" one shouted at me the other day, as I tried to convince her to agree to go to a hospital against her wishes. As much as anything else, this book is an attempt to see which of us is correct.

PART I

1940-1970
How
Deinstitutionalization
Supposedly Took
Place

One of the most common fallacies about change is the conclusion that if something is bad, its opposite must of necessity be good.

—PAUL WATZLAWICK, JOHN WEAKLAND,
and RICHARD FISCH,
Change: Principles of Problem Formation and Problem Resolution (1974)

To understand the present, one must begin in the past. Inevitably, deinstitutionalization's past is the history of the mental hospital. With this fact in mind, I begin my study of the history of deinstitutionalization with a brief review of the rise and fall of the asylum as our premier instrument of psychiatric intervention. Next, I separate the several strands of what I believe to be the fiber of which the concept of deinstitutionalization is woven, which is to say its social, political, medical, philosophical, and economic roots. I examine each strand in turn, both as it contributes to the notion that the mentally ill should live in the regular world and as it was eventually permitted to distort the realities of that life and of clinical practice.

Deinstitutionalization's past is a very recent one, which deprives us of the luxury of looking at it in retrospect. What's more, deinstitutionalization is a phenomenon at once social, political, philosophical, medical, and economic, both in nature and in substance; moreover, it is all of these, all the time. It is important to bear this cumbersome thought in mind, because the critics of deinstitutionalization have tended to attack one element of the whole idea or one aspect of its implementation at a time, thus missing the totality and the enormity of what has been, after all, a huge shift in our social policy.

Deinstitutionalization happened because political ideas about dependent populations changed, which happened because our culture's ideas about deviants changed, which happened because our concepts of psychiatric treatment changed, which happened because our technology changed, which happened because it became economically sensible to spend our mental health dollars on something other than custodial care. How all this came to pass over a mere twenty years is the subject of Part I.

CHAPTER 1

◆

The Historical Context
for Deinstitutionalization

In those receptacles where living beings, bearing the
image and superscription of men, were cut off from all the
sympathies of fellow-men and were rapidly completing
the ruin of their immortal nature, there were scenes of
barbarity and moral desolation which no force of language
can adequately describe.
—ISAAC RAY, *A Treatise on the Medical Jurisprudence of
Insanity* (1838)

THE roots of what we now call deinstitutionalization are firmly lodged in a cyclical tradition of institutional reform: Each reform flourishes briefly, is implemented and becomes routine, then is forgotten and neglected by its creators and the general public until a kind of institutional rot sets in, whereupon another reform movement replaces it. In the eighteenth century, Americans began turning to institutions to care for their mentally ill, first in workhouses and almshouses, next in asylums and hospitals, and finally in large state-run mental hospitals. As each corrective measure went into place, advocates for the mentally ill applauded the achievement as vastly more humane than whatever had passed for care before, which was invariably characterized in vivid and dramatic terms as unspeakably horrible, misguided, and worthless. For many years, in fact, large state-run mental hospitals were themselves instruments of reform, enjoying a moment in the sun before being supplanted in the wake of scandals and exposés.

In America's infancy, care for the few mentally ill citizens in the thinly populated colonies fell to their families, and only as a last resort to the local community. Under the English poor laws of 1597 and 1601, community leaders could either compel recalcitrant relatives to live up to their responsibility or, if that failed, to place the deranged person in the local workhouse. There, the mentally ill person shared the facility with a group known collectively as "the poor," a generic designation that included people with all kinds of disabilities—the mentally retarded, the physically handicapped, the homeless, and the otherwise deviant. Interestingly, colonial residents viewed poverty as God's full and just punishment for wrongdoing, so that actual care of the indigent in publicly funded workhouses was not intended to be punitive. Even when deviants were considered destructive or criminal, they were at most subject to public humiliation in the form of whippings or the stocks, never to incarceration.[1]

As America's population grew throughout the late seventeenth and early eighteenth centuries, so too did the number of dependent persons. Gradually, illness was differentiated from the other disabilities found among poorhouse residents, and in 1751 the first public hospital was built in Philadelphia by Dr. Thomas Bond. Bond derived considerable inspiration for this enterprise from a trip to Europe, where he had been greatly impressed by England's Bethlehem Hospital (the notorious Bedlam), where treatment methods such as bleeding, baths, and physical restraint were provided to the insane, who were also on public view for a fee, payable to the hospital superintendent. Such a therapeutic approach to the mentally ill represented a tremendous advance over previous European techniques such as casting the mentally ill adrift on the open sea, crammed onto "ships of fools," or auctioning them off to the bidder who would undertake their care at the lowest cost to the public.[2]

The Heyday of Moral Treatment

Establishment of asylums for the care of the severely mentally ill, where a humanitarian approach was adopted in a form that came to be known as "moral treatment," occurred at the end of the eighteenth century in both Europe and the United States. The institutions pioneering this approach included William Tuke's York Retreat in England; Bicêtre in Paris, where Philippe Pinel dramatized his reform efforts by personally removing the chains from lunatics incarcerated there for years; and the "Original Thirteen" in the United States, including the Bloomingdale Asylum in New York, the Hartford (Connecticut) Retreat, and the Virginia Eastern Asylum in Williamsburg.

The essence of moral treatment was its belief that mental patients could learn behavioral self-control through a corrective relationship with a benign authority figure, a process that William Tuke equated with childrearing. Even more important, probably, was the fact that the pioneers of moral treatment expected to *cure* mental illness, not just to treat its victims by housing them. Heavily dependent on the personal charisma of its founders, moral treatment assumed a close personal relationship between each patient and the superintendent of the asylum, which itself had to be small and to provide a pleasant environment. In this idyllic setting, internal restraints on behavior were sought and rewarded, idleness was frowned upon, and patients were treated as rational adults. The superintendents had complete control over their institutions, most particularly over admissions, which enabled them to select their clientele with great care. Not surprisingly, they tended to choose patients who came from affluent families, and to admit no more than 200 to 250 patients, as recommended by one of the Original Thirteen superintendents, Thomas Kirkbride.[3]

By all accounts, moral treatment was startlingly successful, even in terms entirely familiar to today's administrators—discharge and readmission rates. The Bloomingdale Asylum, for example, which is now known as New York Hospital, Westchester Division, admitted 1,841 patients between 1821 and 1844. Of these, 1,762 were discharged, including 672 cured, 104 much improved, and 318 improved; *cure* was defined as minimal function within both the patient's family and society at large. Most of those discharged were not readmitted.[4]

In view of their success, which the superintendents did not keep to themselves, the treatment model embodied in the asylum was widely copied. At first, the imitators were private institutions incorporating the beliefs and practices of moral treatment much in the original spirit of its founders, but thanks in large part to the well-publicized reports of success by the early asylums, the idea that asylum care could eliminate insanity gained currency. In those days, insanity was thought to be the result of brain lesions made worse by social stress and instability, an assumption that readily fostered a belief that publicly supported institutions would provide an ideal venue for society to right its wrongs. The goal of the asylum was to create a model community, one in which the mentally ill could relearn life skills in an atmosphere free from tension and chaos. The model public institution was to be built in a rural area, where land was inexpensive and where the environment could be controlled, and the daily routine was to be calm, fixed, and free from the pressures of society. The treatment plan for all inmates was to be the same: hard physical work on a rigid daily schedule for a minimum of three to six months.

The ideas behind the move to adapt moral treatment methods to fit the public sector initially had all the qualities of true belief: the Original Thirteen superintendents believed deeply in the virtues of their practice and in the value of their calling, which was to cure mental illness. As tends to happen to true believers, their zeal for their own cause easily overcame their respect for truth, and they oversold their case by inflating their rates of cure. They also, like shrewd true believers everywhere, formed an organization to promote their efforts politically. Founded in 1844 as the Association of Medical Superintendents of American Institutions for the Insane (AMSAII), the organization is now known as the American Psychiatric Association (APA). The AMSAII's early efforts to promote its model of care were undertaken at precisely the same moment that the definitive crusader Dorothea L. Dix undertook her own promotional campaign to close down the county-run almshouses.

Moral Treatment Meets Chronicity, and They Both Meet Dorothea Dix

Dix's consummate skill as an eloquent advocate for the indigent and dependent who were also mentally ill went a long way to ensure the creation of state-run mental institutions. Not only did she articulate the misery and squalor she saw firsthand in her visits to almshouses in the strongest terms, but she regularly visited state legislatures to suggest an alternative: creation of special institutions expressly for the insane, whom she portrayed as pitiful, helpless, and sick. As it happened, the AMSAII was simultaneously involved in an effort to have the term *asylum* replaced with *hospital*, where medical personnel might treat mental "illness;" and every state responded to the siren calls of science and humanitarian ideals. In a typically enthusiastic passage, the New York State Senate reflected the optimism of the times:

> Science, aided by humanity, has dispelled ignorance, overcome prejudice, conquered superstition, and investigated the causes, character and curability of mental disease, and has gloriously demonstrated that insanity can be made to yield to the power of medicine and medical treatment, and to moral discipline. The mystery which once enveloped it has vanished. The condition of the insane is now calling forth the warmest and most powerful exercise of the compassion and philanthropy of the age. In their behalf, the sympathies of the civilised world are growing stronger and stronger continually. The noble and efficient exertions of the present age are rapidly making amends for the neglect and cruelty of past times.[5]

Such heady optimism proved premature, of course. The harsh realities of the public caseload overwhelmed the design of the asylum, which depended on small size and a controlled environment. American cities in the mid-1800s had a huge influx of immigrants, many of whom could not cope with the stress of their new lives and broke down. Not only did many immigrants require admission to asylums, but they also often did not speak English, which made therapeutic relationships with asylum staff extremely unlikely and moral treatment impossible. Promoters of moral treatment dissolved their public posture of consensus and bickered publicly over whether or not asylum superintendents had inflated data in order to acquire public support.[6]

The Chronic Caseload Proliferates

What really destroyed the ideal of moral treatment, however, was the steady growth of a group of patients with chronic mental illness who failed to respond to treatment and who came to be considered incurable. This group's very existence challenged the basis of moral treatment's support by threatening the idea of successful treatment of the mentally ill: here, for all to see, was a large and growing number of individuals for whom the claims to cure simply did not apply.

The chronic caseload has always been the bête noire of mental health planners, and we shall meet it again and again on the road to deinstitutionalization. This group, for whom the state hospitals were created in the mid-nineteenth century, was made up of alcoholics, people with dangerous behavior problems, deranged individuals who had been rejected by the almshouses, and most particularly the senile elderly, who alone made up 10 percent of all admissions to state hospitals between 1830 and 1875.[7] The chronic caseload has stymied mental health planners, chiefly because its numbers have kept growing as chronic patients have accumulated in various public facilities that haven't really wanted them. Clinically, too, the chronic caseload has traditionally posed two major dilemmas: First, the only known treatment models have generally been geared to acute illness, which is usually expected to remit; yet the chronic mentally ill proved to be far too sick ever to be discharged as cured or even improved. Second, no acute-care facility needed a lot of treatment failures around undermining the confidence of other patients or the staff in the very treatment they either received or provided. No wonder the chronic mentally ill were unwelcome everywhere they were sent.

Hello, State Hospital; Goodbye, Moral Treatment

The creation of the large state hospital to house the chronic mentally ill was an inevitable solution, given the sheer size of the caseload, and so was the gradual abandonment of the grand plan to provide moral treatment in such a setting. Instead of rewarding patients' efforts at self-control, physical restraint proved more practical for staff, who had to manage large wards filled with deranged and unpredictable psychotics. Managing large numbers of chronic cases in physical restraint was no job for a charismatic father figure; so a difficult, boring, and unrewarding task went to untrained aides, who were paid low wages for long hours, and among whom high turnover and low morale were the rule. The idea of therapeutic interaction with supportive parental figures, key to the design of moral treatment, was clearly out of the question in such a setting. Administratively, too, the state hospital system quickly got out of hand; the census grew, as did the costs. The states' response to this problem was then what it is now: centralize, bureaucratize, and regulate in an attempt to control the uncontrollable, which in this instance applied both to the patients themselves and to their increasing numbers. The net result was the creation of a class of mental institution in which cure was not a goal and treatment was not a priority; custody alone was expected and only custody was delivered.

It is ironic that such a genuine and enthusiastic effort at reform as that undertaken by the combined forces of Dorothea Dix, asylum superintendents, and nineteenth-century state legislatures should have as its principal legacy the large, custodial state hospital; but it would be unfair to judge the era's social reformers by results alone. Clearly, events overwhelmed intentions and abilities, so that the nineteenth-century reform era wound up with far less than it had hoped for. The state hospital system was governed by a regulatory system that focused on what it could monitor—namely, order and efficiency, rather than the uniform treatment methods that the small asylums had stood for and whose relative success had led to the call for state-supported facilities in the first place. Noble intentions notwithstanding, the reform era ended with the creation of a new, less-than-desirable class of custodial institutions with which to replace the old, less-than-desirable class of custodial institutions. It has been said of the nineteenth-century social reformers that

> the most impressive fact is the relative absence of malevolence or for that matter consistency of behavior. What emerges more closely resembles a tragedy, in which most participants, to a greater or lesser degree, were well intentioned, but their actual behavior gave rise to less than desirable results.[8]

The creation of the state mental hospital, in retrospect, confirms the proverbial wisdom that the road to hell is paved with good intentions.

Science and Advocacy

At the end of the nineteenth century, two trends emerged simultaneously in the field of mental health: (1) the gradual effort by psychiatry to establish itself as a science and (2) the tentative development of groups dedicated to advocacy on behalf of the mentally ill. Although these two had little in common otherwise, their emergence at roughly the same time decisively influenced the ongoing development of institutional care for the mentally ill.

The New Scientific Psychiatry

Psychiatry had to contend with the uncomfortable fact that its base was the custodial institution, where a doctor was probably more concerned with the physical plant than with the physical patient. Meanwhile, medicine was fast becoming more scientific, which put psychiatry under enormous pressure to abandon its moral and religious roots. Psychiatrists came under steady attack by neurologists, who denounced the rival specialty and barred psychiatrists from membership in their professional organization in 1875; adding insult to injury, they proclaimed the asylum superintendents to be charlatans. The psychiatrists responded by changing their organization's name to the American Medico-Psychological Association in 1892, expanding its membership, and embracing scientific topics as its focus. Mostly, though, psychiatrists managed to differentiate themselves from the state asylums only by denouncing the asylum as an emblem of the old, unscientific, ineffective psychiatry. The new, scientific psychiatry was increasingly practiced privately and in clinics, completely bypassing the state hospitals and their patients, notwithstanding the fact that those patients made up the bulk of the mentally ill.

Advocacy and the Control of Asylums

Advocates for the mentally ill first began organizing in the 1860s, when a Mrs. E. P. W. Packard, who had been committed to the Illinois State Hospital for the Insane by her husband, succeeded in securing her own release and immediately mounted a campaign for general reform and the recognition of patients' rights. By 1868 the law had been changed so that mental patients could be freed by obtaining writs of habeas corpus, and this achievement put pressure on the states to monitor their facilities. At the same time, the National

11

Conference of Charities and Corrections, the precursor to the National Association of Social Workers, put similar pressure on localities to administer various forms of welfare in a planned, organized, and accountable manner—referred to at the time as "scientific charity."

The most obvious result of all the pressure for change was the increased centralization of asylum care in state government, even as the medical superintendents lost their longtime autonomy. The first state to centralize control of its asylums was New York, which created the position of State Commissioner of Lunacy in 1873. The first occupant of the post had as his goal moving all the mentally ill then in almshouses to the state asylums under his control, on the grounds that the counties provided inadequate care. The county governments strenuously denounced the idea as too expensive because they would have to pay the state a share of the cost of each inmate's care—$2.75 per week per inmate, as opposed to the $1.50 per week it cost to keep one person in the poorhouse.[9] Nevertheless, the commissioner convinced the legislature to pass the State Care Act of 1890, requiring that New York's counties send all of their mentally ill to state hospitals for care in centralized facilities. The immediate result of this act was a staggering increase in the population of the state hospitals: in the decade following passage, the state hospital census in New York State went from 5,402 to 21,815, largely because the counties opportunistically reclassified their senile elderly as mentally ill and shifted much of the cost of their care to the state.[10] The State Care Act quickly became a model for the rest of the country.

The Mental Hygiene Movement

The next great wave of social reform was the mental hygiene movement, which occurred during the Progressive Era. Its founders shared a grand mission: to eliminate insanity by attacking the problem at its root in the community rather than in full flower in the asylum. Motivated only in part by the poor quality of public mental hospital care, they were not in fact dedicated to reform of the state hospitals or treatment of the chronically ill, as their predecessors had been, but to a whole new approach to care through prevention. The early Progressives' agenda was built on their firm, if mistaken, belief that

> institutions (prisons or mental hospitals) could coexist with, and even sponsor, non-institutional programs . . . Institutions dominated the system so as to make other options almost impossible to realize. . . . They imagined that non-institutional programs might take away some clients from the institution, that probation

might spare an offender from a term in a state prison, that a community clinic might spare a patient from a stay in a state hospital.[11]

These overoptimistic views led to a spate of well-intentioned, if naïve, reforms.

Adolf Meyer's Vision: The Psychopathic Hospital and the Aftercare Clinic

The mental hygiene movement was led by Adolf Meyer, a psychiatrist who gave the movement its name and did more than anyone else to shift the focus of organized psychiatry away from hopeless cases by breaking the asylum superintendents' hold on the profession. Meyer's campaign was a deliberate effort at professionalization and medicalization of psychiatric care, and its cornerstones were two new institutional designs: the psychopathic hospital and community-based aftercare. The new hospital design was envisioned as a clearinghouse, or what is now generally referred to as a receiving hospital, in which acutely ill patients were to receive high-quality treatment that would most likely prevent the need for long-term care in an asylum, if only because the new facilities would enjoy the prestige of association with medical schools.[12] At the same time, the psychopathic hospital staff were to act as gatekeepers for the state hospital system by identifying and referring chronic cases for long-term care after having done a thorough diagnostic examination. The aftercare clinic, intended to facilitate follow-up of acute cases to ensure their successful return to community life, centered around the new profession of psychiatric social work. Originally envisioned as a kind of friendly visiting, the aftercare model was soon defined as an important adjunct to a psychiatrist's treatment, in which the social worker not only helped the patient adjust after discharge but also modified the home environment that had provoked his symptoms in the first place.

To no one's surprise, the asylum superintendents were extremely threatened by Meyer's vision of a frontline approach to the treatment of mental illness in which they were expected to play a very secondary position. In fact, Meyer never called for the elimination of the asylums, which he renamed "hospitals," but he did see their role as one of providing backup to his acute-care facilities; he intended that a sharp delineation should prevail between acute and chronic patients and their care. In practice, cooperation between the two systems proved an elusive goal, and the distinction between *chronic* and *acute* more problematic than anticipated: *chronic* was taken to mean *insane* by the staffs of the psychopathic hospitals, who resisted any and all involvement in their care. In the end, the mental hygiene movement accomplished nothing for the institutionalized mentally ill; the reality of neglect and poor-quality custodial care went unchanged, of no particular concern to a specialty striving to define its mission in medical and scientific terms.[13]

Proponents of the psychopathic hospitals ultimately failed in their attempts to change the mental health system. The asylum superintendents maintained their power base, chiefly because very few of the new hospitals actually opened—Boston Psychopathic Hospital, New York State Psychiatric Institute, Bellevue, and Albany Hospital were some that did. Also, early on, the new hospitals' preferred tasks of teaching, diagnosis, research, cure, and prevention were quickly swamped by the work entailed in receiving patients on their way to state asylums. In part, this corruption of the psychopathic hospital design resulted from a genuine lack of knowledge on everyone's part about how to treat, much less cure, the seriously mentally ill; but it also turned out to be quite convenient to commit patients to asylums by way of receiving hospitals.

It was the fate of the early aftercare clinics to fail as a device of reform as well, for interesting reasons. First, although clinics did get started—chiefly child guidance clinics funded by private philanthropies—ties to state hospitals did not materialize, either fiscally or politically. Ironically, the state hospitals, notoriously overcrowded, almost never bothered to use "parole status," as they called it, and they showed no interest in creating aftercare clinics to promote discharge or parole. Instead, the patients who could have been paroled probably were kept on the wards to work. Besides, a typical caseload for a state hospital social worker, whose job it was to plan discharges, totaled some 775 patients, which alone suggests that discharging patients was not a priority.[14] The huge industry that grew up to maintain the chronic caseload was in no hurry to shrink itself, for whatever reason.

Although the mental hygiene reform movement did not benefit the chronic mentally ill, it did leave its mark on clinical practice, thanks to the reformers' unwavering belief in the efficacy of science as the weapon of choice against their enemies, which included disease, environmental hazards, and hereditary deficiencies. In that spirit, mental hygienists endeavored to create a better society through aggressive use of scientific principles rather than by obeying the laws of chance.

Clifford W. Beers, Zealot

Another figure at the forefront of the mental hygiene movement was Clifford W. Beers, a Yale graduate who had several psychotic episodes in his early twenties and was subsequently hospitalized in both private and public hospitals. Probably a manic-depressive, Beers expended enormous energy on extraordinarily ambitious schemes, succeeding at many of them.

Chief among Beers's achievements was his classic book *A Mind that Found Itself,* a firsthand account of his mental illness and treatment. He somehow managed to convince William James, whom he had not met, to read the book. James was apparently so impressed with book and author that, until his death in 1910, he supported Beers financially. Nevertheless, publication of the book eluded Beers even with James's help, and it was not until Adolf Meyer took a hand that the book appeared. Beers's plan was to expose and thus correct the terrible conditions he knew to exist in state mental hospitals, and to do this he planned to start a national association on behalf of the mentally ill to follow up on the impact he expected his book to have. Meyer persuaded Beers to tone down his criticism of psychiatry and to shift the focus of the advocacy group away from its original and, thought Meyer, too narrow concern of institutional reform. Meyer advised Beers, instead, to embrace the vague, all-inclusive concept of mental hygiene.[15] Beers and Meyer eventually split over the question of whether laypeople or psychiatrists should have charge of the new organization, which was formed in 1909 as the National Committee for Mental Hygiene and exists today as the National Association for Mental Health.

Beers's organization pursued a variety of ambitious aims, including protection of the public's mental health; promotion of research into the etiology, treatment, and prevention of mental disease; and establishment of aftercare clinics, educational programs, and state societies for mental hygiene, among others—a hefty agenda that veered about as far from the specifics of institutional reform as one could get. Eventually, the organization founded the journal *Mental Hygiene,* undertook to research both conditions in state hospitals and the relationship between mental illness and social maladaptation, and in general became such a tool of organized psychiatry that after the First World War its director was psychiatrist Thomas Salmon, whose primary interest was the prevention of delinquency. Poor Beers remained active in his own organization, if only as a figurehead; but in 1939 he was readmitted to a psychiatric hospital, where he died in 1943.

Prevention of Mental Disease at All Costs

In the first half of the twentieth century, the mental hygiene movement got farther and farther away from any thought of reforming the state hospital system because it focused more and more on preventing disease through science. The prevailing thinking of the times was cordial to such a pursuit, since this was an era favorable to public health initiatives generally. Moreover, the government was quite alarmed to find serious mental health problems in soldiers who had served just prior to the First World War: 20 percent of all men discharged disabled from the army in 1912 were found to have mental illness, and the rate of mental illness found among those discharged in 1916 was triple the national norm.[16] Public interest in prevention efforts was a godsend to the sizable segment of the psychiatric profession most eager to dissociate itself from the increasingly embarrassing public mental hospitals, where there were no scientific achievements worth publicizing and where conditions deteriorated steadily, provoking constant public criticism. Inadvertently, then, the mental hygiene movement made it very easy for psychiatry to turn once again from the chronically mentally ill, whose only value for the prevention specialists was as candidates for the widespread use of sterilization to prevent the reproduction of the unfit.

Sterilization was a scientific tool that appealed to social reformers eager to perfect society by any means at hand, and in the United States at the turn of this century, they found a political climate which was receptive to their crusade. In 1882, Congress clearly articulated the national fear that other countries were using the United States as a dumping ground for their unwanted nationals, including criminals, the infirm, the crippled, and the mentally ill; and in the 1920s, Congress established immigration quotas partly to respond to that fear. The same turn of mind that could blame long-standing social problems on immigration and could then look to science for concrete answers prompted experimentation with sterilization, which was easier and more effective than more neutral measures like education, marriage laws, and segregation of the sexes in institutions. Michigan first legalized the sterilization of the feebleminded and certain kinds of criminals in 1897; Indiana passed a law mandating sterilization of criminals, rapists, idiots, and imbeciles in 1907, and by 1940 a total of thirty states had followed suit. By 1949, 45,127 persons had been sterilized involuntarily in the United States, 21,311 of them "insane" and 22,153 "feebleminded."[17]

Before the Second World War, any public debate on forced sterilization of the unfit was restricted to concern about legal or scientific matters; moral and ethical considerations were irrelevant, because the prime motivation behind the practice was the scientific prevention of social ills at all costs. Eugenics, according to one of its more fervent advocates, "protects the mentally defective against an anticipated overload of offspring and the community against the risk of increasing the number of defective children to be supported by public means."[18] While sterilization of the unfit may strike the contemporary reader as a quaint custom of days gone by, in fact it has a very recent past. A total of 467 institutionalized persons were sterilized involuntarily in 1963, and in 1965, at least two welfare fraud cases in California were settled with plea bargains that included sterilization of the guilty parties.[19]

Gradual Exposure of the Snakepit

Despite the mental hygienists' best efforts at prevention, the population in the state mental hospitals grew at an alarming rate, expanding from 150,000 to 445,000 between 1903 and 1940. During these years, the proportion of patients admitted with a diagnosis of senility grew just as dramatically. Whereas only 18 percent of first admissions to state hospitals in 1920 bore that diagnosis, 31 percent did so in 1940.[20] There were two reasons for this shift: First, the elderly population increased nationwide as the mortality rate dropped among younger age groups. Second, in an unanticipated consequence of the State Care Act of 1890, the almshouses died out between 1880 and 1920. For the aged, the senile, and the indigent, the state hospital was the only place left to go after 1890.

Of course, the state mental hospital was also the only refuge for those with epilepsy, alcoholism, drug addiction, pellagra, or mental retardation. For all the talk about science and treatment of the mentally ill, the truth was that for the most part, state hospitals housed people with severe mental and physical problems who could not care for themselves. Even more important, they could reasonably be expected to need this care until they died. Why the state hospitals were given this enormous burden seems fairly obvious: fiscal policy on the local level encouraged the practice, clearly, and the state hospitals were, after all, available, capacious, and out of sight. It is less obvious why the hospitals so readily accepted the burden, although one assumes some need of their own was being met by being overcrowded, probably not least a need to justify their existence in a professional climate that openly disdained their contribution to the field. Certainly, institutional survival was assured for the state hospitals as long as they provided custody for society's ragbag of dependents; and after all, survival of the institution, not patient care, was the prime consideration of any facility that accepted the caseload yet provided nothing more than subsistence.[21]

A Survey of State Mental Hospitals Turns into an Exposé

Predictably, the Great Depression hit the mental hospitals hard; staff were short and money was scarce. In 1931 the American Medical Association (AMA) put additional pressure on the hospitals when it decided to develop an official policy toward institutional care of the insane and formed a study panel headed by John Maurice Grimes, a physician (but not a psychiatrist). From the first, the American Psychiatric Association objected strenuously to the study and accused the AMA of "entering territory sacred to another organization," but the AMA persisted, provoked by rumors of scandal and mistreatment of patients. To accomplish their survey, Grimes and three colleagues visited 600 of the 631 state mental hospitals then extant in 47 of the 48 states (Massachusetts refused to participate); and they circulated a questionnaire to state hospital directors, receiving an extraordinary return of 75 percent. From both visits and questionnaire data, Grimes saw at once that conditions in state hospitals were deplorable, and he dutifully prepared a preliminary report to that effect. As politically naive as he was meticulous about facts, Grimes was shocked to find his preliminary report unexpectedly "subject to radical revision," and he was fired before he could write a final report. In Grimes's view, such powerful opposition to his committee's findings had come, clearly, from the APA, which had objected to the AMA's undertaking from the first and had clearly been able to make a deal with the AMA, one that sacrificed Grimes and toned down the report in order to preserve the reputation of organized psychiatry.[22] In the end, someone else wrote the official report, basing it entirely on questionnaire data and ignoring the information collected during the visits to all 600 hospitals; that person was not, obviously, a member of Grimes's original committee and so wrote without any firsthand knowledge of the hospitals themselves.

Determined to publish the real committee's unanimous findings, Grimes put out the final report on his own, and the findings were indeed provocative. First, Grimes pointed out that the popular belief that one out of every two hospital beds was occupied by a mental patient was a distortion: mental patients filled only 10 to 20 percent of the beds.[23] Unquestionably, however, the mental hospitals *were* overcrowded, and patients had nothing to do except work for the hospital staff. Hospital staff were mostly patronage appointees, and the staff–patient ratio ranged from one to six to one to twenty-six, the national average being one to thirteen. Grimes demonstrated that patients were kept locked up solely to reduce the staff needed to keep wards orderly. Many patients seen by the surveyors were senile elderly people who had been hospitalized unnecessarily, probably, Grimes surmised, because their families could not afford to care for them in hard times and no alternative existed. As a physician, Grimes was particularly offended by the use of terms like *patient* and *hospital* to describe a setting that merely housed neglected, chronically disordered people; he considered the attendants no more than "guards." Quoting a superintendent, Grimes observed that "a mental hospital, to be called a hospital, must *cure* its patients"; and pointing out that many private mental institutions managed to do so, he dismissed as self-serving the states' repeated justification of their failures as the result of their having taken on a herculean task. The states preferred to complain, he decided, rather than update and improve their antiquated methods of care.[24]

Grimes's recommendations were prophetic. He proposed what he called "de-institutionalization," to include immediate parole of all suitable patients to aftercare clinics, where they would be seen by social workers under medical supervision. He suggested other improvements, as well: conversion of all state hospitals to acute-care facilities run on the model of medicine, not that of corrections; renovation of existing chronic-care wards to promote the aggressive training of long-term patients in the skills of daily living and work with an eye to their eventual discharge; and development of better ties between hospitals and the communities in which the patients had lived prior to admission.[25] Grimes had an unerring eye for the core problem posed by unthinking use of public institutions as warehouses for the dependent: he perceived that if "scores of social workers" were hired, "hundreds or even thousands of patients" could be paroled instead of piling up in the back wards, "occupying beds that must therefore be duplicated in new institutions to receive the thousands of other patients coming in."[26]

The Legacy of the 1930s

Grimes arranged for private publication of his report because he felt his message was too important to suppress, and he was well aware of the efforts of organized psychiatry to cover up his findings by silencing him.[27] One direct result of those very political machinations that haunted Grimes during the Great Depression is something that plagues the state hospital system to this day: the deteriorating condition of the physical plant. In the 1930s public funds were especially short, of course, and money was saved at the time by postponing major repair as well as capital construction; moreover, by the time money was available in at least some of the states, the mental hospitals were in disrepute and thus not a public priority. Generally, the state hospital buildings of today are old, huge, dilapidated, outmoded, and expensive to maintain or replace.

Another hand-me-down from the 1930s is our ongoing interest in biopsychiatry, which in the Depression years was the province of a group of European doctors in flight from Hitler. They brought to the United States an interest in such practices as insulin shock therapy, prefrontal lobotomy, fever therapy, and electroconvulsive therapy (ECT, or, popularly, shock treatment).[28] For some years these new clinical interventions dominated the field, and in some instances they still hold sway—interest in psychosurgery, for instance, has never quite gone away, and ECT is still in use. Although these methods have never proved as useful as their promoters have wished, they certainly have reflected an optimism and a genuine faith in the ability of science to rescue psychiatry from its insoluble problem—too many hospitalized incurable patients.

The Second World War: Psychiatry Discovers the Worried Well and Forgets about the Chronics

The Second World War era provided a very potent opportunity for psychiatry to shine: as it had in the First World War, the military found many men unfit to serve because of mental deficiencies. Out of 15 million men examined by the army, 4,800,000 were turned down, 1,091,000 for neuropsychiatric disorder, of whom 856,000 were mentally ill and 700,000 mentally retarded.[29] The unhappy discovery that of all the young American males called to serve in the great cause, a full 17 percent should be unfit for psychiatric reasons was sobering to the military and renewed official interest in finding quick solutions. The army's interest in solving its psychiatric problems peaked when officials realized that during 1945, one million patients had been admitted to army hospitals with psychiatric disorders, at a rate of admission of 45 per 1,000 troops, or 6 percent of all admissions—to which must be added the 149,281 psychiatric patients in the navy.[30] Military psychiatrists viewed these statistics with alarm, because they suggested a level of psychopathology in the general public that was far greater than had been generally assumed.[31] Since in 1945 the army's psychiatrists included the highly respected Menninger brothers,

Karl and William, as well as Francis Braceland, their findings carried weight and prestige.

The military sought from science answers to its questions about the evident increase in psychopathology among draftees. The military's psychiatrists set out to study situational stress and its effects, which led to the novel idea that perhaps brief hospitalizations might benefit some individuals more than would traditionally long stays. They studied hypnosis, group psychotherapy, narcoanalysis using sodium amytal and sodium pentothal ("truth serum"), and stress-related psychosomatic diseases. Mostly, they studied how to screen out the unfit and how to recognize and treat battle fatigue, or situational stress, quickly and effectively. It was in these enterprises that the military's psychiatrists achieved a new credibility for the entire profession, one that unfortunately turned very quickly to arrogance and grandiosity. It is said of this period that

> a lesson should have been learned that was not learned. Never before had such a large proportion of potential draftees been rejected because of psychiatric diagnoses in an effort to preserve the armed forces from mental disorders, but never before had such a large proportion of the armed forces been found to be inadequate for military service because of mental disorders. The idea that psychiatrists knew how to screen and select people at low risk for mental disorders so as to produce a low occurrence rate should have died from this experiment. But it didn't. On the contrary, the effort to screen and predict grew, and the effort to diagnose and dispose of also grew.[32]

And as organized psychiatry got more and more involved in pursuit of its grand ambitions, it got farther and farther away from the asylum, the state hospital, and the chronic caseload.

Meanwhile, Back at the State Hospitals

Even as psychiatry was growing in authority as a direct result of the war, the hopeless failure of the public mental hospital system was discovered once again, this time by the conscientious objectors (COs) sent to hospitals to perform their alternative to military service. Often highly educated and always highly principled, the COs were shocked to find the mentally ill, the handicapped, and the aged living in helpless squalor, victims of long-standing neglect and with little hope of ever receiving humane care, not to mention treatment. The COs formed the National Mental Health Foundation (NMHF) to renew Clifford Beers's campaign to reform the state hospitals, abandoned some twenty years earlier by mental hygiene's preference for education over advocacy. Under the umbrella of the NMHF, the COs publicized the fact that care in the state mental hospitals had deteriorated dramatically during the 1930s. One argument they used to prove the charge of government neglect centered on the fact that while the federal government spent twelve dollars per day per patient in the psychiatric wards of the Veterans' Administration hospitals, the state, city, and county mental hospitals were spending four dollars per day per patient—still the case as late as 1960. The COs' goal was to get federal funds allotted to improve a decrepit and underfinanced system; to get it, the COs were not above making promises they and the system could not possibly keep.[33]

The conscientious objector–led reform movement was able to succeed where Grimes had failed only because it surfaced at a moment in history when the members of the American Psychiatric Association were engaged in a bitter internal struggle over what direction organized psychiatry would take in the future. According to their president, Harry C. Solomon, the APA found itself to be "too stuffy and too inept to meet the needs of the time" when called upon to address the compelling mental health problems identified by army psychiatrists during the war. A straightforward reorganization effort headed by Karl Menninger led to "enormous strife" within the organization, which split into two factions, one of which asked the APA to "bring new life and leadership to psychiatry;" the other of which chose a more conservative and traditional stance. Solomon reported that the ensuing struggle for control was intense and lasted until 1948, and that, moreover, it produced a "separatist movement [that] threatened the unity of the Association."[34] Throughout its internal battle, though, the organization was unusually vulnerable to public criticism of its efforts in the state hospitals, and unwittingly, the COs took advantage of the fact.

Psychiatry's Glorious Future

The postwar enthusiasm for giant programs of social reform cannot be overemphasized. The United States was on a high, on a roll, on the ball, and on the job—whatever needed to be done, we could do it. Flushed with their own wartime victory over their old public image as proprietors of lunatic asylums, the psychiatrists who had manned the military posts returned to postwar public practice and immediately succeeded in expanding psychiatry's social and political influence on a significant front: they sought and obtained enabling legislation to establish a national, federally funded mental health institute on the order of the National Cancer Institute; and in very short order, the National Institute of Mental Health (NIMH) was created. Then in 1950, the National Association for Mental Health (NAMH) was formed from Beers's National Committee for Mental Hygiene, the COs' National Mental Health Foundation, and the American Psychology Foundation; and together with the new NIMH, what was then and is now a most powerful lobby came into existence. As the 1950s began, the NIMH was consolidating its strength in readiness for what they expected would be psychiatry's glorious future, the NAMH was regrouping under new leaders who planned to take an activist stance by demanding increased federal support for mental health care, and the people who paid the bills were counting and recounting what it was costing them to support truly staggering numbers of chronic patients in the state mental hospitals.

CHAPTER 2

◆

How No One Planned
Deinstitutionalization:
It Would Have Happened Anyway

Most of them were located in or near great centers of
culture in our wealthier states such as New York, Michigan, Ohio, California, and Pennsylvania. In some of the
wards there were scenes that rivaled the horrors of the
Nazi concentration camps—hundreds of naked mental
patients herded into huge, barnlike, filth-infested wards,
in all degrees of deterioration, untended and untreated,
stripped of every vestige of human decency, many in
stages of semi-starvation.

The writer heard state hospital doctors frankly admit
that the animals of near-by piggeries were better fed,
housed and treated than many of the patients in their
wards. He saw hundreds of sick people shackled, strapped,
straitjacketed and bound to their beds; he saw mental
patients . . . crawl into beds jammed close together, in
dormitories filled to twice or three times their normal
capacity.

—ALBERT DEUTSCH, *The Shame of the States* (1948)

THE idea that deinstitutionalization
was a piece of deliberate social planning seems so rational and so obvious as
to go without saying, to people both in and out of the mental health field. It's
not true. Deinstitutionalization, which did not even have a name when it
happened, was the product of only dimly related forces: the "can-do" postwar
American mood, which was one of optimism, faith in the future, and enthusiasm for scientific breakthroughs; the latest in the long line of shocking exposés
of heinous conditions in state mental hospitals, which appeared in the late
1940s and the early 1950s; the organized activity of the states, which had

recognized that the costs to them of lifetime care for the chronically mentally ill were prohibitive; and the profession of psychiatry, which was caught up in a longstanding conflict about the chronic mental illnesses and how best to deal with them. What we now call deinstitutionalization did take place—but it was not planned; it simply happened.

After the Second World War, itself a great triumph for the United States, the country was in a mood to make a radical change in the way it dealt with its chronically mentally ill. This occurred partly because postwar America was a prodigiously optimistic place, and partly because medical science in those years was unusually powerful and popular, thanks in no small measure to its successful campaign against polio in the mid-fifties. Deeply feared, even though it was by no means the most prevalent nor the deadliest disease of the day, polio was a most effective cause for the March of Dimes and other organizations devoted to raising money for medical research. When the Salk vaccine was made available in 1955, the public was wildly enthusiastic and passionately grateful to medical research. "The magic of science and money had worked. And if polio could be prevented, Americans had reason to think that cancer and heart disease and mental illness could be stopped, too."[1]

At the same time, the public's conscience about its hospitalized mentally ill underwent one of its periodic shakeups, this time because of a national newspaper scandal concerning the traditional neglect of hospitalized mental patients. The conscientious objectors had formed their organization, the National Mental Health Foundation (NMHF), and their demands for hospital reform had attracted no less a spokesman than Albert Deutsch, a journalist whose articles in *PM* about the terrible conditions in American mental hospitals were published in 1948 as a widely read book, *The Shame of the States.* An effectively gruesome novel called *The Snake Pit* was published in 1946, whose author, Mary Jane Ward, was said to have been a nurse in a state hospital; if anything, the book's effectiveness and popularity were surpassed when a movie starring Olivia de Havilland appeared two years later. Additional studies of chronic mental illness and institutional care from this period included ones by Lucy Freeman *(Fight Against Fears)* and Mike Gorman *(Every Other Bed);* clearly, the topic was timely and the issue ubiquitous.

The Council of State Governments versus the State Hospitals

What we now call deinstitutionalization came out of the postwar period. One central factor spurred efforts to reduce the state hospital population: state officials could read a spread sheet, and they knew that their continued single-handed support of the huge state hospital patient population would ensure their own bankruptcy. In 1949, the forty-eight state governments took the step—unusual for them—of coming together to discuss what to do about one specific problem, the chronically mentally ill.

Identifying State Needs

In preparation for their meeting, officials in each state conducted surveys to establish the baseline condition of their state's hospitals and to determine future needs. All the states reported severe overcrowding of hospitals; a desperate need for modern equipment and facilities, as well as for trained personnel; a preponderance of special-problem patients such as alcoholics and the elderly; a need for preventive treatment; outmoded laws and terminology that tended to emphasize custodial care rather than active treatment; an overuse of involuntary commitment; admissions and discharges based on legal, rather than clinical, considerations; and far too many hospitalized patients who could be discharged if only there were community-based alternatives.[2]

The states were convinced that their principal problem was the sheer volume of the caseload: "The number of mentally ill persons, *under institutional care,* increased nearly 188 times in the hundred years from 1840–1940. During the same period the population of the United States increased about eight times,"[3] they pointed out, citing data from the U.S. Census. The states identified seven reasons for the enormous increase in hospitalized mentally ill: (1) growth in the general population; (2) an increase in the older population, who are subject to senility; (3) the fact that the more beds a hospital has, the more patients wind up in them; (4) increased public knowledge of existing services; (5) a tendency of people to view more of life's problems as mental illness; (6) greater patient longevity, thanks to improved care; and (7) the pressures of urban life.[4]

According to the council, the single biggest obstacle to provision of the kind of care the states felt under pressure to deliver "as never before" was cost. The report pointed out that mental health costs, unlike the other of the "big four" state expenditures—education, welfare, and highways—were borne entirely by the states without federal assistance. Federal aid, however, was not solely what they were seeking. In their surveys, the state officials found that "there are many persons in state hospitals who are not *now* in need of continuing psychiatric hospital care. *Out-patient clinics should be extended and other community resources developed to care for persons in need of help, but not of hospitalization.*"[5]

Before they even met, then, the state governments were committed to the notion that what state mental hospitals needed was not more money to do better work, but fewer patients to house in the first place.

This approach to the formulation of public policy toward the mentally ill was unparalleled. Previous efforts to improve the mental hospital system had focused on building, expanding, or improving hospitals, whereas the 1949 council intended to shift the focus from the hospitals to extrahospital treatment. They realized perfectly well that the body of practical knowledge then available was insufficient to support the goal of discharge to the community, and turning to psychiatry, they called for expanded research into the etiology and treatment of the severe mental diseases:

> A few new discoveries could result in money savings (and in a saving of human misery) that stagger the imagination. First admissions to all mental hospitals in the United States have averaged about 150,000 persons annually in recent years and are now approaching 200,000 per year. . . . The discovery of a cure for one disease entity—schizophrenia—might eventually empty one-half of the mental hospital beds and, more important, keep them from being filled.[6]

The council was determined to set new goals and explore new approaches, but only if their fundamental aim of reducing the hospital census once and for all was part of every plan.

The Governors Stir Public Interest

The governors held their conference in February 1954, in Michigan, with all the states represented except Arizona and Nevada. At once, the tone was set by G. Mennen Williams of Michigan, who called for a cooperative effort by all the states to reverse the trend of rising hospital population and costs by promoting prevention, early diagnosis, and shorter hospital stays. Dr. Henry Brill, Assistant Commissioner of the New York State Department of Mental Hygiene, forecast a 250 percent increase in the patient population between 1930 and 1965 unless trends changed. A recurrent theme reported from the conference was the charge that states spent too much money on hospital construction and not enough on research that would render those hospitals obsolete. For the first time, the state leaders pledged to pool their experiences with administration, personnel recruitment, and research; one contemporary observer was particularly impressed by the representatives' eagerness to sponsor research that might eventually restore mentally ill citizens to normal life rather than to devise ever more elaborate structures for locking them up.[7]

So they held their conference in 1954, got a lot of publicity for an issue that usually stayed in the background of state government, and in a way, raised the nation's consciousness. The Council of State Governments' role in determining the fate of the chronically mentally ill has not generally been acknowledged by students of deinstitutionalization, which is unfortunate, because the council represented a group with an intimate knowledge of the problems endemic to the postwar state mental hospital as well as an undeniable stake in solving those problems. Thus, the council constituted a superb source for the political and strategic thinking that led inexorably to deinstitutionalization and, ultimately, to the problems we face today. The state representatives' concerns were real, practical, immediate, and even moral, although one cannot overlook a certain disingenuousness on their part as they suddenly noticed undesirable practices their own states had been implementing for over a hundred years.

Although the governors' activities were impressive and their recommendations novel, the council's proceedings cannot be described as a formal planning meeting at which the future of the state hospitals was decided in an organized and thoughtful way, complete with the thorough design of alternative systems of care for the patients then in the states' mental hospitals. Theirs was a first step—and a tentative one at that. For movement on a larger political scale, the federal government had to be involved; and for professional authority and endorsement, the mental health establishment—which is to say, organized psychiatry—had to be included.

Mainstream Psychiatry Creeps toward Change

Much of the political activity of organized psychiatry at that time took place under the aegis of the National Institute of Mental Health (NIMH), which in those years was expanding at an amazing rate: from its initial appropriation of $870,000 in 1950, its budget grew to $18 million in 1956 and to $68 million in 1960, all of it, unlike the money that supported the chronic patients, in federal dollars. From the beginning, the NIMH, which was to set the course for the mental health field for years to come, did not have as its focus either the public mental hospitals or the severely mentally ill. Its first director, Robert Felix, wrote off the chronically mentally ill by calling for "an attack on mental illness [that] must reach beyond the more serious hospitalized cases to those persons in the community with psychoneuroses and

28

character and behavior disorders that cause untold suffering and economic loss."[8] Thus, one of the most prestigious professional organizations in the field of mental health openly turned away from the chronically mentally ill and the institutions charged with their care; instead, the NIMH favored patient populations that could be expected to prove more rewarding to practitioners. Ironically, the initiative originally undertaken by the states to address the needs of the hospitalized mentally ill in a new way by expanding the scope of psychiatry to the community had become the occasion for their abandonment by mainstream psychiatry.

Solomon's Vague New Plans

Five years later, the president of the American Psychiatric Association (APA), Harry C. Solomon, made his organization's intention to give up on the state hospitals and their problems equally clear in his presidential address to the organization's national conference: "I do not see how any reasonably objective view of our mental hospitals today can fail to conclude that they are bankrupt beyond remedy. I believe therefore that our large mental hospitals should be liquidated as rapidly as can be done in an orderly and progressive fashion."[9] Citing Massachusetts' diminishing state hospital patient census as an example, he observed that "the first signs of self-liquidation are already evident. . . . This suggests that if the trend continues less bed space will be required." Less callous and indifferent to the needs of the already diagnosed than his counterpart at the NIMH, Solomon was nonetheless startlingly woolly-headed and vague as he outlined his amorphous plans to relocate the state hospital caseload in general hospital psychiatric wards, new clinics, day hospitals, night hospitals, private mental institutions, rehabilitation or aftercare programs, and new facilities for the elderly—all of which he cheerfully, if naively, believed to be extant. Similarly, he made enthusiastic plans for psychiatrists in private practice to take on the chronically mentally ill, declaring them to be "equipped for and interested in" the population—an amazing and unbelievable statement for which he offered no documentation. Next, he mentioned a proposal he admitted was sketchy and incomplete to resettle the long-term chronic patients in "a colony or home rather than in a hospital," with rehabilitation as the central service and a multidisciplinary staff. Admitting that he had no idea how to implement his plan, he nevertheless made an admirably honest assessment of the state of the art in his day: "One must face the fact that we are doing little by way of definite treatment of a large number of our chronic hospital population. It is not even the case that we are providing them with first class environmental care, much less loving and tender care."[10]

Solomon spoke in the vague, high-flown language of the late 1950s, an era that Daniel Patrick Moynihan has characterized as "a political culture that rewarded the articulation of moral purpose more than the achievement of practical good:"[11] mental illness was about to be "cured," thanks to wonderful "new approaches" and "brilliant new solutions" that had no need of the terrible old mental hospitals, which were nothing but "pesthouses" where patients were indefinitely confined in hopeless misery. Daniel Blain, medical director of the APA, predicted in the *New York Times* that very shortly, "the 750,000 patients now in this country's mental hospitals" would be returned to the community—"cured."[12] In early 1955, the brilliant new approach by which psychiatry planned to empty the state hospitals was community-based treatment. No longer was the state hospital to serve as the "primary tool for treating the mentally ill; in future a network of community services would exist to forestall or prevent hospitalization if possible or to shorten it if not," according to American Medical Association (AMA) and APA testimony given to the House Interstate and Foreign Commerce Committee, then in the process of hearing requests for grants to do research. Contemporary newspaper accounts record the politicians' views as newly critical of the "construction approach" to mental illness, strongly preferring the idea of replacing state hospitals with networks of community services as suggested by the nation's experts.[13]

This rosy vision of community treatment was understandably vague, for this approach to mental illness had not yet been explored in great depth; the most recent experiment with outpatient clinics was the abortive attempt at aftercare undertaken by Adolf Meyer and his followers. To visualize the reality behind the grand design, one must remember that community mental health clinics simply did not exist in the 1950s: the hospitals and the seriously mentally ill existed; in most parts of the country that *was* the mental health system. The planned shift to community-based care was a radical notion: move a nonexistent service to an untried market. The assumption underlying the shift was that the chronically mentally ill would be accommodated in hypothetical new clinics along with the mildly troubled, but no one knew just how this would work, since it had never been tried. It is possible that everyone involved, from the NIMH and the APA on down, firmly intended to ensure that the new clinics would treat the seriously ill; but it seems extremely unlikely that the truly deranged were much on the minds of those thrilled with the prospect of a glorious new day of significant medical advances in the treatment of the mentally ill in the community.

Community Mental Health: The Federal Agenda

The federal government got involved in the mental health issue when the combined pressures of the nation's governors, the NIMH, the APA, public health organizations, and various citizens' groups prompted them to undertake a full-scale study of the mental health needs of the country. Based on a similar study done in 1953 by the World Health Organization, which had concluded that community-based treatment was essential, as well as on a joint conference held in the same year by the AMA and the APA, the federal study was cosponsored by senators John F. Kennedy and Lister Hill and was initially known as the Mental Health Study Act of 1955 (PL 84-182). The act appropriated $1,250,000 for research into the diagnosis and treatment of mental illness and established the Joint Commission on Mental Illness and Health. The joint commission, under its director, Jack Ewalt, spent five years in deliberation and study, issuing its final report, *Action for Mental Health*, in 1961.

The Joint Commission's Grand Design

Much of the commission's report was written with optimism and faith in the efficacy of medical science; but once again, the report's authors were shocked to find out what they should have known—namely, that the state hospitals were dreadful and outdated institutions, with 80 percent of the facilities providing only custodial care. The bottom line, according to Ewalt, was that

> with present knowledge put to use, the nation could more than double the number of chronically ill mental patients returned to the community . . . to end [the mental hospital's] isolation—where backward, custodial systems still thrive—and bring it out into the community where it may be observed and criticized.[14]

To this end, the commission recommended huge outlays of federal funds to abolish the state hospital system as then constituted in favor of community-based treatment facilities coordinated with the old hospitals in smaller form, with additional funds for research and professional training.

As it happens, the process of emptying the state hospitals had been under way for over five years by the time the joint commission's report came out; in fact, the event was taking place even as it was under examination and debate by the commission in its effort to plan for mental health's future—so much for strategic planning and long-range thinking. In retrospect, this placement of the cart before the horse seems particularly unfortunate, for among the commission's most salient observations were some it made about the readiness of the general public to accept the mentally ill, whom it had stigmatized and banished for years. In the commission's view,

> One reason the public does not react desirably is that the mentally ill lack appeal. They eventually become a nuisance to other people and are generally treated as such. . . . People do seem to feel sorry for them; but in the balance, *they do not feel as sorry as they do relieved to have out of the way persons whose behavior disturbs and offends them.* [15]

The commission recommended an interesting solution for this longtime problem: they called for a leader, a battle commander, in a war against mental illness; and they ruled psychiatrists ineligible for this role, because they had already proved unequal to the task, hence the mandate for the study. The report mentions, rather wistfully, "gossip in mental health circles" to the effect that once the polio vaccine had been developed, the National Foundation for Infantile Paralysis might take on mental illness—"at last the movement against mental illness would have the benefit of driving leadership, strong organization, and a 'success' formula." However, the foundation declined, put off by the immensity of the problem, the enormity of the patients' need, and the absence of any real support for the cause among either interested professionals or the general public.[16] Last but not least, the joint commission clearly recognized the severely limited possibilities for community-based treatment as then available, and the report "stress[ed] the necessity for community planning around all of the mental health resources, instead of around the clinical treatment services only, as is the current tendency," specifying welfare, family agencies, churches, and the like as vital to the cause of mental health in the community.[17]

Prevention versus Long-Term Care

Obviously, the key to successful implementation of the proposed overhaul of the state hospital system was the community-based network of services, with its intended relationship to the remnants of the old hospitals. Unfortunately, a philosophical split in the field of psychiatry surfaced at a critical point to render integration of the two impossible. The political accommodation of the factions by the federal government probably wrecked the government's ambitions for community-based care for the mentally ill and laid the groundwork for most of the failures we have come to associate with deinstitutionalization. This is what happened: President Kennedy read the joint commission's report and appointed the secretary of Health, Education, and Welfare (HEW), Abraham Ribicoff, to head an interdepartmental task force to develop proposals to implement the commission's recommendations. The task force, which included doctors from the NIMH and officials from various public health organizations, was composed exclusively of professionals, and as such declared itself to be unalterably opposed to endorsement of the state hospitals in any form. At the joint commission, on the other hand, Chairman Ewalt had shrewdly arranged for a variety of unlikely lay organizations to be represented on the rather large panel in order to guarantee broad-based support. These groups included psychiatry's former nemesis, neurology, for example, as well as representatives of the Defense Department, a Roman Catholic organization, and the American Legion; their attitudes were much more flexible than the professionals'. Among their more creative suggestions was one that unwittingly echoed the recommendations of the whistleblower silenced by the APA in the 1930s, John M. Grimes (see chapter 1): they called for a kind of retooling of the old state hospitals into smaller, chronic-care facilities that would be but one part of a comprehensive service delivery system.[18] (The astute reader will realize at once that it is precisely the *absence* of such settings for long-term chronic patients that bedevils the mental health system today.)

Within organized psychiatry, however, the split over the future place of the mental hospitals in the hierarchy continued. One contemporary observer described the controversy as he saw it:

> On one side are arranged the "Hospital Busters," a group dedicated to the abolition of the public mental hospital as we know it. This faction uncritically assumes that everything about the public mental hospital is evil, that the mental hospital should be razed to the ground and the site sown with salt. . . . The opposite camp are the "Hospital Savers." These are partisans in favor of the mental hospital. Typically, they have grown up professionally in mental hospitals and derive their strength from the mental hospital constituency. They are equally uncritical in their overevaluation of the hospital. They refuse to find anything wrong in the mental institution except that staff are too few and the public "apathetic."[19]

The argument was largely a philosophical one about prevention of mental illness: one side, represented by the task force, wanted to promote it; the other side, represented by the joint commission, did not.

The Rush for Prevention

A key spokesman for the proprevention group was Robert Felix, the first director of the NIMH, who summarized his group's beliefs as follows:

> Too many social agencies and welfare departments are concerned principally with those who are already ill and do too little promotion of mental health and psychological welfare. Too much of the work of these agencies is devoted to "patching up," to dealing with existing problems rather than planning ahead in order to forestall the onset of problems.[20]

For this group, creating a system geared to the work of primary prevention was the only worthwhile goal for psychiatric reform. The 1960s saw more of the same heady optimism that had characterized the 1950s with regard to the imminent obsolescence of mental illness—HEW Secretary Ribicoff predicted that "mental illness might be brought under control in a generation or so"[21]—in addition to renewed psychiatric grandiosity. Thanks to the high profile that attended the politically popular community mental health center, psychiatry was able to offer its services as a newly recognized authority on all matters of community life; and one of its most eminent practitioners, Karl Menninger, wrote happily of his vision of a glowing future, one in which psychiatry would intervene in society's difficulties on many levels, including church, factory, medical clinic, hospital, schools of all sorts, prisons, and detention homes; the psychiatrist would become "a kind of twentieth century general practitioner."[22] Society did not disagree with psychiatry's expanded view of its role: when Supreme Court Justice William O. Douglas spoke to the 1963 annual meeting of the APA, he urged psychiatrists to "help all efforts to bring peace to the world."[23] Certainly, the agenda of psychiatry had shifted way beyond the scope of the mere state asylum as its practitioners pursued universal primary prevention on the highest levels of abstraction.

The Dilemma of Chronic Mental Illness

The joint commission members' view, on the other hand, derived from their doubt that prevention methods were particularly effective. They saw a democracy as unsuitable for the kind of social and cultural engineering implicit in a search for either the best minds or the "manifestly unfit": "Even if we could agree on what kind of men and women we wanted to produce, we could not predict the outcome in a given family due to the multiplicity of uncontrolled variables—such as the mathematics of inherited characteristics. Thus, primary prevention of mental illness has remained largely an article of scientific faith rather than an applicable scientific truth."[24] What is more, the commission members seem to have realized that ignoring the fact of chronic mental illness would not make it go away. They were convinced it was treatable—an episodic, rather than a total, condition, unworthy of incarceration at a remove from the community, and no more awful than cancer or diabetes, both equally incurable diseases.[25]

Psychiatry Ignores the Obvious

The philosophical debate within academic psychiatry over whether or not to include long-term hospitals in the overall design of the community mental health centers was argued on the highest intellectual plane, which is to say it was made so abstract as to be removed from reality and therefore of questionable usefulness. At the time, practicing psychiatry's most pressing problem was that it had a great many patients stuck away in decrepit old buildings where very little of therapeutic value was going on. To appear to weigh the relative merits of dealing with those patients, on the one hand, or addressing larger issues, such as reaching out to the community to prevent future problems, on the other, seems disingenuous at best and downright dishonest at worst. After all, prevention and planning for psychiatry's future could easily have been begun even as the profession went on dealing with its preexisting problems, so there was no imperative to neglect old tasks in favor of the new. The chronic caseload, needless to say, existed no matter what the profession did. Nevertheless, the pretense of compelling choice was used to justify irresponsibility—not for the first time, and probably not for the last. But in the 1960s, such trifling matters could not really be referred to so eminent a group as psychiatrists were then, briefly, when the rest of us expected them to bring peace to the world and fix things in schools and prisons and all the neighborhoods of America; and so the unresolved issues never really got addressed. The result, unhappily, was continued lack of interest in the chronic mentally ill, then as now the bulk of the patient population.

Organized psychiatry had turned its back on the chronic patients in the mental hospitals before, during the mental hygiene era. (In fact, whenever psychiatry feels insecure as a medical science, it tends to reassure itself, reasonably enough, by pointing to its successes, not to its failures. And there can be no question about it: the chronic mentally ill certainly do look like therapeutic failures.) In the mental hygiene era, however, organized medicine was neither as powerful nor as prominent as it was in the early days of what is now called deinstitutionalization; this time there was a much bigger impact when medicine withdrew its investment from the asylum and the chronic caseload. The important thing to bear in mind is that the investment was not that great to begin with. Not since the superintendents of the nineteenth-century asylums has there been a particularly dedicated involvement in the care of the state hospital chronic caseload on the part of a substantial proportion of the profession: psychiatrists have tended to dismiss the state hospitals as merely a venue for a small part of their training—early on, of course—and as a place where they can always get a job.

The profession's primary interest has generally been elsewhere. The power and prestige positions within medicine have been found in medical school–connected medical centers, "which instead of being organized around the immediate needs of patients," have been "oriented primarily toward research and training"[26]—and psychiatry is nothing if not part of medicine. As such, it is sometimes better at polishing its public image than in performing public service, and some of its public-relations efforts have looked a little opportunistic. In the immediate postwar period, for example, psychiatry exploited the scandals that filled the popular press after the conscientious objectors organized to seek reform of the state hospital system. Deutsch, for one, wrote a widely read exposé of state hospital conditions in several states; and among his recommended remedies was a much-increased role for psychiatrists, in whom he expressed considerable faith: "It is because modern psychiatry is a stranger to so many hospital wards that many more patients don't return to their communities as cured."[27] Endorsements like Deutsch's helped psychiatry sell Congress on the legislation that created the NIMH in 1946 and again to boost its appropriations by huge increments beginning in 1948. The NIMH used the money to attract young doctors to the specialty, as well as to expand the profession's reach dramatically; but somehow the state hospitals and their patients never saw much of the benefits. "If young psychiatrists took advantage of the public purse and then practiced among the well-to-do, this choice had to be accepted. It was no business of public policy to influence it . . . [and] federal aid must not compromise professional autonomy."[28]

The Chronic Mentally Ill Lose Again

In the end, professional psychiatry prevailed over the curious consortium assembled to be the joint commission. The task force sent President Kennedy programmatic recommendations that called for creation of community mental health centers, funds to staff them, funding for states to acquire inventories of existing resources in order to plan for the future, federal support to improve the quality of service in state and county facilities, federal encouragement of insurance companies to cover psychiatric treatment, and the apparently obligatory funds for professional training and research. As ultimately negotiated, the Community Mental Health Center Construction Act of 1963 (PL 88-164) represented a compromise between the hospital-oriented joint commission and the community-oriented task force; it provided for grants to build community mental health and research centers, which were to provide comprehensive mental health services, particularly to those who could not pay. As countless critics after the fact have complained, the five clinical services that the centers were mandated to provide were, and are, woefully inadequate for the chronically mentally ill. Those services include inpatient (for acute cases), outpatient, partial hospitalization, twenty-four-hour emergency, and community consultation/education services; they utterly exclude, as we now know to our chagrin, the chronic, long-term mentally ill, whose needs far outstrip what is readily available under the rubric of the five essential services. Clearly, the primary prevention lobby had succeeded after all.

If anything, what we now call deinstitutionalization was brokered, not planned. The die was cast when the states realized that hospital costs had to be contained at a time when the postwar sentiments were propatient as a result of 1940s books like *The Snake Pit* and *The Shame of the States.* The question was not whether the locus of treatment of the mentally ill would change but where the next locus of treatment would be. As we have seen, the community mental health center, which everyone took for the replacement of the old state hospital, was never designed to be any such thing—certainly not after the professionals on Ribicoff's task force overrode the recommendations of Ewalt's joint commission. Care for the chronic mentally ill became a bargaining chip in a political negotiation—a chip for the side that lost.

Deinstitutionalization was not planned; it just happened. It would have happened someday in any case, and maybe it would have worked better with a little more advance planning. At certain points in its course, the shift of the chronic population from hospitals to communities proceeded like a juggernaut; and one of those moments occurred in the mid-1950s, when everyone's prayers seemed to have been answered: the miracle drug to cure mental illness had been found.

CHAPTER 3

---◆---

May the Sales Force Be with You: Psychotropic Medication, the New Magic Bullet

> The very desire for success can distort the facts, subtly and pervasively, often without one's being aware of it. In the great majority of cases—where results are presented prematurely, where success is overestimated and dangers underestimated, where there are biases in the selection of patients, and where failures are explained away as exceptions—the physicians responsible have been genuinely convinced of the validity of their conclusions. Self-deception is by its very nature difficult to guard against—almost impossible when fueled by unbridled ambition.
>
> —ELLIOT S. VALENSTEIN,
> *Great and Desperate Cures* (1986)

> We oppose the medical model of "mental illness" because it justifies involuntary psychiatric intervention including drugging.
> We oppose the medical model of "mental illness" because it dupes the public into seeking or accepting "voluntary" treatment by fostering the notion that fundamental human problems, whether personal or social, can be solved by psychiatric/medical means.
>
> —*Declaration of Principles*,
> TENTH CONFERENCE ON HUMAN RIGHTS AND
> PSYCHIATRIC OPPRESSION, TORONTO (1982)

EVER since the mentally ill left the state hospitals in large numbers, it has been an article of faith that it was the discovery of the phenothiazines[1] alone that made it possible for those patients to go home. So common has this assumption become that professional writings rarely even mention any other causes. The party line goes something like this:

38

For many years the major problem of the state mental hospitals was the endless increase of their population. The peak was reached in 1955 and with a figure of 559,000 for the United States and 93,600 for New York State, where the census had been doubling every 25 years. Then, coincidental with the introduction of new chemotherapies, the increase was replaced by a slow decline nationwide and in other countries.[2]

Another version goes like this:

The phenothiazines, in particular the long-acting types, have been credited with helping to salvage (even if partially) hundreds of thousands of lives, with opening psychiatric hospital doors, and with promoting the growth and viability of community-based treatment.[3]

On the face of it, this assumption about the beginnings of deinstitutionalization is compelling because it provides such a simple, straightforward explanation of the origin of the complex problems we face now. But the assumption is not only inaccurate, and misleading in itself; it is also a piece of spectacularly fuzzy thinking that has allowed much of modern psychiatry to pretend for over thirty years that the psychotropic medications would do far more than they can.

In fact, medications were but one part of the overall process by which patients were moved out of institutions. This process, once initiated, met so many fiscal and political needs that it became the preferred method by which people otherwise uninvolved in the provision of mental health care solved the problem of the mentally ill. Psychotropic medication happened along at an extremely convenient moment and made the inevitable that much easier to accomplish—thanks to the prophetic vision of certain drug companies. Prominent though Thorazine and other such medications have been in the unfolding of deinstitutionalization, they did not cause that event, for mental hospitals would have had to change even if the drugs had never been discovered. Besides, the idea that psychotropic medication caused deinstitutionalization is really part of a carefully tended mystique the companies who hold the drugs' patents have worked hard to develop on their products' behalf. To a stunning extent, the crucial role supposedly played by Thorazine in the depopulation of state mental hospitals was simultaneously a cause and a result of drug company hype, thanks to the accidental discovery of that drug at just the right time.

The Selling of Thorazine

The timing was so perfect that it must have seemed like a gift from the gods. In February 1954, three months before the first of the neuroleptic drugs, Thorazine, was introduced in this country, the states sponsored a National Governors' Conference on Mental Health. During this conference the representatives of all forty-eight states agreed that their states would almost certainly go bankrupt unless they did something with the chronically mentally ill other than continue to support them for life in state hospitals. But then medical science stepped forth, ready to revolutionize care for the mentally ill with a wonderful new drug. The cure for mental illness had arrived just in time, and best of all, it took the form of a pill—small, easily administered, and inexpensive. It was what doctors call a "clean" method—uncontroversial and unlikely to upset relatives and journalists, unlike lobotomy or shock treatment. In the general euphoria, no one cared to remember that only fifteen years earlier, lobotomy and shock treatment, too, had been touted as almost certain cures for mental illness.[4]

The Thorazine Marketing Blitz

Hailed as a miracle of modern science, the new medication, chlorpromazine (CPZ), known commercially as Thorazine, was really a miracle of modern promotional technique. First synthesized in 1883 by a German chemist analyzing chemical dyes, CPZ was rediscovered in 1937 by French chemists searching for a synthetic antihistamine to counteract anaphylactic shock in allergies, and in 1944 French and American chemists tested it as an antimalarial drug. In 1951, French navy surgeon Henri Laborit reported CPZ's usefulness as a tranquilizer: he called it "a veritable medicinal lobotomy"[5] and described its effect on surgical patients as "artificial hibernation," or consciousness associated with marked indifference to one's surroundings.[6] In 1952, French psychiatrists Jean Delay and Pierre Deniker reported that CPZ affected mood, thinking processes, and behavior in psychotics. In 1955, they coined the term *neuroleptic* to describe drugs that appeared to reduce nervous activity.

The international psychiatric community was extremely skeptical of Delay and Deniker's claims for their discovery. Nowhere was opposition stronger than in the United States, where the French pharmaceutical company that held the patent for CPZ had to make pitches to several American drug companies before finally persuading Smith, Kline & French (SK&F) to accept a licensing agreement to market the drug in the United States. Using the trade name Thorazine, SK&F introduced chlorpromazine in 1954.

At first, the American scientific community was far more invested in developing chlorpromazine as a medical or surgical drug than in exploring its antipsychotic properties. Of 563 articles about CPZ published between 1954 and 1956, only 39 were concerned with their role in psychiatry.[7] The bulk of the clinically oriented articles suggested possible roles for CPZ in preparing patients for surgery. Not until early 1957 did a dramatic upsurge in scientific exploration of the phenothiazines' use in psychiatry occur. In that year, 113 of the 348 articles published in the first six months alone concerned the drugs' use in psychiatry. Surprisingly, several raised the possibility, evidently ignored by practitioners at the time, that long-term phenothiazine use might easily lead to serious parkinsonian side effects, as we now know it does. The shift in interest from medical and surgical to psychiatric uses coincided neatly with a dramatic restructuring of the sales force at Smith, Kline & French.

From May 1954 on, the history of chlorpromazine has been one of brilliant marketing. In a 1971 interview, Charles Bolling, SK&F's product manager for Thorazine, and Frazier Cheston, director of hospital sales, recalled,

> When SK&F marketed Thorazine, we found that we had a concept problem with office practice psychiatrists. They were generally separable into two groups, the electroshock people and the analysts and related psychotherapists, both with a great commitment to their years of experience and basic training philosophy, and some resistance to the use of drugs. Then we began approaching mental hospitals, and found that they were more interested in trying Thorazine. But the hospitals did not have enough money to use the drug, as they were provided only with small drug budgets. . . . By the end of 1954, then, we recognized that we had to overcome these two problems. . . . In the mental hospitals we visited, we found a heavy atmosphere of custodial care. One reason that the staffs were highly conditioned to this type of care was that anything else meant money, more than the average of $2.50 per day that most institutions were spending on their patients. . . . [We] saw there would be a need to educate supervisors, business managers, and staff people about the potential therapeutic value of Thorazine and the vast administrative savings it offered in reduced damage to plant and reduced inpatient population. We also saw that we would have to go to work with, and similarly educate, state legislators on the need for higher drug budgets for the state hospitals.[8]

The SK&F managers quickly found that their regular sales team was too small to tackle the professional and legislative resistance to Thorazine, so Cheston hired a special Thorazine task force of about fifty men—enough to station one in each state capital. This group was to tackle legislators and state hospital administrators, especially to help them plan their state hospital budgets for "intensive care," an SK&F euphemism for drugs. Some states

> were so apathetic to the idea of funding intensive-treatment programs that the Task Force sometimes had to use "drastic" procedures. In one state, for example . . . a special legislative session took place at one of the state mental hospitals, with the governor's and the legislative leaders' blessings. The entire session was filmed by the "Today" show, and, in that state, it was the breakthrough that eventually committed the legislature to funding an intensive-treatment program for the state hospital system.[9]

One of SK&F's other activities on behalf of their new drug included establishment of a speakers' bureau, through which they helped hospital administrators present their medication budget requests most effectively. SK&F also created statistical summaries relevant to the marketing of Thorazine, including such useful information as the cost of custodial care compared to the cost of treatment with Thorazine, staff turnover before and after Thorazine, broken hospital window replacement costs before and after Thorazine, and so on. The company helped fund various rehabilitation programs, including one in Massachusetts that aimed at returning stabilized patients to work in local industries, and one in Pennsylvania that produced a film of Thorazine's remarkable effect on catatonic patients under the auspices of a program called "remotivation." The SK&F task force members even convinced themselves that they were engaged in a disinterested, altruistic enterprise, for, as they put it, "The work of the Task Force with state legislatures and at mental hospitals was not lobbying per se. It was a true educative effort, done with the sanction of the state mental health commissioners and at the request of the legislative committee heads in various states."[10]

According to the task force, the effort to introduce Thorazine to the state hospitals was an uphill battle, since at first, only New York made a commitment to widespread hospital use of the drug. New York's commitment was made by the deputy commissioner of mental hygiene, Henry Brill, who apparently acted largely on his own and, perhaps as a result, encountered considerable opposition from his own bureaucracy. Whatever risks he took to pursue his interest in chemotherapy for mental patients paid off handsomely, however, for Brill ultimately made quite a name for himself as author of three of the most widely read professional studies of the impact of psychotropic medications on New York state hospitals.[11] In spite of Brill's tireless efforts, the task force reported that

> New York's example was not readily followed; we saw a lot of state provincialism in some of the resistance to large-scale hospital use of chlorpromazine. Eventually, though, CPZ was recognized as important enough so that for 3 or 4 years intensive treatment of mental patients was a number one item at the annual meeting of the Council of State Governors, in terms of things such as mental hospital building costs, drug budgets, and so forth.[12]

Outside of New York State—which, besides having Brill, was the only state with the money to experiment freely with drugs on a large scale—SK&F had to overcome American psychiatrists' long-standing resistance to drug therapy. Having had earlier unsuccessful experiences with psychoactive drugs, psychiatrists were more invested in the shock therapies in the early 1950s. Initial attempts to interest America's research psychiatrists in studying CPZ met with stiff opposition from doctors who suspected it of being a glorified sedative and somehow connected with sleep therapy, never a popular treatment in the United States. In SK&F's view, CPZ was unique, not at all like the barbiturates already in existence; and they tried to demonstrate this by testing the new drug's effect on a large number of mental disorders, admittedly with varying degrees of success.

Apparently, the key to overcoming American psychiatrists' skepticism lay in the laboratory data reported by the French, which suggested that CPZ had the ability to abolish conditioned reflex responses in laboratory animals; if true, one skeptic commented, this "offered an entirely new treatment concept."[13] From this evidence, which SK&F circulated widely, U.S. psychiatrists gradually decided that CPZ might help conditions that had so far eluded all known treatment methods, conditions like severe obsessive-compulsive neurosis, chronic hypochondriasis, chronic schizophrenia, and agitated senility. To test this potential, SK&F sponsored studies at medical schools. One of these, conducted by N. William Winkelman, Jr., at Philadelphia's Sidney Hillman Medical Center, led to the first article on CPZ to be published in the United States.[14]

Winkelman reported the clinical response to CPZ of 142 ambulatory, noninstitutionalized, and for the most part, nonpsychotic patients. The researcher assessed the drug's ability to relieve psychomotor overactivity caused by tension and anxiety, mild to severe agitation, hypomanic behavior, delusions, hallucinations, and various obsessive-compulsive-phobic conditions. As if that range of

43

target symptoms were not broad enough, Winkelman also gave the drug to patients with epilepsy and paralysis agitans. The 142 patients took the drug for two to eight months, and its effect was measured by self-appraisal, comments from families and friends, and psychiatric evaluation, presumably performed by the author himself. On the strength of this rather unscientific study, Winkelman concluded and announced that while CPZ was no panacea and no substitute for analytically oriented psychotherapy, it could, nevertheless, "reduce severe anxiety, diminish phobias and obsessions, reverse or modify a paranoid psychosis, quiet manic or extremely agitated patients, and change the hostile, agitated, senile patient into a quiet, easily managed patient."[15] Despite Winkelman's disclaimer that the drug was no panacea, the impressive list of accomplishments he claimed for it certainly suggests the miraculous.

A second SK&F-sponsored study was undertaken by John Vernon Kinross-Wright at Baylor University College of Medicine in Houston. Kinross-Wright gave CPZ to some thirty patients in a study that was particularly important because it suggested for the first time that schizophrenics taking CPZ were more accessible to psychotherapy. Indeed, he wrote, "patients often discuss their deep-seated emotional problems spontaneously."[16] This was a little like saying the crippled had taken up their beds and walked.

SK&F marketed Thorazine largely on the strength of these two studies and a third done in Canada,[17] in addition to the research done earlier in France, much of which had been concerned with extrapsychiatric symptoms like nausea and vomiting. Those three trials involved a skimpy total of 243 subjects. Many contemporary scholars have commented on the flimsiness of the design of the early research, and certainly by the standards we take for granted today, SK&F's research was sloppy, uncontrolled, and amateurish.[18] In fact, skepticism among psychiatrists about chlorpromazine's effectiveness proved so persistent in the early days that at least two experts attribute the creation of many of today's research methods directly to the slipshod research practices associated with the introduction of Thorazine.[19] Nevertheless, SK&F could claim that only eight months after its introduction to the American market, CPZ was being given to two million patients.[20] Even considering that SK&F may have inflated the figures—the company was, after all, in the business of selling drugs—it is astounding that such widespread administration, on the basis of so little information so inadequately acquired, could even have been contemplated. (Today's drugs must undergo at least two years of testing, on from 400 to 1,000 subjects, in carefully controlled stages—and some critics do not consider these Food and Drug Administration requirements stringent enough.) Yet this tiny fund of results was used to hail the discovery of "a simple chemical agent with which to treat mental illness."[21]

The Voice of Caution, Easily Overwhelmed

There was another side to this story, all but forgotten in today's total reliance on medication to control the seriously mentally ill. Brill and Patton's first two articles, one published in 1957 and the other in 1959 in the *American Journal of Psychiatry,* each appeared along with the comments of outside readers. In both articles the outside readers urged caution in overcrediting neuroleptics with the whole of the change in the state hospital population. The reader of the 1957 article, Sidney B. Eisen, of Chicago, observed that within the mental health field in general, an increased optimism regarding the treatment of schizophrenics had been developing slowly over the years and might be responsible for a portion of the positive developments in the population studied by Brill and Patton. As a final observation, Eisen said, "The chief questions I raise involve limitations in the historical control method when observed over *too short a time,* and with a tendency towards unicausal explanation which masks slower moving and subtler changes."[22] The reader of the 1959 article, Joseph Barrett, of Virginia, stated emphatically that drugs were but one of several factors behind the migration of patients out of hospitals, including increased staffing, better trained staff, and improved attitudes on the part of staff and families toward the mentally ill.[23] And by the time Brill and Patton wrote their third paper, published in 1962, they, too, had retreated a little from their earlier claims and confessed to uncertainty about the true extent to which drugs had been responsible for the census reduction in state mental hospitals. Somewhat belatedly, they warned that "striking and valuable as the recent improvements in hospital results have been, it is also possible to exaggerate them."[24]

The Promise of Relief for Hospital Staff

The combined effects of SK&F's tireless promotion of Thorazine and the dramatic clinical reports of the effects of the phenothiazines make it easy to understand how champions of these drugs triumphed so quickly, overwhelming all their early opposition. If you have ever spent time with a floridly psychotic person who is expressing himself in behavior that was supposed to have been extinguished in childhood, you will never forget how terrifying it is to see someone so utterly out of control. But now imagine yourself in a huge, old building that is visibly falling apart, in charge of sixty to eighty adults, all acting like one-, two-, and three-year-olds in mid-tantrum—such were the patients that the state hospitals, alone and unaided, kept in their wards for over

45

a hundred years. A doctor from that era described a women's ward at New York's Pilgrim State Hospital before the introduction of phenothiazines:

> [They were] so wild I couldn't keep them decent. They'd soil themselves, tear their clothes off, smash the windows, and gouge the plaster out of the walls. One of them would even rip radiators right off the wall. We'd sometimes have to surround them with mattresses in order to give them sedative injections, and these would help for a while, but then they'd get addicted to the sedative and we'd have to take them off it.[25]

By contrast with this ugly picture, the promise that psychotropic drugs could provide hospital staff with relief from such a terrible burden must have seemed like the answer to centuries of prayer.

Hospital staff quickly found that medicated patients were quiet patients, a discovery that guaranteed ongoing use of medication for behavioral control and cemented its reputation as the lifesaving fruit of the latest revolution in psychiatry. In their 1961 report, the Joint Commission on Mental Illness and Health, which was formed in 1955 to assess the needs for mental health services nationwide, proclaimed, "Unquestionably, the drugs have delivered the greatest blow for patient freedom, in terms of nonrestraint, since Pinel struck off the chains of the lunatics in the Paris asylum 168 years ago." The commissioners went on to observe that "the most noticeable effect of the drugs is to reduce the hospital ward noise level,"[26] begging the question of whether patients or staff had achieved the greater liberation. In any event, the new drugs made the wholesale removal of patients from hospitals imaginable and then possible, which in the end became one of the most effective selling points of the new medications.

From the beginning, effects the medications had on actual patients were mentioned by their promoters almost as an afterthought. The most emphasized quality of the new drugs, couched strictly in clinical terms, was that they rendered patients more accepting of treatment—that is, they became easier to handle. At the time, all anyone could see was how much better things were on the wards. Psychiatrists nationwide described the joys of using CPZ for the first time, and SK&F eagerly compiled these observations. Here is a sampling:

> The opinion seems to be almost unanimous that patients who exhibit psychomotor activity, assaultiveness, hostility, and negativism show a reduction in their motor output with the administration of the drug.[27]

Despite our sophisticated pessimism, these new medications seemed to work. . . . We consented to use phenothiazines, erroneously pushed them to toxicity— and found that they worked anyway. Patients became quieter, wards became quieter, and psychiatric aides became quieter.[28]

To say that there has been considerable improvement in the general activity and behavior of the patients under treatment, would be the real understatement of the year![29]

The ability of the new drugs to alter ward atmosphere, unarguably a major achievement in and of itself, came to be proof of their efficacy and justification for their further use. With time, unfortunately, psychotropic medications' low cost, availability, and ease of administration helped them become the treatment of choice—the *sole* treatment of choice in far too many cases.

Weighing the New Drugs' Impact

Understudied, overpraised, and oversold, the new medications swept the field. Early professional literature on CPZ was not entirely admiring, but as the editor of an enormous collection of papers on psychopharmacology published in 1958 pointed out, "It is almost impossible to convince the public and even the general practitioner that in many cases psychotherapy, shock therapy, and even hospitalization cannot be replaced by pills."[30] Unhappily, this romance with the *efficacy* of the medications brought on near-universal amnesia about their *purpose*, which was to make patients more amenable to *other* forms of therapy. As anyone who has worked in a psychiatric facility in the last thirty years knows, the drugs' use as an adjunct to therapy got lost somewhere as their role in the management of patients expanded, until finally the management role was the only one left.[31]

Notwithstanding the enthusiasm of the manufacturer or that of the hospital staff and psychiatrists whose work life was made vastly more pleasant by the new medications, Thorazine and its analogues did not cause deinstitutionalization to occur, although the new medications certainly made it easier for states to continue to depopulate their hospitals. A 1956 study of drug use by all the states, prepared by the California State Senate one full year after the state hospital census had begun to decline nationwide, revealed that by mid-1956, only some of the patients hospitalized in the forty-one states surveyed were taking CPZ or reserpine, an alkaloid agent known to India for centuries. The percentage of patients on medication at that time ranged from a high of almost 50 percent (of 93,000 cases) in New York and 80 percent (of 4,500) in Kansas, to 20 percent (of 48,000) in California, 13 percent (of 37,000) in Ohio, and 10 percent (of 7,250) in Alabama. Most states were medicating between 10 percent and 30 percent of their patients out of total hospital censuses that ranged anywhere from 700 (Wyoming) to 30,000 (Massachusetts). The national totals of the states reporting to California's study came to some 103,000 patients receiving the new medications, or about 19 percent of the total of 551,400 patients.[32] One student of deinstitutionalization has noted that from 1946 to 1954 the mean increase in discharge per state was 172.39 percent, as opposed to a mean increase per state of 164.19 percent between 1955 and 1963. He points out that the lower rate of increase in discharge after 1955 may have been partly the result of the absence of places to which patients could be discharged, and he concludes that "the drugs, then, were an opportunity, not an imperative."[33]

Thorazine: A Cash Cow

No one should be in any doubt, however, that psychotropic medication was and is capable of generating enormous amounts of money. As early in the life of hospital-administered Thorazine as 1956, California found that most states were spending substantial sums on their SK&F-inspired "intensive care" budgets: the total spent annually on the new drugs already totaled $4,781,035 (in 1956 dollars). Although this represented a significant investment by state governments, the average cost of medication, $46.42 per year per patient, seemed a bargain, because it represented only 5 percent of the 1956 cost of custodial care, or $912.50 per year per patient.[34] By 1970, Thorazine alone was bringing in $116,500,000 for SK&F, one part of the $500 million total that year that manufacturers took in from sales of all psychoactive medications.[35]

The Disappointing Reality

Sad to say, the miracle drugs never proved as effective as their true believers promised they would be. First, the mental health industry jumped on the pharmaceutical bandwagon and introduced the drugs across the board long before anyone knew just what they could deliver. No one could deny the drugs' potential usefulness; they still play a vital role in the care of agitated and deranged patients and have profoundly changed the atmosphere of hospital wards and residential settings. However, thirty years' experience has shown us some of the very real limitations of neuroleptic medications: They may ameliorate one set of problems, specifically psychotic symptoms, but they also aggravate and may even cause another set of severe and at times irreversible problems.[36] In treating symptoms, they may mask the real problems of the disease like extreme social isolation and autistic thinking.[37] Furthermore, their use can temporarily obscure but not undo the patient's "poor premorbid . . . behavioral disorganization."[38] We have had to learn the hard way that if the patient's underlying disorganization goes unaddressed—as always occurs when medication is the sole treatment—then in the long run even medication is worthless; its use only postpones the inevitable relapse that will follow any change in the patient's regimen *and* adds the risk of irreversible long-term side effects.

Acknowledging Limitations

The drugs simply do not work as well as we hoped they would. Psychotropic medications control some symptoms, such as agitation, confusion, or disorganized thinking, without fundamentally altering the underlying condition that provoked them in the first place. So for years psychiatrists have had to resort to prescribing them for long-term maintenance, only to learn too late that the drugs have dangerous side effects and can lead to irreversible neurological toxicity. The irreversible neurological condition that is most feared, tardive dyskinesia, results from brain tissue damage and usually appears in patients who have taken antipsychotic medications for a long time, although occasionally it appears in patients after only a short period of drug use. Other than that, little is known about the horrible, disfiguring condition, which involves involuntary and abnormal movements of the tongue, mouth, arms, and legs.[39] Thus, the unknown long-term effects of psychotropic medications turn them into something of a modern Pandora's box. One has only to think back to 1889, when the German pharmaceutical company Bayer marketed a cough suppressant called heroin, which it firmly believed to be nonaddicting, to see how dangerous unquestioned acceptance can be.[40]

Present-day psychiatry offers its sickest patients little besides psychopharmacology. Having put all our therapeutic eggs in the medication basket, we closed off a lot of inquiry into other options, and now we're stuck:

so completely have we adopted medication as the treatment of choice in the management of severe mental illness that we have long since stopped using or exploring other methods, except maybe hospitalization. As one author in the standard textbook puts it, "It is safe to say that drug treatments in psychiatry have been more thoroughly assessed than have psychotherapeutic methods."[41] And studied they have certainly been. Virtually every article and book about psychopharmacology mentions that about 10,000 papers have been written on antipsychotic medication, either to demonstrate or, occasionally, to challenge their efficacy.[42]

A curious quality of the argument about whether psychotropic medication is effective or not, one that has so far escaped notice in the literature, is that it is an argument *post hoc propter,* a logical position that uses a phenomenon to explain itself—this is what happened, which is why it happened, similar to medicine's diagnosis *ex jurantibus,* or diagnosis by "what helps." According to the literature, the efficacy of psychotropic medication was demonstrated, once and for all, by the mere fact that thousands of patients were able to leave the mental hospitals in the mid-1950s; never mind that the reason they are supposed to have left in the first place is that they were given psychoactive medication. One author puts it this way:

> The shift in the fate of mental patients is the most convincing proof of the efficacy of those agents. The normalization of psychosis was so impressive that the use of chlorpromazine spread quickly throughout the world. Indeed, the drug produced an improvement in schizophrenia heretofore unknown.[43]

In other words, we know the drugs were effective because the patients left the hospital, and we think they left the hospital because of the availability of the drugs. Any way you look at it, this has not been the most carefully thought out event in modern science.

In fact, of course, we know that neuroleptic medications did not play the key role in deinstitutionalization that has been assumed for them, if only because the assumption does not hold true elsewhere in the world. On the one hand, in certain countries where neuroleptics have been used in massive quantities, there has been no move to deinstitutionalize patients at all; examples include Austria, Germany, and most of eastern Europe.[44] On the other hand, in countries where deinstitutionalization has occurred, scholars view that as more of a political than a clinical revolution, not so much a change in the methods by which patients are controlled—one in which chemicals are substituted for straitjackets and asylums—but a larger change in society's attitude toward deviance.[45]

A More Likely, If Less Glamorous, Scenario

What actually happened is that phenothiazines appeared at a most opportune moment in American psychiatry. Hospitals were filled beyond capacity with deranged mental patients, states were grumbling about costs, psychosurgery and ECT (shock treatments) had both turned out to be overrated, and psychiatry was under self-generated pressure to catch up with the rest of medicine and devise a truly scientific method of treatment for mental illness, preferably one that could be touted as a breakthrough. Small wonder that a kind of desperation set in as psychiatry failed to keep up with its own ideological commitment to the medical model.

Having touted the drugs to everyone else, psychiatry, with the eager and enthusiastic assistance of the pharmaceutical industry, then sold itself a bill of goods. Millions were given the drug before anyone knew what the long-term effects would be. Also, the earliest studies of the effect of CPZ on the state hospital population never dealt with the likely contaminating presence of the "Hawthorne effect," whereby study results are put in doubt because the mere fact of being studied may have changed the subject under study. The term derives from the so-called Hawthorne studies done in 1939 to test the theory that physical conditions affect work output. The researchers found that while their theory was correct, their testing was seriously flawed because the workers in the experimental group were so well aware that *they* were being studied that that fact alone accounted for much of the increase in output. Although the Hawthorne researchers used this insight to expand their theory to include social as well as physical conditions as important influences on workers' productivity, the term *Hawthorne effect* has come to refer to any research whose results risk contamination by the fact of the researchers' presence.[46] Such an oversight with the early CPZ studies may well have led to an overoptimistic assessment of the drugs' efficacy by confusing their usefulness in ward management with their actual effect on patients, a distortion that we compound every time we assume hospitalized patients are better because they have taken a neuroleptic agent. As John S. Strauss and Hisham Hafez pointed out in 1981, every clinician who claims such a result for a drug "seems to ignore the fact that the patient in entering the hospital has also (1) left his usual environmental context and (2) entered a particular treatment setting within which the structure, expectations, relationships, and other aspects may have powerful treatment potential."[47] Of such overgeneralizations and overreliance on cause-and-effect relationships, they say, is our field currently composed.

Patients, unfortunately, have been paying the price ever since, by taking the blame for the drugs' failure, which is euphemistically known as noncompliance. As discussed in some detail in chapter 5, once the patients got out of the hospitals and were on their own, many chose not to take the drugs regularly or at all. By then, however, mental health professionals had become addicted to their use—whether they worked or not, whether patients would take them or not. Mental health professionals had committed the error of believing their own public relations, and it falls inevitably to the patients to pay the bill.

CHAPTER 4

What Happened to the Myth that Mental Illness Is a Myth?

> In the context of our present pervasive madness that we call normality, sanity, freedom, all our frames of reference are ambiguous and equivocal. A man who prefers to be dead rather than Red is normal. A man who says he has lost his soul is mad. A man who says that men are machines may be a great scientist. A man who says he *is* a machine is "depersonalized" in psychiatric jargon. A man who says that Negroes are an inferior race may be widely respected. A man who says his whiteness is a form of cancer is certifiable. . . . The statesmen of the world who boast and threaten that they have Doomsday weapons are far more dangerous, and far more estranged from "reality" than many of the people on whom the label "psychotic" is affixed.
>
> —R. D. LAING,
> *The Divided Self* (1960)

IN 1961 four books that were to have an enormous influence on the contemporary practice of psychiatry appeared: the Joint Commission on Mental Illness and Health's *Action for Mental Health,* Erving Goffman's *Asylums,* the American Bar Foundation's *The Mentally Disabled and the Law,* and Thomas Szasz's *The Myth of Mental Illness.* Just one year earlier, R. D. Laing's study of the essence of madness, *The Divided Self,* had been published in England as well. The collective impact of these books cannot be overstated, and in many ways we are still reeling from it; the terms of our discussion about mental illness and how to treat it have been totally altered, and the care and feeding of the mentally ill can never entirely go back to the innocent days of enforced custody and control.

In 1961 the population of the state mental hospitals declined by a few thousand nationwide, although no one realized yet that the depopulation of the hospitals was taking place, and the word *deinstitutionalization* would not be used for another ten or so years. In retrospect, however, one can see that the process had begun in earnest, owing in part to the thorough rethinking of many of our most fundamental assumptions about mental illness and the mentally ill. Without significant revision in the official attitude toward the mentally ill—what they can tolerate and what they need—their eventual resettlement in community settings would not likely have taken place to the extent it eventually did. More than just a reform movement, the crusade to change public and professional attitudes toward the seriously mentally ill derived much of its zeal and most of its respectability from a growing body of scholarship that explored new ways of looking at the phenomenon of mental illness. Without such a solid theoretical base, and without the endorsement of the academic and scholarly wing of the mental health field, the enormous upheaval in social policy and practice known now as deinstitutionalization probably would not have gained the broad-based public and political support it enjoyed from the earliest days.

Mental Illness Redefined

In the wake of the books' appearance in the early sixties, an apparently new idea emerged in our collective consciousness: that mental illness is not always nor solely a function of patients' unique disabilities but may reflect the culture of which they are a part, and that merely being deranged does not necessarily render them unintelligible or incomprehensible. From this point of view it proved possible to conceive of mental illness as an artifact occurring naturally in the social system and thus something that deserved society's routine and open attention; moreover, it became possible to imagine the mentally ill person as someone with a right to such attention.

These rather speculative and highly abstract notions found a ready, if unlikely, home in an extremely literal application of their content to the specific and concrete realities of direct practice. It became fashionable, for instance, to believe, or at least to say you believed, that mental illness per se didn't exist. Early efforts to put into practice the idea that mental illness doesn't exist were undertaken occasionally by self-declared "radical therapists," whose goal was to destroy the system by exposing its hypocrisy and hidden fascism. Operating on the premise that the mentally ill were victims of judgmental labeling, it was clearly the duty of any right-thinking therapist to sabotage the system by only pretending to treat the misunderstood and much-maligned victims while really secretly liberating them from the controlling bondage of their label. The bottom line: mental illness does not exist, and to pretend it does by propping up the corrupt system of social control is to allow oneself to be co-opted and used.

Far-fetched though such an attitude may seem today, it was a powerful part of self-consciously enlightened care of the mentally ill all through the late sixties and early seventies. Two vivid memories from my own early practice in that era come to mind. In one case, a state hospital social worker boasted that he and his supervisor had colluded to concoct phony written records of their traditional work with patients, while his real activity had been to meet with the patients in lengthy encounter sessions whose focus was to undermine the hospital's authority and promote the idea that patient rebellion might not be a bad idea. The second example involved a psychiatrist in another state hospital, whose chief endeavor was to eliminate the artificial barriers between patients and staff by the simple maneuver of conducting all interviews sitting on the floor, insisting that patients call him Charlie, and refusing to prescribe any medications.

What is most striking today in these examples of enlightened clinical practice is the fact that what were doubtless sincerely held beliefs had been indiscriminately, though zealously, misapplied in an arena that could not possibly handle them in any form—traditional treatment facilities for the chronically mentally ill. In the accepted view of the time, the state hospitals were chosen for the implementation of the new idea that mental illness did not exist, because the worst, longest-standing social oppression of the mental patient had occurred there. It is more likely, however, that the state hospitals were selected because it was easy to get jobs in them, and the administration was sufficiently distracted not to put a stop to peculiar clinical approaches. Besides, everyone knew you couldn't really *hurt* the state hospital patients; they were too far gone.

Reframing the Concept: R. D. Laing

In themselves, the ideas that reformulated our public awareness of mental illness were not politically motivated so much as they were *radical,* in the word's purest sense: Laing, Szasz, and Goffman took us back to our fundamental assumptions and beliefs about patients and their symptoms, and our supposedly sane response thereto, in order to "reframe" our concepts and premises. According to a book much admired by enlightened therapists of the 1960s and 1970s,

> To reframe, then, means to change the conceptual and/or emotional setting or viewpoint in relation to which a situation is experienced and to place it in another frame which fits the "facts" of the same concrete situation equally well or even better, and thereby changes its entire meaning.[1]

In this spirit, Laing, a great reframer, pointed out in 1960 that to call another person psychotic is not so much to render a scientific or dispassionate judgment as it is to express a social one: in the absence of a reciprocal agreement as to each other's sense of self, and if mutual efforts to resolve differences in perception fail, "there is no alternative but that one of us must be insane . . . [when] sanity or psychosis is tested by the degree of conjunction or disjunction between two persons where the one is sane by common consent."[2] Put more crudely, if you tell me you're Jesus Christ, and I say you're nuts, and provided I'm established in the eyes of the world as a normal person, then you *are* nuts, regardless of the validity of your view of yourself. The key elements of the determination rest on one person's acknowledged, superior claim to sanity and the fact that the judgment is made on the basis of a social encounter—and could easily go the other way. Whatever else can be said about the process of diagnosing mental disorders, and despite all the efforts of the people who write diagnostic manuals, it cannot be honestly described as scientific, which is to say objective, value-free, and capable of being replicated uniformly.[3]

Laing also objected to the marshaling of clinical data to support one's determination of the psychosis of another, as evidence not so much of one's superior knowledge of the disease process as of ignorance about the person who is psychotic. Laing made this objection on the grounds that by adopting a detached, clinical posture based on the assumption that a psychiatrist, say, knows better than a patient what his or her thinking is really about, the psychiatrist will never be able to understand what the patient, psychotic or not, is trying to say.

> It is just possible to have a thorough knowledge of what has been discovered about the hereditary or familial incidence of manic-depressive psychosis or schizophrenia, to have a facility in recognizing schizoid "ego-distortion" and schizophrenic ego defects, plus the various "disorders" of thought, memory, perceptions, etc., to know, in fact, just about everything that can be known about the psychopathology of schizophrenia or schizophrenia as a disease with-

out being able to understand one single schizophrenic. Such data are all ways of *not* understanding him.[4]

Implicit in Laing's argument is a startlingly obvious point that no one else before him had made much of a case for: that the mentally ill person is a person who sees things differently from the rest of us and who has interesting and even valuable perceptions to share if we would but listen. This, Laing reminds us, we cannot do if we concentrate on maintaining and even emphasizing the differences between the patient and ourselves, as psychiatrists in particular tend to do, by such routine and self-reassuring maneuvers as calling patients by their first names while insisting on being addressed as "doctor."

Some critics have charged that Laing, like so many others, based his observations of schizophrenics in particular and psychotics in general on work with the lighter cases. Peter Sedgwick, for one, believes that Laing generally treated only single-episode, acute cases, patients who had had just one psychotic episode and who clear up in a "once-for-all remission of symptoms." He quotes the general secretary of the (British) National Schizophrenia Fellowship as having said, wryly, "Whoever he has been seeing, they are not our patients."[5] While it is certainly possible that Laing's caseload has been acutely, and not chronically, impaired and thus more accessible to therapeutic intervention, this hardly seems to invalidate his observations on the nature of the condition. It is tempting to credit the condition for the cure with the fact of its being "single-episode;" however, one can never know for sure whether the single episode was self-limiting or was kept in check by good treatment, which was Laing's point.

Laing's greatest contribution could well be the idea that the mentally ill may be more like the rest of us than they are different, if we can just leap the chasm made by both their strangeness and our own communication, limited as it is by the imperative of logic. The chasm can be very wide indeed, and our rational thinking very limited as well. I remember being completely unable to bridge the gulf on behalf of a patient who had been arrested for a bizarre crime. According to the district attorney's office, he was charged with sexual harassment in a subway station while waiting for a train to take him to his day treatment program. According to him, what witnesses called "harassment" had in fact been a prudent precaution on his part: convinced he was allergic to hairspray, he had systematically sniffed the head of each woman on the platform in order to determine which ones had used hairspray so he could stand elsewhere.

Ironically, one of the women whose head he sniffed was an off-duty policewoman, who instantly charged him with sexual harassment; and since this incident took place in a city that was in the midst of a big public campaign against sex crimes, this admittedly peculiar behavior was viewed with predictable alarm. Once in custody, the patient's characteristically irritating, but essentially harmless, antics became his entree to the criminal justice system. The world of criminal justice is particularly inhospitable to the truly eccentric and offbeat; the patient's crazy behavior would have looked peculiar anywhere, but nowhere so much so as in terms of the criminal code. Unhappily, we were only able to get him off the hook by demonstrating that by history, he was every bit as crazy as his behavior on the subway platform suggested, which hurt his feelings very much.

Mental Illness as Metaphor: Thomas Szasz

Laing's reframing of the essence of madness was of a piece, in a way, with the reframing of the concept of mental illness that Thomas Szasz has provided. Szasz makes a crucial distinction between illness of the body and the metaphor that is mental "illness," a metaphor he says we take too literally by confusing it with something that doesn't exist—a diseased mind.

> Only when we call minds "sick" do we systematically mistake and strategically misinterpret metaphor for fact—and send for the doctor to "cure" the "illness." It is as if a television viewer were to send for a television repairman because he dislikes the program he sees on the screen.[6]

Much of Szasz's concern in *The Myth of Mental Illness* is his sharp criticism of the process whereby psychiatric disorders are diagnosed. Too often, he says, diagnoses are little more than pejorative labels applied to persons whose behavior offends or annoys others. By and large, he observes, patients who seek help on their own are classified as neurotic, whereas people whose behavior has provoked others to seek help for them are often classified as psychotic; this, he says, suggests that "mental illness is not something a person has, but is something he does or is."[7]

In Szasz's view, which is nothing if not consistent, where there is no mental illness, there can be no treatment, no hospitalization, no cure, nor can there be an insanity defense, a declaration of incompetence to stand trial or handle one's finances, nor any rationalization of socially inappropriate behavior on grounds that the actor doesn't know any better. In addition, for Szasz, "there is no medical, moral, or legal justification for involuntary psychiatric interventions. They are crimes against humanity."[8] All individuals, in his view, should take responsibility for their own behavior, and depriving them of that burden and privilege is unethical.

Echoing Szasz's disregard for the standard practices of establishment psychiatry, not to mention its beliefs, E. Fuller Torrey criticized the application of the medical model to mental illness in *The Death of Psychiatry,* published in 1974. In Torrey's dramatic characterization, the chronically mentally ill are

> the people who are out of the mainstream of our society—the people drifting along in the side eddies both unnoticed and unnoticing. For them, the miracle of their birth is a heavy yoke to be dragged from day to day. . . . To call such people "sick" is absurdness *in extremis.* It is like calling a ladder "sick" for being too short to reach the roof. . . . Our use of the adjective "sick" for such people shows only our own arrogance in believing the mainstream as we define it is "well."[9]

Clearly, as Szasz and Torrey both acknowledge, there are people with a legitimate claim to the condition that has been known as mental illness, and they exist in substantial numbers. They deny not the disability, but the claim that it is a disease. Szasz and those who accept his fundamental premise stress that the difficulties encountered by the disordered constitute problems in living, with which the individuals in question are singularly ill equipped to cope. This view has been articulated in commonsense terms by Robert Perrucci, who sees such individuals as people who

> experience severe *problems of living* that involve interpersonal difficulties with family, friends, and employers. Many also experience life under conditions of extensive deprivation, both economic and emotional. . . . They begin life, therefore, as victims of a system of inequality of resources and life chances that places them at the bottom of society with little prospect for improvement. . . . Commitment to a mental hospital has less to do with having a disease called "mental illness" than with being without sufficient resources to deal with problems that are experienced by many people, most of whom do not become mental patients. Mental illness is therefore best understood as a social process rather than as a medical one. It is a process that starts with everyone, including the victim, believing that [he] has a mental illness and requires hospitalization.[10]

Perrucci's thoughts are similar to those articulated by a trio of researchers who endeavored to describe the actual behavior of hospitalized mental patients in an effort to demonstrate that schizophrenics "have all the characteristics of ordinary human beings," and that what passes for their "illness" is but a manifestation of their "not-altogether-irrational attempt to cope" with the day-to-day problems of life.[11] The authors believe that the psychiatric perspective on mental illness has got in the way of our understanding the phenomenon as it occurs in those we have identified as schizophrenic, with the unfortunate result that we not only do not have a particularly good knowledge of the disorder or its victims, but we also have wound up demeaning the sufferers even as we mismanage the "illness."

Sociology Writes the Mental Patient's Job Description

The antimedical view of mental illness has based some of its argument on the work of sociologists whose focus has been on the links between traditional views of mental illness and perceived social deviance. One of these, Thomas Scheff, believes that disordered people embrace the "sick" role because doing so helps them organize their feelings and behavior; even more, it gives them something to be. When the role is validated by psychiatrists and others in authority, according to Scheff, the patient is launched on a "career of chronic illness."[12] The idea that there might be such a thing as an implicit job description and even what he calls a career for mental patients has also occurred to sociologist Erving Goffman, who has written that hospital life appeals to patients if only because it is the one place where they know they'll fit in:

> It is thus a tribute to the power of social forces that the uniform status of mental patient can not only assure an aggregate of persons a common fate and eventually, because of this, a common character, but that this social reworking can be done upon what is perhaps the most obstinate diversity of human materials that can be brought together by society.[13]

Sociologists have long been interested in the process by which patients acquire the label "mentally ill." To look more closely at the inner workings of traditional psychiatry, Scheff arranged to be present when psychiatrists at a mental hospital interviewed prospective patients to decide whether to admit them, and he discussed those decisions with the doctors afterward. Scheff concluded that the decisions were routine and reflected economic and social pressures rather than any objectively defined condition; he was particularly struck by the prejudicial judgments made and defended by the doctors, who justified their decisions with remarks like the following:

> On the schizophrenics, I don't bother asking them more questions when I can see they're schizophrenic because *I know what they're going to say.* You could talk to them another half hour and not learn any more.

The petition cases are pretty *automatic*. If the patient's own family wants to get rid of him you know there is something wrong.[14]

The sociological argument that "mentally ill" is a label—one that when affixed to people tends to become a self-fulfilling prophecy as well as a lifetime sentence—has profoundly affected us all; it is one of those uncomfortable insights that never quite gets argued away by its detractors, probably because it is essentially true. However, the argument presents its own pitfalls: even if accurate, the idea that mental illness is a stigmatizing label stuck on people for political reasons is not particularly helpful when one must deal with flesh-and-blood patients, who may well be the victims of labeling, but whose problems are very real nonetheless.

Avoidance of the use of the dread label exerts its own tyranny by forcing the terms of discussion away from the obvious and concrete into a vague never-never land of abstractions. By way of an example involving an unlikely cast of characters, I recently had occasion to meet with a ward of designated mental patients who had encountered serious problems in living together and who were extremely vigorous in their denunciation of the destructive behavior of the problem people in their midst. However, they flatly refused to permit *any* characterization of the problem behavior or of the obvious perpetrators in terms that they referred to as "labels"—it was all right to make loud general remarks about stealing, for example, but to face the fact that Denise, say, was stealing or to identify her as a thief was to "label," and I, for one, was soundly criticized for trying to do so in my misguided effort to address the problem.

Mental Illness as Artifact of the Larger World

Other efforts to define the condition traditionally called mental illness have led a diverse group of scholars to link the condition to circumstances extending far beyond the limits of the medical model even at its most grandiose. A sociologist named M. Harvey Brenner makes a compelling case for his observation that "the prevalence of treated and untreated psychopathology is inversely related to socioeconomic level,"[15] a relationship he established by way of a painstaking review of both employment statistics and admissions to state mental hospitals in New York over more than one hundred years. He concluded,

From a sociological viewpoint, then, adverse economic changes bring about severe social and personality disorganization for a considerable number of persons in the

61

society. This process of disintegration is so marked and thorough that, as a result, individuals are defined and treated by the society as mentally ill—a label that prevents the use of common-sense understanding and ordinary supportive mechanisms for reintegrating the displaced individual.[16]

Brenner's work was very much in line with that of his teacher, August B. Hollingshead, whose famous 1958 study *Social Class and Mental Illness* established beyond question that a "distinct inverse relationship does exist between social class and mental illness. . . . [The lowest class], almost invariably, contributes many more patients than its proportion of the population warrants."[17] The larger perspective of sociology, then, has contributed to our understanding of mental illness the notion that it may well be a function of phenomena entirely beyond anyone's individual control and certainly outside the limits of the case-specific, individually oriented, medical model of the condition. It is easy to imagine how unsettling has been the suspicion that by "treating" the mentally ill, we are really pretending to "treat" the economy, say, or the unacknowledged American class system, and in any case struggling to do the impossible. It is even easier to imagine how people involved in the extremely difficult task of caring for the mentally ill have tended to grasp at whatever looked like an answer to the problem of mental illness—and what could be more appealing than a total redefinition of the term? Reframed, "mental illness" became the much more benign sounding "problems of living," for which, clearly, the traditional venues of care were no longer suitable.

The Mental Hospital Revisited

Throughout the 1960s, as in the two prior decades, the most traditional setting for the care of the now-redefined mental patient, the state hospital, was being thoroughly and convincingly written off as a noxious, countertherapeutic, inhumane, and subhuman environment. This time, however, the criticism carried the weight of empirical evidence and scholarly technique, because the authors were psychiatrists and sociologists instead of journalists and advocates. Beginning with *The Mental Hospital,* published in 1954 by psychiatrist Alfred Stanton and psychologist Morris Schwartz,[18] the literature on mental hospitals as self-contained social systems beset with chronically unresolved problems grew by leaps and bounds, although it was not until Goffman published *Asylums* that considerable attention from outside the field was attracted to the topic.

Something about Goffman's book appeals to a wide audience in much the same way that the frankly sensational novel *The Snake Pit* did in the 1940s and Ken Kesey's more metaphorical *One Flew Over the Cuckoo's Nest* did in the 1960s and 1970s. Despite their obvious differences, all three books give the impression that they are revealing secrets about an otherwise hidden and unknowable, but terrifying, world to lucky outsiders, letting them in on the real story by putting them in the know.

To write *Asylums,* Goffman spent a year doing fieldwork at St. Elizabeths Hospital in Washington, D.C., which then had a census of over 7,000 patients. Perfecting the technique of participant-observer research, he sat among patients day after day, openly taking notes, which he later used to write the series of essays that comprise the book. His field of inquiry is what he calls the total institution, of which the mental hospital is but one example—others being jail and the army—and he takes as his particular focus the nature and quality of the inmates' lives wherever they are housed. It is Goffman who has revealed most clearly the dehumanizing, demoralizing, and humiliating effects of life in the total institution on the inmate, and he has done this partly by pointing out how very different the institution is from what it says it is.

> Many total institutions, most of the time, seem to function merely as storage dumps for inmates, but . . . they usually present themselves to the public as rational organizations designed consciously, through and through, as effective machines for producing a few officially avowed and officially approved ends.[19]

Goffman's revelations made it increasingly difficult for hospitals to pretend to be anything other than the warehouses for society's unwanted human refuse they really were; thanks to his relentlessly matter-of-fact presentation of the stultifying pseudo-life led by patients, the facilities' cover was blown, once and for all.

The Nature and Quality of Institutional Life

Probably the most enduring insight from *Asylums,* in view of its currency in subsequent literature, is found in Goffman's convincing argument that the identity of the mental patient is formed not so much by the illness as it is by life in the institution; once an individual has assumed the role of patient, his behavior probably will fall well within the norms for that role. Life in the mental institution in many cases creates the very behavior that we have come to associate with mental illness.

I used to work with a young man whose extensive use of hallucinogenic drugs had rendered him intermittently psychotic and whose personality was unstable, even fragile, to begin with. This young man was not *very* mentally ill—he still looked quite normal and could, if and when he chose, act like the middle-class, college-educated young man he was. On one occasion, though, his Supplemental Security Income (SSI) checks stopped for no apparent reason, and he told me how he planned to cope with this problem: "First, I'll go to the emergency room and act crazy. Then I'll tell the psychiatric resident that I'm hearing voices that tell me to kill a psychiatrist. That'll get me into the hospital and then I'll get the social worker there to fix my SSI." This strategy for coping with unforeseen catastrophe was hardly something he had learned at Oberlin but was entirely the fruit of his repeated, if brief, stays in various mental hospitals.

Goffman's observation of how destructive life in a total institution was on its inmates' sense of the normal has been echoed by several writers who have looked at institutions from varied vantage points. One, an anthropologist who posed as a depressed patient in order to be hospitalized, found that "it was difficult to resist the force of others' expectations, expressed in both subtle and obvious messages."[20] Similarly, a family who took in an uncle upon his discharge from a state hospital where he had spent thirty years, found that he shook with fear if called on to answer the phone, had to be led around the block by the hand in order to walk the dog, and maintained a daily routine limited to sitting around. His psychiatrist's comment to the family was, "The state of Pennsylvania did a better job of brain-washing your uncle than the Red Chinese could ever do."[21]

It is important to underscore the fact that what Goffman and others like him have pointed out is that much of what looks crazy in a chronic mental patient may very well be the product, and not the cause, of life in a madhouse. J. K. Wing, a British psychiatrist, has called this phenomenon "institutionalism," a syndrome he defines as "dependence on the institution, apathy about leaving, lack of interest in events outside, lack of competence in extramural activities, resignation towards the institutional mode of life, and so on."[22] Wing has acknowledged that these behaviors can be and often are attributed to schizophrenia in chronic patients, but like Goffman he is convinced that the deadening effect of life in a total institution produces its own set of symptoms, and many other clinicians agree. One psychiatrist considers hospital life the source of "secondary invalidism. . . . Each day in the hospital [the patient's] disabilities increase, and if given enough time he will become a patient with such severe 'hospitalitis' that he will live a totally 'crazy' existence."[23] Another calls it "a way of life, a career for which [the patient] is trained in the school of the institutional experience itself"[24] and goes on to characterize what passes for treatment in mental institutions as equivalent to rescuing a drowning man, teaching him to ride a bicycle, and putting him back into the water.[25]

The Mental Institution's Real Purpose: Social Control

Where clinicians see institutionalism in individual patients, outside observers, who have mostly been anthropologists and sociologists, see the old-style mental institutions in a very different light. To them, the very premise on which care in large institutions has always been based is questionable. For one thing, according to their collective findings, total institutions do not exist to *care for* anyone but rather to function as a means of largely inept social control; and for another, the institutions are crazy places in and of themselves. As sociologist Kai T. Erikson put it:

> Indeed, the institutions devised by human society for guarding against deviance sometimes seem so poorly equipped for this task that we might ask why this is considered their "real" function at all. . . . Many of the institutions built to inhibit deviance actually operate in such a way as to perpetuate it. . . . Such institutions gather marginal people into tightly segregated groups, give them an opportunity to teach one another the skills and attitudes of a deviant career, and even drive them into using these skills by reinforcing their sense of alienation from the rest of society.[26]

The mental hospital, like other total institutions, is an entity with a hidden purpose very much at odds with its stated goal of providing treatment and care to the helpless—namely, social control of the deviant. Such a paradoxical situation can only lead to organizational confusion and self-deception of a sort to which the mentally ill, with their severe perceptual disorganization, are especially vulnerable.

Thinking about this kind of institutional duplicity, I remembered a really difficult patient named Paul, a big, fat baby of about nineteen who found it extraordinarily difficult to cope with his life after his parents, whose only child he was, got a divorce. Paul had retreated from a world he found too demanding and too hostile into a state hospital, but he did this at the height of the deinstitutionalization movement, which meant that his therapists were always pushing him out into community settings that he hated. For months the two forces, the defiantly regressed Paul and the determinedly progressive hospital staff, fought an unspoken, unacknowledged battle for control of his life. At one point, Paul's attempt to prove to us how crazy and helpless he was—which is to say, how much in need of the hospital he felt—meant that he regressed to a preverbal level, abandoning toilet training and refusing to eat solid food. All of this, by the way, occurred despite *high* doses of antipsychotic medications. Yet each time he got a little bit better, the hospital kept trying to discharge him: once they drove him to his residence, where he jumped into the nearest cab and got back to the hospital before the hospital van did. Surely, Paul was a patient for whom rapid discharge was not indicated but one for whom the traditional hospital role of asylum and shelter was not available; unquestionably, the conflict between what he felt he needed and what the hospital would let him have made him much sicker than an extended stay would have done.

True Institutional Self/False Institutional Self

Sociologist Ivan Belknap uncovered a variant of the paradoxical role of the mental hospital during the three years he studied a public mental hospital system in an unidentified state. Belknap was particularly struck by the paradox implicit in an institution whose stated goal of treating the mentally sick was at odds with its legal mandate to restrain the irrational from injuring persons or property. He decided that the paradox rested on a contradiction: reliance on the hospital as the sole treatment for the illness instead of the combination of prevention and rehabilitation known to be essential for good care. He further decided that the treatment offered the mentally ill was "not medical in origin at all. Rather it is clearly an accommodation forced on medicine in the sociopolitical development of [the state hospital]."[27] In Belknap's view, the upshot was the creation of an institution geared to the provision of custody alone, a "hospital" that was a medical facility in name only.

Psychologist William Ryan believes the main function of the state hospital is "to store away people who are troublesome or frightening, and who, in addition, have the unfortunate habit of acting crazy."[28] Sociologist Leona Bachrach points to the array of functions performed by mental hospitals, including the provision of "a sort of hiding place outside the community for some of its less attractive members, or providing an economic base for the hospital community. . . . Some of these roles were not originally intended, but have evolved."[29] And Nicholas N. Kittrie, a lawyer, feels that the growth of the state hospital system owed much to the reluctance of the legal system to tread on psychiatry's toes, with the result that the therapists thus became total masters of empires they did not seek in the first place and for whose administration they were never granted the proper supports and tools. Frequently, the true powers of the therapeutic state finally devolved upon custodial staffs, and considerations of custodial security often took precedence over individual treatment. As a result of this unconcern and abdication, human beings have languished in institutions which can do nothing for them and have been subjected to drastic invasions of mental and bodily integrity, all in the name of therapy.[30]

Bit by bit, observers willing to look beyond the hospitals' public assumption of the role of caregiver were able to discern a very different set of functions served by the state hospital, functions at once valued—like control of deviants, and surreptitious—such as providing a dump for the unwanted.

The Mental Hospital: Nutty as a Fruitcake

As if exposing the ill-considered, poorly executed mission of the state hospital were not indictment enough, the scholarly literature delivered yet another blow to the institutions' tattered reputation, this time in the form of the often humorous revelation of how really distorted and crazy the hospitals themselves had become. Psychologist Robert Perrucci tells the story of a woman who sought discharge from a state hospital in that hospital's usual way, by presenting her case to a medical staff conference. She told the doctors about the job she had arranged for herself and commented that being in the hospital had represented a loss of personal freedom, so that she was looking forward to a return to community life. One of the doctors present denounced her comment about not being free as "the most paranoid statement I've ever heard," and discharge was turned down on the grounds that she was too paranoid. The patient told Perrucci that all she had learned from this exchange was not to tell the truth: next time, she vowed, "I'll keep my big mouth shut and I'll lie like hell."[31] The mistake she had made was to appear to be too sane, which is never seemly in a patient, even one seeking to leave the hospital. Another patient, this one a mother who had been hospitalized with her son and husband on a research ward whose focus of study was "mother–son symbiosis," realized how phony the data being collected was because the hospital environment was so unnatural and so divorced from normal life. This consideration had apparently not occurred to the researchers, who undoubtedly wrote off her criticisms of their research design as defensive resistance.[32]

The sum total of all the revelations of and the anecdotes about life in the total institution was to create considerable doubt in the minds of many as to whether or not a hospital milieu, such as it was, was a suitable setting for human existence, much less for restorative therapy. The confusing and contradictory institutional missions, hovering uncomfortably between custody and care, coupled with the uncertainty as to whether the goal of hospitalization was to benefit the patient or the community, led to the growing sense among scholars and advocates that the therapeutic model represented by the state hospital had become thoroughly bankrupt, incompetent in design and ineffective in execution. Not least of the model's flaws was its paradoxical assumption that anyone can get "well" by community standards in a thoroughly artificial setting, removed in every sense from that community. As it turned out, identifying the fallacy on which the state hospital concept was based probably led to the single most compelling argument in favor of treatment in the community for the mentally ill. This argument, so obvious and inarguable, neatly reframed the idea of mental illness as something people could and should deal with openly. Following this reasoning, community care of the mentally ill became inevitable, if only because the pretense that anything resembling treatment took place in a state mental hospital became impossible to maintain.

Ideas Taken Too Literally

Unfortunately, the new ideas were only *ideas* about hospitals, custody, environments, care, and problems in living. Some of the ideas gave us brilliant insights into a phenomenon that had been too long neglected, and many of them were profoundly *right* and can never be ignored totally again. But ideas, however brilliant, profound, and morally correct, could not by themselves reshape the treatment facilities whose purpose and goal they had reframed and whose hidden agendas they had exposed. In our collective zeal to right the conceptual wrongs of hundreds of years, we forgot that theory and practice often diverge, and we forgot what chronic mental patients were like. Worse still, we ignored the obvious once again: while it may have been theoretically sound to return mental patients to the community, in part because "treatment" in a remote hospital setting had been declared theoretically impossible, the patients themselves had spent thirty and forty years in that theoretically impossible situation and could be guaranteed to show the effects thereof. So the ideas, while compelling on the printed page, needed modification in reality in order to accommodate the fact of the mentally ill themselves, not to mention the residue of their incarcerations; but this step in the realization of an ideal was left out in the name of ideological purity.

The revelation that mental illness was a myth was unfortunately not shared with those thousands of ex-patients whose lot it had been to be so designated for many years, with the result that they often did not know how to act under the new circumstances. Let out of their obsolete, insane state hospitals into the harsh light of the community, they continued to function in their acquired role of chronic mental patient, complete with its characteristic indifference, lack of ambition, and passive dependence on others. As for enlightened mental health professionals, we allowed ourselves to forget that the mental patient was a product of the very system now in disrepute, and we forgot what chronic mental illness looked like, even though we had certainly had every opportunity to see it during our years in the old institutions. An anonymous critic of the mental health system put it this way in 1839:

> What would be the consequence, if we were to take a sane person, who had been accustomed to enjoy society and . . . were to lock him up in a small house with a keeper for his only associate, and no place for exercise but a miserable garden? We should certainly not look for any improvement in his moral and intellectual condition. *Can we reasonably expect that a treatment which would be injurious to a sane mind could tend to restore a deranged one?*[33]

In retrospect, it is easy to decide that the idea of returning the mentally ill to the community for ongoing care and, for once, real rehabilitative treatment, was naive. I don't think that is entirely accurate. Certainly, the execution of the transfer was inept, but the impetus for the change was based on solid evidence and a body of highly creative thought of the sort that doesn't turn up every day. Part of the trouble with deinstitutionalization, we can now see, was that the new ideas replaced the old without much thought for the remnants of the past, so that thousands of ex-patients, long schooled in the tradition of the shuffling institutionalized mental patient, suddenly found themselves in community settings for which they had no skills or recoverable past experience on which to draw. The justification for such a thoughtless move was the happy assumption that once we reframed the idea of mental illness, it would be reframed in the past as well. This was not only sloppy thinking based on false belief and wishfulness, but in the long run, may prove destructive of some of the best and most visionary of the ideas of the time.

CHAPTER 5

◆

Treatment of Choice:
Community Care
(Whether It Exists or Not)

> This is a field where fads and fancies flourish. Hardly a
> year passes without some new claim, for example, that the
> cause or cure of schizophrenia has been found. The early
> promises of each of these discoveries are uniformly unful-
> filled. Successive waves of patients habitually appear to
> become more resistant to the newest "miracle" cure than
> was the group on which the first experiments were made.
> The one constant in each new method of psychiatric treat-
> ment appears to be the enthusiasm of its proponents, and
> most probably such enthusiasm transmits itself to patients
> in beneficial ways. Even when some small success is
> gained, however, the major problems in the field still seem
> to remain as insoluble and obdurate as before.
> —JOINT COMMISSION ON
> MENTAL ILLNESS AND HEALTH,
> *Action for Mental Health* (1961)

ALTHOUGH no one realized it at
the time, deinstitutionalization had already begun long before efforts to fit
ex–mental patients into nonexistent community agencies and provide them
with inadequate services got under way. From the start, the depopulation of
state mental hospitals was an undertaking that began, flourished, and ended
with an astounding lack of awareness on the part of those actually responsible for its realization—state hospital officials—of just what it was that patients were being discharged to, and just how this enterprise was to be
managed once patients were outside hospital walls. Policy was completely
divorced from clinical reality, probably not for the first time and certainly
not for the last.

In 1955 the Joint Commission on Mental Illness and Health was charged by Congress with the task of "survey[ing] the resources and [making] recommendations for combating mental illness in the United States,"[1] a task they took up with enthusiasm. Even as the social planners associated with the survey were in the throes of assessing community resources, needs, attitudes, and prejudices as regarded the mentally ill—an enormous task that had never been done before and one that took five years to complete—a steady stream of discharged mental patients was leaving state mental hospitals, moving back to the very communities then under study. By 1960, for example, census data clearly showed that the total population in the country's mental hospitals had been reduced by about 30,000 from its all-time peak of 550,000 in 1955, despite an overall increase in admissions during the same period. In 1958 epidemiologists had recorded the fact that "the resident population of the public mental hospitals of the nation was lower at the end of fiscal 1956 than would have been expected on the basis of the trend of these populations during the period 1945–1955. . . . [It was] also lower than expected in 45 states."[2] There was no need to unlock the barn door, for the horse had already bolted; the joint commission was busily planning something that had already taken place.

The basis for the planning and the rationale for the wholesale relocation of the patients began, as we have seen, with the idea that state mental hospitals were terrible places that did bad things to people, and a corollary assumption that anything else would be better. The joint commission report acknowledged that the state hospitals had served as

> a "dumping ground" for a variety of problem persons, particularly certain kinds of troubled and troublesome individuals in the lowest socioeconomic classes, [whose presence] combined with the high proportions of aged and chronic patients seems to be particularly conducive to the custodial and apathetic atmosphere that is a striking feature of our State hospitals, including the better ones.[3]

Even the psychiatric establishment, some of whom were represented among the commission's membership, had figured out that the mental health system over which it presided was less than adequate to its task. The joint commission spelled out the ideal—individualized care, a therapeutic environment, and an absence of barriers between hospital and community—and regretted that by its own estimate, "no more than 20 percent" of mental hospitals then in existence (including public, private, Veterans' Administration, and general hospitals) approached that therapeutic ideal, "in keeping with the modern trend."[4] Not surprisingly, no state hospitals were included among that 20 percent.

Mental Health, Not Mental Illness

Crucial to the joint commission's work was its definition of mental health as a positive concept: something to be sought after, worked for, and achieved. Clinical treatment was to be used as a means to that end when necessary. One of the joint commission's chief goals was to wipe out the stereotype of the mental patient as deranged lunatic in order to promote the idea that normal people could, and did, seek psychiatric help. Psychiatry's focus, then, had to shift from caring for the mentally *ill* to maintaining mental *health,* a distinction that was to take many forms. One thing that greatly impeded the joint commission's efforts, as it had all previous reform movements, was the very existence of the untherapeutic mental hospitals, which represented no one's idea of mental health. The joint commission argued that a long-standing social distaste for the mentally ill was responsible for our historic tendency to incarcerate them, and they suggested that "one way around the impasse of public and professional attitudes that we appear to have erected would be to emphasize that persons with major mental illnesses are in certain ways *different* from the ordinary sick,"[5] thus explaining and maybe even justifying society's traditional rejection of the deranged. To make the seriously mentally ill more normal and familiar, the joint commission said, it was essential that patients be treated in the community:

> Community mental health clinics ... should be regarded as a main line of defense in reducing the need of many persons with major mental illness for prolonged or repeated hospitalization. . . . The principal functions of a mental health clinic ... should be (1) to provide treatment by a basic mental health team ... for persons with acute mental illness, [and] (2) to care for incompletely recovered mental patients either short of admission to a hospital or following discharge from the hospital.[6]

The implications are clear: treatment of the seriously mentally ill should take place in the community, where the patients would be better off because they would be spared the stigma of long-term hospitalization even as they lived within the mainstream of American life.

To a great extent, this optimistic plan depended on an illusion. The authors of the community-based model of psychiatric care made an easy extrapolation from their own experience of the normal: people who are discharged from hospitals go back home—where else? This was, in fact, what had happened to the first wave of mentally ill who left the hospitals in the mid-1950s; but they had been the easiest patients to place—those who had a home to go back to and a family interested in helping them readjust. Ironically, a group of empirical studies that sought to pin down the whereabouts of recently discharged mental patients collected all its data from this first wave of discharges, and so inadvertently confirmed what had been assumed yet was not really the case: that mental patients could be expected to find niches in the community upon discharge. According to the studies, more than 65 percent of discharged mental patients, even schizophrenics, had families to go home to—35 percent to 40 percent had spouses, the same percentage had parents and other relatives, leaving only 20 percent to 25 percent who wound up on their own.[7] A study done in the 1970s during the early stages of deinstitutionalization in Alabama, a state that was among the last to depopulate its state hospitals, found essentially the same thing: 72 percent of ex-patients returned to families, 14 percent went to nursing homes, 5 percent to foster homes, and only 3 percent went to live alone.[8] The first wave of discharges were clearly the lucky ones.

By the mid-1970s, progressively fewer studies turned up considerably smaller percentages of patients with families to go back to. One study, done in rural Virginia in 1974, found that only 48 percent of recently discharged patients lived with relatives, 10 percent were in boarding homes, and the remaining 31 percent were in hotels, rooming houses, and apartments by themselves.[9] Two studies done about a decade apart in New York City demonstrate the shift quite clearly: whereas in the mid-1960s two-thirds of discharged patients had returned to families, by 1975 only 23 percent did so, while 38 percent went to hotels, 11 percent to nursing homes, and fully 28 percent "to places unknown."[10] By then, of course, it was too late; the damage had been done. Wholesale discharges had become the rule, and regardless of where patients really went, governments and institutions for whom there was a decided value in depopulating state hospitals could always justify their actions on the entirely accurate, if misleading, information that studies had shown that most patients would return to their families and live happily ever after.

Discharging the Chronic Patients

As it worked out, the more patients were discharged from state hospitals, the more the hospitals were able to dislodge longtime residents from the back wards—the hapless "chronics" who have since turned out to be such a problem, wandering around in the streets just as they had done on the wards, openly hallucinating and bristling with hostility. Chronic patients, currently referred to by the mental health bureaucracy as the CMI, for chronically mentally ill, are truly the creation of Goffman's dehumanizing asylum. Dazed and often

73

disoriented, they function extremely poorly outside the comforting perimeter of the hospital—no surprise, since when the depopulation of the state hospitals began in the mid-1950s, fully 40 percent of the patients then resident had been there for at least ten years.[11] Chronic patients, moreover, have *never* been discharged in large numbers to their families. As early as 1960, a study in Pennsylvania found that only 33 percent of discharged chronic patients returned to their families, while 22 percent went to boarding homes and 45 percent to rooms and live-in work. Similar studies in California, Illinois, Texas, and Canada demonstrated even lower percentages of chronic patients living with relatives and much greater concentrations in boarding homes.[12] A 1977 study done in Utah found fully 53 percent of discharged patients to be "living in an institutional setting such as a nursing home, a hospital, or a halfway house."[13]

Patients, Once "Warehoused," Are Now "Dumped"

As epidemiologist Kenneth Minkoff observed in 1978, when problems stemming from reckless discharges of chronic patients, uncared for and unwanted wherever they went, surfaced in virtually every corner of the country,

> it is clear from the data presented that many chronic patients live alone in unsupervised facilities. For "better-adjusted" patients, this works out very well. Serious problems can arise, however, when a hospital must discharge chronic patients who are not well-suited to living alone but for whom no other resources are available. . . . Problems of this sort have arisen most commonly when public policy has mandated or forced deinstitutionalization at a time or in a location where suitable resources were not available.[14]

In retrospect, it seems hard to believe that state hospital bureaucracies could have been so mean and hard-hearted as to unload their unwanted chronic caseload onto community streets, knowing, as they must have, that there were nowhere near enough suitable facilities for the patients to live in; but that is unquestionably what happened. It is ridiculous to pretend that the bureaucrats didn't know what they were doing. The literature on the subject was so substantial that Minkoff, for one, could cite ninety-seven sources full of convincing empirical evidence—the *numbers* so sacred to bureaucrats everywhere, not the single-case anecdotes collected by therapists and always dismissed as flimsy and unscientific—to show both the absence of community residential facilities for the chronic population as well as the significant rate of failure encountered by chronic patients after discharge. By 1972, for example, the percentage of state hospital admissions that were readmissions had risen to fully 64 percent, up from only 25 percent in 1950.[15]

The drive to discharge chronic patients from the back wards was well known to practitioners all during the 1970s, whether documented or not. Inpatient social workers in many state facilities were given quotas of discharges to plan. At the state hospital where I worked for most of the 1970s, it was an article of faith among outpatient and day hospital workers that our own inpatient unit would only keep patients a maximum of twenty-one days, no matter what. After one colleague left our hospital to become team leader of an inpatient unit at another state facility, he told me that he quickly learned that when all else failed, staff were expected to discharge patients to an address that turned out to be a vacant lot in a remote part of the city. One of the greatest advantages of this procedure was that the vacant lot was part of another state facility's "catchment area," or area of accountability, so that discharged patients could be expected to wind up on someone else's back ward when, inevitably, they needed to be rehospitalized.

Also common in those years were creative, if cynical, treatment strategies designed to empty back wards of chronic patients. One of these was documented in 1977: an unspecified large state hospital "on the East Coast" undertook to "clean out" its back wards by instituting a strict token economy system predicated on the unusual notion that the patients' condition was really a resistance to participating in capitalism; the patients were viewed as "alienated from the prevailing economic order," which they expressed by being mentally ill. Treatment was designed to reintroduce the values of capitalism so as to dislodge the patients by the same system that had driven them in: patients had to "earn" things, like psychotherapy, that had previously been free to them. The state in question viewed the program as a great success, simply because the wards were emptied. As is usually the case with articles of this sort, the successful outcome is the end of the story; no mention was made of where the patients went or what happened to them afterward.[16]

Treatment for Chronic Patients?

With all the emphasis on getting the chronic patients off the back wards, it seems reasonable to wonder what was intended for them in the way of community-based treatment. In 1961, when it was already five years too late to plan for the discharged patients who were then in the process of leaving the state hospitals, the joint commission predicted that this would be a problem. Their ideal, however, was very clear:

> The fullest development of outpatient and ex-patient services would reduce the mental hospital to a temporary phase in a total program for the mentally-ill—a way station as it were rather than an institution at the end of the road. The hospital then would be truly open, in this case, *open-ended* in the process of treatment. So extended—that is, into treatment services short of hospitalization and subsequent to hospitalization—the modern mental hospital might then emerge as the center of an integrated mental health service to the community.
>
> But here we discuss principles far more than practices.[17]

This passage contains all the elements of the dream, even as it acknowledges the limitations thereof: the community mental health center was expected to address the mental health needs of everyone before, during, after, and instead of hospitalization.

The center was to be complete and self-contained instead of fragmented and scattered, and it was to be an integral part of the specific neighborhood it served, one that would reflect its special needs and unique character. All constituent services—inpatient, outpatient, and aftercare—were to share the same quarters, the better to coordinate services and see that patients received the required treatment. Although the hospital would be at the hub of the model, as befitted a medical facility, it would be but one piece of the whole package. It sounds wonderful, and in a very few cases it really was. I once had the privilege of treating an outpatient who underwent a psychotic episode requiring emergency hospitalization under circumstances that approximated the joint commission's model of community-based care. The clinic was part of a one-building community mental health center with an intake department on the first floor, an outpatient clinic on the second, a day hospital on the third, and an inpatient unit on the fourth. Within seconds of my call from the outpatient clinic to the inpatient unit upstairs, a psychiatrist, a nurse, and an aide appeared at my office door. We conducted the admission interview together, and the patient was whisked upstairs within minutes, with no fuss.

The community mental health center did sound wonderful, and its designers made implementation seem so easy that the program model sold itself. Even a spokesman for the state hospital, the new model's only natural competitor, claimed that community programs had already started in some states and that the proposed community mental health centers were thus an extension of services already in existence.[18] This was far from true, but it sounded good and said what, for different reasons, politicians and professionals wanted to believe, particularly since it came from the only likely defenders of the status quo. As the joint commission realized, advocates for community-based care somehow gave the impression that ex-patients actually received aftercare services even though they emphatically did not: in 1958, there were only nine halfway houses, fewer than two dozen day hospitals, only eight rehabilitation centers, and some seventy ex-patient clubs in the entire United States.[19] The joint commission, of course, believed it was commenting in advance on future needs; but, in fact, the state hospitals were discharging patients into this meager treatment network of 1958 and not into community mental health centers as envisioned then and for the future.

Helping Psychiatry or Patients?

The literature of the community mental health center model paid lip service to the hospital as the center of the system, probably because the state hospital system represented the greatest political threat to passage of the legislation that would ultimately be needed to fund creation of the proposed mental health centers in communities all over the country. Actually, the real center of the theoretical model was the outpatient clinic, defined as "the fulcrum of efforts to remove the barriers isolating mental hospitals from the community,"[20] and, more important, the key to improving psychiatry's image by separating the profession from the memory of the public mental hospitals and their terrible caseload of lunatics. The idea of a national network of community-based mental health clinics was very attractive to those who wanted to see psychiatry firmly ensconced in the mainstream of American life rather than relegated to the back wards, so in many ways the clinic was the heart and soul of the community mental health center model and movement—as it still is. Chief among the joint commission's recommendations to the federal government was the goal of creating "one fully staffed, full-time mental health clinic available to each 50,000 of population."[21] With modifications of the size of the population served, theirs was the model that was eventually expanded from clinics to centers.[22]

The joint commission went to some trouble to ascertain the nature and extent of psychiatric clinics already in existence by the mid-1950s. In so doing, they found a 1955 study done by the National Institute of Mental Health (NIMH), which provided a good idea of what exactly there was available in the community to take care of the patients after they left the state hospitals. The NIMH found 1,294 clinics in the United States, 962, or 74 percent, of which were located in only fifteen of the states. Fifty-two percent of the patients treated by the clinics were children under eighteen; roughly a third of the clinics served children only, over half served children and adults, and about 10 percent served adults exclusively. The report mentioned that the clinics saw a rapid turnover during any given year and were most diligent in treating psychoneurotic disorders. Only 19.5 percent of the clinic patients were diagnosed as psychotic, and they did not do very well, improving in only 45 percent to 55 percent of cases, by contrast with 70 percent to 80 percent of patients with neuroses. The joint commission concluded that "the present operation of clinics leaves much to be desired if we continue . . . to set adequate or sufficient therapeutic services as our goal."[23] Unquestionably, community-based services were not in place at the time the state hospitals began to discharge the patients to the communities.

No One Wanted the Chronic Caseload

Even when the clinics did exist, and even in states that had substantial numbers of them,[24] the seriously mentally ill were not very welcome. One psychiatrist, writing early on in the development of the community mental health center system in Kentucky, justified maintenance of the state hospital aftercare network, such as it was, to augment the services available through the new centers. He listed as grounds for his recommended maintenance of the state aftercare system three considerations: (1) the centers were not ready for the chronic caseload; (2) they would be swamped with ex–state hospital patients to the exclusion of others; and (3) "it would not have been good for a center's community image if it were to be seen solely as a place for the care of former state hospital patients."[25] In other words, the centers simply did not want the state hospital patients, and the state hospitals were well aware of the fact as early as the 1960s.

To this day, clinic workers at large, successful nonprofit social agencies feel compelled to "discourage the chronically mentally ill from continuing services, after the initial evaluation reveals that the client needs more than individual casework,"[26] according to a student in a social policy course I taught in 1988. She based this allegation on discussions with intake workers at several large and prominent community-based social agencies, as well as her own direct experience working in various clinics. As it happened, I knew what she was talking about, because a few years earlier, I had directed a program specifically for deinstitutionalized mental patients at one of the agencies she had mentioned. In my capacity as agency "expert" on the population, I had been consulted by the staff of one of the largest of their traditional outpatient clinics about a problem they were having with people they described as "homeless schizophrenics." Apparently, the people in question dropped into the clinic and hung around in the waiting area, unable or unwilling to say what they wanted, staying unreasonable amounts of time, and behaving "inappropriately." My expertise was sought in how to get rid of them and prevent their return. I found the problem extremely puzzling, because the attitude of the clinic staff was so profoundly hostile and rejecting that I could not imagine why schizophrenics, who are normally very sensitive to rejection, would continue to visit such an unrewarding place. The answer: "Oh, we give them money to get rid of them."

In my own experience in the early 1970s, acquired by doing intakes in community-based, state hospital–connected clinics, the message of rejection to chronic patients was more subtle, since the state clearly bore an immediate responsibility for the caseload that the nonprofit agencies did not share. In one clinic, the weekly staff meeting invariably included a lengthy discussion of ways to make the waiting room uninviting to chronic patients, who tended to come hours or even days early for their appointments—partly because they had confused ideas of time and mostly because they had nothing else to do. In another clinic, elaborate rules for the use of the bathrooms and strictly enforced rules prohibiting smoking and eating in the waiting rooms proved very successful in driving out schizophrenics, for whom smoking, drinking coffee, and eating are the three great essentials of life. And in a third clinic, housed "temporarily" for years in a disused hospital ward, the waiting room was set up in a tiny cubicle that could fit, at most, four people at a time and was thus inhospitable to people of all diagnostic categories, let alone to psychotics. In all three clinics, patients quickly got the message and dropped out of treatment, whereupon our staff meetings took to featuring regular discussions of how bad the clinics looked to the parent hospitals, which were very critical of the number of dropouts the clinics were reporting. Staff invariably blamed this on the patients, who were termed "unmotivated" and dismissed as "resistant to treatment" and "chronic dropouts."

Far and away the most effective strategy I ever saw for getting rid of unwanted chronic mental patients was one adopted by a dreadful day program run by a notoriously inept municipal hospital that is now, mercifully, defunct. Before the hospital was made redundant, it shifted its outpatient facilities from one community-based center, which it had shared with the clinic where I worked, to another. One weekend, the staff moved the program lock, stock, and bingo game to its new location and deliberately avoided telling certain patients when the move was to take place and where the new clinic would be. On Monday morning, all those selected for abandonment showed up at the empty site and stood, helpless and befuddled, until someone found the courage to break the news of their betrayal. I was a junior worker at the time and was horrified by such cavalier treatment of people who struck me as particularly pitiful, if only because their whole lives clearly revolved around such an awful program. "Oh, don't be such a bleeding heart," my hard-bitten supervisor said. "They've got institutional transference, that's all; they're attached to the *building,* not the program. Besides, they'll give up and go somewhere else."

Community-Based Treatment Means Drugs

When clinics did take on seriously mentally ill patients, treatment plans generally focused on one intervention exclusively—psychotropic medication. The authors of an article about postdeinstitutionalization treatment in Hawaii, for example, pointed to "a pervasive belief among staff that nothing very useful can be done for [chronic] patients, except perhaps to maintain them on high doses of antipsychotic drugs if they request help."[27] Not much has changed since that article was written; in fact, I recently heard a program administrator say to a group of colleagues, "We all know what you do with schizophrenics—you medicate them and that's it." Psychotropic medications, after all, were marketed specifically for their ability to control psychotic symptoms, and from the first that has been what they were expected to do. In the heady days of wholesale discharge of long-stay chronic patients, when all things looked possible, it was easy to assume that the improvements in patient behavior seen in the hospital would naturally accompany them to the streets.

The Failure of a Promise

But the new drugs failed to live up to their billing. Positive changes on hospital wards did not transfer uniformly to outpatient settings; gains in symptom reduction only persisted as long as patients were in controlled environments; and the unanticipated need to medicate chronic patients indefinitely led to unpleasant, disfiguring, and potentially irreversible side effects. Still worse, the much-touted new medications were not, after all, the psychiatric equivalent of antibiotics. They made patient management a little easier but cured nothing; in fact, if patients stopped taking the medications, they probably returned, gradually, to whatever wild state led to their being diagnosed psychotic in the first place.

80

Ironically, patients' lives since deinstitutionalization have shown us that patient management through chemistry is only possible if patients are willing to be managed. This is fairly easy to achieve on a controlled hospital ward, but much less so out in the world, where patients can and do tinker with their medication. As any postdeinstitutionalization mental health clinician knows, an enormous factor in the treatment of any chronic mental patient is the monitoring of what is known as his medication compliance. Before we even ask a patient's name, we ask: Is he taking his medication? All the time or sporadically? Does his medication history include a history of noncompliance? It is an article of faith among practitioners that patients' failure to comply with their medication regimens is a ticket back to the hospital, and most authors consider this the single most significant cause of readmissions. In the rather self-oriented values of the mental health worker, a "good" chronic patient is a compliant chronic patient, in or out of the hospital; moreover, noncompliant chronic patients soon find themselves back in rather than out.[28]

Even though we believe that failure to take medication is the reason most patients need rehospitalization, and even though we know failure to take medication is one reason people think deinstitutionalization has failed, we don't seem to have worked very hard to learn why some mentally ill people stop. In fact, compliance with prescribed medication among chronic mental patients is apparently an issue that concerns practitioners much more than it does scholars and researchers. It is only very recently that the topic has appeared in the literature on psychotropic medication at all, and when it does, it is generally worth no more than a paragraph or two, suggesting that it is merely a pesky problem entirely tangential to the big picture; little if any of the attention given to chemotherapy in psychiatry has been directed to the question of *why* some patients simply will not take their medication. When psychiatrists writing for journals do address the question of noncompliance, which they also call "drug deviance" or "default," they mostly tend to list standard hypothetical causes for the problem's existence. These include patients' ignorance, the absence of family involvement in the administration of medication, drug regimens that are too complicated, patient and/or family resistance, cost, denial of illness, and the patient's desire to control the therapy.[29]

Noncompliance: Resistance or Rejection?

The literature is less than helpful or systematic about what to do with the noncompliant patient. In one study of thirty-one involuntary patients, fifteen of whom indicated that they would, given the choice, refuse prescribed medication, the researchers concluded that the wish to refuse reflected a symptom, "schizophrenic negativism," which they defined as "a tendency among severely disorganized psychotic patients to refuse to do things that are expected of them."[30] Leaving aside the question of precisely how "disorganized" someone is who is entirely willing to oppose an entire hospital staff, especially someone with the experience to know just how risky such opposition can be, it is important to point out that in this study, as in so many others, no one ever thought to ask the patients *why* they would refuse. For the most part, the medical solution to noncompliance has been to devise medications that are harder for patients to fail to take, such as long-acting drugs given by injection once a week or even once a month. Of course, even the slowest chronic patient can figure out how to avoid or foil that regimen, by refusing the injection, coming to the clinic on a day other than the one for his injection or on the day the nurse isn't there, or dropping out of treatment altogether. It never seems to occur to most psychiatrists that perhaps patients have a point of view toward medication that is worthy of exploration; with all the arrogance many of us have come to associate with medicine, psychiatrists prefer to assume that medication compliance is somehow within *their* control. I have a memo from one psychiatrist in charge of a large program that says, "The failure of compliance has to be thought of as a failure of the system to help the patients comply."[31] Note that the patients' only role is that of passive recipient of both medication and the extra services intended to make them take it; the patients have no voice in either. No wonder they don't comply.

Medication and Self-Determination

The truth, apparently vouchsafed only to the people who actually work with the chronic mentally ill and not available to researchers or the authors of handbooks, is that a considerable number of patients simply do not like taking medication, however beneficial it may be. One objection I have often heard from patients is that whenever they are told they will have to take medication for the rest of their lives, they feel they are also being told that their illness is incurable and hopeless, which, not surprisingly, is one message they simply do not want to hear. Patients' built-in dilemma is clearly illustrated by one young man who said to me, "You tell us we're going to get better if we take medication, so how come we're never well enough to stop taking it?" Patients who are feeling better often say something like, "I'm better now; I don't need it anymore." And you never know what unexpected concerns might be behind a refusal to take medication: I once interviewed the family of a patient who steadfastly refused medication as well as food, to the point where his life was threatened. It turned out that just before this crisis, his family had secretly decided to grind his medication up in his food in order to make absolutely sure he was taking it; subsequently, he refused all substances his family offered him on the grounds that there was "poison" in everything. On the whole, in my experience, patients have perfectly understandable questions and concerns about medications, concerns that generally go unaddressed by the doctors who prescribe them. Angry refusals to continue to comply have always struck me more as expressions of hurt disappointment than of anything else: the patients have done what we told them to do, but it wasn't enough, and it didn't work. It isn't as if they *want* to be mentally ill, after all.

One documented attempt to elicit patients' ideas about psychotropic medications was undertaken by anthropologist Sue E. Estroff during the two years she spent living in an informal colony of deinstitutionalized psychiatric patients. Estroff solicited thirty-two patients' views about their medication—generally, Prolixin Decanoate, a long-acting phenothiazine administered by injection—and found only three who felt positive, seven who were ambivalent, eleven who were neutral, and another eleven who were negative, three of them so much so that "they had to be forced by court order to take it."[32] The group Estroff interviewed expressed a number of shared objections to the effects of the drugs, among them a common fear of becoming addicted, of losing control over one's life, and perhaps most important, a fear of losing one's access to the desirable aspects of being crazy, identified as the "license for eccentricity, flights of fancy, and fun."[33]

To be thorough, Estroff arranged to take Prolixin in pill form herself for six weeks, an event that she found "confirmed for me what clients had said. . . . By the time I stopped the Prolixin, I was very thankful I did not have to take it forever, for my ambivalence toward it was getting stronger each day."[34] She carefully kept a diary of her thoughts and reactions to the medication, noting changes in behavior and attitude. The most interesting aspect of some of the changes she observed in herself is how much they resemble mannerisms associated with chronic schizophrenics—as time went on, Estroff became irritable, impatient, "antsy," distracted, "foggy," intolerant, and self-isolating. Some of the phenomena she recorded even sound like descriptions of psychosis written by people who have experienced it: for example, Estroff wrote one day, "[I] felt *very* light and loose and shaky when I got home. A bit discoordinated. Conversation racy and animated, but part of me feels flat. Like I'm functioning differently on different levels." Toward the end of her regimen, she noted, "It is harder than usual for me to wake up in the A.M. and I am sleeping sounder. Very shaky in the mornings. Thoughts are more focused, less racy. Scared that might mean I'm a little crazy."[35] She summarized her findings:

> For clients, Prolixin held a variety of meanings. The medication evoked mixed feelings, neutral to negative, about self and others identified with the drug. Clients struggled to evaluate the role of Prolixin in their lives, accepting or rejecting their need for it and weighing its costs and benefits. In a sense, the choice was not theirs to make. Medications played a pervasive role in their environment, coloring their relationships with mental health professionals, with their families, even with their landlords. . . . The web of persuasion surrounding the clients was powerful. Those who chose to try it without meds [medications] ran known risks, to be learned firsthand. Despite this, the persistence of their negative or ambivalent feelings and their attempts to erase meds from their lives reveals a paradoxical dilemma of patienthood, even in the community, that deserves attention.[36]

I know a lot of psychiatrists, all of whom prescribe neuroleptics, but I have met only one who did what Estroff did and took some himself. The doctor I know was well regarded by patients, universally perceived as someone who *never* overmedicated. Staff, of course, mostly viewed him as more than a little nutty, given to incomprehensible, if not bizarre, practices like eating his lunch in the patients' dining area and chatting with those patients sitting outside his office whenever he had some time to spare.

So far, little professional attention has gone to the dilemma of the ex–hospital patients who are free to live on their own in the community yet are not free to do so without wearing what many of them view as a chemical straitjacket. In the hospital, patients can be forced to take medication against their will, in certain limited circumstances dictated by the law that governs the use of involuntary treatment of those individuals from whose dangerousness society is entitled to be kept safe. This law obviously cannot be used to control patients who are outside a hospital, because by definition they are not dangerous enough to themselves or others to be in a hospital, much less to be forced to take medication against their will. If mentally ill individuals who are free to refuse medication seek help with their problems only to learn that that help will be limited to the prescription of drugs they neither want nor trust, then what are they to do?

It is ironic that so far our only response to this dilemma has been to push for amended mental hygiene laws, changes intended to make it possible to force outpatients into treatment, which will certainly mean forcing them to take medications. For example, in New York State, as of fall 1989, a bill was

84

before the state senate to provide for a pilot program of involuntary outpatient treatment; the bill is known as S. 3804, "Outpatient Commitment." Involuntary outpatient treatment is defined by the bill as including the following:

> Medication, individual or group therapy, day or partial day programming activities, services and training, including educational and vocational activities, supervision of living arrangement, intensive case management services . . . to treat the person's mental illness and assist the person in living in the community, or attempt to prevent a relapse or deterioration that may reasonably be predicted to result in the need for hospitalization. . . . In order for the court to order the involuntary administration of anti-psychotic drugs as part of the treatment program, the court must find that the hospital has demonstrated by clear and convincing evidence that the patient is incapable of making a treatment decision, as a result of mental illness, and that the proposed treatment is clinically appropriate.[37]

What sponsors of political initiatives such as this fail to recognize is that involuntary treatment is enforced social control wherever it takes place. It is hypocritical to pretend that involuntary outpatient treatment has anything to do with mental health, something that depends on a certain degree of autonomy and self-determination.

Medication and Community Care: Overused and Oversold

One point cannot be overemphasized: Deinstitutionalization depended on the ability of the mental health field to maintain its long-term patients outside hospitals for the first time since colonial days; to do this, mental health professionals have relied above all else on psychoactive medications. Their great mistake was to assume, arrogantly and condescendingly, that chronic patients would go along with the plan and would view the medications with the same enthusiasm as therapists. No one who has had the sometimes dubious privilege of sitting through a case conference or a team meeting or a grand rounds in a psychiatric facility could ever doubt the ubiquity and predominance of medication in the treatment arsenal; the topic *always* comes up. Clinicians rely on medication when they are feeling frightened of certain patients or of their conditions, when they do not know what else to do, and when they want to control behavior. A psychiatrist I know is working at a famous and highly regarded hospital on a new research project in which patients with very serious mental illness are treated without medication for a few weeks. One of the requirements for admission to the project is that the patients cannot ever have taken psychoactive drugs in the past, and not surprisingly, the project staff is having a very hard time finding suitable candidates—in fact, after four months in existence, they had only found six.

Looking back, it is easy to see that community mental health care got its start thanks to unwarranted optimism about the efficacy of neuroleptic medication, a touching faith in the interest of mental health clinics in preventing rehospitalization of the previously hospitalized by treating them, and most of all, a wishful fantasy about the future availability of community resources to take the place of the asylums. The community mental health movement was overwhelmed before it even began by events over which it had no control, most particularly by the fact that patients had already been discharged long before the only serious national effort to plan for their release got under way. With the advantage of hindsight, it seems clear that the members of the Joint Commission on Mental Illness and Health were overly optimistic and even naive about the extent to which the system that provided care to the seriously mentally ill would and could change, just because it was time for it to change. As one illustrious psychiatrist put it in dissenting from the final report:

> Had I been writing the report, I do not think I would have been quite as positive about some things. One gets the feeling in spots of a slight air of belligerence, but I know it was not intended. Besides, I guess my efforts would be designated as pusillanimous, and I guess one is as bad as the other.[38]

No systemic change of the magnitude of deinstitutionalization could ever have happened smoothly or efficiently. The wonder is that it happened at all, given the weight of history and tradition and the fact that what was being done had never been done before, so that no one knew what to expect. The truth is, though, that the change did not happen because of ideology or even because of the availability of new psychopharmacological agents or interest in the community mental health center model; it happened because hospital-based custodial care cost too much.

CHAPTER 6

How Deinstitutionalization Never Saved Us a Dime

An economy can afford to spend whatever it desires to spend. All that is necessary is that we spend less on something else. . . . What society can spend (and ultimately what society should spend) depends on the value system that society holds to. It is obvious that society *can* spend much more on mental illness (or on anything) than it presently is doing. Whether or not it chooses to do so is another question.

—RASHI FEIN,
Economics of Mental Illness (1958)

The recommodification [from *commodity*] of the mental patient possesses an irresistible combination of virtues. It saves money while the ex-patients are alive (though to some degree only by transferring costs between levels of government); and it dramatically accelerates the speed with which crazy people move along the pathway to the grave.

—ANDREW SCULL,
A New Trade in Lunacy (1981)

I N New York City, where I live, there is a street hustle called three card monte, a version of the old shell-and-pea game of carnival fame. In both these games, the operator moves one object (a pea, or a red card in monte) around very fast among three identical hiding places (the shells or the black cards); and spectators are invited to bet money on which shell hides the pea or which card is the red one. In fact, the whole game is an elaborate device used to set up a "fish," or victim, so that he will bet large sums based upon his false belief that he *knows* where the object is, a belief to which he has been very carefully led by the operator. The foolish fish is separated from his money because he, like the operator, is eager to get

87

something for nothing: the fish is convinced he can beat the operator at his own game; and the operator shrewdly challenges and exploits the player's greed and confidence in his superior talents.[1] It is an ugly and cynical game on both sides, played either by sociopaths looking to part self-satisfied "vics" (victims) from their money, or by narcissists who cannot believe that some street hustler's intelligence could possibly rival their own; and the whole thing reminds me very much of contemporary mental health funding.

Deinstitutionalization: A Cost-Cutting Measure

For some reason, early advocates of community-based treatment of the mentally ill decided to use the argument that placing patients in the community would save the government money, or maybe the government decided on its own that this would happen. In any case, the belief persists to this day that to deinstitutionalize the mentally ill was to save money, even though everyone knows perfectly well that the United States spends more today than ever before on mental health care, and that the bulk of that money is still going to support the old state mental hospitals. But as any three card monte operator knows, what someone thinks depends entirely on what card he is shown, and his willingness to believe what he is shown will depend largely on his need to be right. Community-based care advocates convinced themselves that it would be cheaper to treat patients outside the hospital, and politicians, who did not necessarily share the advocates' philosophy nor their interest in the well-being of the disabled, leapt to the conclusion that it would be cheaper for patients to *live* outside the hospital as well, with or without treatment. Both conclusions appear to have been drawn almost entirely on wishful thinking. For politicians, as for purveyors of mental health care, enlightened self-interest proved to be a powerful motivating factor and one that enabled them to believe the most amazing things.

Traditional Funding Sources

The background to the current picture of funding for mental health starts with the reform movement initiated in the mid-1800s by Dorothea Dix and Horace Mann. Their plan for centralizing mental hospital care, known as the Dix–Mann formula, replaced a failed attempt by states and localities to share the per diem costs of custodial care for indigent inmates of state facilities with a grandiose plan for large, state-supported institutions that were expected to help create a good society. Dix's ultimate goal, which she fought for years to achieve, was to secure federal funding for the public mental hospitals. In fact, she saw legislation pass both houses of Congress, only to lose her campaign to President Franklin Pierce's veto in 1854. Ironically, nineteenth-century reformers viewed state hospitalization as a therapeutic intervention that was likely to prevent long-term care, especially if provided early on in the course of what reformers had helped to redefine as an illness.[2]

The Dix–Mann formula for public funding of mental hospital care remained the rule nationwide until 1954, when New York State passed its landmark Community Mental Health Services Act (CMHSA), the first attempt by a state to develop mental health services in local communities with fiscal support from both state and local sources. Although the stated purpose of New York's legislation was the promotion of coordinated services for the prevention and treatment of mental illness, its real purpose, judging from Governor Thomas E. Dewey's budget message for fiscal 1955, was to reduce the state's fiscal responsibility for its institutionalized mentally ill by promoting the idea of aftercare for ex-patients in community clinics.[3] CMHSA passed the state legislature unanimously and with no debate on 3 February 1954 and was signed into law a few days later. Until 1957, when California passed the Short–Doyle Act, CMHSA was the nation's only such law, although by 1967, twenty-seven states had passed equivalent legislation.[4]

Both the New York and California laws authorized communities to develop local mental health services, with half the funding in New York and 90 percent in California to come from the states in question. Although the authors and implementers of New York's legislation preferred in retrospect to emphasize the high-minded ideals and pioneering spirit of their efforts, stressing the "expansion of the spectrum of care" that would become available to the mentally disordered as a result of their efforts,[5] it is clear from contemporary newspaper accounts that New York's CMHSA, at least, was introduced to reduce the state hospital census and thus its cost. Certainly, it was publicized that way.[6]

The States Draw the Line

The impetus for the effort to redesign the funding patterns of over a century was simple: the costs of maintaining mental patients for life in total institutions were growing steadily and rapidly, and those costs threatened to bankrupt the states. Prior to the 1954 National Governors' Conference on Mental Health (see chapter 2), the Council of State Governments sent each governor a questionnaire to be answered about his state's hospitals, and the council got a remarkable return of 94 percent. The council used data from thirty-seven states—all except Arizona, Georgia, Indiana, Kentucky, Maine, Minnesota, Mississippi, North Dakota, Oklahoma, Tennessee, and West Virginia, whose data were evidently incomplete at the time of compilation.[7] The data thus acquired enabled the council to establish the fact that nationally, states had experienced an increase in total expenditures for mental health care that was truly staggering, as indicated in table 1.

The council, which functioned as a sort of lobby on behalf of its members, also pointed out that in the decade following 1939, the median annual cost per patient in the nation's mental hospitals had risen from $246 in 1939 to $636 in 1949.[8] The members further observed that individual states were affected to different degrees by the overall rise in mental health care costs, so that the poorer states were particularly hard hit. Over the decade that followed 1939, the ten states whose mental health expenditures showed the biggest increases included Idaho (which experienced an overall rise of 394.3 percent), North Carolina (318.8 percent), New Mexico (301.4 percent), and Iowa, Illinois, and Ohio (201.4 percent each). By contrast, the council pointed out, the consumer price index for the same period rose from 100.2 to 171.4, a substantial increase to be sure, but nowhere near as steep as the rise in mental health costs.[9]

TABLE 1

State Mental Health Care Appropriations/Expenditures
1939–1950

	1939*	1949*	% Increase 1939–1949	1950†	% Increase 1939–1950
Capital[a]	$11,626,685	$61,867,498	432.1	$143,070,733	1130.5
Maintenance[b]	98,581,557	297,599,191	201.9	334,104,628	238.9
TOTAL	110,208,242	359,466,689	226.2	447,175,361	333.0

SOURCE: Council of State Governments, *The Mental Health Programs of the Forty-eight States* (Chicago, Ill.: The Council, 1950), p. 107.
*expenditures
†appropriations
[a]*Capital* included new construction, additions, and improvements to old facilities.
[b]*Maintenance* included wages and salaries, fuel, power, water, and miscellaneous expenses.

The States Battle Rising Costs

The reasons for the inexorable rise in costs to the states, particularly after the Second World War, were clear and well understood. First, the bulk of the patients in the hospitals wound up staying indefinitely, often leaving only when they died. Second, medical science had succeeded in lengthening life expectancy in general, so long-stay patients could be expected to be in hospitals longer before dying, and the pool of older people at risk for senility and other conditions associated with aging was growing as well. Third, as more patients stayed for longer periods, added strain was put on the physical plants, which wound up requiring more and more additions and improvements as time went on. Just to make the picture even gloomier, in many cases the hospital buildings themselves dated from the mid-nineteenth century, and as a result were expensive to heat and difficult to repair. Other costs, like food and clothing, went up steadily as well, just as they did for all consumers. Fourth, the admission rate kept going up: "First admissions to all mental hospitals in the United States have averaged about 150,000 persons annually in recent years and are now approaching 200,000 per year," worried the council in 1950.[10] The council offered several suggestions as to the cause of the overall rise in admissions, among them the assumption that the more beds a hospital has, the more patients will be found to fill them, and the notion that more and more people in the United States had come to view life's problems as a function of mental illness.

The crux of the matter for the states was the fact that they had to bear the expenses of the state mental hospitals alone. Unlike the other three of the "big four" state-level public expenditures—education, highways, and welfare—mental health costs had traditionally been borne entirely by the states. The council noted that "mental institutions . . . receive no federal grants-in-aid; they are operated by political subdivisions in only a few instances; and expenditures for their construction, maintenance, and operation are financed almost entirely from state revenues."[11] The states, then, faced a grim future in 1950: based on their uniform experience over the past century, they could expect more admissions of more people who would stay longer, at prices that could only rise, presumably by the same or even more enormous increments.

Since the states were hardly extravagant in their spending for mental health care, they could not hope to save much by cutting costs: on the contrary, their expenditures were extremely low relative to those found in private and Veterans' Administration (VA) hospitals. In 1949, the average annual expenditure per patient in a state mental hospital was $720, compared with $2,133 in the VA hospitals, $2,500 in the private hospitals, and $5,104 in the psychopathic hospitals (an invention of the mental hygiene movement of the early twentieth century, roughly comparable to the psychiatric units of today's teaching hospitals[12]). The American Psychiatric Association estimated that to meet the APA minimum standards for care, a hospital would have to spend $1,825 per patient per year, or $5 per day. Interestingly enough, compared to the average per diem cost of care in medical hospitals, mental hospital care was dirt cheap and had risen nowhere near as fast over time: between 1888 and 1948, the average per diem cost of medical hospitalization had gone from $1.40 to $14.61, whereas the average per diem cost of mental hospitalization had only doubled, from $1.00 to $2.00. But the bottom line was what worried the states, whose total bill for public mental hospital care in 1949 was $405,107,901—and that money only covered the cost of day-to-day maintenance.[13]

Part of the states' problem was (and is) that while no one really minds spending tax dollars to cure disease, it is easy to resent the relative fortune it costs the taxpayer to provide custodial care for intractable, disabling illnesses, like tuberculosis and polio earlier in this century or chronic mental illness and acquired immunodeficiency syndrome (AIDS) now.[14] Clearly, it is much harder to get people or government or both to foot the bill for what is in essence long-term, even lifetime, maintenance of hopeless cases than it is to rustle up the one-time cost, however exorbitant, of reattaching the severed hand of one accident victim, using the dramatic and expensive technique of microsurgery. Grudging public support of those constantly in need only makes the difficult work of caring for the incurable that much harder. In 1960, a former New York State commissioner of mental hygiene lamented

> the financial straitjacket placed upon the mental hospitals, which are expected to operate a modern medical facility with a full program of psychiatric treatment on a fiscal pattern designed for a nineteenth-century poorhouse. Psychiatric care in a general hospital today costs from $25 to $40 a day. Yet, throughout the country, state hospitals are struggling to provide the same kind of care on an average of less than $5 a patient per diem. . . . Plans can be implemented only to the degree that they are supplemented by cold cash.[15]

As they got together in 1954 to consider ways of lightening the financial burden imposed by their total responsibility for the mentally ill, state governments were worried about the money they were already spending and even more worried about what that same burden would amount to in the future. In the long run, custodial care is much more expensive to provide than is state-of-the-art medical technology—a CT scanner, say—because the latter often represents just one hefty initial investment, followed by relatively small costs for upkeep and the few technicians needed to operate the equipment during more or less normal business hours. In contrast, custodial care is labor intensive, and the workers generally belong to a union and have to cover three shifts, twenty-four hours a day, 365 days a year, including holidays—and *that's* expensive. By 1984, the states' direst predictions had come true: in thirty-five years, the annual cost of exactly the same custodial care for one patient had risen from $720 in 1949 to $41,651.[16]

The States Seek Alternatives to Hospitalization

The solution the states came up with in 1954 to reduce their burden was not to look to the federal government for financial aid, as one might expect, but rather to find alternative means by which to care for people then in state hospitals who no longer really needed to be there—in other words, they began to look seriously at the possibility of escaping their burden of sole responsibility for the public caseload altogether. *"Out-patient clinics should be extended and other community resources developed to care for persons in need of help, but not of hospitalization,"* they wrote.[17] The states' prophetic shift of focus away from the hospitals to vaguely defined "community resources" and nonexistent clinics may well have marked the birth of what came to be called deinstitutionalization, for in one bold move, the states redefined the terms of public discussion of mental illness, probably forever. Adroitly, they changed the subject from the standard topic for newspaper exposé—the terrible, unscientific, too expensive, scandalous state mental hospital—to the mentally ill themselves, as people who might conceivably be better off somewhere else. By completely recasting the terms in which mental illness was discussed—or reframing the argument, in the jargon of the times—the states finally relieved themselves of their burden of total financial and moral responsibility for the chronically mentally ill in a way that no federal financial aid could possibly have done.

The States Get Lucky: Federal Government Funds

The first real ray of fiscal hope for the states came in 1960, when the federal government offered a helping hand in the form of Medical Assistance to the Aged (Medicare), a method of subsidizing general and chronic hospital care, as well as nursing home and home health care services for income-eligible elderly patients and welfare recipients, under Title I of the Social Security law—provided the care was *not* given in state-run institutions, deliberately excluded by the federal government as approved service sites. This financial aid for long-term care of the frail elderly was followed up in 1965, when Title XIX and Title XX of the Social Security law provided for Medicare and Medicaid (health care reimbursement for the poor) to be made available to states to subsidize care outside institutions; the same amendment to existing law also established the Old Age Assistance (OAA), Aid to the Permanently and Totally Disabled (APTD), and Old Age and Survivor Insurance (OASI) entitlements.

The first thing the states did to take advantage of new funding sources willing to support community-based settings was to begin moving the elderly out of the state mental hospitals into nursing homes. The states had two good reasons to choose the homes for that particular group of patients: for one thing, the elderly made up fully 30 percent of the state hospital caseload, and for another, Medicaid—called by the U.S. General Accounting Office "the most important federally sponsored program affecting deinstitutionalization"[18]—reimbursed the states for between 50 percent and 78 percent of eligible costs incurred by the 30 percent of its total caseload once the patients entered nursing homes. Not until 1977 did the federal government notice that it had failed to enforce its own rules requiring the states to develop alternatives to institutional care and had in fact made it doubly rewarding for them not to do so by providing the states with financial relief as well as a chance to unload almost a third of their hospital patients.[19] This sudden shift of 30 percent of the state mental hospital caseload into local communities failed to cause an uproar at the time because the elderly mental patients themselves tended not to provoke controversy—they were unintimidating, rarely committed crimes, and infrequently performed dangerous, deranged acts.[20]

In a way, the federal government has only itself to blame for the failure of states to develop genuine, community-based alternatives to institutional care for the mentally ill, because Medicaid did not reimburse many of the mental health services that knowledgeable practitioners considered essential for the chronic population even in those early days—specifically, clinical services such as day hospitalization and nonmedical services such as casework, advocacy, and vocational counseling. Because the new funding streams—as the bureaucracy insists on calling money it is making available to be spent—were tied to medical providers, the net result of the introduction of Medicaid money into the mental health field was to promote the expanded use of alternative *institutions* rather than genuinely alternative *care*. As Ernest Gruenberg has pointed out, after Medicare and Medicaid became available, the balance shifted over remarkably from mental hospital occupancy rates for the elderly to an epidemic of nursing home construction and nursing home place-ments. . . . The amendments to the [Social Security Act] had an even larger impact on the care of mentally ill people than the actions associated with the creation of the mental health centers. While some leaders in public health and psychiatry played an active part in the formulation of Medicare and Medicade [*sic*] legisla-tion, they had little interest in or understanding of the implications of chronic mental illness here in this country. The impact of these amendments on the financing of state mental hospitals, nursing homes, and mental health centers was not appreciated for a number of years by those responsible for setting policies with respect to those agencies.[21]

The impact of the existence of Medicaid and Medicare was decidedly not lost on all social planners; otherwise, the states would not have exploited their potential with regard to the elderly in mental hospitals quite so efficiently, and the nursing home industry would not have seen so clearly the opportunity to cash in. Beginning in 1965, the state mental hospital population decreased steadily each year, while at the same time, the nursing home population increased. In 1960, all categories of mental hospitals nationwide housed 630,046 people, while "homes for the aged," as the Bureau of the Census calls them, contained 469,717; in 1970, however, the mental hospitals had only 433,890 inmates, while homes for the aged counted 927,514.[22] Statistical evi-dence on such a scale, combined with the gigantic shifts in placement of such large groups of people, does not accumulate without someone noticing. Fur-thermore, the very tidiness of the shift strongly suggests it was a deliberate fiscal maneuver on the part of one or more government entities. The switch from mental hospital to nursing home as the locus of care for the senile elderly—at someone else's expense, no less—was no accident.

Private Enterprise Touts the Nursing Home

The use of nursing homes to rehouse the mentally ill proved so convenient and profitable for states that overuse was inevitable—it simply didn't pay not to use such an eager, willing resource. In Massachusetts, for example, state officials quickly learned that while Medicaid would reimburse them for 50 percent of nursing home expenses, it would pay nothing toward the care of patients under sixty-five in mental hospitals. The 50 percent reimbursement was available for patients over sixty-five in either location, *but* in the case of hospitalized elderly, the money went into the state's general fund, not back to the mental health system.[23] The federal government was saying, in effect, that it would help states support the senile elderly as long as they were not in state mental hospitals, which were still the states' sole political and fiscal responsibility. From the states' point of view, nursing home placement for the elderly mental patient brought a double payoff, anyway: the state not only got half the expenses reimbursed by the federal government for each patient placed in a home but it also saved all the money that otherwise would have been spent to house the same patients in state hospitals. A state's mental health department would have had to be stupid not to climb aboard this particular gravy train.

The States Hit the Jackpot: SSI

Useful as Medicaid and nursing home placements were in enabling states to reduce the burden of the chronically mentally ill on their hospitals and their entitlement rolls, nothing proved quite so valuable a resource as did SSI. The Social Security Amendments of 1972 (PL 92-603) provided the nation's first program of guaranteed income for certain groups with a new entitlement called, in full, Supplemental Security Income for the Aged, the Disabled, and the Blind, but known to everyone as SSI. The enabling legislation, which passed the Congress on 30 October 1972 and went into effect on 1 January 1974, was considered unique in the annals of welfare legislation because it established nationally uniform eligibility requirements based on presumed need rather than on a means test applied on a case-by-case basis, which is the inelegant expression the welfare industry uses to describe the process by which it decides whether someone is poor enough to be eligible for a specific program. SSI, by contrast, is available to anyone who meets the requirements of age, blindness, or disability sufficient to render him or her incapable of entering the work force, as determined by a doctor.[24]

SSI presented the states with several obvious advantages. Unlike Medicaid, for one, which required a state contribution, SSI was fully federally funded—although in recognition of the fact that the cost of living varied from state to state, the program allowed for states to make an additional payment direct to the recipient, on a strictly voluntary basis. Even more important from the states' point of view, SSI was to be administered by the federal government; that fact alone has indeed saved the states a huge amount of money.[25] The advantages to SSI usually mentioned by students of the system include the relative absence of stigma attached to Social Security as opposed to welfare, and the often substantial rise in benefits paid out to eligible recipients in the poorer states—in 1978 in Mississippi, for example, an SSI client got $129.47 each month, which compared dramatically with the $13.58 the average Mississippian on public assistance received at the time.[26] What little has been written about SSI and its impact on the lives of the mentally ill has inadvertently misled us all by focusing exclusively on the recipients and the presumed advantages to them of the entitlement. The real beneficiaries have been the states.

SSI found a natural and unusually broad base of supporters among groups who normally opposed and distrusted each other—patient advocates and therapists as well as the mental health bureaucracies. The federal government touted its new program as one that helped "to make it possible for [mentally disabled persons] to be released from institutions;"[27] and propatient groups hailed the new entitlement for its finessing the stigma that has always plagued welfare and its recipients. State mental health bureaucracies, needless to say, immediately and vigorously promoted the new entitlement, which not only offered a potentially useful device for patient support outside their hospitals but also had the unique characteristic of being a welfare program that patients could apply for before leaving the hospital. Thus, before their discharge, patients—and more important, their hospital discharge workers—were assured that bills would be taken care of, which made applying to certain community-based settings much easier because the settings were assured of payment. Home relief, or welfare, by contrast, would not permit an institutionalized person to apply for benefits until after discharge. In practice, this meant that discharged patients had to find and brave their local welfare office before they could apply for, much less get, any money. One can readily imagine how difficult this task proved for patients discharged after twenty years, say, in an institution.

SSI and the State Hospitals

Understandably, mental health workers and bureaucrats everywhere hailed SSI as a godsend for the thousands who took immediate advantage of it. The state hospitals' population declined by 10.8 percent nationally between 1972 and 1974, undoubtedly because the legislation enabling the creation of SSI was passed in 1972 to take effect on 1 January 1974, and most states wanted to make sure their patients were "grandfathered in," or made eligible automatically. It certainly looks today as if states worked hard to declare as many of their dependents eligible in advance as possible: from 1970 through 1973, adult recipients of the predecessor entitlement, Aid to the Permanently and Totally Disabled (APTD), increased from 866,000 to 3,000,000, a gain of 247 percent (by contrast, the APTD rolls had expanded by a mere 106 percent in the entire preceding eight years[28]). In 1974, the first year SSI was available, state hospitals saw a nationwide decrease in population of 13.3 percent, the largest decrease ever.

Promoting Disability

What SSI did not do was make *any* demands or *any* requirements that its recipients receive *any* form of treatment or aftercare, nor, apparently, did the Social Security Administration particularly care where its beneficiaries went to live after leaving the hospital. SSI is a benefit paid directly to the recipient, who is presumed to be free to choose, from among existing resources, where to live and how to receive treatment, if any. SSI does not require the mentally ill recipient to seek treatment any more than it requires the blind recipient, say, to purchase a seeing-eye dog. But since SSI represents the sole support for vast numbers of deinstitutionalized mental patients, many of them housed at considerable expense to taxpayers in proprietary institutions (see chapter 7), one can reasonably see that when states shifted their fiscal burden to the new federal entitlement, they gave up any chance of controlling the whereabouts or treatment status of the caseload.

The only requirement SSI makes of its recipients is that they stay disabled if they want to stay on the rolls—a requirement that says, in effect, we'll support you as long as you're too crazy to work; get better, and we'll stop sending you money. This implicit threat became very real in the early years of the Reagan presidency, when approximately 33,000 mentally disabled recipients of SSI were summarily dropped from the program in one year alone, on the grounds that they were not *really* disabled, as part of the Reagan administration's drive to save money.[29] Consequently, SSI has wound up promoting dependency and disability, by paying for it, at the same time that SSI's very existence has made it all too easy for states to get patients out of their hospitals *and* give up having to worry about them after they have gone. Since no one has been required to oversee the patients' posthospital treatment, no one has done so.[30]

Cutting Costs, Cutting Care

By the 1970s the states had got the message and had figured out how to maneuver much of their caseloads onto one or another of the federal entitlement rolls. Lest anyone think this happened by accident, a look at California should prove instructive. Under then-Governor Ronald Reagan, a major initiative to cut taxes by cutting expenses was under way by the 1970s, and as usual, one of the expenses slated for deep cuts was mental health. To this end, the Reagan administration devised two schemes by which to guarantee that the number of patients admitted to state hospitals would be minimized. One was called a "county-bounty:" each community had a target goal for the number of admissions Reagan's people considered reasonable per year, and if the community came in below that number for the year, it got 15 percent of the per diem cost of care for each patient not admitted—careful communities could thus get state money to spend as they wished by *not* sending patients to state hospitals. The particular treatment needs of the patients themselves were of no consequence in this endeavor, whose only purpose was to reduce state expenses.

The other scheme involved the cynical use of the otherwise liberal legislation known as L-P-S (for its authors Lanterman, Petris, and Short), which passed the California state legislature in 1967, went into effect in 1969, and is mostly known for its promotion of mental patients' rights and its stated aim of promoting community-based alternatives to hospitalization. The Reagan forces, among whose goals was the total elimination of California's state hospitals, used L-P-S by including provisions that had the effect of making state hospital admission criteria more stringent and making it more difficult to keep patients against their will. Although California did not, in the end, shut down all its mental hospitals, as Reagan had hoped, it did make significant inroads into the state's caseload, which went from 26,567 hospitalized patients in 1966 to 7,011 in 1971.[31]

The Hidden Costs of Saving Money

The overall result of the availability of Medicare and Medicaid in 1965 and SSI in 1974 was to enable states to discharge huge numbers of mental patients in the certain knowledge that they would have money to live on. Since the states could get reimbursed for money they spent to house ex-patients in nursing homes, and since SSI came with no strings attached to aftercare, there was no pressure on anyone to come up with the treatment-oriented, community-based housing alternatives everyone longs for today and wonders why the so-called planners of deinstitutionalization did not build twenty years ago.

The fact was, nobody built community-based housing because no organization would—which means had to—pay for it. Medicare didn't, because it was never designed to pay for the treatment of the mentally ill, even though it was used to support elderly nursing home patients who happened to be mentally ill.[32] Medicaid didn't, because its funds, to which SSI recipients eventually became entitled, would only pay for clinic treatment, not housing. (Medicaid, ironically enough, is a federal–state matching program that from its inception has specifically prohibited paying for psychiatric care for people aged twenty-two to sixty-four in what the Medicaid people call institutions for mental disease, or IMDs, on the grounds that mental health care was a traditional responsibility of the states.)[33] And SSI didn't, because SSI is an individual entitlement and a social, not a medical, program that by definition will not pay for treatment.

Who Is in Charge Here?

These multiple funding sources, unrelated and completely confusing to everyone except, presumably, the authors of the enabling legislation that spawned them, create such an ambiguous and shifting picture of finance that it is extraordinarily hard to keep track of the subject. It is this kaleidoscopic effect that reminds me of three card monte, because anyone who looks at mental health funding after deinstitutionalization never quite knows whose money is paying for what. First, there are thousands of ex–mental patients, let out of state hospitals, some after years of care at state expense. Second, there is federal money available to pay for nursing home care *if* the patients qualify as old and dependent enough. Third, there is SSI, which provides a small monthly payment to those who live with family or friends, a larger amount to those who live alone, and the largest amount to those who live in proprietary board-and-care homes.[34] If the patients are not SSI eligible, or are but have to wait the usual several months before first receiving SSI checks, they have as interim support public assistance, home relief, or welfare, which is paid for by the state and/or the local community. Then there is Medicaid, which in some places is paid for by federal, state, and local governments collectively, and which is available to pay for visits to mental health clinics and medication at a pharmacy willing to take Medicaid. When patients get crazy again, they can go to their local hospital emergency room, where treatment will be paid for by the local government—although if the trip to the hospital takes place in an ambulance, Medicaid will pay for the ride. If the patients really get out of hand, the state hospital may take them back, briefly; and, of course, the state government still foots that particular bill. If all this seems confusing, imagine mastering the different eligibility requirements and payment schemes.

What is not clear is where the responsibility for former patients lies. The fact that someone pays the bill generally implies acknowledgment of responsibility for the condition, but in the current overlapping conglomeration of multiple funding streams, it is often impossible to establish exactly who is paying for what service on behalf of which government entity. State mental health departments used to have all the responsibility for the mentally ill indigent, but states have shed more and more of that burden as they have shed the expense, by shifting patients around, taking advantage of likely alternative funding sources as those emerged. No one can fault states for wanting some help with the crushing financial burden of the public caseload of chronic mental patients, but in retrospect it does seem as if they have operated in financially opportunistic and self-serving ways, showing no particular regard for the human beings who made up that caseload. In this they have acted very much like three card monte operators, who shrewdly exploit their targets' weaknesses to their own advantage, setting the victim up to fail by encouraging him to think he is calling the shots when in fact he is way behind. In just that fashion, state funding for community-based care has encouraged advocates thereof to think they were developing innovative mental health programs for patients newly placed in community settings, when the real function of those settings was to make it possible for states to unload an unwanted fiscal burden.

What Does It Cost?

We come to the bottom line: Have we actually saved any money by moving patients out of hospitals into community settings? The answer hinges on the tough task of knowing how much it costs to care for today's mentally ill. To calculate the total cost, the obvious thing to do first would be to compare what it used to cost to support one patient for a year in a state hospital, say, with what it now costs to support him or her out of a hospital, but right away we run into two problems. First, there are a lot more things to count outside of a hospital and budget items that get paid for in all kinds of ways, unlike the single-source spending that total institutional care represents; and second, much of the information available to answer the question is of dubious value because it is so clearly slanted in support of one political position or another.

The first problem, though fairly straightforward, is vexing, because it is hard to decide just what should be included in adding up all the living costs for a hypothetical, deinstitutionalized mental patient.[35] Obviously, we add up the amount of his SSI, the cost of his day hospital, outpatient, and/or vocational treatment, plus that of his medication. The total, which will vary depending on the state he lives in and will probably be pretty small in any case, should represent the cost to the taxpayer of the patient's life outside a hospital. Realistically, though, there is no reason to expect our hypothetical patient to *stay* outside a hospital for his whole life, so we have to consider the cost of an occasional rehospitalization and guess at a reasonable formula that would take such unpredictable, but expensive, episodes into account.

There are also very indirect costs that some people think should be factored into the equation, like the cost of police time to escort our patient to the emergency room if he has to be taken there against his will, or the cost of mental health lawyers, should he decide to challenge an involuntary hospitalization. Furthermore, some scholars estimate that only one-fifth of all mentally ill Americans ever see a mental health professional—three-fifths, they think, see general medical practitioners for vague complaints that are treated with psychoactive medications[36]—so maybe we need to count in a share of that expense, too. It is next to impossible to get everyone with an interest in mental health funding to agree on what component expenses are essential in a tally of the total; experts' choices will vary, depending largely on whether they want the total to be high or low. Such divergence only adds to the uncertainty surrounding the whole question.

Who's Adding Up the Bill?

The other problem, politicization of mental health costs, is quite a troublesome one, because it illustrates the old Mark Twain joke about there being three kinds of lies—lies, damned lies, and statistics. Different people and groups use numbers to tell stories in particular ways, often distorting and even concealing facts in order to make their points that much more compelling, trusting in the authoritative sound of numbers to persuade others of the rightness of their position. An example, which for obvious reasons I cannot document, comes from the height of the depopulation effort in New York State in the early 1970s, when hundreds of patients were being rehoused in various community settings. All of these placements were monitored by a special department within the state, one set up for the express purpose of identifying problem placements early on in the process. A psychiatrist I worked with at the time told me that a friend of his had charge of that department, someone who was a firm believer in institutional care for the mentally ill and who saw his job as a great opportunity to collect all the data that came his way to use as evidence of the failure of deinstitutionalization.

The data Dr. X acquired, while doubtless entirely accurate, was also entirely deceptive because it was so one-sided: the whole purpose of his department as defined by its creators was to identify problems and mistakes as they happened in the course of implementing the depopulation effort, so all he ever heard about was what had gone wrong. For him to tell the tale of discharge gone wrong as if it were the whole story of deinstitutionalization was bad enough; but if my source was correct, his friend had deliberately sought a job that would give him access to data and anecdotal material he could use to further his own campaign to return both patients and policy to the asylum. If true, this was surely deceitful—and his very position as head of an agency dedicated to oversight of a practice he did not believe in only added to his authority and credibility, even as it made it easier for him to deceive.

And We Haven't Even Saved a Dime

Bearing in mind that in the three card monte school of mental health economics, statistics can be and have been used to manipulate and fool us into seeing things from a preselected point of view, then, here are two interesting attempts to assess the total costs of mental health care in the days of community-based, noninstitutional services. In one, former Massachusetts Congressman Robert Drinan demonstrates the enormous growth of a state system that spends more and more even as it cares for fewer and fewer patients, by comparing numbers that speak for themselves:

	1969	*1974*	*1977*
Number of patients in the state system	21,000	11,688	3,262
Massachusetts budget for the mentally ill	$116,000,000	$188,000,000	$233,000,000

Drinan comments that nationally, the annual cost per known mental patient jumped from $5,626 to $20,924 between 1969 and 1977.[37]

In the other attempt, Steven Sharfstein, a psychiatrist who frequently writes about mental health economics, used the real-life story of "Sylvia Frumkin" told by Susan Sheehan in her book, *Is There No Place on Earth for Me?*, as a case study of fragmented and uncoordinated mental health care. Sharfstein and his coauthors "conservatively" estimated the direct costs of Ms. Frumkin's care, given in forty-five settings over eighteen years, to have been $636,000— and their estimate did not include the cost of outpatient treatment, emergency room treatment, general health care, law enforcement, social services, or what it cost the Frumkins to support Sylvia during the periods when she lived with them.[38] Even at New York's 1984 rate of $41,561 per patient per year, eighteen years in a state hospital would only have cost $145,718 more, and probably the hospital would have wound up costing less were we to add in all the costs Sharfstein and his coauthors left out.

What Has Our Mental Health Money Bought?

One of academic psychiatry's strategies for promoting itself as a scientific enterprise has been to deploy statistical evidence and rigorous data analysis of every question it faces. The cost of care is frequently fodder for such analysis, although the use of economic analysis to structure the provision of services has its weaknesses. Although it is tempting to seek comfort in the certainty implied by numbers and graphs, one has to bear in mind who is doing the counting and what is being measured. The whole question of benefit–cost analysis of care for the chronically mentally ill is a dubious one, considering the relative ease of measuring cost compared with the total impossibility of establishing a standard by which to measure benefits. One of the favorite benefit indices is a patient's length of stay outside a hospital, which is used as a measure by almost everyone, probably because rehospitalization costs so much—yet what possible meaning can rehospitalization have as a measure of anything in the case of chronic mental illness, which is known beyond question to require periodic rehospitalization, almost by definition? And if we are honest, we will recognize that it is the mental health field and the taxpayer who enjoy that particular benefit, not necessarily the patient.

What no one has come right out and said is that there *are* no fiscal benefits to caring for the chronically mentally ill, save the existence of the mental health and social service industries engaged in providing their care; there are only costs. As one economist has pointed out,

Although it makes sense to consider the cost versus benefits in any decision, including those involving health care, both costs and benefits must be regarded in order to maximize the probability of finding the best bargain. Where one party in a market transaction can fix costs, the other party has severely limited options. In the market for health care, where it is so much easier to measure costs than benefits, the tendency may well be to keep costs at a level third-party payers feel comfortable with, and simply to assume that adequate levels of benefit will somehow ensue.[39]

After years of inconclusive struggle to measure the most elusive of concepts—things like "loss of productivity from schizophrenia," measured in dollars,[40] or the benefit–cost ratio of case management services given to thirty-six patients in rural New York State over fifteen months[41]—we have yet to come up with a particularly useful or even a comprehensible statistical measure of mental health. Our worst problem, one we try to distract ourselves from with all this fascination with the empirical, is that chronically mentally ill people are not likely to disappear from the face of the earth just because the costs of their care may well outweigh the benefits—to us. (No one ever bothers to consult the mentally ill themselves on this point.)

The Benefits of Hidden Costs

The fact is that politically, it is extremely fortunate that so many of the costs of caring for chronically mentally ill people are hidden, because that fact covers up a lot of problems. For one thing, responsibility is diffuse and accountability even more so—if no one knows for sure who is working with or maintaining or merely tolerating the presence of the mentally ill individuals, then who gets the blame when they go crazy and stab people or set themselves on fire? Certainly, not all those government departments and agencies that got rid of the responsibility. No one outside the mental health business, except maybe lawyers, would believe the scrambling that goes on behind the scenes when a person known to be violent and destructive is about to hit the streets; it's every agency for itself as they all try to foist any future liability for the person's behavior off on someone else—just in case.

There are many advantages to the mental health system in an amorphous and chaotic setup like America's current one, in contrast to the state-dominated and -controlled one of the past. But as in three card monte, what you see is not necessarily what you get, and nowhere is that principle in operation to greater effect than in obscuring the whereabouts of the mentally ill, not to mention the costs of keeping them there. Strictly from the states' point of view, the mentally ill were and are better off living somewhere "in the community," where they are on somebody else's entitlement rolls and maybe even in someone else's catchment area.

Leaving aside the theoretically important but unanswerable question of whether the benefits of community life for the mentally ill outweigh the hidden costs, it is important to emphasize that it is probably the fact that the costs *are* hidden that makes them so high, because most of them are incurred in response to one or another failure of our disorganized and frankly crazy mental health "service delivery system," as the (expensive) regulatory bureaucracy insists on calling it. If thirty years ago we had faced up to the obvious and built appropriate housing for the state hospital patients we were discharging, we would probably not now need to rely so much on law enforcement and emergency rooms. If we had been committed to treatment rather than custody and maintenance, then we would not have designed an entitlement program like SSI, which punishes people for getting a little better—say, by working in a sheltered workshop for fifty cents an hour—by taking away part or all of their benefits, and which pays much more for a patient to live in an adult home than alone or with her family.

By hawking community mental health as a cost-cutting device, we mental health professionals sold ourselves a bill of goods. Even worse, we were shortsighted enough to sell the same bill of goods to people who delude themselves that all social problems are trivial and could be solved readily if only all the grasping, liberal experts would step aside—the kind of self-indulgent ignorance that promotes the conceit, for example, that serious mental illness can be cured by a reading of Norman Vincent Peale's *The Power of Positive Thinking*.[42] Just so does the three card monte operator exploit his victim, by recognizing the "hook" they have in common: the desire to get something for nothing.

PART II

1970 and Beyond
The Aftermath of
Deinstitutionalization

> First, identify a social problem. Second, study those affected by the problem and discover in what ways they are different from the rest of us as a consequence of deprivation and injustice. Third, define the differences as the cause of the problem itself. Finally, of course, assign a government bureaucrat to invent a humanitarian action program to correct the difference.
> —WILLIAM RYAN, *Blaming the Victim* (1976)

ALTHOUGH the practice of discharging mentally ill people to communities had begun at least fifteen years earlier, it was not until sometime in the 1970s that the idea of large-scale depopulation of the state mental hospitals took sufficient form in the world of mental health to get a name. Surprisingly, the term *deinstitutionalization* is not indexed in the clinical literature before 1981, and the federal bureaucracy did not enumerate deinstitutionalization among its planning goals before 1976. Once it had a name, of course, it could be studied and talked about and planned—which was all very well, except that what was being planned was a process that had been under way for fifteen to twenty years, and one that was accelerating rapidly even as mental health policymakers began to plan for it.

As it turned out, what mental health bureaucrats hoped to achieve with their belated planning was not *deinstitutionalization,* as that term refers to the depopulation of mental hospitals or to the resettlement of mentally ill persons in regular neighborhoods, but rather an appearance of having had the whole process under control all along. This meant that mental health bureaucracies had to address the aftereffects of an event none of them had designed or directed. Once it was a foregone conclusion, however, clinicians and policymakers alike scrambled to make it look as if they had intended to deinstitutionalize the mentally ill all along; perhaps they even convinced themselves that they had. Part of this initiative included naming the phenomenon after the fact, and here the bureaucracy's choice of language is instructive: the term *deinstitutionalization* makes it sound as if the phenomenon focused on the removal of mental patients from institutions, rather than the reduction of state expenditures. In effect, the mental health industry was writing discharge plans for patients who had already been discharged for ten years.

Because mental health professionals were so slow in realizing that the depopulation of state hospitals had long since come to pass, the job of making the phenomenon succeed after the fact was to prove herculean, if not impossible. Even the earliest literature written in reaction to deinstitutionalization bespoke failure: ex-patients were "shuffling to oblivion," the mentally ill were "dying with their rights on," the mental hospital had become "a revolving door," and contemporary mental health practice represented a "return to the Middle Ages." Out of such cheerful and optimistic attitudes had to come the clinical and programmatic answers to any and all unexpected problems created in the wake of wholesale discharges of mental patients, some of whom had been locked up in a kind of sensory deprivation for thirty years and were therefore unprepared, to say the least, for what the world had in store for them.

Just as the initial impetus to relocate the mentally ill had been rationalized and justified in theoretical and clinical terms long after the fact, ignoring its economic and political origins, so too the task of coping with the aftereffects of such an enormous change in public mental health policy fell in time to what were probably the wrong people—namely, those who had a vested interest in maintaining the status quo. In this instance, they were psychiatrists and high-level social services bureaucrats, few of whom were likely to want, much less know how to create, radically new and different ways to conduct their business. By the same token, neither group was eager to volunteer to accept responsibility for something they saw as a programmatic failure, and both sought to blame someone else for the mess that deinstitutionalization was turning out to be. New myths gained currency, myths that accounted for the failures and mistakes of the past even as they diverted attention from the ineptness of those groups most closely identified with the treatment of mental illness. Finding increased numbers of ex–mental patients among the homeless and in jail was useful in this enterprise, if only because the failures of governmental housing agencies were so glaring and because the criminal justice system, as always, offered such a broad and easy target for criticism.

Deinstitutionalization of the mentally ill undoubtedly added to serious social problems that would certainly have emerged without it—homelessness and overcrowded correctional facilities, for example. Other problems, however, should have been anticipated by people who knew perfectly well what the mentally ill are like and should therefore have known how they would fare in community settings. As much as we would like to think that we have developed modern, up-to-date treatment methods for the age-old, universal affliction that is chronic mental illness, the fact is, we have not. Our society's safety net and talisman, the medicinal drug, has let us down very badly in this regard, holding out the promise of behavioral control but never quite delivering. The habit of lying to ourselves dies hard, though. In one issue of a 1989 journal for psychiatrists I noticed as usual that *all* the ads for neuroleptic medications depicted white, middle-class people functioning on the job despite alleged mental distress that was impossible to discern from the pictures. In the case of the chronically mentally ill—the very population in whose name deinstitutionalization was undertaken and the very ones for whom neuroleptic medications were developed—the *last* thing they usually look like, even under the best of circumstances, is white, middle-class people functioning on the job. Continuing to lie to ourselves about who they are and what they look like is truly irresponsible.

As we shall see in chapter 7, most of the thousands of mental patients released from long-term state hospitalizations were well over forty and had been locked up for long periods of time, some as long as fifty years. I once tried to convince one, whose name was Hilda, to go for a walk in the neighborhood where she had lived her whole life until she wound up in a state hospital, the neighborhood to which deinstitutionalization had brought her back, some thirty years later. This time, she was living in an adult home in Coney Island, where whole blocks had been razed during the 1960s in the name of urban renewal, so that all the old two-story, two-family homes she had grown up among had been replaced with random colonies of high-rise apartment buildings interspersed with rubble-strewn vacant lots. However, the ocean and the boardwalk were still there, and I thought she might want to see at least that much again. "No, thank you," she said. "I went out once but I couldn't find my way around. They moved all the buildings." Hers would be a disappointing homecoming for anyone—you go away for thirty years and come back to find all your remembered landmarks gone. Sadly, it is precisely people afflicted with chronic conditions like hers who deal least well with disorientation and confusion. Unable to face geographic dislocation on top of the disorganization characteristic of schizophrenia, Hilda retreated more and more into the life of the home, which so resembled life on the back ward where she had spent the past thirty years. Hers was a stultifying routine, made up mostly of long stretches of inactivity punctuated with meals, the occasional bingo game, or TV soap operas glimpsed through a haze of cigarette smoke on the one standard-size black-and-white television set shared by the home's 200 residents. And there she waited to die.

Hilda is representative of the bulk of deinstitutionalized mental patients who now live in adult homes or nursing facilities. Another group, much smaller but much likelier to be in the public eye, is not eligible for nursing or adult home placement, because they drink, take illicit drugs, commit crimes, or "act out," the all-purpose mental health term for misbehavior that can somehow be attributed to mental illness. By now, everyone has seen what these people are like: they mutter dire imprecations to themselves, they suddenly shout curses at strangers, they throw light bulbs onto subway tracks, they surround themselves with unspeakable body odors, and they approach strangers to ask for help in getting rid of spies they insist are following them. Sometimes they are homeless and have had to jerry-build lives for themselves, using their inadequate physical, financial, and cognitive resources to come up with solutions to the dilemma of homelessness that are certainly peculiar but represent a disordered person's best shot at adapting to an impossible situation. Sometimes they are in jail because they have been caught committing a crime that may or may not have been an expression of a mental disorder, a crime that may even have been the product of a desperate attempt to find a home. "I like jail. It's better than the shelter," more than one homeless ex–mental patient has told me. (Such comments invariably prompt the thought that one would really *have* to be crazy to like jail—which tells us a lot about homeless shelters.) These problem patients who wind up in the least suitable settings for the mentally ill because they do not fit the requirements of programs designed for psychiatric patients definitely do not look like the people depicted in pharmaceutical ads.

Chronic mental illness is more than a collection of symptoms. It is a disorder of perception and communication, so that its sufferers see and hear things differently from the rest of us *and* probably have trouble telling us how things look to them. Often, their peculiar mannerisms and behaviors represent their best attempt to communicate something important, and everyone else's failure to comprehend can be extremely frustrating and enraging to the sender, just as it can be frightening and threatening to be on the receiving end of some bizarre communiqué. No matter how failed the transmission, though, there is *always* a message buried somewhere in the peculiar and bizarre behavior of the mentally ill person, and it *always* makes sense to him or her. For example, one woman I know spends her life as a kind of itinerant preacher of economic justice. She views herself as a contemporary Robin Hood who does not steal but is content merely to berate those whom she identifies as rich, accusing them of crimes against humanity, conspicuous consumption, wretched excess, and general unfairness. The fact that she has chosen to do this in a popular shopping area of New York City gets her in no end of trouble, as you might imagine, especially since her chief tactic involves following women in fur coats and yelling at them. Her methods break the law, but that does not mean her behavior is as irrational as it may seem; she is fully aware that she risks breaking the law, although she regards our legal system as yet another example of economic injustice and therefore worthless. My point is that if you only look at what she *does* and interpret it according to how the rest of us act, you will have defined her as deviant, but you will not have understood what she is trying to say.

Obviously, understanding what crazy people are trying to communicate is very hard work and will certainly not appeal to everyone, and there is no reason why it should. I mention it only to explain why I think the mentally ill have done so badly in community settings, for reasons neither they nor anyone else could help, and for reasons mental health professionals could and should have anticipated. I think we allowed ourselves to believe that the treatment of the chronically mentally ill properly involved expecting them to act like the rest of us, which they could not do, just because they were not in hospitals anymore. We also allowed ourselves to forget that they were not in hospitals anymore because it had become economically and politically convenient for us to move them out. Expecting them to know how to act normal was like inviting a bunch of four-year-olds to a formal dinner and expecting them to act like adults without prior instruction; ex–mental patients have done about as well in the community as four-year-olds would at a dinner party. We have compounded our short-sightedness by blaming the patients for what is really our failure. We have blamed them for swelling the ranks of the homeless, for helping to crowd our jails, for stinking up our subways, for yelling in our streets, for being crazy, and for being out where we have to look at them. We have told ourselves we do not know how to take care of them, which is not true; we have frightened ourselves with the belief that they are dangerous, which is only sometimes true; and now we are trying to convince ourselves that they need to go back to the hospital again for their own good, even though we still can't afford it.

CHAPTER 7

Where the Patients Really Went

The reduction in the register of patients . . . has been
achieved through the creation of a rhetoric of "commu-
nity-care facilities" whose influence over policy in hospital
admission and discharge has been particularly remarkable
when one considers that they do not, in the actual world,
exist.
—PETER SEDGWICK,
Psycho Politics (1981)

Ideologies tend to shift more rapidly than actual practices;
in fact, many movements in the history of psychiatry took
place only in people's minds.
—BARBARA J. FELTON and MARYBETH SHINN, "The
Ideology of Deinstitutionalization" (1981)

WHENEVER people write about
contemporary mental health services, they usually say something like this, by
way of establishing the background to the current picture: "The state mental
hospital census decreased from 558,000 resident patients in 1955 to approximately 140,000 in 1980."[1] Although the accuracy of this routine observation
is not in question, it is nevertheless a misleading assertion, for like the very
term *deinstitutionalization,* it suggests that the whole story of the phenomenal
shift in the caseload can be told by counting all the discharges from all the state
hospitals. The assumption under which the mental health industry has operated for many years is that patients were transferred from institutional care
in state mental hospitals to "the community," where they would presumably
receive "treatment" and "services." The myth in this instance is not that the
state hospital census decreased, which it did, but that patients left institutional
settings for the community, where they benefited from a change in the form
in which publicly supported care was provided to the chronically mentally ill.
The professionals' and the public's folly has been to assume that once patients

were outside mental hospitals, they were outside institutions. Nothing could be further from the truth.

The Aging Caseload

Well before deinstitutionalization began in the mid-1950s, public mental hospitals had become home to the elderly and were to some extent serving as old-age homes for those elderly individuals who were mentally or physically incapacitated or both. Increased longevity among Americans in general added considerably to this hefty portion of the state hospital caseload: in New York, for example, the percentage of first admissions to state hospitals whose diagnosis was senile psychosis rose from 18 percent in 1920 to 31 percent in 1940, and the average age at first admission rose from 42.69 years old to 48.47.[2] Since the senile elderly were not the patients most likely to be discharged in great numbers to loving families, they tended inevitably to get stuck on the infamous back wards, trapped in the hopelessness of their conditions, whether Alzheimer's disease, psychosis secondary to arteriosclerosis, or some other physical problem equally unlikely to respond to psychotherapy. In an age newly rededicated to the task of portraying the mental hospital as a therapeutic facility, as the years just after the Second World War were, the mental health bureaucrats who longed to rehouse the senile elderly at someone else's expense got unexpected support in their efforts from psychiatrists, who viewed patients who would never get better as a liability and an embarrassment. It thus became a clinical and political priority to relocate this unwanted and untreatable population. As it turned out, relocating the senile elderly was a pretty simple thing to accomplish.

The States Redefine Admissions Standards

In a brilliant bureaucratic move that has never received much attention in the clinical literature, the states, beginning with New York, California, Massachusetts, Hawaii, and Utah, rewrote their criteria for admission to the state hospitals in the mid-1960s, making it virtually impossible to use the state hospitals for the long-term custodial care of the senile elderly: they redefined the state hospital as a facility solely for the treatment of the severely mentally ill. As one state's internal guidelines put it in 1968,

Individuals would not be accepted for state hospital admission if care and treatment would more appropriately be given by another facility. . . . Patients should
not be admitted when their problems are primarily social, medical, or financial or
for the convenience of some other care facility.[3]

States, in other words, would deal with the chronic elderly mental patients by
simply refusing to admit them.

The model for the new configuration of the state hospital as acute-care
facility was a highly successful program developed in 1957 in Saskatchewan,
Canada, and exported to the United States five years later by two Canadians,
Hugh Lafave and Frederic Grunberg, who emigrated to New York State to
become, respectively, assistant commissioner and deputy commissioner of the
Department of Mental Hygiene. Lafave and Grunberg made three profound
changes in standard state hospital program design: (1) hospitalization was to
be sought only if treatment was not feasible within the community, (2) no one
was to be admitted for custodial care, and (3) no one was to be retained in the
hospital who could possibly live outside. All this was predicated on the assumption that everyone, however chronic and however crazy, was capable of
some type of community life. The Saskatchewan Plan boasted excellent rates
of discharge as well as promising follow-up studies suggesting that their ex-
patients were doing very well.[4]

To reproduce the Saskatchewan Plan in the United States, some place other
than state mental hospitals would have to have taken on the burden of the
traditional custodial caseload, specifically of the senile elderly. By the 1960s,
though, the states had figured out that as long as mental hospitals remained
available for this unwanted, unrewarding group, there was no pressure on
other governments to develop alternative placements. Alvin M. Mesnikoff, an
early participant in the reformulation of the role of the state hospital in New
York, remembers that for years the state hospitals

were being used to really dump the geriatric population, even though what these
people needed was not to be in state mental hospitals, but nursing home care; so
this was an easy out for years. The state thought . . . talking about it wasn't going
to get anywhere, because nobody listened. What they did was to say that we're
not going to admit [the geriatric patients], and that you, as a local government,
have to provide alternate facilities. You have to build nursing homes, you have
to provide care. . . . I think it was an attempt to take the power that was available
and use it to produce this kind of social change.[5]

Clearly, the states were well aware of the likely impact of their altered
admission practices, but they were probably entirely correct in assuming that

endless "talking" about the problem in various intergovernmental configurations—what bureaucrats would probably call "interfacing"—would lead nowhere as long as the states were taking care of the actual problem, which meant that no one else had to. Mesnikoff has called the states' finesse of the system "a striking example of the making of social policy by administrative order."[6]

The Rise of the Nursing Home

Luckily, nursing home placement soon became available to those who could no longer qualify as mental patients, chiefly because nursing homes became eligible to collect Medicaid payments. Beginning in 1965 with the original enabling legislation, Title XIX of the Social Security Amendments, any participating state had to offer its eligible residents five essential services, among them skilled nursing home care for persons aged twenty-one and older. The enormity of the opportunity that Medicaid suddenly offered the states, chiefly by expanding "the principle of 'medical indigency' to all welfare categories,"[7] cannot be overstated: the states had a chance, which they took, for vast expansion in public assistance medical services as well as a rethinking of their related goals and philosophy. Thanks to Medicaid, the states now had not only the alternative source of funding that would enable them to relocate the senile elderly, but also a considerable advance in their campaign to redefine the state hospitals as therapeutic agents rather than custodial facilities.

That the senile elderly left the state mental hospitals during the decade from 1965 to 1975 is without question. In study after study, scholars have found that by far the bulk of the patients discharged during this period wound up in nursing homes. In Boston, for one, the population of Boston State Hospital went from 3,000 patients in the late 1940s to 2,000 in 1963 to around 300 in 1978, thanks to an aggressive campaign to discharge any and all back ward patients. One nursing supervisor colorfully illustrated this campaign by literally throwing each newly emptied bed out the window after each discharge to show that it could never be filled again.[8] Of the 1,500 patients discharged in the mid-1960s to late 1960s whose whereabouts could be ascertained through a follow-up chart review, fully 1,200 went to nursing homes.[9] In California, as the rate of hospitalization of the senile elderly declined from 400 to 200 per 100,000 population, so the rate of admission to nursing homes rose from 200 to over 400 per 100,000, according to a retrospective study published in 1978.[10] One Massachusetts study followed 2,174 schizophrenic patients whose mean age was fifty-five, who had been in continuous hospitalization in state psychiatric facilities for an average of nineteen years, and who had been chosen precisely because they represented poor candidates for discharge. Of these, two-thirds of the chronic long-stay patients from Grafton State Hospital and Foxboro State Hospital, and more than half the patients discharged from Boston State Hospital, had gone to nursing homes. An additional 17 percent of the total sample were discharged to adult homes after an intervening stay in a different state hospital.[11]

The elderly were not alone in the great migration from state hospitals to nursing homes that took place in the late 1960s and early 1970s; a substantial number of younger ex-patients were sent to nursing homes as well. In Texas, a study done from 1975 to 1977 found fully 28.5 percent of nursing home residents throughout the state to be chronic schizophrenics under the age of sixty; a 1979 study done in Chicago found 50 percent to be mental patients under sixty-five; Alabama officials reported in 1973 that 15.5 percent of that state's nursing home patients were under sixty; and similar findings were reported in Utah.[12] The biometricians at the National Institute of Mental Health (NIMH) found that between 1964 and 1969, the number of senile elderly patients in nursing homes in the United States had seen an average increase of 143.8 percent;[13] and the U.S. General Accounting Office (GAO) reported in 1977 that nursing homes had become the "largest single place of care for the mentally ill" of all ages, despite what the GAO saw as the total inadequacy and inappropriateness of such an exclusively custodial setting for the population. Nevertheless, at the time the GAO did its study, nursing home care represented 29.3 percent, or $4.2 billion, of the costs of direct care to the mentally ill, by contrast with state and other public mental hospitals, which then accounted for 22.8 percent of direct costs.[14] The GAO report scornfully referred to the wholesale transfer of patients from one custodial setting to another as mere "reinstitutionalization."[15]

The reality of reinstitutionalization, or more trendily, *transinstitutionalization,* is brought home by the discharge sites used for the relocation of 641 chronic patients by Grafton State Hospital (Massachusetts), and reported in 1973:[16]

283 went to other hospitals
131 went to nursing homes
59 were on their own
57 went to rest homes
52 died within twenty months of discharge
26 went to residences
23 went to supervised apartments
8 went to other states

1 went to foster care
1 went to the Salvation Army

Of the total of 641, some 497 patients—78 percent—wound up in institutional settings. If we leave out those patients who died (8 percent), we find that only the remaining 14 percent can conceivably be said to have been deinstitutionalized.

Back Wards in the Community: The Adult Home

A phenomenal growth occurred in the nursing home industry in response to the huge influx of paying customers from the state hospitals, and part of that growth took place in a sort of corollary setting, known variously around the country as board-and-care homes, adult homes, rest homes, and PPHAs (private proprietary homes for adults). Created out of old hotels (New Jersey and Long Beach, New York), old motels (Queens, New York), or hastily renovated garages and chicken coops (California), these facilities mushroomed in response to need. As one observer of the phenomenon points out,

> Like nursing homes, board and care homes are not the result of careful planning and well-conceived social policy. On the contrary, they sprang up to fill the vacuum created by the rapid and usually haphazard depopulation of our state hospitals. Suddenly, many thousands of former state hospital patients needed a place to live, and private entrepreneurs, both large and small, rushed in to provide it.[17]

The suddenness of the demand cannot be overstated. For some years I directed a program whose mission was to meet the aftercare needs of chronic state hospital patients discharged to two adult homes. One of the home's operators used to tell the story of how he took the job of managing what was supposed to be a nursing home, until state inspectors measured the hallways and found that two wheelchairs abreast would not quite fit in the corridors, thus rendering the home ineligible for the requisite license. All was not lost, according to the inspectors: had the operator considered becoming a PPHA? Any objection to housing ex–mental patients, all safely medicated and guaranteed nonviolent? Funding all arranged by SSI? Eager to turn the profit required by the home's absentee owners, a group of physicians, the operator said he would give it a try. According to him, it was only a matter of days before two huge tour buses pulled up in front of his home, and out piled the first shipment of some

400 ex-patients from the state hospitals, who filled his home to capacity. With replacements as needed from the same supply, his home has stayed filled to this day.

A Deregulated Industry

Too-rapid discharge of ex-patients to adult homes during the years of aggressive placement of chronic patients in the community had its negative consequences, certainly, although nothing interfered with the steady flow of patients to the homes. When the need for adult home beds exceeded the supply in the early days of wholesale discharge, some states solved the problem by lowering their standards. In Hawaii, large numbers of state hospital patients were placed in what were called, and licensed as, boarding homes. When those were filled, the hospitals did not stop discharging patients; instead, they switched to unlicensed homes. Similarly, Nebraska used boarding homes licensed by the Department of Agriculture to rehouse its state hospital chronic caseload; but when local citizens complained about the low quality of care the patients were receiving, the state removed the homes' licenses—but left the patients in the unlicensed homes.[18] In California, where during the Reagan governorship the state's goal was to close down all its mental hospitals, the pressure to discharge patients was keen, and state mental health bureaucrats made it as easy as possible to place ex-patients in what California calls board-and-care homes. Specifically, they lowered the license fee to $10.00 and overlooked violations of minimum safety standards, with the result that the California state hospital census dropped particularly dramatically, from 26,567 in 1966 to 7,011 in 1971.[19]

The issue of licensing is particularly important. As the Nebraska example suggests, licensing and oversight of the adult home industry are not necessarily functions of the same governmental bodies that oversee nursing homes—themselves not the most tightly controlled of institutions—much less psychiatric facilities. For the mental health bureaucracies of most states, once chronic patients were placed out of sight in community-based facilities, they were truly out of mind and, more to the point, out of the agency's jurisdiction. There is a great value, from the point of view of a bureaucracy looking to shift a problem to someone else's area of accountability, in being able to rewrite policy in such a way that a particularly vexing problem ceases to exist. I tried once to find out the answer to what to me seemed, and still seems, a legitimate question: How many ex–mental patients live in either nursing or adult homes? Nobody knew. Finally, a friend who is a mental health bureaucrat in New York

City explained why these particular statistics are not kept by agencies who normally count everything: "There is no regulatory reason to do this as mental illness is not a criterion for admission or service."[20] It was possible, then, for a hospital to place its chronic patients in an unrelated setting with accountability, if any, to another discipline or political entity, and to write the patients off their own books without a trace—because no one at the receiving end was keeping any record that would lead directly back to the hospital. And if the placement were to fail, no one could ever prove faulty discharge planning was responsible.

In 1981, statisticians and epidemiologists at NIMH did in fact try to guess how many chronic mental patients there were in the United States and where they were housed. They came up with a total of between 1,700,000 and 2,400,000, of whom 900,000 lived in institutions (defined as mental hospitals, nursing homes, and prisons). Of the others, the 800,000 to 1,500,000 living in communities, NIMH guessed a quarter were living with families and at least 400,000 were living in adult homes.[21] Using their estimates, then, at least 1,300,000 chronic mental patients—anywhere from 54 percent to 76 percent of the total, depending on which of their estimates are used—were living in institutional-type settings, and that number does not include shelters for the homeless. So much for the notion of deinstitutionalization.

Maximum Profit, Minimum Care

Another reason it is hard to find out how many ex-patients live in adult homes is that the homes are, and always have been, essentially free agents. Curiously, clinicians and advocates cannot seem to grasp this essential point but are forever being shocked and horrified by what they view as the short shrift given to patient care by adult home operators, when all the operators are doing is running their business operations. Unlike mental health agencies, which are designed with patient care in mind, the first priority of the adult home or the nursing home is to make a profit. In the case of the adult home, whose rates are fixed by SSI, the only way to make a profit consistently is to cut expenses, only some of which can be tinkered with to any useful extent. Ironically, the easiest items to economize on are those that most directly affect patient care, like food or recreational supplies, as opposed to fixed costs, like insurance or real estate taxes. To maximize profits, it pays an operator to have a large home, to maintain a sizable population, and, ideally, to have a chain of large homes. One of the best ways to save on costs is buying food in bulk, which means meals will be generally of low quality, starchy, routine, and lacking in fresh produce. Another measure is hiring people to work in the home for the lowest possible wages, which inevitably leads to a high rate of turnover, an excessive reliance on students and/or volunteers, or employees who are less than ideally suited for the job at hand. One of the adult homes my program worked with met its staffing needs with a vast network of illegal aliens, none of whom spoke English and all of whom seemed mystified by the home's rather bizarre residents and gave them a wide berth.

To maintain a high census, the canny home operator uses aggressive public-relations techniques, including bribery, to keep referrals coming. Also, to keep patient-related expenses to a minimum, he or she can probably contract with outside practitioners willing to come to the home to dispense "treatment" and "services" at Medicaid rates.[22] The home and its services are designed not to meet the needs of its residents, who are a dime a dozen, but to maximize profits, so we really should not be surprised when those needs go unmet in the interests of maintaining a healthy bottom line. I was once frankly shocked when a home operator told a state hospital representative that he would consider admitting a known sniper to his home, a young man who had spent a couple of years in and out of forensic hospital units while the courts decided what to do with him. His crime had involved shooting strangers out his apartment window with a rifle. I thought this an unwise addition to a home mostly populated with elderly ex-patients, not to mention a home located in the middle of an entirely residential neighborhood, in a remote section of the city. The operator was furious with me for, as he put it, "screwing up his business" by jeopardizing his relationship with his supplier.

The opportunities for abuse, fraud, theft, malpractice, and cruelty to helpless and dependent residents are rife, of course. It is the rare home operator who does not turn a blind eye and a deaf ear to the niceties of patient care in favor of the more prosaic requirements of doing business. Even where regulation and monitoring by state agencies are in place, the low-level bureaucrats who actually provide the oversight are no match for the industry, which is made up of individual entrepreneurs who can act quickly, without having to stop to meet the finicky requirements of a policy and procedures manual—and who are very likely devoid of conscience and by no means above breaking a law here and there in the interests of their pocketbook.

Exploitation, not Rehabilitation

To anyone but a dedicated mental health professional or a zealous patient advocate, the sleazier activities of the adult home industry might well be seen as corrupt examples of more or less normal business practices, but advocates *only* look at the patients and their needs, thereby missing the point: patients were placed in substandard facilities because no one else would take them. Our bargain with the devil in charge of the adult home industry was that in exchange for an acceptable-looking setting in which to house thousands of ex–mental patients on very short notice, we would overlook the fact that they were being handed over to people who knew how to, and would, turn a profit on this new commodity that had come their way. As one industry critic observed not long ago,

> The larger implications of handing over the long term care of a substantial fraction of the mentally disabled to the free play of the marketplace likewise require intensive scrutiny. . . . There are obvious dangers attached to an approach which structures economic incentives so that they systematically reward neglect and exploitation.[23]

Nevertheless, a deal is a deal, and we're stuck with this one.

The hyperdramatic, revolting, horrible stories get public attention in the newspapers—for example, stories about pitiful chronic patients in Queens, New York, living with a corpse for days on end, or living in concentration camp conditions at an unlicensed boarding home in Mississippi, or found starving and filthy in unlicensed homes in New Jersey.[24] However, the truly terrible story about the modern version of the almshouse is the extent to which it exploits the very dependency on institutional care that community-based care was supposed to eliminate. From the point of view of the profit-seeking businessman, patient turnover is not desirable; therefore, any efforts at genuine rehabilitation are anathema (bingo games are fine, but vocational training is out of the question), as are any efforts to move the patient to a more independent life. Clearly, no attempt to treat the population with a goal of personal growth and a return to mainstream society at any level of involvement will suit the needs of the business; so real treatment, as mental health practitioners understand it, is out of the question.

One of the adult homes I worked with had a most interesting resident for about six months. Mickey was a jazz drummer with a master's degree in music who had had bouts of psychotic depression and had wound up in a series of state hospitals, the last of which cared for him briefly, wrote him off as a chronic, and placed him, heavily sedated, in the home. Because he was not a very convincing chronic mental patient, it occurred to us that it might be a good idea to take him off his medication—for the first time in years, as it turned out—and he turned back into a normal person. The home's owner, who operated the facility himself, had a fit at the thought of an unmedicated resident in his home (quiet patients require less staff time, which lowers costs), and he reassigned the "case" to a special psychiatrist he brought into the home two evenings a week from no one quite knew where, whose job it was to medicate potential troublemakers at Medicaid's expense. The tactic, which usually worked pretty well, backfired this time, because Mickey had no intention of becoming a "zombie," as he put it, ever again, and he had the sophistication to realize he could refuse the treatment offered by the house psychiatrist. Much to the home owner's disgust, Mickey left, got an apartment, got a job, and amazed us all about a year later by sending us his wedding picture. I have never forgotten this story, because it was the first, though certainly not the last, time I was under strenuous pressure *not* to help a patient get better.

Mental Health Meets Big Business

The adult home industry is, by and large, a spinoff of the nursing home industry, and in some instances the two are for all intents and purposes one and the same.[25] The nursing home industry got its start when the Social Security Act of 1935 specifically excluded payment of federal money to the residents of public institutions for the elderly, which called the attention of entrepreneurs to the business potential in caring for the aged. Subsequent federal entitlement programs, particularly Medicare and Medicaid, provoked periods of fabulous growth in the industry, so that by 1971, nursing homes' take from Medicaid alone—$1.7 billion, which amounted to one-half of all the money paid to the homes in that year—exceeded the total spent by all funding sources on nursing home care only five years earlier.[26] In 1977 the industry billed $12 billion, 60 percent of it to Medicaid.[27] Such incredibly rapid growth was no guarantee of high-quality care; to the contrary,

> money was suddenly pumped into a system that had neither the capacity nor the desire to expand rapidly, with the result that much of the new money disappeared into higher costs rather than into more service for those who needed it. . . . In effect, the sponsors of Medicaid and Medicare said to the industry: "Let us give you the money, and we won't look too closely at how it's spent."[28]

Indeed, a GAO survey conducted in New York in 1971 found that in just five years, nursing home operators had received a return of 450 percent on their original investment, on top of which the owners could count on an additional profit of unknowable size from fraud, kickbacks, and service not provided to residents, all of which were known to be endemic to the industry.[29]

A Hands-Off Approach

As critics reported more and more evidence that the nursing home industry was contaminated with corruption and possibly even criminal activity, it became difficult not to notice that this particular part of the private sector was operating virtually without regulation by government agencies. As at least three critics of the industry have pointed out, the homes could not possibly promote their own economic interest to the extent they do without government indifference or collusion.[30] The most likely explanation for the government's failure to regulate the homes is that not doing so represented a compromise made during the protracted legislative battles preceding passage of the 1965 amendments to the Social Security Act establishing Medicare and Medicaid, a compromise made by politicians with the two groups that had lobbied most vigorously against the amendments: the American Medical Association (AMA) and the American Hospital Association (AHA). By promising to stay out of medicine's future business even if it was paying the bills, the federal government secured passage of popular legislation it had little hope of enacting otherwise.[31]

Nursing home abuses are a familiar story by now, featuring such dubious financial activities as capital-finance fraud, illegal tax sheltering, mortgage and ownership deals, and pyramiding, whereby owners mortgage their nursing homes in order to finance unrelated enterprises such as frozen-drink stands and helicopter-leasing firms. Other common abuses include the embezzlement of patients' assets, extortion of assets from patients' families through the sale of phony "lifecare" contracts, vendor kickbacks, patient abuse, employee theft, phantom medical "gang visits" billed to Medicaid, and filling homes with relatively healthy patients who require the least care.[32] The two forms of patient abuse that have particularly jeopardized the well-being of the nursing home resident with a history of mental illness are the chronic overuse of psychotropic medication and the threat of involuntary rehospitalization, especially when used to stifle protest. The use of psychotropics in nursing homes has been well known for years. Medicaid estimated in 1974 that fully 40 percent of the drugs given to nursing home patients were tranquilizers, for which it paid $200 million that year; however, it is entirely possible that as much as half of Medicaid's money went for padding—the GAO has reported kickbacks of 25 percent and price markups as high as 1,650 percent.[33] Whatever the financial truth, fully half the residents of all nursing homes, not all of whom have a psychiatric history, receive tranquilizers or sedatives.[34]

Money: The Central Issue

Much more insidious, however, is the fact that all aspects of patient care for this sizable population are determined exclusively by the profit motive, the single engine that drives the nursing and adult home industries. The life dictated by the homes' need to make a profit is at least as monotonous and regimented as it ever was on the back wards, despite the fact that, as one observer has pointed out, we may be able to say that the toilets and linen supply are probably better in nursing homes than they were in the custodial state hospitals, and the stigma of living there is probably less.[35] Inmates' days, however, are spent in the kind of pointless, mind-numbing, time-wasting activities that are all too reminiscent of the total institution, where the high point of the day is the meal. Nancy Scheper-Hughes, an anthropologist, has collected some entries in a journal kept by a resident in a halfway house:

> *Monday.* Record playing is a good recreation if you're losing interest. It might work. Sometimes you might read, or play cards. Take a load off your feet. Well, nothing to complain about today. Everything is going well, except the plumbing. . . .
> *Thursday.* The simple life is good, providing you don't become too simple. Try to be basic. A coffee break or a cigaret will keep you going. Not that life needs to be any more simple.[36]

Whatever else one can say about the kind of marginal, uneventful, and unproductive day that is typical of the community-based back ward, it can be provided cheaply and therefore profitably. And the profits can be enormous: according to the U.S. Senate Special Committee on Aging, one nursing home partnership made $300,000 on $1,000,000, another made $185,000 on $400,000 (partly by spending fifty-eight cents per patient per day on food), and a home in Chicago yielded a return of $185,248 on an initial investment of $40,000—all in 1976.[37] Far from being a drain on the public purse, as they were in the state hospital, ex–mental patients in a community-based institution have become a profitable commodity, a useful component of the free enterprise system, and a hidden symbol of deregulated industry. In truth, according to one critic, the states have long since realized their goal of getting out from under the crushing cost of care for the chronically mentally ill by successfully shifting the burden of responsibility to

> various combined welfare–private profit systems that cost the state less and provide numerous entrepreneurial opportunities. This transfer of money and responsibility has been facilitated politically by statutory and case law, policies relating to federal fiscal incentives and revenue-sharing practices, welfare payments, insurance coverage, and patients' rights in and licensure requirements for the institutional control of deviant populations.[38]

As long as there is money to be made by housing the chronically mentally ill in community-based institutions, they will probably continue to be a primary source of housing for the easy-to-manage portion of the population. Whether it is of particular therapeutic value to that population is a question that really cannot be asked at this point, because it does not matter: the homes are there, the patients are in them, the industry is protected by friendly regulators as well as by its own aggressive lobbying efforts, and it is too late now to do much more than wonder whether we did the right thing twenty years ago. Nevertheless, the literature directed at academics and some practitioners continues to promote a pointless debate about whether nursing homes, for example, are providing a useful service to chronic patients who otherwise are inadequately served by community mental health programs, if only because they provide a practical alternative to the state hospital.[39] Questions like these miss the point: as long as nursing and adult home operators can turn a profit by housing the chronically mentally ill, and as long as the states can save the cost of hospitalizing them by fostering use of alternatives like the homes, they will be used, whether clinicians like it or not.

The Hospital Carries On

Even as community-based institutions such as nursing homes and adult homes were being created to absorb a large segment of the formerly hospitalized, the dream of eliminating the state hospital altogether was slowly disintegrating. This was partly the result of patient need—life outside the hospital appeared to be too difficult for too many of the ex-patients, and intermittent rehospitalization was the only backup facility available to those in charge of their aftercare—and partly the result of hospitals' refusal to die. In both instances reality gradually overcame wishful thinking, and it became harder and harder not to recognize the naivete of many of the assumptions underlying deinstitutionalization, in particular the notion that people who were used to hospital life, whether patients, staff, or residents of surrounding communities, would willingly give it up. Much of the overall failure of the attempt to relocate the chronically mentally ill permanently stems from an inadequate appreciation of the ability of systems, structures, and people to resist the efforts of others to change them and their ways.[40]

For one thing, the state hospital, grim and antitherapeutic as it no doubt was in the decades prior to 1955, was nevertheless a valuable resource for its host communities, which were often small, remote, and poor. Hospitals brought jobs, livelihoods, and customers to local businesses, so local residents doubted assurances that jobs lost in hospitals would be replaced automatically with jobs in community-based treatment programs. The extent to which state hospital employees fought against this fundamental piece of the ideology of community mental health was most evident in California, where then-Governor Reagan fully intended to jettison all the state mental hospitals as a cost-cutting move in the late 1960s. Hospital employees fought back by helping journalists write exposés of the horrors of the ex-patients' lives in nursing homes and board-and-care facilities. This led to an investigation by the state legislature, which subsequently refused to close any more hospitals. Even though Governor Reagan vetoed the legislation maintaining the hospitals, the legislature overrode him, the first such override of a California governor's veto in twenty-three years.[41]

Rising Readmission Rates

Even as employees of state hospitals resisted political efforts to shut them down, the realities of housing large numbers of ex-patients in loosely structured community-based settings led inexorably to the bane of community psychiatry: increased readmission rates. From the earliest days, the success of community-based care has been measured by reference to a single index, namely, whether or not a discharged patient returns to a hospital. Unfortunately, chronic mental illness by definition involves intermittent periods of poor functioning combined with increases in symptomatic behavior, a condition that American psychiatry has traditionally dealt with in a hospital, so that the idea that rehospitalization reflects a therapeutic failure of some magnitude is profoundly and destructively misleading both to the people who take care of the patients and to those who do the counting. In an article that has enjoyed wide circulation since it was written in 1973, two psychiatrists made the point that the critical index of the [state hospitals' discharge and admission] policy's efficiency should reflect the quality of life outside the hospital, rather than the length of time before readmission or deterioration. . . . We should not be asking "How long has he remained out of the hospital?" or "How quickly can he be discharged?" but rather, "How is he getting along day by day, what is he doing, and where is he going?"[42]

Nevertheless, the index of good clinical work with the deinstitutionalized chronically mentally ill has continued to be the length of their stay outside the hospital, especially as measured by those who control public funds. Not long ago, I had to write some lengthy descriptions of an aftercare program for which we sought state funding. Among the language I was told I had to use in order to sell the program was the promise that if implemented, this program would certainly reduce the number of readmissions to state hospitals, a promise I had no reason to know we could keep. I also remember the horrible feeling of personal failure I used to feel, secretly, as a line worker whenever I had to rehospitalize someone: I had done a bad job. The idea that one's work is to keep chronic patients out of hospitals by any means necessary is firmly and thoroughly entrenched now, even though clinically it is a useless measure of success and failure, given the episodic nature of chronic mental illness.

As hospitals shifted their approach from long-term custodial care to brief and rapid interventions in acute exacerbations of a chronic condition, the way patients used the hospital changed. As a result, the episodic quality of the chronic illness, which in the old days was invisible because patients never left the hospital, began to show up more and more in the statistics. Over the years of rapid discharge from state hospitals, the readmission rate climbed rapidly, according to the National Institute of Mental Health: in 1956, 178,000 readmissions represented 27 percent of all intake to mental hospitals; and by 1975, 376,000 readmissions represented 65 percent. Simultaneously, the average length of stay in a mental hospital declined sharply, from 211 days in 1955 to a mere 38 in 1974.[43] It is this pattern of rising readmission rates as stays grew shorter and hospital censuses dropped that led to the belief that mental hospitals had installed "revolving doors" for patients who presumably went in and out all the time, refusing to stay in the community and in effect refusing to be deinstitutionalized. As Ernest Gruenberg, a psychiatric epidemiologist, pointed out in 1976,

Deinstitutionalization is a slogan which confuses issues. Institutional censuses did drop with community care programs because the "easy-out" practice shortened hospital stays even faster than the complementary "easy-in" practice raised ad-

130

mission and readmission rates. Hence a hospital census drop with rising readmission rates became an *indicator* of a service system moving toward a good pattern of community care. To call a policy "deinstitutionalization" substitutes this indicator for the desired phenomenon—something like a child trying to push the speedometer needle to make a car go faster.[44]

Unfortunately, a whole industry has grown up around this confusion of indicators with desired ends, so for the moment, we are stuck with it.

Community-Based Care: Plus ça change

Whatever else was accomplished during the years of rapid discharge of chronic patients to "the community," it seems clear that "the hospital" has maintained its position as the centerpiece of the system, the focal point, the hub around which the rest of the system revolves. For all the brave talk about how "the primary locus of care must be shifted from the hospital to the community,"[45] our obsession with readmission statistics and the "revolving doors" on all the public hospitals makes it perfectly evident that nothing has really changed. The old-guard chronic patients, by and large, were moved in the 1960s to community-based institutions that were not very different from the state facilities, where they mostly fit right in, having been well trained in the technique of docile compliance by years of incarceration. Newer patients had not had the benefit of the years of training, so they did not do as well in community-based facsimile state hospitals, and their fate is less clear. Called "young adult chronics" in the literature, they seem to have discovered the revolving door to the public mental hospitals, public shelters for the homeless, the streets, and especially drugs. We cannot really think of these younger patients as deinstitutionalized, for they never were thoroughly indoctrinated in the skills of hospital life, which, ironically, is the source of many of their current difficulties in the community.

As for those who supposedly were deinstitutionalized, the truth was that *plus ça change, plus c'est la même chose.* For them, the nursing home–adult home–shelter circuit is more like the hospital than not, and at best can only offer a "haven in which unwanted members of the larger society can be 'stored,'" according to two anthropologists who studied board-and-care homes in California by living in them, disguised as patients.[46] While offering a haven to those in need is not a negligible achievement, a facility is not much of a haven when it re-creates the very conditions it was intended to replace, which is the best that can be said of the perfectly awful life provided in most community-based institutions. A former state hospital patient and adult home resident in California told participants at a conference,

> I believe the majority of board-and-care residents live in an isolated, removed, seldom-changing, untouched world. . . . There are many aspects of board and care home living that "institutionalize" a person just as much as does some hospital care. Both of these forms of treatment can have a depersonalizing, dehumanizing effect.[47]

It is easy to look at this situation and find some group or vested interest to blame—the states for being callous, the adult and nursing home industries for being greedy, the mental health professions for being naive, for example—but to point the finger is not likely to lead to greater understanding of how the mistakes were made in the first place. One glaring error seems to have been the failure of early advocates of depopulation of the state hospitals to realize that simply having patients leave the state hospital would not be enough, that merely treating psychotics like everyone else would not make them any less psychotic, and that expecting ex-patients to be eager to leave the institution might be self-serving.[48]

Unrecognized Opponents of Change

For the chronically mentally ill, the hospital, with all its drawbacks, may well be a reassuring and comforting environment, not only because they know the setting, have the skills to survive in it, and sometimes even to do well there, but also because for once in their lives, they fit in. The chronically mentally ill who have spent years in hospitals really do not fit in anywhere else, nor do their skills adapt to other settings particularly well, as we have seen on the streets of our cities in recent years. And what no one seems to have appreciated was the perhaps peculiar fact that some people really *like* to live in total institutions and give them up unwillingly, if at all:

> Institutional life . . . obviously has many advantages. First of all, one moves into a world that will provide some sense of temporal stability; it is as if one steps out of a maddening, swirling river onto the comforting, immobile shore. Second, it is a simpler world. . . . Third, leisure time activities and, in general, a hedonistic pursuit of them, are not only possible but are embedded into the very structure of hospital life itself. Such an environment . . . would be appealing to *anyone,* but

especially to a person for whom the outer world is a source chiefly of melancholy and despair.[49]

Early advocates of community-based care really were naive about the political opposition of those who stood to benefit from the maintenance of a large network of public and private institutions, geared to provide custodial care to the chronically mentally ill. If they thought about it at all, advocates underestimated the extent to which hospital employee unions would be able to force state governments to preserve their hospital jobs intact, even in the face of a vastly reduced patient census. This, and this alone, is why the bulk of mental health funding still goes to the state hospitals, even though the patients really are not there anymore.[50] Advocates also miscalculated where the private sector was concerned: they optimistically assumed that voluntary mental health agencies would want to treat the chronically mentally ill, which they did not, and allowed themselves to think that community-based facility operators would take chronic patients into their homes with the intention of rehabilitating the patients and moving them on into the mainstream of society. (I realize this seems unbelievable, but the original proposal for the program I administered involving the residents of two large adult homes was explicit: the goal of the program was to "mainstream" the residents.) And finally, everyone involved in the earliest days seems to have assumed—contrary to evidence, experience, and the merest common sense—that the chronically mentally ill were a homogeneous group presenting a discrete set of problems that could be addressed with a single solution: removal from the hospital. In the words of one of the early architects of community-based care of the chronically mentally ill, "A more modest appraisal of our capacities for change, by professional and patient alike, might have produced a more tempered process. . . . But that is not the stuff of which such movements are made."[51]

CHAPTER 8

Maybe It's Easier to Be Homeless If You're Crazy

> When we approach the vagrant in the spirit of charity, we merely advertising ourselves in order to seduce him into our ideology; when we approach him juridically, we are trying to justify ourselves by means of his annihilation. He shows us our weaknesses, and he shows us the utter equivocation of our morality. We cannot in good faith say that he is as he is because he is wicked; because we know only too well the ethical poverty of our own more successful practice. Our safest bet is to call him mad.
> —PHILIP O'CONNOR,
> *Britain in the Sixties: Vagrancy* (1963)

> It must be some kind of experiment or something, to see how long people can survive without food, without shelter, without security.
> —HOMELESS WOMAN (1980)

EVERYONE, it seems, has a theory about the homeless—who they are and how they got that way. Everywhere there are articles, books, and even television shows about the homeless, some scholarly, some impressionistic, some anecdotal, and some full of wishful thinking. What is it about homelessness that commands the attention so forcefully? There are, after all, other poignant and dramatic social problems. None other—not even AIDS—has caught the public attention and imagination quite so consistently over so long a time.

Among the assumptions reviewed in any discussion of homelessness and its causes is, inevitably, the thought that some large proportion of the homeless is mentally ill. There are variations of this idea—deinstitutionalization is identified as one of the prime causes of homelessness, for example, if not *the* prime cause—but the core belief is always this: homeless people are crazy. This pervasive view of a social problem of horrifying magnitude is appealing, probably because it implies an easy explanation for why such an advanced society finds it so difficult to provide something as simple as housing across the board. Besides, if the homeless are all crazy, then we have a built-in solution: treat mental illness, and homelessness will go away, too. The trouble with simplistic thinking about complicated issues is that it is so tempting to look at complex problems as if they were clear and straightforward and easy to solve that we fool ourselves into believing what we really know isn't true. But the truth is so much more horrible that we come to prefer to delude ourselves, hoping meanwhile that someone will come up with answers to all the problems that won't go away. Blaming the frightening notion of homelessness on mental illness has been especially easy to do because, in fact, some of the homeless are inarguably crazy.

The way in which homelessness and mental illness are generally related in the popular press is reflected in a recent feature article about the homeless mentally ill:

> Years ago, these people might have spent their lives in institutions. But new drugs and treatment that often controlled their symptoms made it possible for them to live outside. In the 1950's, more than half a million people were institutionalized. Now, about 110,000 are. The problem, experts say, is that the country has failed to supply the range of alternative care that much of the mentally ill population needs.[1]

If one were looking for a single explanation for a highly visible problem, he could find it in this brief passage: the 400,000 people who are not in hospitals and who do not get the range of care they need must obviously be on the streets. This surmise will certainly go a long way toward explaining the presence of the ragged man with body odor in the public library, or the old, tattered woman asleep with her shopping cart in a doorway, or the furious individual shouting at cars while crossing a busy intersection.

The Roots of Homelessness

Whatever else homelessness in the latter part of twentieth-century America is, it is not a simple problem, although it is one that probably could have been prevented. Its roots are deep and of long standing; and the more precise relationship between homelessness and untreated mental illness is one of similarity—the same short-sighted public administration decades ago has left us a legacy that features both. In the case of homelessness, the intricately interrelated causes identified by students of the phenomenon are unemployment, a chronic scarcity of low-cost housing, cutbacks in public assistance of various kinds, and, of course, deinstitutionalization.[2]

Homelessness and Unemployment

When the federal government counts the unemployed, they count those who collect unemployment insurance. They do not count those who have never worked, who used to work but have given up looking, or those who are underemployed, meaning that they work at unskilled, low-paying jobs. They also do not count those who have used up their unemployment benefits without finding new jobs, or those whose skills have been rendered obsolete by changes in the labor market. Any way you look at it, the national figures for unemployment are misleading and deceptive; and it should go without saying that the unemployed homeless are squarely among those who go uncounted.

Homeless people found in public shelters across the country are predominately black or Hispanic males, whose median age is thirty-four; and fully 40 percent of them attribute their homelessness to job loss. In spite of the economic recovery reported enthusiastically by the Reagan administration throughout the 1980s, recorded unemployment increased by an average of 49 percent between 1980 and 1983, and unrecorded unemployment increased as well, although no one knows how much. One pair of authors willing to guess in print has come up with the following speculative figures for 1984: 5,544,630 "officially" jobless plus 1,457,000 "discouraged" jobless, for a total of 7,001,630 unemployed.[3] The difference between the two totals is, of course, considerable.

Perhaps least appreciated of all as a group at great risk for homelessness, however, are the so-called underemployed (also sometimes referred to, I regret to say, as "bottomdwellers"). These are people who work yet who earn too little to afford more than their own subsistence, people whose resources are inadequate to enable them to survive a blow like an illness or a rent increase. The U.S. Conference of Mayors estimated that 22 percent of the homeless served by their cities in 1987 were people with full- or part-time jobs, and they predicted that the percentage, already up from 19 percent the year before, would continue to rise.[4] The jobs the underemployed are likely to hold are not, of course, either particularly lucrative or very desirable; typical examples include hotel maid, security guard, dishwasher, or low-level assembly worker.

These are all jobs that pay at or close to the minimum wage, last set by the federal government in 1990 at $3.80 an hour.

Minimum wage employment adds up to $152 for a forty-hour week or $608 per month, before any deductions are taken out. It should be easy to see how difficult it must be to manage on so little money, and how impossible it would be to weather a crisis. For example, one man living for two months with his fourteen-year-old son in shelters, on the street, or with relatives, earned the minimum wage and had been just able to pay the rent on a small apartment in a building that burned down. As he pointed out, starting over would require a month's security deposit and the purchase of furniture plus equipment, none of it within the reach of one with so small an income. It is entirely possible that the city shelter in which he lived was one of those demanding as much as 75 percent of the income of its employed residents, to pay for services rendered and to "encourage those who can afford their own housing to get it rather than linger in the shelter system."[5] It is hard to see how anyone can hope to escape the shelter system if all he or she has to work with is one-quarter of the minimum wage.

Homelessness and the Housing Shortage

Even if a homeless person has a job and can save the amount needed to rent an apartment, he has to confront the other big social problem behind homelessness—the chronic shortage of low-cost housing. There are many reasons for the shortage, none of them particularly admirable. For one thing, federal subsidies for low-income housing have been on the decline—the Reagan administration was proud to announce a $30 billion cut in housing assistance provided by the Department of Housing and Urban Development between 1981 and 1983[6]—and from the outset of their years in office, the Reagan administration intended that the number of households receiving housing assistance was to be held to an absolute maximum of 3.8 million. Before the Reagan era, housing assistance had been available to all who qualified for help, so this represented a major change in U.S. housing assistance policy, one whose immediate effect was to make housing assistance a limited entitlement program.[7]

The loss of housing assistance for all but a limited portion of the needy was thus no accident but part of a calculated shift of government priorities away from the poor, "a fundamental redirection in U.S. housing policy" as it had stood since the 1930s.[8] In 1985, for example, a deputy assistant secretary of HUD said at a National Urban League Conference, "We're getting out of the housing business. Period."[9] And since the federal government considers the taxes that homeowners do not pay because they are entitled to deduct mortgage interest—$44,000,000,000 in 1985[10]—from their federal income tax to be part of the money it "spends" on housing, it is clear that federal housing policy, as reflected in expenditure, greatly benefits middle- and upper-income families[11] even as it provides a convincing fiscal excuse for not providing more housing assistance to the needy. Any way you look at it, U.S. housing policy in the late twentieth century is not geared to address the needs of the people at risk for homelessness.

There is more bad news. Each year about 2.5 million people are involuntarily displaced from their homes by gentrification, economic development schemes, eviction, or inflated rents. Another half-million housing units of low-rent dwellings are lost each year to arson, co-op or condo conversion, abandonment, demolition, and inflation.[12] In the case of abandonment, New York City alone estimates that 15,000 to 25,000 housing units (apartments or single-family houses) are abandoned each year, for a variety of reasons: population shifts; aging buildings and neighborhoods; rent control; rising costs of taxes, financing, and maintenance; tenant malfeasance; governmental harassment; incompetent maintenance; inadequate inspections; and the lack of follow-up building code enforcement.[13] A study of rental buildings in a very poor area of New York City, buildings that had been abandoned by their owners after years of gradual deterioration, turned up some unexpected findings. For one thing, very few of the landlords interviewed for the study felt that the much-disputed system of rent control should be abolished; some of the actual rents in the study area were lower than those allowed by rent control, which suggested to the investigators that rent control may have operated to keep rents higher than they otherwise might have been.[14] The study mostly found a distressing ineffectualness on the part of the city government to provide any services at all that might stem the tide of building abandonment, a failure to do anything "other than to keep records until a building was virtually unsalvageable."[15] Clearly, in New York City, at least, maintaining the low-income housing stock has not been on the agenda at all, which means that New York City has not done anything it could have done to prevent homelessness.

Homelessness and the Death of the SRO Hotel

Another interesting example of governmental indifference to the part of its citizenry that exists at the outer limits of respectability can be found in the death of the single room occupancy (SRO) hotel, where for years marginal isolates could find shelter that was often quite decent. These hotels were located on side streets in undesirable neighborhoods and were often assumed to be a source of criminal activity. In fact, the SROs performed a useful social function: they tolerated a variety of residents who had in common that they were alone, socially marginal, and for one reason or another, chronically dependent on the dole—the old, the mentally ill, the blind, the permanently disabled, the addicted. Joan Hatch Shapiro, the lone scholar of the SRO phenomenon, observed in 1971:

> There simply is no alternative housing available to [the SROs'] single clients. A series of discriminatory practices in public and private housing severely limit choices for "undesirable" people. Public housing regulations specify twenty-one personal characteristics which are considered disqualifying. SRO tenants rarely are acceptable.[16]

Shapiro believed that the SRO hotel was not necessarily as awful an environment as most of its critics assumed, because it offered some social support to its residents and made very few demands on them. The hotels also housed a lot of less-than-desirable tenants, including ex–mental patients, when no one else would.

It may come as a surprise to learn that SRO hotels have long played a part in a great variety of American communities and are by no means purely a function of large urban areas. According to the U.S. Senate, SROs have been a part of the following communities: Charleston and Huntington, West Virginia; Big Stone Gap, Virginia; Louisville and Lebanon, Kentucky; Utica and Syracuse as well as New York, New York; Des Moines, Cedar Falls, and Sioux City, Iowa; Portland, Oregon; St. Louis, Missouri; and San Diego and Santa Barbara as well as Los Angeles, California.[17] Traditionally, SROs have housed the elderly more than any other single group, particularly in the smaller towns and cities, as the following survey taken by the Senate's Special Committee on Aging in 1977 suggests:

- Benton, Illinois, population 6,800, had 4 SROs, 48 units, all for the elderly;
- Syracuse, New York, population 197,000, had 7 SROs, 519 units, 25 percent occupied by the elderly;
- Denver, Colorado, population 500,000, had 42 hotels, 48 percent used to house the elderly; and
- San Diego, California, population 697,000, had 32 hotels with 2,300 rooms, mostly housing the elderly.[18]

SRO hotels, unhappily, were (and are) unattractive, and their residents were anything but desirable as neighbors, so municipal governments came under fairly steady pressure from angry neighborhoods and ambitious real estate developers to get rid of them. According to an information paper prepared for the U.S. Senate's Special Committee on Aging, "It was the urban renewal efforts of the sixties that brought the existence of SRO hotels to public attention. The gutting of old hotels in favor of condominiums and high-rent apartments sent thousands of residents into the streets to search for other low-rent accommodations."[19] In Seattle, Washington, for example, fully half the SRO units in the city, or 16,200, were demolished either to make way for a freeway, parking lots, or office buildings or to avoid the cost of complying with a new fire code.[20]

Urban Renewal Takes Its Toll

The human side of urban renewal had its ugly side. In August 1977, for instance, forty elderly Chinese and Filipino residents of a San Francisco SRO were evicted at 3 A.M. by 330 police officers and sheriff's deputies, after a nine-year legal battle was lost, a battle, ironically, in which the elderly had enjoyed significant support from civic leaders. Too late, in the wake of this unhappy incident, it became clear that SRO housing had been the norm for many non-English-speaking residents of all ages in San Francisco's Chinatown, and SROs had made up fully half the Chinatown housing stock. Only after a four-year legal battle ensued was any substitute housing built to replace the 4,000 low-cost units that had been lost to area development, and the new housing was built in a high-crime area far from the Chinatown-area services residents had long depended on. Subsequently, the waiting list for public housing, which had been three years in San Francisco as a whole, soared to twelve years in Chinatown.[21]

In another example of spectacularly stupid planning, New York City passed its Housing Maintenance Code in 1967, one section of which (D 26-33.11) specifically called for the elimination of all SROs by 1977, because the code's drafters "assume[d] that the population they house would not then be in existence."[22] To the contrary, the very population served by the hotels—urban hermits whom no one else particularly wanted to house—was growing dramatically even as the code's drafters were at work signing the hotels' death warrant. Owing to early discharge from state mental hospitals, increasing longevity among the elderly, shorter medical hospitalizations thanks to the rising costs of chronic care, and continuing growth in the number of people addicted to various substances, the pool of candidates for the SRO hotels' low-cost facilities was expanding rapidly. New York City planners certainly made their prophecy come true: the 98,400 people living in SRO housing in 1965 had dwindled to 50,454 by 1975, to 28,332 by 1979, and to 18,720 by 1986.[23]

The common assumption among social planners and critics, that SROs routinely housed drunks, criminals, lunatics, and junkies, made it extremely easy to consign the hotels to oblivion because they could be, and were, written off as magnets for low-lifes. As it happens, though, the assumption was faulty. In New York, for one, a 1980 survey found that fully 42 percent of the SRO residents left were employed; while it was true that 32 percent received either public assistance or SSI, 29 percent were elderly, not welfare cheats. The study also noted that while 20 percent of SRO residents surveyed identified themselves as alcoholics, only 15 percent had a history of any kind of psychiatric treatment, and of them, just 10.9 percent had been hospitalized psychiatrically. Only 15 percent had ever been in jail, for an average stay of two weeks; and the largest category of residents, 39.5 percent, reported having no problems.[24]

Even though the people who had lived in SRO hotels may have been nowhere near as objectionable as had been assumed, real estate developers capitalized on public fears; the hotels were gradually gobbled up throughout the boom years of the 1970s, and developers realized huge profits by converting them to condominium and cooperative housing for the affluent. Too late, the same neighborhoods that in the late 1960s and 1970s had been so vocal in their opposition to the hotels' presence realized that they were now hosts to the homeless. In New York City, officials tried too late to stem the tide of real estate conversions by denying tax incentives to some developers.[25] A bitter irony emerges in the fact that because of federal requirements, SROs themselves were not eligible for federal funds for rehabilitation, such as mortgage insurance or direct loans, because under HUD rules, only "self-contained units"—namely, those with private baths and kitchens—were eligible for those programs. Under HUD's conditions, rehabilitating an SRO would mean not only the loss of half of the units but also a substantial increase in the rental cost, which would, of course, render them useless as SRO housing.[26]

We can't say we weren't warned. In 1971, watching the dismantling of the SRO network and knowing full well that SRO tenants truly had nowhere else to go, Shapiro warned of "a homeless beggar culture more reminiscent of Dickens' London than twentieth century America."[27] Her prophetic sense of the future, now our present, was shared by Howard Bahr, a sociologist who studied skid rows in several U.S. cities even as the areas were changing and losing their traditional population. Writing in 1973, he made the following prediction:

Among the concomitants of the decline in the skid row population will be an increase in the number of multiple-problem persons there, higher rates of mental illness, alcoholism, and violent crime, and fewer clients for social control agents. The clients who remain will have more severe problems, or a wider variety of problems, and the chances of successful treatment will decline. Consequently, disappointment and frustration among social control agents on skid row can be expected to increase. Although the traditional skid rows may lose population, there is no evidence that the number of homeless persons in metropolitan areas will decline. Homeless persons will be "deprived" of their skid row subculture, and the "support" it provided.[28]

Bahr's prediction seems now to have been uncannily accurate.

Homelessness and Poverty

Throughout the decade that saw the gradual elimination of traditional housing for the very poor who were also social isolates, median rents nationwide rose by 63.2 percent though wages did not. Thus, while in 1970 families with an income of less than $3,000 per year paid only 34 percent of their money for rent, by 1980 half of them were spending more than 72 percent of their income for housing. Demographically, this group, which comprises about 10 percent of the rental market, is made up of single-parent households headed by nonelderly females; there are 2.7 million of these households in the United States.[29] These are the people who become homeless in whole families rather than as solitary individuals, and who have received a great deal of attention, chiefly because their numbers are mostly made up of very small children. Poor to begin with, homeless families have been squeezed by the simultaneous overall rise in rents over the last decade and the erosion of welfare benefits.

To understand how so many welfare-dependent families have become homeless, more statistics are in order. First, the U.S. Census Bureau pegged the national increase in the number of poor Americans at 3.6 percent between 1978 and 1982, when it went from 11.4 percent of the population to 15 percent, the highest rate of increase since 1968. Nevertheless, the United States changed its working definition of poverty in the early 1980s and made fewer people eligible for various kinds of aid, reducing the total Aid to Families with Dependent Children (AFDC) caseload by some 3 percent even as the percentage of people below the poverty line rose by as much as 10 percent, depending on where in the country they lived.[30] One million food stamp recipients have been cut from that program since 1981, while the average recipient lucky enough to be kept on the program has had his or her benefits reduced by about 14 percent. Far from being the profligate handout Reagan's people would have had the public believe, the average stipend provided by the food stamp program in 1984 worked out to forty-seven cents per person per meal.[31]

By the same token, the average payment to a recipient of AFDC has decreased in real value—by 69 percent between 1969 and 1981, with a drop of 30 percent between 1979 and 1981 alone. The deterioration in the value of the benefits looked like this:

	1975	*1982*
Average AFDC monthly benefit	$72.40	$102.80
1967 equivalent monthly benefit	$44.89	$ 35.67

For a point of reference, consider that in the same years, average *weekly* gross earnings in industry were $190.79 (1975) and $330.65 (1982).[32] Not only do welfare benefits, which are always lower than wages to begin with, go up much more slowly than wages, but the value of money has been going down over the years, and this affects welfare recipients just as it does the rest of us. Government spokesmen can and do claim to have raised AFDC benefits by 45 percent between 1975 and 1982—which doesn't tell us either how little money that was to begin with, nor how small the benefit is relative, say, to minimum wage. The $102.80 that was 1982's average monthly AFDC benefit is a *lot* smaller than the $536.00 that the then minimum wage (which was awfully small at the cash register) brought in each month.

Soaring Rents

As should be painfully obvious by now, this decline in welfare income to families was accompanied by a huge increase in rents. At the same time, the federal government made it a virtual certainty that poor people would be unable to afford housing, by requiring each state to set a maximum rent allowance for its welfare recipients, a uniform national standard that unfortunately did not specify how to adjust rental allowances to market conditions. In places where housing costs tend to be especially high, like New York City, this meant that for the first time the state *could not* help its welfare recipients pay their rent if it went higher than the new maximum, even if it wanted to. What happened was all too predictable: rents rose by 100 percent between 1975 and 1984 in New York City, while the maximum rent for New York State stayed at 1975 levels until it was finally raised in 1984—by 25 percent. The 1984 maximum rent allowance of $270 per month was clearly not adequate in a city where the median rent was $330—where, it must always be borne in mind, some 2,000 units of low- and moderate-income housing were being lost to the market altogether each month.[33]

What happens, according to families who become homeless, is that welfare recipients and low-income workers alike wind up paying far too large a portion of their income for rent and can all too easily fall behind if they need to buy food *and* pay the light bill. Since their income is so small to begin with, people living at the margin are never able to catch up. To a great extent, the first remedy sought by families unable to pay their rent has been to double up with relatives and friends: 52 percent of the families in New York City shelters reported in a 1986 Human Resources Administration study that they had come from shared households.[34] In general, the issue of doubled-up families has been most controversial: advocates insist there are millions of people in this precarious position, teetering on the verge of homelessness; but governmental bureaucrats have so far refused to accept any of the advocates' predictions of more homelessness to come. The doubling up was even noticeable on the 1980 U.S. Census: the census takers found the first rise since 1950 in the number of housing units shared by two or more unrelated families, from 1.2 to 1.9 million.[35]

Nor is all this just a New York City problem. In some places, some people have managed to hold on to their homes by using soup kitchens and taking advantage of the increasingly infrequent federal handouts of surplus cheese and peanut butter. Cleveland and Detroit, for example, are both home to laid-off blue-collar workers and have seen business at their soup kitchens rise by as much as 32 percent in one year.[36] Other families have lost their homes and have had to turn to public shelters. In Chicago, where the rate of mortgage foreclosure is the highest in the country (1.6 percent), city-run shelters opened for the first time in 1983 and have operated at more than 100 percent capacity from the very first night. Fully 80 percent of Chicago's homeless families reported becoming homeless after being evicted when their AFDC or other government entitlement was cut.[37] In Tulsa, Milwaukee, and Denver, unemployment doubled during the early 1980s, which led to an increase in homelessness as businesses went bankrupt; skilled workers took day laborers' jobs, forcing the unskilled into unwanted unemployment; and migrants moved into these cities looking for work.[38] Homelessness is by no means exclusively an urban problem, for there are more and more farm foreclosures, currently at a post-Depression high. Unquestionably,

> in the past few years, homelessness has changed radically from a comparatively rare phenomenon of the deteriorated inner-city regions, to the increasingly common lot of the desperately poor everywhere. . . . The only thing it can be asserted with confidence they all share is the one thing they all lack: a home.[39]

The Politics of Homelessness

With so many compelling explanations for the increase in homelessness across the country, it seems decidedly odd that deinstitutionalization should continue to get the blame, but it does. In a poll conducted nationwide in early 1989, 82 percent of those asked believed homelessness to be the fault of "mental institutions for releasing patients who aren't able to lead normal lives," either "a lot" (44 percent), or "some" (38 percent). Only drug and alcohol abuse came in for a greater portion of the blame—90 percent.[40] Certainly, the mentally ill homeless are among the most visible and unsettling of the larger group and may well be the most memorable, thus the ones who come to mind when the poll taker calls up. That could explain why the average citizen blames deinstitutionalization, but it doesn't explain why people who really know better, like advocates, experts, and social planners, do so. Here are the *facts* of homelessness, put as directly as anyone has:

> On any given night, New York City provides shelter to more people in families (4600 families consisting of 16,500 persons) than to single individuals (10,500). More children—11,000—live in the city's emergency housing system today than the total number of homeless single individuals, and homeless children are the fastest-growing segment of the City's homeless population. . . . Family homelessness is typically a housing and income problem: the unavailability of housing and the inadequacy of public assistance income.[41]

In spite of the fact that homelessness afflicts mostly families with small children in both rural and urban settings, deinstitutionalization routinely appears on everyone's list of reasons why we have homelessness in our country; and incredible quantities of time, energy, and money have gone into counting how many of the homeless are, in fact, mentally ill. The motivation behind the counting seems to be the perfectly valid assumption that we cannot properly care for the homeless unless we understand who they are and how they got that way. As we shall see, however, the real reasons for our obsessive counting of the homeless are much less benign.

HUD versus Everyone Else: Counting the Homeless

In 1984, the Reagan administration issued its official document on homelessness, a report by HUD. The report represented an attempt on the part of the federal government to achieve a legitimate and useful goal: an accurate count of the homeless. Ostensibly, knowing this number would enable planners to come up with realistic responses to actual need, and services could thus be targeted appropriately, to use the language of the bureaucracy. This noble aim was in fact subverted by the political agenda that has plagued homelessness from the very first; and the HUD estimate came in *so* much too low, in the view of the advocates and agencies who were actually trying to cope directly with the problem, that it was dismissed by them as transparently political. The battle between advocates and service providers on the one hand, with HUD and the Reagan White House on the other hand, was not so much concerned with learning once and for all the dimensions of the homeless population as it was with establishing accountability and thus fiscal responsibility. A high estimate—three million is tops so far, and even the U.S. Department of Health and Human Services guessed two million for the 1983–84 fiscal year[42]—suggests that homelessness stems from a profound failure of the Reagan administration's social and economic policies, one that will require a massive deployment of federal resources to put right. But a low estimate—HUD came up with 250,000 to 300,000[43]—suggests the problem is not a national one but one that can be dealt with on the local level.[44] In the end, the HUD report was widely criticized for serious methodological weaknesses by many of the experts brought in to testify about it before Congress, and it wound up being further discredited by evidence that its consultants had been pressured by HUD to keep their estimates low.[45]

Counting and recounting the homeless has proved to be a great distraction from the much more difficult task of figuring out what to do about the conditions that create homelessness, and we have become very creative in our counting techniques and our debating tactics when needed to defend those techniques or to rebut others' counts. In fact, judging from the literature on the homeless, we have focused on determining who is homeless, how many of them there are, where they came from, and especially, whose fault, responsibility, and/or problem homelessness is, with a great deal more dedication and interest than we have so far shown in facing up to the obvious: we do not have enough low-income housing in the United States, nor do we have anywhere near the quantity of specialized housing we need to care for the disabled and dependent. In 1984, Mitch Snyder, a well-known advocate for the homeless who is based in Washington, D.C., was asked by a congressional committee how many homeless people he thought there were. He answered, "These numbers are in fact meaningless. We have tried to satisfy your gnawing curiosity for a number because we are Americans with western little minds that have to quantify everything in sight, whether we can or not."[46] The National Coalition for the Homeless has echoed Snyder's comment, saying, "We have made no pretense of arriving at a statistically valid measure of the problem of homelessness. We doubt that such a measure can be obtained."[47]

City versus State

Conveniently, we have been able to distract ourselves from the magnitude of the problem of homelessness, and the profound implications thereof, with the idea that the homeless were on the streets because mental hospitals put them there. Here is a story, entirely factual, that illustrates both the peculiar machinations of large bureaucracies faced with a crisis they are under political pressure to address and the tendency of social programming to take the shape required by whatever funding is available. In 1981, when homelessness was first being discovered in a big way, a social worker then with the New York City Department of Mental Health, Mental Retardation and Alcoholism Services[48] was asked to write a plan for delivering mental health services to the homeless. He recalls that the city officials for whom he worked "started to talk about the homeless as though it was a big surprise, and they kept talking about how all these homeless people were crazy, and I kept saying, they're not crazy," based on his observations during visits to the city shelters in the fall of 1981. "I saw [shelter] clients who did not look nuts—they looked black, they looked Hispanic, they looked mostly male, they looked poor. Some were a little nuts, but the majority did not seem crazy. . . . There were behavior problems—you know, hustlers, people who had to hustle to survive."

The city department for which he worked had control of millions of state dollars earmarked for aftercare for ex–state hospital patients, money that it had been spending on mental health services for the ex-patients then housed in SRO hotels. Since the SROs were in the process of being converted to luxury housing, and the SRO caseload was therefore politically irrelevant, the department had come under increasing political pressure to use that money for

homeless people instead. The social worker was told to write a plan to determine how to accomplish the substitution of the mentally ill homeless for their
SRO equivalents. Whether or not the homeless were, in fact, mentally ill was
irrelevant. The social worker remembers being

> under a lot of pressure to be really critical of the state policies of deinstitutionali-
> zation and restrictive admissions. It was really hard to make a case for that,
> because we couldn't figure out that any of these people would have been in a
> hospital, anyway; they didn't seem that crazy. Then the Coalition for the Home-
> less became very active and discovered the mentally ill as a constituency group
> that they could jump on and take full credit for having discovered.[49]

In his opinion, early public responsibility for homelessness fell to the mental
health bureaucracy solely because it had the money on hand. Besides, the only
other likely candidate for the job of doing something about the homeless, the
state Department of Social Services, had no equivalent available funds. In
short, using mental health money meant that "no one had to go to the legislature to ask for funds. Instead, it proved expedient to demonstrate that all the
homeless were crazy."

Once New York City had successfully identified and paid for a significant
portion of its programs for the homeless with mental health funds, on the
grounds that homelessness was a direct result of deinstitutionalization, it became easy for other cities to do so, too. The question of whether the city or
the state would take responsibility for the homeless was debated in Philadelphia in 1982, where the controversy involved the Department of Public Welfare and the Department of Health:

> The source of this controversy was not simply disinterested social research, but
> the division of responsibility between the state and the city. If the homeless were
> considered a welfare problem, the city had ultimate responsibility. If they were
> considered a mental health problem, the state needed to act.[50]

Counting the Mentally Ill Homeless

Clearly, it would indeed be helpful to know how many homeless people to
expect over, say, the next twenty years, if only to predict how many soup
kitchens and shelters we will need. It would also be helpful to know how many
of the homeless are going to be mentally ill, in order to know what they are
likely to need to continue to survive. These are not really our reasons for

counting the mentally ill homeless, though: what we really want to know, up front, is who is going to get stuck with the bill. It is all too easy to focus on the numbers and the dollars and forget that they represent human beings, all real and in terrible trouble.

Somewhere along the line, mental health professionals stopped concentrating on treating the chronically mentally ill—or trying to—and got thoroughly caught up in counting the mentally ill homeless instead: by 1987, the field had produced at least twelve major empirical studies designed to nail down once and for all how many of the homeless are mentally ill. These studies report findings that vary so widely as to be collectively useless, yet endlessly debatable. When planners and pundits get tired of arguing about how many homeless there are, they can always shift their attention to quarreling over whether the low percentage of mentally ill homeless (15 percent to 25 percent) or the high one (97 percent) is the more accurate.[51] They can distort each other's findings in defense of their own political views, as Ellen Bassuk says has been the case with her own much-cited finding of an extraordinarily high percentage of mentally ill among the homeless in a Boston shelter, a finding that Bassuk says was first reported by someone who misused her data in the popular press.[52] They can also argue about methodology, of course—some studies rely heavily on anecdotes and clinical findings, whereas others strive for rigor and sneer at competitors for "oversampling" shelters simply because that is the easy way to find the homeless.[53] Further, the homeless constitute such a diverse group that they present interesting methodological challenges, such as the fact that some of them are very mobile and have a tendency to "roam."[54] Defining "mental illness" raises some provocative questions, such as whether to count substance abuse as a primary diagnosis or not (some studies do, some don't), not to mention how diagnosis is arrived at (interviewer rating or psychiatric examination), and who made it. Any way you look at it, the possibilities for ongoing discussion are endless; and even better, so are the opportunities for more research.

How the Mentally Ill Homeless Got That Way

Although some of the homeless are indeed crazy, it is more precisely the case that they have been a group easily made homeless by circumstances over which they have even less control than the rest of us, rather than that their existence on our city streets has brought homelessness to the rest of us. In other words, the failure of many mentally ill persons to acquire stable homes in the wake of deinstitutionalization is but one aspect of homelessness, one of its more discernible features; and the presence of ex–mental patients among us did not shrink the housing stock any more than did the existence of children on AFDC or food stamps. The mentally ill, like the children of poverty, are among the people most likely to become homeless. To have stretched this simple fact into a causal relationship has been most destructive, for it has encouraged all of us to avoid looking at the serious weaknesses in our larger housing and welfare policies.

Being Homeless Could Drive You Crazy

Something that has not been studied to any appreciable degree, surprisingly, is the relationship between life without a home and mental status. Living on the street or in a shelter, as many homeless people do, cannot possibly have a positive effect on one's self-esteem or provide much in the way of gratifying experience; and homelessness itself is a state of such unremitting crisis that one would expect it to provoke some kind of emotional or mental disorder, in and of itself. For the most part, though, the detachment prized by science has allowed researchers to look at specimen homeless people so objectively that the possibility of their having been driven mad by worry, fear, grief, guilt, or shame has not seriously entered the observers' minds. A typical example of the party line can be found in a review of existing empirical research into homelessness. The author concluded that the connection between mental illness and homelessness is too strong to be ignored, yet she devoted no more than one sentence to the idea that homelessness itself could conceivably provoke mental disorder.[55]

Trying to expand the field of inquiry into the phenomenon, one group of researchers studied a thousand homeless adults in Texas in some detail, trying to identify those with diagnosable mental illness. They decided that only 15 percent of the subjects showed any evidence of mental illness, noting that 10 percent of them had a history of psychiatric hospitalization as well. The Texas group concluded that the homeless, far from being mentally ill, are for the most part America's losers, people caught in low-paying, dead-end jobs without much hope of advancement, unable to amass enough extra money to be able to cope with disasters that potentially threaten us all, such as illness, fire, or eviction.[56] A second group looked at just under a thousand homeless people in Ohio and considered whether the mental illness they found was the cause or the result of homelessness. This group decided it would be impossible to say with any certainty, since the two conditions were so inextricably intertwined in the lives of the subjects.[57] A third group has written a critical attack on what its members view as exaggerated estimates of mental illness among the homeless made by other researchers: they attribute this empirical hyperbole to the "tendency among observers to interpret as serious psychopathology behavior that is either an adaptation to the condition of homelessness, a reflection of nonpathological personality, or cultural differences between the homeless and their observers."[58] In their view, most homeless people are in severe, short-term, first-time crisis and cannot legitimately be diagnosed otherwise.

In direct practice with a population at constant risk for homelessness, one periodically comes across people whose fragile equilibrium has been swamped by losing their homes. I remember an elderly gentleman who had lived for years in a low-rent apartment in a neighborhood undergoing vigorous gentrification since the 1960s. He had never lived anywhere else, and even though he had to all appearances been a fully functioning member of society—that is to say, a normal adult wage earner—he was actually a very limited person with coping skills in no way adequate to the stress of sudden devastating change. He was evicted when his landlord sold his lifelong residence to a developer, and not knowing how to manage or where to go for help, the elderly gentleman slipped into homelessness. The police found him wandering the old neighborhood in a daze, talking to himself. They took him to a hospital, which put him in a state hospital, which discharged him to an adult home, where he was labeled "chronic mental patient," even though he really was not. The subject of Brian Kates's *The Murder of a Shopping Bag Lady* provides a similar example: the shopping bag lady was someone whose history had not been particularly consistent with schizophrenia, the diagnosis she was given at the very late age of fifty-one; yet her response to a number of profound losses culminating in the devastating trauma of becoming homeless made her appear deranged, as indeed she was, but whether by the effect of more than her fair share of life's cruel blows on a relatively insubstantial personality or an internal process of deterioration no one troubled to determine while she was alive.[59]

Disposition: Homelessness

For all the time and money that have gone into studying the homeless in order to decide how many are mentally ill, we do not know much more than what should have been obvious from the outset: some are, some are not; and the mere fact of being homeless cannot be ruled out as a factor in the creation of the condition. One of the most disturbing findings of the Ohio group was that only 7 percent of those homeless who were unquestionably mentally ill were receiving any services from the Ohio mental health system.[60] But more unsettling is the fact that none of the other research groups even thought to ask. Some of the relationship between mental illness and homelessness could have been anticipated and was in fact documented in advance of the revelation of the scandal that is American homelessness. One article, written three years before Ellen Baxter and Kim Hopper called the nation's attention to the huge number of homeless people on New York City's streets, noted that throughout the decade during which large numbers of chronic mental patients were discharged from state hospitals, public shelters were often used routinely by hospitals as places to send discharged patients.[61]

I can corroborate this allegation, since I worked for state mental hospitals in the 1970s, and I clearly remember case discussions in which we deliberately planned to discharge patients to the public shelters and thought nothing of it. Sometimes we even discharged them as "undomiciled," which meant we gave the patient a slip of paper with the address of a welfare center on it. The center was believed to cope with the patient's homeless state in some way, although I now realize we had no evidence that they ever did anything of the kind; we probably were discharging all those people to the streets and were too gullible to realize it. In those days, all the public shelters were in another hospital's catchment area, so once the patients left us, they were effectively lost to aftercare and follow-up.

Adult Home Evictions

Another way in which mentally ill people have become homeless was, and doubtless still is, the direct result of relying on private enterprise to house the deinstitutionalized chronic population. Since board-and-care homes are not regulated by the mental health system, they are not accountable for providing postdischarge follow-up, as is now the rule when one hospital discharges into another's catchment area. Adult homes can and do discharge to shelters, welfare centers, and the streets. Two examples come to mind from my years of running an aftercare program in two adult homes. The first was Sandra K., a woman in her fifties who had been placed in an adult home in Brooklyn by a state hospital in another part of New York City.

Sandra was not an easy person for the home to deal with, because she was a great believer in personal freedom and made it a point to question any and all rules she was required to obey; this quickly got her labeled a "pain in the ass" by the home's staff, who passed her on to the home's owner-operator once they had run through their limited repertoire of methods for coping with inquisitive residents. The owner quickly became exasperated with Sandra's defiance and undertook a campaign of threats of eviction if she did not comply with his rules. Many of the rules were quite trivial and arbitrary, although some were perfectly sound; however, Sandra opposed regimentation on principle and clearly enjoyed the combat. I left before the owner succeeded in dislodging her, which must have taken quite a while, because she was intelligent enough to realize that he had to follow standard eviction procedures, which she fought tooth and nail. I was nevertheless not particularly surprised to see Sandra a couple of years later, barefoot and dressed in a plastic garbage bag, rooting through trash cans on Madison Avenue, a good twenty miles from the home.

The second example, Joe D., was a schizophrenic man in his late twenties whose condition had been greatly exacerbated by his steady use of hallucinogens. Joe had lived for years on freight trains, which he used as transportation on his endless quest for the job of his dreams: Mafia hit man, a profession he had chosen on the strength of a recommendation by a high school buddy, who had assured him hit men earned $50,000 per year (characteristically, Joe seemed interested only in the steady source of income and oblivious to what it was hit men actually *do*). Eventually, Joe wound up in a mental hospital, which placed him in an adult home. Joe presented no problem to the home that I could see; he seemed like a quiet person who smoked a lot and mostly hung around in an aimless fog. For some reason, though, his appearance bothered the home's manager, who took to nagging Joe to get a haircut and wound up threatening to cut off his weekly allowance if Joe didn't comply. Joe, who was not reassured by our insistence that such a move on the manager's part would be illegal and could be stopped, got the haircut and then got angry, which in his highly individual view of things meant it was time to move on. He vanished one day, and I ran into him about six months later, wrapped in a green electric blanket and shuffling along in front of the New York Public Library. He was friendly enough on the street and seemed gratified to hear how worried his caseworker was about him, but it was sadly clear that he had determined to move on; I never saw him again.

SSI Terminations

The best-known means by which mentally ill people became homeless began in 1981, when the federal government under Ronald Reagan took advantage of an opportunity to cut costs in the Social Security program by throwing as many people off the disability rolls as they could. This short-sighted and destructive activity had its origins in 1980, when Congress overreacted to reports that fraudulent applications had been filed for disability payments. The congressional remedy was to mandate case reviews every three years to weed out all the freeloaders who were not permanently disabled; but Reagan's expense-cutting zealots "began the review several months ahead of schedule in 1981 and with an enthusiasm that has concerned many of those involved with the mentally disabled."[62] Widely publicized by the press at the time, this low point in the history of public charity hit the mentally ill particularly hard: half the cases reviewed were denied further payments, stranding over 500,000 recipients suddenly without benefits, a disproportionate number of whom were mentally ill—even though only 11.2 percent of disability recipients were mentally disabled, they made up over 28 percent of those who lost their benefits.[63]

The Reagan administration's action in this matter has long since been thoroughly repudiated by the judicial system: fully 60 percent of the cases brought to appeal within the Social Security Administration system itself were reversed and benefits restored; the General Accounting Office found improprieties in the process by which mentally disabled persons were ruled ineligible; and in 1986, the government lost a class action suit filed in 1983 by the city and state of New York jointly with representatives of the class.[64] Nevertheless, by the time this disgraceful episode finally came to an end in 1984, a lot of damage had been done to people profoundly vulnerable to sudden and arbitrary deprivation; and almost certainly many of the individuals who lost their benefits joined the ranks of the homeless.

Homelessness versus Hospitalization

To the apparent surprise of onlookers, many of the homeless mentally ill have made it clear that they prefer life on the streets to life in an institution. Take the example of Rebecca Smith, who died at the age of sixty-one in a cardboard box in New York City in 1982:

> She froze to death in the home she had constructed for herself inside a cardboard box. She preferred it, she said, to any other home. Rebecca Smith had spent much of her life in a state psychiatric hospital under treatment for schizophrenia. Life in the box was preferable.[65]

This should not be taken to mean that the homeless mentally ill should be living on the streets, but rather that they do not necessarily regard it as helpful to be offered the alternative of involuntary mental health care. Agencies whose workers visit their homeless clients on the street are adamant that what home-less people, mentally ill or not, need and want is homes and money.

Unhappily, homes for them are in terribly short supply, and money has been a problem, too. When a program called Project Reach Out first tried, in 1981, to help the mentally ill homeless get SSI benefits, they found that *all* their clients applying on the basis of psychiatric disability were turned down.[66] By and large, outreach programs in existence to serve the mentally ill homeless have made strikingly few referrals for psychiatric services—as few as 2.2 percent of an entire agency's contacts, in one case.[67] The reasons are simple: survival needs come first. Commenting on the fact that mental health workers assigned to a public shelter had seen hundreds of chronic mental patients yet had placed only fifteen in any facility or program, observers pointed out that:

> The problem is not primarily a function of large, unwieldy caseloads; it is rather that very little can actually be done in the absence of supportive shelter or housing resources. The linkage to services holds virtually no meaning when immediate survival needs remain under constant threat.[68]

Still we persist. Money is found for programs such as Project HELP, inaugurated in 1982 in New York City. Vans are driven around to pick up homeless people so the psychiatrist on board can examine them and take them to a public hospital, where the public funds needed to house and treat them for a few days are available and are not begrudged. In its first ten months of operation, this extraordinarily expensive service had performed 2,218 evaluations of 574 persons—only ten, or 1.7 percent, of whom could be hospitalized involuntarily. Sixteen percent of the evaluations resulted in voluntary referrals to shelters, detoxification programs, or hospitals, and the rest remained on the streets.[69] Ironically, the same individuals who receive such services are routinely turned down for SSI and public assistance because they have no fixed residence, among other reasons. The picture of the homeless person as a solitary, deranged individual, dumped unfeelingly by a state mental hospital on a street corner and told to sink or swim, never quite leaves the public imagination—even though the "dumping" took place twenty years ago and even though we *know* most of the homeless are single-parent families with small children.

More than any other group, the mentally disordered have been linked in the minds of the public to the production of aberrant individuals: the image of the homeless person has changed from the public inebriate to the potentially dangerous "crazy" person. The degree to which this stereotype has real substance is unclear.[70]

Why this should be is something of a conundrum, since it involves what one sociologist points out has been a huge shift in public attitude toward the mentally ill homeless person, a shift from the attitude prevalent during the Great Depression, when the mentally ill played the role of a "dangerous class" that tended to stigmatize the "sturdy unemployed" with whom they shared the streets. The opposite view obtains today, she notes: the homeless mentally ill are pitiful and deserving of both our sympathy and a hospital bed in which we can protect them from themselves, whereas the unemployed are presumed to be lazy, shiftless drug addicts unworthy of our support—the "undeserving and dangerous poor."[71]

The Current View of the Homeless

The contemporary fantasy of homeless people as helpless, crazy hermits probably has two sources: first, it is a uniquely tidy explanation for a messy social problem, with an implicit built-in solution in the form of return to the asylum; and second, the fantasy conforms to the politically conservative view of social problems as relatively small, local events in no need of federal intervention. That both ideas are irresponsible and false is, of course, irrelevant. The myth has served its purpose by providing us with the distraction we need to avoid facing the overwhelming problems inherent in the question of whether a free enterprise system of private ownership can and will support publicly funded housing for the low-income portion of our population.

Homelessness in the midst of what is touted as a great economic boom is a terrible irony. It strongly suggests that the boom is not real, or at least not consistent. It throws the cold water of reality on the fantastic idea that the Reagan revolution in social programming has been a success. No wonder then-Attorney General Edwin Meese felt it necessary to bluster about reports of hunger among Americans as being "purely political" and to make the preposterous charge that people who eat at soup kitchens do so "because the food is free and that's easier than paying for it."[72] How much more reassuring to the conservative sensibility to continue to believe that the homeless are mentally ill persons for whom "institutions already exist" and that "the people in the shelters have not been helped yet."[73] More than any other single public problem, homelessness makes it clear that the American dream of ever-increasing affluence and conspicuous consumption is not for everyone, that "the system" is not evenhanded, and that equality of opportunity remains out of our reach.

CHAPTER 9

True or False? Deranged Criminals Are at Large and the Mentally Ill Are in Jail

Violence is a part of life, a component of the personality of every one of us, and only more conspicuous in criminals because it has—for many interesting reasons—escaped control in a way that hurts or frightens us.
—KARL MENNINGER, *The Crime of Punishment* (1968)

The most securely imprisoned population that exists is the general public that is uninformed about the nature and consequences of imprisonment as practiced in America today. They are imprisoned in a mass delusion which, in the long run, punishes society far more severely than society can ever punish a convicted criminal.
—HANS W. MATTICK, "The Future of Imprisonment in a Free Society" (1965)

IN the wake of deinstitutionalization, some ex–mental patients have become involved with the criminal justice system—something they are singularly ill equipped to deal with. Observers, depending on their particular interest in the subject, have so far tended to look at this artifact of the deinstitutionalization process in one of two ways. On the one hand, the popular media have seized upon certain crimes involving the sudden and dramatic killing of innocent victims by vicious killers, whom they eagerly identify as "escaped lunatics" or "psychos on a rampage"—something, in any case, that inextricably links the alleged killer to mental disorder. On the other hand, mental health professionals have been quick to expose what they view as the unfair and unnecessary incarceration of mentally ill individuals for trivial crimes, which the professionals characterize as the criminal justice system's unwarranted intrusion into the mental health business.

Both versions of reality share the core idea that deinstitutionalization is at the root of the problem; moreover, both views logically result in a call for rehospitalization of the mentally ill, either because they are unfit to live in polite society or too vulnerable to survive an intolerant society's discrimination and abuse. The cause is the same, the remedy is the same, and all that has been lacking is empirical evidence of what we all assume to be self-evident: that deinstitutionalized mental patients either are criminals or are treated like criminals. Almost everyone does seem to agree, though, that the process of enfranchising mental patients by restoring their civil rights has somehow gone too far: in seeking to free captive mental patients, liberal zealots have managed to enslave the rest of us in a world of danger and overcrowded prisons. Deinstitutionalization, of course, is presumed to be directly responsible for this sorry mess.

Like most simple explanations for complex social problems, this one is too neat. Although it is true that there are mentally ill people in jail, just as there are some violent criminals who are out of their minds, this fact has little to do with deinstitutionalization. Some criminals have always been crazy, and some crazy people inevitably wind up in jail—that is nothing new. What is true is that crazed criminals and incarcerated mental patients show up more, now that the alternative of lifetime mental hospitalization for the deviant is out of the question. In fact, now that the mentally ill are out and about where we all have to look at them every day, we have to face it: deviant behavior is unpredictable, illogical, and even, sometimes, dangerous.

One thing deinstitutionalization has done is to deprive us of a handy device for sorting out deviants. In the old days, crazy people went to the hospital, while bad people went to jail. By the same token, people driving by a mental hospital could be pretty sure it housed crazy people; if they chanced to see a jail or a prison, they could safely assume bad people were inside. Now, though, it's a lot less clear who is crazy and who is bad, which is making the rest of us more than a little anxious.

Mentally Ill Criminals

According to the tabloid press, our lives are punctuated with horrible, senseless crimes committed entirely at random by violent, uncontrollable people colorfully described as "crazed," "berserk," or "mad." The obvious extension of this observation is that our communities are full of dangerous lunatics who are all too likely to strike out without warning: the potential is always there, because the maniacs are always there, lurking in dark alleys everywhere, waiting to attack the innocent. The belief that hundreds of thousands of ex–mental patients were turned out of mental hospitals on purpose by irresponsible, liberal do-gooders has only made the fantasy that much more vivid and real. In the various investigations of public attitudes toward the mentally ill that have been made over the years, the one thing everyone agrees on is that "the most influential factor behind negative attitudes [toward the mentally ill] is the perception of the mental patient as dangerous."[1]

The public perception of the mental patient as threatening and potentially violent is not particularly new. What is new, or what is at least a new twist, is that some members of the mental health field have perceived what they like to call the "criminalization" of mental illness in the wake of deinstitutionalization, "a shunting of mentally ill persons into the criminal justice system."[2]

Public versus Professional Views

The views of both the general public and mental health professionals are based on the myth that mental illness and violent behavior are somehow inextricably linked; the difference between popular and professional perceptions is that the frightened public just wants the dangerous lunatics locked up, while the mental health field wants to dictate the nature of their confinement. The public imagines dangerous maniacs out on the streets, whereas the mental health professional imagines mentally ill persons "arrested for minor criminal acts that are really manifestations of their illness, their lack of treatment, and the lack of structure in their lives."[3] The kinds of crime mental health professionals assume mentally ill persons are arrested for include loitering, vagrancy, or "socially inept and unacceptable behavior like urinating on lampposts or wandering aimlessly. . . . This seems to be the belief not only among mental health professionals but also among most educated, liberal, and thoughtful people."[4]

The paradox is striking: On the one hand, the public, as reflected in the media, seem convinced that much violent, terrifying crime is so irrational that it must be caused by madness. On the other, mental health professionals hold the opposite view, namely, that the criminal justice system picks on the mentally ill, charging them unfairly and inappropriately with trivial, victimless crimes. Violent criminal acts can thus be pointed to by the one group as support for their view that deinstitutionalization has resulted in the saturation of communities with insane killers; just as the other group, the mental health professionals, can look at the fact that the mentally ill are no longer in hospitals and assume that they must be in jail instead.[5] In truth, there are terrible crimes committed by people who are undeniably psychotic—for example, in New York, the "ferry slasher" and the "St. Patrick's Cathedral killer," both of whom were clearly deranged but had been denied admission to city hospital psychiatric wards shortly before committing their crimes—just as there are terrible crimes committed by people who are entirely sane; and in truth, there are mentally ill people in jail, just as there are mentally ill people out of jail. The unanswered question seems to be whether or not there is a causal relationship between mental illness and criminal behavior, or one between deinstitutionalization of the mentally ill and the prodigious growth of the prison population.[6]

Criminals Who Are Crazy: An Old Story

There is nothing new about the fact that occasionally a gruesome, newsworthy crime will turn out to have been committed by a psychotic. In 1954, for example, Judge Saul S. Streit of the New York State Court of General Sessions accused the state of having "foisted dangerous maniacs on the public with the most dire consequences," because an ex–Veterans' Administration hospital patient had murdered a Columbia University secretary; then-Governor Dewey responded, "We must not be stampeded into unwise action by hysteria engendered by occasional widely published acts of violence."[7] Quite apart from the fact that this particular incident–cum–political skirmish could just as easily have taken place last week as thirty-six years ago, it is important to note that it took place *before* large numbers of patients were discharged from state mental hospitals. It is easy to forget that random violence is not contained or controlled by the existence and intervention of institutional care but goes on everywhere and always. It is also easy to forget that the old state mental hospitals were knowingly used not so much for treatment of the insane as for protection of society from the random acts of a violent few. Summing up the findings of visits by four physicians to 600 U.S. mental hospitals in 1931, John Maurice Grimes, one of the four, wrote:

> In all or nearly all the states the legal aspect of the care of mental patients is predominant. *Patients are hospitalized, not because they are mentally ill, but because of unsocial or antisocial manifestations.* The primary aim of the care provided is not cure, but custody.[8]

The relationship between mental illness and crime is an old story, as is the incarceration of violent criminals, whether their crimes are viewed as the result of their illness or not.

Mental Patients in Jail

Assuming that Grimes was accurate in his observation that the actual function of the state hospital was to protect the public from the irrational acts of the deranged, and knowing that the state mental hospital as Grimes saw it no longer exists, then surely that important social function has now had to fall to some other public institution. Some people contend that the jail/prison[9] system has taken up this particular slack (although the public shelter system is probably helping, in the great tradition of the almshouse), and that is certainly where we have always tended to put many of our most difficult problems. As one writer put it:

> The jail *idea* does not change. It is still the lockup, the place of ill repute, the place the town is ashamed of (or should be). It is apt to be one of the lesser political areas for the employment of men of nondescript skills, or of difficult assignment. No jail in the country—so far as I know—has been dignified and elevated to being the cornerstone of community security and justice.[10]

It would make sense, then, for ex–state hospital patients to wind up in jail now that the back wards are closed, for them to have left one discredited place of ill repute for another. That has been the basis of the assumption made by mental health professionals who seek to address the "criminalization" of mental illness.

The Realities of the Jail Environment

What makes sense to the detached and scholarly observer, however well informed, is not necessarily evident in the real world. Inmates, their crimes, and their problems are looked at very differently in the world of jail than they are in the world of the mental health professional—so differently, in fact, that ideas fundamental to each system of thought and practice cannot even be translated from one jargon to the other. I have worked in a jail, providing mental health services to inmates. Once, acting in that capacity, I had a most amazing conversation with a high-level bureaucrat from the state office of mental health. At the time, I found our conversation intensely frustrating, yet it ultimately proved quite illuminating in that it showed me just how divergent the two systems can be regarding the most mundane events.

We had in our jail a young woman, whom I will call Kelly, from another state, who had driven to our state in a car "borrowed" from her mother in order to pester her ex-boss with her fixed delusions concerning their upcoming (imaginary) marriage. When the man in question rebuffed her advances, Kelly got angry and plotted her revenge, which began as unceasing telephone calls and wound up as some sort of physical assault, the crime with which she was charged.[11] To all eyes, Kelly seemed normal and sane, except for her fixed belief, which persisted in jail—she fully expected to be rescued from incarceration by her "fiancé." Because she had spent some time in a mental hospital in her home state, she was referred to us. Kelly's mother was both zealous and resourceful in her efforts to have her daughter transferred from jail in our state to a hospital in her own, and to this end she contacted our state's office of mental health.

The bureaucrat in our state who got the case, because her bailiwick included liaison with other state mental hospital systems, called me and ordered me to turn Kelly over to her office. I said I could not do that, that the patient was in jail and would remain there until released by a judge, explaining as best I could how people charged with crimes, yet suspected to be insane, are dealt with by the criminal justice system. "Yes, but we want to put her in a *hospital*. She's *mentally ill*," was the response. I tried again to explain how the jail system works, how only a judge can order an inmate's release; and the bureaucrat said, "But I'm a *psychiatrist!* Why can't you just let her go so I can get her into a hospital?" In the end, the only way I could convince her was to point out that if all it took to get out of jail was a phone call from someone claiming to be a psychiatrist, all the jails would be empty within hours. Eventually, Kelly was transferred through the courts and was returned to the mental health system—and I had learned a lesson I will never forget: two monolithic bureaucratic systems do not necessarily know how to talk to each other in even the simplest of terms.

This insight would be of only passing interest were it not for the fact that the criminal justice system and the mental health system are intertwined in many ways, none of which works particularly well, and as a result, they can operate collaboratively only very rarely, if at all. Another example from the world of mental health in jail involved a mentally retarded woman named Carol Ann, whose IQ we estimated to be about 50, maximum.

Carol Ann had been in jail before, on the same charge of shoplifting, which usually carries a brief sentence of only a few days. Carol Ann, however, got stuck in jail for several months, for two reasons. First, she refused to complete the physical examination required of all inmates on admission, because it involved a gynecological exam, and she had been very thoroughly taught never to allow anyone to touch her genitals. Her refusal carried with it automatic isolation in a cell in case she was carrying an infectious disease, a serious concern in jail; this made her very lonely and homesick, and the other inmates reported that she cried all night for her mother (I proposed giving her a teddy bear to hold, and to their credit, the jail's administration seriously discussed the idea but decided in the end it would set a bad precedent, one that could lead to a security risk, the precise nature of which I never quite understood). Second, Carol Ann got stuck in jail because she was not supposed to be there. In New York, it is a violation of the rules governing the corrections department that a seriously mentally retarded person be in jail in the first place; Carol Ann was supposed to have been rerouted to the developmental disabilities system at the point of arraignment.

To do so once the retarded person has been incarcerated, however, is easier said than done, as we quickly found out when we tried to move Carol Ann from a jail run by the city to a residential facility for the retarded run by the state. As it turns out, the corrections system and the developmental disabilities system do not connect at any point, so it is impossible to communicate directly from one to another in any really useful way; and in any case, the actual decision to transfer the inmate had to be ordered by yet a third system, the judiciary. In Carol Ann's case, we got lucky: a corrections officer lived in her neighborhood and knew her mother. It turned out that the mother was in her eighties and senile, unlikely to have realized that her daughter was missing because her own sense of time was so confused. Carol Ann had for years attended a day program for the retarded a few miles from her home, to which she traveled by bus (it was while waiting for the bus that she did her "shoplifting"—pretty colors in nearby shops caught her eye and she simply took things, much as a child might); and we were able to arrange for the staff of the day program to go to court on her behalf. The judge ordered her into a state developmental disabilities center, and eventually, "the state" came and got her. The whole thing took many weeks, much longer than the original charge of shoplifting usually warrants—not out of harshness or cruelty, but out of the clumsiness caused by enormous bureaucracies that don't interconnect, can't communicate, and won't accommodate to individual case needs.

Managing the Mentally Ill in Jail

Bureaucratic isolation works the other way, too. The jail system doesn't tolerate defiance or negativism well, not surprisingly; and within the self-contained world of the incarcerated criminal, deviance is no more welcome than it is on the outside. Those inmates who are viewed as management or behavior problems are often written off and dismissed as "crazy," dumped unceremoniously into the rubbish heap labeled "mental" or "fruit loops." Truly crazy behavior creates anxiety among the other inmates and the officers, who respond with alarm and a particular kind of overreaction, one that involves a refusal to acknowledge that even the disturbed can be held to account for their acts, the fundamental premise on which corrections is based. If possible, according to corrections logic, disturbed inmates should be in a hospital; having once written an inmate off as "mental," the facility will thereafter try to avoid getting in a position where it is called on to contain or limit that inmate's behavior in any way.

The tendency of corrections to shrug off responsibility for deranged behavior it neither understands nor feels capable of dealing with poses a particularly vexing problem in the case of certain inmates sent to jail charged with assault, say, by mental hospitals. Occasionally, such patients will prove to be such a handful that mental hospital staff give up on them, on the grounds that they present "out-of-control management problems." The hospitals' remedy? Send them to jail. These inmates/patients live in a terrible kind of administrative limbo, often charged with gruesome crimes, which their attorneys blame on a psychiatric history of deranged behavior. Nobody wants these patients—neither the hospitals, which do not feel secure enough to contain them, nor the jails, which do not understand them.

Where the Twain Meet: The Forensic Unit

The bureaucracies' solution has been to create a hybrid—the forensic hospital unit, where people suspected of insanity are sent by the courts for observation of their ability to stand trial and where really crazy criminals are supposed to be cared for. In practice, the forensic patients are preferred—they are often quite interesting, and their stay is time-limited in advance. In contrast, the out-of-control criminals inspire the same reaction they get everywhere, which usually means their cases are reformulated on paper to demonstrate that they are best served somewhere else.

Here is an example: Larry was diagnosed as schizophrenic during his single admission to a state hospital, and upon discharge, he was fortunate enough to be accepted to one of the very few apartment programs available to young adult schizophrenics in New York City. While there, he was given a room that he had to share with another patient, a circumstance he felt forced to accept unfairly. His response was to kill the roommate, hack the body into bits, and distribute the parts around the city so he wouldn't get caught (his original goal, he told us, was to sever the head and put it on the desk of the staff person who forced him to share his room, to teach her a lesson, but the knife was too dull). Larry talks quite openly about his crime, shows no remorse, wishes he had hidden the body more successfully, and says he would do the same thing again. He is spooky and unnerving to be with but not a particular management problem; however, the judicial system cannot quite believe the results of several forensic examinations that show him to be fit to stand trial. As a result, he perpetually shuttles back and forth between jail, where he waits for the trial that never gets started because a succession of judges doubts his competence, and a state hospital with a forensic unit, which is ordered by the judges to treat him until he is fit to proceed. So far, Larry has spent two years in custody, and no signs yet indicate any pending trial. As I write this, he is back in the state facility for the third time.

Two psychiatrists, Robert Liss and Allen Frances, have written of their experience with providing hospital-based treatment for the mentally ill offender, whom they view as a "nomad caught between the jurisdiction of law and psychiatry, neither of which knows quite how to deal with him."[12] They tell a story very much like mine about "Larry," illustrating the tendency of courts to confuse competency to stand trial with "sanity," or more precisely, "nondangerousness." The confusion is easily exploited by the manipulative inmate/patient who is willing to be self-destructive in order to gain the benefits of a hospital stay instead of jail time: thus "the 'incompetent' patient protects himself from prosecution by remaining incompetent," and the courts are unwitting participants in the charade.[13]

In Liss and Frances's experience—which is probably not unique, although they may be the only ones to have written about it—the mentally ill offenders who wind up in psychiatric hospitals fall into three categories: (1) the psychotics who are too deranged to be held accountable for their actions; (2) the "manipulators who are in the hospital because it suits them better than prison does;" and (3) a third group peculiar to corrections—the inmates whose ordinary outlets for impulsive and explosive behavior, like crime and drug abuse, are cut off by incarceration, thus rendering them vulnerable either to psychosis or depression in response to captivity and the special features of jail life. It is this last group, they think, who are at greatest risk for being caught between the psychiatric and correctional/judicial systems; although these patients may look quite disturbed in jail, they generally get better once they are in a hospital, away from the temptations and stresses of life behind bars.[14]

Counting the Mentally Ill in Jail: Not as Easy as It Looks

The trouble with trying to pin down the nature and extent of mental illness among the offender population is that nowhere—except presumably in totalitarian countries—is it quite so clear how relative and even political psychiatric diagnosis can be. Clearly, some alleged criminals benefit from portraying themselves as too insane to stand trial, and loopholes like the insanity defense offer precisely the kind of challenge and opportunity for exploitation that sociopaths most enjoy. Although fairly common behind bars, malingerers are only "mentally ill" for the duration of their time in jail and certainly should not be counted among genuine sociopaths. Oddly enough, certain kinds of patients who *are* seriously disturbed do fairly well in jail, which after all is a highly structured setting, useful to the disorganized precisely for the order it imposes on their chaotic thinking; since these individuals function in the setting, they are unlikely to be brought to the hospital or even, sometimes, to the in-house clinic and so do not get counted among the mentally ill. In the jail where I worked, we briefly had a very retarded young girl in the facility who was not referred to us for weeks because she had been "adopted" by the other inmates, who cared for her every need, shielded her from exposure, and protected her from predators.

For the most part, people identified as mentally ill by corrections personnel are, not surprisingly, those who cause them trouble. This may or may not mean they are mentally ill, since even the slowest sociopath can detect a potentially useful situation in appearing to be mentally incompetent to corrections staff. (An amusing example of this was a first-time inmate, free of psychiatric symptoms, who asked to see "mental health" in order to obtain "a character reference" in an effort to get out of jail.) Furthermore, correctional facilities are run exclusively by correctional personnel, who are and always will be the gatekeepers to their on-site services: no clinical service personnel, however well-designed their services, can ever get around the fact that they see those inmates sent by corrections personnel.

An example of this phenomenon appears, ironically, in one of the few studies of the mentally ill inmate done not by mental health professionals but by criminologists, a survey of 339 New Jersey inmates. The author defined mental illness as having been hospitalized psychiatrically sometime in the past, and she identified 10.9 percent of the population studied as falling into that category (she suspected that many more inmates were mentally ill than her own research showed). It turned out that corrections personnel, citing security problems, had deprived the researchers of access to those inmates housed in special custody precisely because the jail viewed those inmates as "really crazy" and therefore too deranged to be safely let into an interview room to be studied.[15] If nothing else, this anecdote clearly illustrates how important it is—doubly so in counting the mentally ill in jail—to know who has identified research subjects, according to what criteria.

Existing Studies

Against the background of political diagnosis and highly questionable control over the usual variables of access to and identification of subjects, researchers have made a stab at figuring out to what extent American mental patients are also criminal offenders. They have done this since at least 1922, when M. C. Ashley looked at the arrest records of a thousand discharged mental patients. Even though twelve studies of the same phenomenon have been done since 1922,[16] it is striking that exactly as many serious studies purporting to count the homeless mentally ill were completed in just the six years between 1978 and 1984: for whatever reasons, determining the number of mentally ill among the offender population has not been anywhere near as interesting a research project as it might have been. As a result, a big part of our current problem, and one nearly every contemporary investigator of the mentally ill offender regrets, is that we have no baseline historical data against which to compare today's findings—that is, we cannot establish whether there are more mentally ill in jail today than there were before deinstitutionalization. As it is, we will never know for sure, statistically speaking. This leaves us at the mercy of such assumptions as the European epidemiological rule of thumb that says there is an inverse relationship between the number of people in mental hospitals and the number of sentenced prisoners (i.e., the more asylums a society maintains, the fewer prisons it will need to build, and vice versa).[17]

Data-Collection Difficulties

I should emphasize that even though some researchers have tried to figure out a way to count the mentally ill in jail, the literature is still very sparse, especially in contrast to the voluminous body of extant material on more compelling and politically "hotter" topics like homelessness. What's worse, the findings we do have are in serious question. The methodologies used in most of the studies have been questioned repeatedly by those who doubt the value of the exercise, not to mention the means by which it has been undertaken so far. As a British scholar pointed out not long ago, of the eleven best studies of the number of mentally ill prisoners,

> they all used different definitions; all were on different categories of prisoners and used different methods and so cannot be easily compared with each other; and none had control groups from outside prison. . . . The answer to how many mentally abnormal prisoners there are cannot be answered with any confidence.[18]

An American author who has reviewed many of the same studies has identified these and other difficulties compromising their results, including varying sample sizes of anywhere from 301 to 10,247, with the smaller samples tending to show an inflated crime rate; varying inclusion of certain problematic diagnostic categories, specifically substance abuse (even though "the common man does not generally include alcoholics and addicts in his definition of mental illness"[19]); and a failure to control for relevant demographics. In this last category, it is worth pointing out that to rely on arrest records to establish criminal activity, as all twelve of the classic studies have done, is to ignore the FBI's standard rule that only one-third of all arrests lead to conviction. To be accused of a crime, after all, is not the same as having been convicted of it. Perhaps mentally ill people get arrested not because they commit crimes at a higher rate than normal people do, but because they lack "adeptness at avoiding capture," as one observer put it, speculating that "it is probable that some of the criminality manifested by ex-patients represents defensive reactions to economic, physical, and verbal assaults perpetrated on them."[20] Given what we know about where and how most ex-patients live, this seems most likely.

Most reviewers have divided the bulk of the studies comparing the arrest records of mentally ill offenders to those of the population at large into three groups: early (1922–1945), middle (1962–1967), and late (1974–present). The early group decided that ex-patients were arrested at the same or lower rates as were normal people; the middle group found either no difference or higher rates for the mentally ill; and the most recent studies have reported markedly higher arrest rates for the mentally ill.[21] The cumulative findings of these studies have struck everyone who has looked at them as contradictory and therefore ultimately inconclusive. As one scholar put it,

From the information presently available, it seems that discharged mental patients as a group are not significantly less likely than others to exhibit dangerous or illegal behavior. At the present time there is no evidence that their mental status as such raises their arrest risk; rather, antisocial behavior and mentally ill behavior apparently coexist, particularly among young, unmarried, unskilled, poor males, especially those belonging to ethnic minorities. It is unlikely that most people would care to have such neighbors even in the absence of a history of psychiatric hospitalization.[22]

At least we know not to blame all their undesirable qualities on their psychiatric history alone, because we can always object to their antisocial traits as well.

But If They're Not in Hospitals, They Must Be in Jail

Judging from the clinical literature, even in the face of such unconvincing and inconclusive research, the assumption persists among mental health professionals that if violent people are no longer in mental hospitals, then they must be in jail or prison—if only on the theory that "the elimination of a social evil often has another unanticipated social cost."[23] Henry J. Steadman, who is one of the busiest of the current researchers of the mentally ill offender, looks at the assumption this way:

A number of suggestions have been put forth to explain the increasing arrest rate among former mental patients. Dominant among these suggestions has been that recent community treatment ideologies and programs have put more persons who are at risk of arrest into the community. Further, this explanation has pointed to the overreactions to such programs in some states that have "dumped" persons not ready for independent living into high crime areas.[24]

In other words, a high crime rate can be blamed on, or at least be explained by, the presence in the community of unwanted mentally ill persons, if we can just prove once and for all that they are the ones committing all the crimes. Actually, says Steadman, the most we can say for sure is that the people in mental hospitals now closely resemble the people who have always committed the most crimes—namely, poor, unemployed, unskilled, uneducated, single black and Hispanic males with inadequately controlled aggressive tendencies.

For all the energy that has gone into the research effort to establish how likely the mentally ill are to commit crimes, the results have not shed much light on the question of whether in fact the mentally ill have flocked to jails now that they cannot get into hospitals. There is a very good reason for this:

it is impossible for clinically oriented researchers to do an accurate study of inmates. Inmates of correctional institutions are very different from mental patients, and they cannot be studied in the same way by the same people using the same techniques and research designs. For one thing, inmates cannot be counted on not to lie, especially if they think telling a researcher what they decide he or she wants to hear will in some way help them with their case or get them out of jail altogether[25]—in fact, inmates should be counted on *to* be lying a lot of the time.

Many inmates are sociopaths, after all, who are extraordinarily skilled at knowing what it is others want to hear—this is how many of them earn their living when they're not in jail. For another, most inmates would no more cooperate with an outsider, like a researcher, than they would squeal ("drop a dime") on a buddy. This does not necessarily mean they would not talk to him, although they might not, but rather that they might well make it a point merely to *appear* to cooperate: many inmates would find it a challenge to fake compliance with a research protocol, appearing to meet the investigator's expectations while actually misleading him, the point being simply to fool a gullible victim (called "getting over," an important survival skill for a group at constant risk for victimization themselves).

Clinicians, who are trained to listen for content plus nuance plus emotion plus subtext, are no match for truly skilled, professional sociopaths, whose determination to misinform and mislead on all levels of communication matches therapists' resolve to hear and understand the patient's point of view. This leads to the ironic situation of one person bending over backward to take what the other says at face value, while the other is working overtime to say what he has deduced the first will most like to hear. There is no empirical truth in that situation, and nothing that can be measured will ever come out of it—unless we could get the inmates to tell us after the fact how many of us they have gulled, over the years. They would be no more likely to do that than we would be likely to want to hear it—and besides, they probably would exaggerate.

Which Behaviors Count?

Another reason traditional methods of doing clinical research are probably worthless in a jail setting is that certain behaviors clinicians use to measure and define psychiatric diagnosis not only are normal for inmates but also are tolerated and even rewarded within the correctional setting. For instance, a mental health clinician might see fighting as evidence of poorly controlled aggression secondary to a psychiatric disorder; but a corrections officer might see fighting as a normal, proper, and even admirable response to a perceived threat. This simple point is not readily understood by clinicians who want to look at incarcerated offenders.

In a striking example of interdisciplinary confusion, a group of researchers sought to obtain a psychiatric profile of the people in prison in New York State, using two survey instruments they had adapted from the state's level-of-care surveys of its psychiatric facilities. Two behavioral measures in the instruments seem so maladroit when applied to the offender population that their inclusion seems like an unbelievable oversight. First, on what they call a "psychiatric disability subscale," the investigators list several routine indices of emotional instability, like depression, confusion, social affect, and interest—and then, "steals or hoards things."[26] Inmates steal. Inmates also hoard, because other inmates steal. Stealing is such a constant in their lives outside jail and prison that of course they carry it over to the institution; and to include it on an "adapted" schedule of clinical indicators of psychiatric disability seems, at best, naive.

Second, the investigators adapted a "Community Activity Dysfunction Scale" that measures functional disability among inmates and includes such tasks as "follow a facility medication schedule," "make commissary buys without help," and "keep cell neat (up to standards)."[27] Without going into a lengthy profile of the typical inmate of a correctional facility, I will just point out that (1) most inmates are drug addicts in various stages of detoxification, who have *no* trouble adhering to drug regimens—provided they want to take the drug in question; (2) commissary, like mail call, is sacred to the incarcerated, and it is difficult to imagine an inmate who would not make it his or her business to get there, no matter what; and (3) jail cells are horrible places *by design,* furnished in battered metal bolted to the floor, offering few opportunities for individual expression by way of "decorating," even by being messy. None of the tasks chosen for the scale reflects much awareness of what life in a correctional setting is like, not even of the fact that inmates technically do not have the freedom to choose whether to perform such tasks. These measures may have proved significant when applied to a mental hospital population, but even "adapted," they seem totally out of kilter with the population being studied.

We know that there are some psychotics and other seriously disturbed people in jail—and for all our studies, that is about all we know for certain. Of the several attempts to quantify the phenomenon, a misleading statistic—that fully 80 percent of the inmates studied in a California city jail "exhibited severe, overt major psychopathology"[28]—is frequently used by those who wish to dramatize the problem of mental patients behind bars. (So widely has this statistic been circulated that it turned up on a promotional examination for corrections officers who seek to become captains in the New York City Department of Corrections—in its distorted form, according to one successful candidate, who asked me, "Did you know 80 percent of all inmates are psychotic?") What those who cite the 80 percent finding omit to mention is that the California study looked at those inmates who had been referred for mental health services, not the entire jail. More precisely, they found 80 percent of 4.5 percent of the total population of the jail to be psychotic, or, to use their own numbers, a total of 80 severely disturbed people among the 5,500 inmates in jail on an average day—a much less alarming 1.45 percent.[29] The investigators, to their credit, noted that several students of the phenomenon had questioned whether the mentally ill in jail had not always been there and were simply being recognized and dealt with more than before. In the end, however, the California researchers decided that "those who would have been hospitalized before deinstitutionalization are now in the community and more subject to arrest."[30] That, of course, is the hypothesis many researchers conducting empirical studies hoped to prove but could not, chiefly because there were no equivalent studies from the predeinstitutionalization era with which to compare their current findings.

Who's in Jail? Criminal Offenders

The California study's finding that 80 percent of inmates referred for psychiatric evaluation were psychotic seemed based on an extremely high estimate to some of us who were providing mental health services to inmates on New York City's Rikers Island, a collection of eight huge jails with a total population of around 16,000 men and 2,000 women. We certainly were not seeing anywhere near that high a proportion of psychotic patients, so we decided to do a modest point prevalence study of our own. We reviewed all the psychiatric evaluations done in one week in two large men's jails at Rikers, looking at the patients' charts for recorded diagnosis and the supporting evidence on which it was based. We found 17.5 percent of the patients referred for evaluation and treatment to be sufficiently disturbed to warrant being diagnosed psychotic. In addition, we compared our results to a control group of inmates admitted during the same week who had not been referred for mental health evaluation, among whom we found no psychotics. It should be emphasized that the total number of patients referred to the mental health services during that week probably represented no more than 2 percent of the buildings' then combined census of 3,800; thus, the rate of psychosis found among inmates on Rikers Island represented a mere 0.28 percent of the total.[31]

The only other study I know of that has sought to pin down the extent to which mental illness was prevalent in a total jail population, regardless of whether the subjects had been referred for mental health services or not, is an unpublished one done in the Cook County Correctional Facility (Chicago). The Cook County investigators reported finding 20 schizophrenics and 41 major depression/bipolar disorders among the 728 male inmates they surveyed, which represented 8.3 percent of the total population. To put these numbers into some perspective, it may help to know that the NIMH Epidemiologic Catchment Area Program determined in 1985 that in three U.S. cities (St. Louis, New Haven, and Baltimore), schizophrenics not in institutions were to be found at a rate of 0.5 to 0.8 per 100 population, that sufferers of major depression were to be found at a rate of 1.8 to 2.6 per hundred, and that all mental disorders were present at a rate of 10.6 to 18.5 per hundred.[32]

For what it's worth, we found at Rikers what the Cook County investigators found: the bulk of the people referred for mental health services were substance abusers. The Cook County sample included 37 percent diagnosed as dependent on alcohol; we found 15 percent. The Rikers population included 31 percent opioid and/or cocaine abusers, whereas the Cook County group found 22 percent.[33] Our inmates, and theirs, were overwhelmingly poor, black or Hispanic, young, uneducated, and unemployed. We found that a distressingly high percentage—32 percent—were homeless when they were not in jail. We also found that 38 percent had prior histories of psychiatric hospitalization, or at least said they did, in addition to multiple incarcerations. This finding confirms a point made by a pair of authors who view mentally ill offenders as "chronic habitués" of both correctional facilities and psychiatric hospitals, "absorbing both mental health and criminal justice resources at an alarming pace."[34] One wonders if perhaps mental illness is not the least of their problems.

The Anecdotal View

Still curious about the current picture of mental illness in jail relative to that of the undocumented past, I abandoned any pretense to empiricism and asked an ex-offender and a warden for their impressions. The ex-offender, whose first incarceration took place during the 1950s and his last in the early 1970s, could recall no mentally ill inmates being in prison at all during his early days as an inmate—"You remember, they were all in the asylum." He provided an interesting perception of mental health services as a commodity, which is how he believes most inmates see things: the same inmate might use one incarceration for a "gym bid," say, meaning he will spend his time bodybuilding in the gym, or for a "dental bid," getting his teeth fixed, "a school bid, or a mental health bid." In this way of looking at things, mental health treatment is not only a commodity, but also a commodity unrelated to diagnosis or need as determined from the outside: it is one among many services available for exploitation.[35]

The warden, on the other hand, saw the provision of mental health services to the inmate population as the key to their improved management: twenty years ago, when he started out in the field, he saw "really crazy" people in jail; "either they were way out or they were zombies on some kind of drugs." He believes the proportion of mentally ill people in jail is no bigger today than it was in the past; moreover, their presence no longer presents the problem it once did to corrections, since there are now services on hand for those inmates: "Twenty years ago, we had a problem. Even seven, eight years ago, no one took care of the mentally ill, and they were a real problem. Now, it's taken care of."[36] Judith Godwin Rabkin and Arthur Zitrin, two researchers known for their work on the question of how many mentally ill offenders are incarcerated, have made a similar observation. They think dangerous patients used to be in the criminal justice system but are now diverted to mental hospitals on the strength of their being dangerous to others, if not to themselves. In the hospital, these inmates/patients are viewed as refractory to treatment and difficult to handle, and they have greatly altered the composition of both systems by making it *appear* that correctional institutions are full of the mentally ill because so many have histories of psychiatric hospitalization, and vice versa.[37]

The Mentally Ill: Responsible for Their Behavior?

In a way, it would be a triumph of the spirit of deinstitutionalization if there were large numbers of ex–mental patients in jails and prisons, because it would show that they were being treated like regular citizens who are held accountable for their actions. It may well be that the mentally ill commit crimes (or get caught) more than normal persons do, but mental illness should not be used as an excuse, a means to escape responsibility for one's actions, a defense likely to keep one out of jail if that's where anyone else caught committing the same crime would go. It's *fair* for mentally ill offenders to go to jail, and for some of them it may be the best possible place to be. I once had a most interesting conversation about this with an inmate who was unquestionably mentally ill yet fully in control of her behavior, who had broken the jail's rules about something for the third time in as many days. The inmate, whose name was Peggy, was waiting for her hearing on these internal charges and knew she was likely to be given time in punitive segregation, a punishment from which only the mental health staff could excuse her, on the grounds that she was too debilitated to do so-called "Bing time." (The "Bing" is the in-house term for the area used for punitive segregation, and time served in that area under sentence is known as "Bing time" by inmates and corrections staff alike.[38]) I said I was not willing to excuse her on such patently false grounds. Angry, Peggy threatened to "cut up the place and throw things around" unless and until I capitulated. We argued fruitlessly until, finally, I countered one of her more detailed descriptions of how out of control she would be with the comment, "Well, then, I guess you're in the right place—jail." That, evidently, was the correct answer, for she laughed uproariously and repeated the comment to everyone else waiting for their hearing.

The legal field has looked at the question of the uncomfortable mix of criminal law and mental health law for some time, at least since California passed the Lanterman-Petris-Short Act (L-P-S), which went into effect in 1969, and the 1972 Wisconsin federal court decision, *Lessard v. Schmidt,* both of which limit the power of the state to commit people involuntarily to mental hospitals. Before these legal watersheds came into play, the system was extremely unfair. As one legal scholar, Norval Morris, puts it, "In principle the criminal-law power of the state is limited by what the criminal deserves for what he did whereas the mental health power of the state is limited only by the patient's death."[39] Morris proposes abolishing the mixing of criminal law and mental health law, even to the extent of doing away with special pleas of unfitness or incompetence, substituting suitable sentencing reforms with which to hold the mentally impaired accountable for their actions. But, says the other side of the dispute, we know we need some kind of official control over the severely disturbed; we always have and we always will, because society has a right to be spared the excesses of their disturbed behavior. Don't forget, say the libertarians, that the track record of existing methods of social control of the severely mentally ill has not been good: the agencies of social control have been abused and overused for years. The dispute goes on in the literature, the emotional tone growing ever more noticeable until it *becomes* the argument: a psychiatrist accuses the libertarians of screwing things up so badly that "patients are dying with their rights on;"[40] and an advocate of liberty for individuals who happen to be mentally ill refers to mental health professionals as "jailers or worse."[41]

Overlooking the Common Ground

This has been the atmosphere in which the question of how to handle the mentally ill offender has been argued. Part of the difficulty encountered by those who seek to learn more about the whereabouts of the mentally ill offender has been that the prevailing tone of the discussion between the criminal justice and the mental health systems has been so rancorous and so mutually accusatory as to preclude what is needed—namely, a joint effort at coming to terms with what is, after all, a shared problem. Stephen J. Morse, a lawyer and psychologist, says:

> Name calling should cease, and advocates should no longer use unrepresentative cases to support their positions, for such evidence produces both poor social science and unsound bases for sensible public policy. What should be clear is that there is no ideal solution to the personal, family, and social problems associated with mental disorder. Maintaining *or* abolishing (or severely limiting) involuntary commitment will create costs and benefits for disordered persons and society at large. What is needed is reasonable and realistic analysis of the likely outcomes of various approaches to the problem of involuntary hospitalization.[42]

To make both the mental health and the criminal justice systems more fair for individuals, of course, has been to create new situations for which old solutions do not immediately work, and what we have been learning the hard way is that old-style mental hospitals and traditional correctional institutions are equally ill equipped to handle the mentally ill offender, who has the right to be treated like any other citizen. One of our oldest solutions, and one that has had immediate appeal to sizable portions of the public, is to blame crime on the crazed, a particularly attractive notion, since it both explains and prescribes in one fell swoop. I think we know it isn't really so, or we wouldn't need daily reassurance from the sensational press that "Crazed Killer Goes on Rampage" or "Psycho Goes Berserk, Kills Mom and Dog."

The impulse to count the mentally ill in jail is probably not all that different from wanting to know that seemingly random violent crime is actually the product of a diseased mind. For years we locked our lunatics up, protecting them, we said, from the pressures of a world they couldn't handle, but really protecting ourselves from the unknowable acts of which we assumed they were capable. Now that they are out in large numbers, we find their behavior has been "criminalized" as a result of the fact that "there may be a limit to society's tolerance of mentally disordered behavior" which might result in "community pressure [to] force them into the criminal justice system of social control."[43]

The truth is that deinstitutionalization has changed nothing but has merely added to the confusion about where we should best put our defiantly deviant. Ex-patients have been welcome in the community only if they act normally—which of course they can't do, since they aren't normal. Now everyone seems sure that mentally ill offenders need to be locked up again; the only dispute is over *where*. This view is not new, however. The "legalization" of the mentally ill had not even taken place before its results were predicted: "If the mental health system is forced to release mentally disordered persons into the community prematurely, there will be an increase in pressure for use of the criminal justice system to reinstitutionalize them."[44] Having warned that wholesale release of patients to the community would cause an increase in the use of jails to take the mental hospitals' place, the anti-deinstitutionalization forces have been at pains to show that they were right all along.[45] The irony of the fact that some mental health professionals noisily object to incarceration of the mentally ill and seek their immediate release merely in order to rehospitalize them involuntarily is apparently lost on those mental health professionals who believe "the social and medical needs which state control is designed to meet are as great as ever if not greater."[46] Surely social control is social control; but it appears that what really matters to the mental health field is that we be the ones to carry the keys.

CHAPTER 10

Backwards into History: Waiting for Moral Treatment to Be Rediscovered

While it is important to understand the social and cultural characteristics that lead patients and their families to resist definitions of disorder and treatment efforts, it is even more crucial for psychiatric services to be aware of how their own patterns of organization may hinder accessibility and effective use of assistance. First, it is necessary to establishment that the treatment program itself is one that a reasonable man or woman could wish to take advantage of. Unfortunately, much of the care available for patients with mental impairments could not pass this rather simple test.

—David Mechanic, "Alternatives to Mental Hospital Treatment: A Sociological Perspective" (1978)

I hope that it will not come to be accepted . . . that community psychiatry is a subspecialty of psychiatry. If this were true it would have totally failed. Community psychiatry is the ordinary practice of good psychiatry.

—J. K. Wing, "Planning and Evaluating Services for Chronically Handicapped Psychiatric Patients in the United Kingdom" (1978)

IF mental health experts from another planet were to visit the United States, they would almost certainly be struck by the vast array of programs and services available, most of them highly specialized and articulated to identify precisely the specific subgroup of the population that they serve. The visitors would also notice, however, that while virtually all of the U.S. programs accept public funds, few of them actually treat the public caseload; and none of the programs is well integrated with any

179

of the others. In short, these experts would see a big, chaotic system, uncoordinated and incoherent, one that utterly fails to fulfill its mission, which is the ongoing care and treatment of the mentally ill.

Except on paper. There, we have an accountable, coordinated, integrated, unified, cost-effective, and comprehensive system of care available to all who seek it at a cost they can afford, tailored to their individual needs. We have hospitals, day hospitals, clinics, clubs, socialization programs, vocational programs, drop-in centers, crisis centers, lounges, outreach services, hot lines, and prevention programs—and still, it isn't enough. Despite the vast array of services and programs, and despite all the money we spend on these, there are seriously mentally ill people all over the country who have been left to manage on their own, without visible assistance from the rich panoply of treatment programs. After all these years, we still seem to be at square one, paralyzed by the sheer size of the problem of a huge and growing caseload of seriously impaired mental patients no one seems to want and no one apparently knows what to do with. After all this time, money, and effort, says one critic of the system,

> The bewildering distribution of responsibility among different levels of government and such varying providers as those of medical care, housing, and disability assistance almost guarantees significant gaps in service and a lack of accountability. The severely disabled inevitably depend on public services, but the public sector is too disorganized and demoralized to respond appropriately to the challenge.[1]

Dismal as this picture is, it is also very deceptive. In fact, we know—and have known for years—what to do with the chronically mentally ill, we know how to treat them, and we know what they need; in this chapter we consider this knowledge. What is more, we have proved what we already know again and again, generally through the "pilot programs" so beloved by the cautious bureaucrat who is eager to avoid the appearance of "throwing money at" problems that are unlikely to go away. What we have not done is to come up with *one* treatment that will simply, effectively, and cheaply meet the needs of *all* the mentally ill, although that has not been for lack of trying. What we have come up with are costly treatment models that take a long time to bear fruit, require the best possible staff, and do not cure mental illness. But they do take care of the patients.

Moral Treatment Revisited

In a way, we have never really gotten past the early nineteenth century and its reportedly successful moral treatment. As noted in chapter 1, moral treatment began life at the end of the eighteenth century as an alternative to forced confinement in custodial care, developed simultaneously in England by William Tuke, who founded the York Retreat, and in France by Philippe Pinel, famous for removing the chains from the lunatics at the notorious Bicêtre. Imported to America by Benjamin Rush, moral treatment had as its essence the belief that the mentally ill could learn self-control by eliciting a positive response from a benign but all-powerful authority figure, a process Tuke saw as roughly analogous to childrearing. The idea was born out of reaction to the early madhouses—Bedlam in England, or Bicêtre in Paris—of whose therapeutic techniques a contemporary once said, "These institutions, as they are generally managed, are far more likely to make a wise man mad than to restore a madman to his senses."[2]

Building on two ideas—one, that institutional care could actually make mental illness worse, and two, that mental patients could learn to control their symptoms—the proponents of moral treatment designed treatment facilities that would best promote their beliefs. They came up with the asylum, a small, pleasant environment where patients could enjoy a close personal relationship with the superintendent, where internal restraints on behavior would be sought and rewarded when developed, where patients would be treated as rational adults, and where idleness would be frowned upon. The so-called Original Thirteen asylum superintendents envisioned their facilities as very small— Thomas Kirkbride limited them to a maximum of 200 to 250 patients each[3]— and they were able to select their clientele very carefully, mostly from among affluent, intact families. Patients in their care, then, could find solace and protection in a setting that was big enough to provide privacy and anonymity when required, and small enough so that one could, if he wanted, get to know everyone else. Staff were friendly and approachable, and the superintendent prided himself on being available in a fatherly sort of way to all his patients.

The asylum staff tried to create a familylike, tolerant, and loving environment—what we would call "supportive" today—without being small and intense, as families, especially dysfunctional ones, often are. Isaac Ray, another of the Original Thirteen superintendents, defined moral treatment in reaction to what he and his colleagues had seen elsewhere:

Instead of the kindness and care, so usually manifested towards the sick, as if it were a natural right for them to receive it; instead of the untiring vigilance, the soothing attention, the lively solicitude of relatives and friends, the patient, af-flicted with the severest of diseases, was deprived of most of all that was ever dear to him, and suffered to remain in his seclusion uncared for and forgotten.[4]

Much of moral treatment is rooted in simple common sense. If someone is too disruptive to remain in polite society, for example, removing him only makes sense, provided the next step includes the chance to learn better, more successful methods of social interaction, something moral treatment was deter-mined to do. Mental illness was assumed to be a sickness and its remedy the same sort of "soothing attention" and "lively solicitude" that is given routinely to most physically sick people—a far cry from the harsh and punitive attitude toward the mentally ill that both preceded and has replaced moral treatment. Perhaps most important was moral treatment's view of mental illness as a relatively routine and unremarkable offshoot of normal life, something that could be dealt with in a temporary, specialized environment designed to maxi-mize social function and promote self-esteem. To the denizens of moral treat-ment, mental illness was no big deal; it was something to be fixed if possible, and coped with in any case. There is something very attractive and soothing about moral treatment: for a patient, it must have been reassuring just to be around an asylum superintendent, with his faith in one's ability to control disruptive thoughts and impulses and learn to act normal. Patients, their families, and asylum staff alike must have derived enormous comfort and support from the simple knowledge that in the eyes of moral treatment, these were not hopeless cases.

Its Success Proved Its Undoing

At first, the originators of moral treatment claimed impressive success, as at the Bloomingdale Asylum, mentioned in chapter 1.[5] Success brought imita-tion, of course, at first in the private sector—in New York State alone, six private asylums were built between 1820 and 1870—and eventually in the public sector as well, where moral treatment met its undoing.

The most avid supporters of moral treatment exaggerated the benefits of institutional care, confusing the care given *in* the asylum with the facility itself by claiming that asylum care in and of itself would eliminate insanity and its effects. The upshot of this overselling of the asylum model of care was the construction of publicly supported model communities in which the mentally ill were to relearn the skills of life in bucolic settings, far from the stress and tension of normal society. Where this had been an enterprise well within the reach of private facilities, which could limit the size and nature of their patient populations, it was one that was doomed to failure in a public venue, which could not. The enlightened goal of replicating the moral treatment model in public institutions gradually gave way to the pressure to expand that was caused by the sheer volume of chronically dependent mental patients, a group made up increasingly of individuals without financial resources or loving families, patients who had nowhere else to go and nothing very much to get well for. One historian of the asylum era believes the superintendents oversold their treatment model in part because their commitment to their vision "made them unreceptive to alternative means or services and largely oblivious to the fact that they no longer met the needs of . . . even all the patients in their asylums."[6]

In retrospect, it seems odd that the single piece of moral treatment to survive replication in state hospitals was the notion that people could get better if they were simply removed from the stressful environment in which they had first succumbed to mental illness. The sole surviving remnant of the asylum's heyday was thus the *fact* of institutional care, although the institutions that replaced the asylum bore no resemblance to the prototype, save that all were located in remote settings—certainly there were few other similarities between Connecticut's original Hartford Retreat and New York's Manhattan State Hospital. The rest of moral treatment got thrown out in the press to house the huge public caseload, who after all were people who had long since been written off as hopeless crazies. This was the public caseload that emerged gradually throughout the rest of the nineteenth century, growing steadily as it absorbed large numbers of immigrants who spoke no English, alcoholics, people with unmanageable behavior problems, and the senile elderly—none of them suitable candidates for moral treatment.

Ironically, moral treatment's essence has surfaced in bits and pieces ever since, as pilot program after pilot program has reinvented the wheel by discovering what the asylum superintendents knew all along. Known variously as "therapeutic communities," "lodge programs," or "community residences," the several revolutions in care of the mentally ill have always borne considerable, if unacknowledged, resemblance to the original asylums, if only in their mutual attempt to deliver what their patients' lives lacked.

What the Mentally Ill Need

Housing

The first thing the mentally ill need, like the rest of us, is a place to live. No one living on the street has any hope of recovering from any illness, regardless of its nature. Besides that, though, the mentally ill need to be able to live in a place where they can belong, where their peculiarities will be tolerated and even better, understood. This point may seem elemental, but it really is not: even people who know better than to try to force chronic patients into appearing normal go ahead and do so anyway, whether out of anxiety (rationalized along the lines of "If the patients look crazy, the neighbors will complain and they'll shut the program down") or simple meanness (I knew an old man in an adult home who used to mutter constantly to himself about what God would say when He came to earth, so the staff of his adult home derived great amusement from faking occasional telephone calls to the old man in which they pretended to be God).

Like anyone else, the mentally ill need a home that is a refuge, a haven, a place where they can loosen up a little, even if in their case, "loosening up" means stockpiling thousands of recipes they'll never cook or writing undecipherable documents to Congressmen to whom they have decided they are related. Interestingly enough, a review of all research comparing the outcome of institutional versus alternative care for the mentally ill noted that it mattered less *where* patients lived than it did what the place was like to live in: a tolerant and accepting custodial institution was better than a hostile community residence.[7]

Outreach

The next thing we know mentally ill patients require is aggressive outreach. It is amazing to me how slow mental health professionals have been to figure out this elemental lesson, but we still haven't fully caught on. The fact that chronic mental patients are notorious for failing to get to their outpatient clinic appointments at all, let alone on time, is invariably attributed by clinic workers to the patients' resistance or their negativism, and there the matter is left until the patient falls apart and needs rehospitalization. Collectively, the chronic population has largely been written off as "inappropriate" for clinic treatment, whereupon a self-fulfilling prophecy takes over at the bottom line of every treatment plan: chronic patients drop out of treatment because they are expected to. One would think that clinic directors should realize that if whole portions of the clientele avoid using their services, then maybe something is wrong with those services; however, in my experience it is the rare mental health program that tailors its services to the requirements and limited abilities of its chronic patients.[8]

What we know, but are rarely willing to incorporate into our treatment facilities, is that severely mentally ill people often do not have a good sense of time, do not always do what they are supposed to, and are used to being able to blame their own failures on their illness—all of which, put together, makes them very poor candidates for infrequent individual clinic treatment. Aggressive outreach, as it is called, means aftercare staff have to call the errant patients up or even go visit them when they do not show up; it also means therapists may have to squeeze them in unexpectedly if they do show up on the wrong day or at the wrong time. Having supervised therapists for many years, I know how unpopular these ideas are with most professional staff, but let's face it: such approaches are what all chronic patients need—and not just the homeless ones.

Ready Access to Hospitals

Another thing the chronically mentally ill need is permission to regress occasionally in the course of treatment and the ability to be rehospitalized at once when they need it. The notion that community-based treatment *had* to be adequate to the task of keeping even the chronically mentally ill out of the hospital forever has been extraordinarily slow to give way to overwhelming evidence that it cannot be done. This does not mean the chronically mentally ill cannot live in the community; it means that they cannot be guaranteed never to need brief, intermittent rehospitalizations. The goal of keeping each and every patient out of the hospital indefinitely is so pervasive as a measure of therapeutic success that for practitioners, each rehospitalization of one of their patients can feel like a devastating personal failure.

Nevertheless, all existing outcome research related to the chronic population has as its primary index of treatment success the length of time patients remain outside a hospital—even though it has long since been established that what they suffer from in the first place are disorders defined, in part, by a perpetual need for intermittent, intensive treatment of a sort traditionally available only in a hospital. Abbott S. Weinstein, for example, says that the number of mental patients readmitted to state facilities has remained constant over the years, as have the percentages of those patients readmitted frequently (three or more times in one year) or rapidly (within three months of discharge). His goal was to correct the widespread, but inaccurate, belief that readmissions to state mental hospitals reflected accelerated returns of prematurely discharged patients.[9] Even though everyone recognizes that the chronic mentally ill require the occasional readmission—practitioners, from direct observation; researchers, from their own and colleagues' findings;[10] policymakers, from hospital census figures—we still seek program perfection in an impossible clinical goal. One potentially damaging distortion of the reality of severe mental illness and its remedy can be found in the denunciations of community-based care by those who use the fact of patients' inevitable brief rehospitalizations to justify their call for a return to the total institutions of the past, which they, knowing no history, have decided are the only suitable setting for the population. Such a simplistic and insupportable conclusion shows just how easy it is to politicize clinical data in defiance of demonstrated patient need.

Skills of Living

The chronically mentally ill need something that in the literature is sometimes called "treatment" and other times "rehabilitation."[11] I have always thought of it as training in the art of acting normal, but whatever it is, the nature of the work is to reeducate the mentally ill in the myriad skills of interpersonal life. Included in such a catchall category are such things as personal hygiene and grooming, shopping, budgeting, traveling, social skills, and polite discourse—all the little skills of civilized behavior that we take for granted. A special task for the severely mentally ill is learning a kind of symptom management: to get along in the world, schizophrenics, for example, need to learn that it is not all right to talk openly to one's "voices" (auditory hallucinations) on a bus or in a store, nor is it okay to menace strangers with dire warnings and threats, however important it may seem at the time to communicate the information. The distinction I try to make in practice, one that seems very important to patients, is that learning to act like normal people does not mean they have to give up their voices or their peculiar thoughts—something they would find a terrifying, even impossible, challenge. The biggest problem with this necessary therapeutic activity is that most psychotherapists much prefer, understandably, to practice a highly verbal psychotherapy rather than to communicate the simplest skills of daily life to people whose tendency is first, to communicate through action rather than speech, if at all possible, and second, to use speech that is almost entirely metaphorical.

Work

Next, the mentally ill need work to do. Most mental patients have nothing to do all day. They had nothing to do all day in the hospital, unless you count the occasional "current events" group or "community meeting" as something to do (I, for one, do not), and they have nothing important or even very real to do out in the world. In my neighborhood there is a large public library with a surprisingly inexpensive snack bar; and since I spend a fair bit of time in the library myself, I have come to recognize a substantial population of discharged mental patients whose daily life is centered there, especially in the snack bar. While it is possible that they are all doing profound and significant research, it seems far more likely that they are in the library because they have nowhere else to spend the day. There is no excuse for this.

Discharged mental patients are never going to learn to live in the real world as long as they are living in the same kind of unreal half-life of empty inactivity that characterized the custodial hospitals. Besides, if normal people work for a living, why shouldn't they? The chronically mentally ill need to be able to work, at real jobs; furthermore, there is no reason why they can't work. In one interesting study, for example, the researcher found that over 80 percent of a group of patients who had been diagnosed schizophrenic and discharged after a single hospitalization went right back to work. The researcher noticed that all the previous studies of work performance among schizophrenics had used hospitalized patients exclusively, a sampling bias that resulted in overstating the relationship between work failure and mental illness. To the contrary, he concluded that "the capacity to perform the work role cannot be wholly or even largely accounted for on the basis of the presence or degree of manifest psychopathology."[12] We must face the fact that we cannot seriously expect the mentally ill to live out their whole lives wasting time—no one, perceiving that to be his future, could seriously want to go on with it. No wonder even a mental hospital comes to look like a better bet.

Cuba has devised a fascinating solution to this problem. The Cubans have identified a series of five or so levels of mental impairment, each keyed to a treatment setting; as patients' mental status improves, they move from hospital to community in a series of graduated steps. Every step, even the lowest, requires each patient to work at a job, and the jobs pay better as the patient gets better and moves to successively less restricted settings. There is thus a built-in incentive to continue to get better—it pays to get well, literally—and there is no "free ride" for the dependent patient, no secondary gain in staying in the hospital.[13]

Cigarettes and Coffee

One of the most important considerations for anyone who is thinking of working with the chronic mentally ill is generally overlooked by mental health professionals: that mental patients nearly all smoke, all seem to drink gallons of coffee, and all love junk food.[14] These days, of course, most mental health professionals abhor smoke and prohibit it whenever and wherever they can. Without challenging professionals' right to spend the day in a smoke-free environment and without endorsing nicotine addiction, it nevertheless should be obvious to anyone trying to develop a program for a population that smokes so heavily that, for example, rules against smoking on the premises may drive patients away. Surely it is wiser to face the inevitable and design smoking areas with the best possible ventilation as standard equipment in the program's physical plant. By the same token, coffee is so clearly viewed as a necessity by the population that surely it is worth a few dollars and a little of someone's time to have a pot available in the waiting room.

In my experience, though, most clinics aren't set up to attract chronic patients, and their waiting rooms are often devoid of ashtrays, while phonily polite signs prohibit the consumption of food or beverage altogether. The excuse generally given is that to allow chronic patients to "hang out" in the waiting room—which they would certainly do if there were free coffee, according to the party line—is to allow "chronics" to drive off the more desirable, middle-class population, who won't want to share a waiting room with crazies. The crazies get the message and drop out of treatment—but that's understood and written off, because everyone knows how resistant they are. Genuine outreach to people who differ from the norm means that services and the manner in which they are delivered have to differ from the norm if they are to be accepted by the target population, even if that means creating a smokers' lounge and providing free coffee.

Treatment Free of Condescension

Above all else, I have noticed, the chronically mentally ill are thoroughly schooled by life on the margins of society in the detection of hypocrisy and condescension, and one of their treatment needs is to be able to have some say about the therapists they will work with. Susan Sheehan's wonderful book about "Sylvia Frumkin," *Is There No Place on Earth for Me?* includes a telling illustration of how important being able to choose one's therapist is, even to psychotic patients, who are all too often written off as "too out of it to notice."

In Sylvia's earliest days as a psychotherapy patient, at her first regular session after the intake interview, she met her assigned therapist for the first time. Since she could read upside down, Sylvia saw that the intake report on the therapist's desk began with an unflattering comment on her appearance. In what she remembered as a deliberate test of the therapist's truthfulness, Sylvia asked her to read the first page out loud. The therapist complied, but she changed the content so it would be less unflattering. Sylvia decided from then on that the therapist was neither trustworthy nor helpful, although she continued in treatment for a year, pretending everything was all right. When in the course of treatment the patient and the therapist completely disagreed about whether she should be hospitalized, Sylvia asked for and got a new therapist, whom she promptly put to the same test. The second therapist passed the test with flying colors by reading the report as written. Sylvia not only decided she could trust this new therapist but went on to develop so strong an attachment to the second therapist that twenty years and countless successors later, Sylvia still remembered her as "the only therapist with whom she would ever try to work out her problems . . . 'something just clicked . . . [she] was my fairy godmother.' "[15]

Two things strike me as important about this illustration: First, seriously mentally ill people are fully capable of making shrewd and lasting assessments about other people even though they often appear out of it and totally indifferent to interactions, which suggests that many of us who work with them are seriously underestimating their abilities to assess *us*. Second, patients probably choose their own therapists whether we permit them to or not. In any case, the need for patients to feel free to make their own decisions about the mental health professionals whom they can trust and therefore work with is rarely acknowledged, much less acted upon. What they *do not* need, any more than the rest of us do, is to be patronized and shut out of all decision making that directly affects their own lives.

Long-Term Illness, Long-Term Access

Finally, chronic patients need our assurance that all of the things described thus far—homes, coffee, cigarettes, rapid hospitalizations, real jobs, and real treatment with therapists they feel they can trust—will be available to them for as long as they need them, even if that means forever. No one likes feeling insecure about the future availability of what he needs, and mental patients are no exception, even if they cannot or will not say so. The odds are that most severely mentally ill people are well aware that they have a lifetime disability, and the concept of "short-term" or "time-limited" treatment must strike them as ridiculously inapposite in the face of that lifelong illness. Nevertheless, many programs and entitlements stress from the outset how very limited they intend their services to be, not because time-limited service is what the population requires, but because policymakers and auditors think they are saving money by preventing long-term dependency.

Even worse, in a way, is the misguided practice of punishing mentally ill people for breaking the rules of a program by kicking them out, or threatening to do so. When people are as anxious and uncertain as chronic mental patients are, this practice can only undermine what little self-assurance they have been able to develop, and it is hard to see how that can be called treatment. Consider the comments of the Joint Commission on Mental Illness and Health, made nearly thirty years ago:

> The mental patient is *not* unconscious of how he is handled, but is usually hypersensitive, quick to resent injustice, and apt to interpret harsh and punitive handling as substantiation of his own sense of guilt or persecution, of being "no good," or of feeling that everyone is against him.[16]

It is crucial that chronic patients be able to feel they belong and fit in somewhere, that their odd behavior and peculiar ways can be tolerated by someone, and that their particular needs will be understood and addressed in some fashion. A program that takes back membership at will, that uses it as a tool or even a weapon to ensure compliance, is providing none of those and can hardly be considered therapeutic. It is not enough simply to dream up and enforce rules among a population whose social skills are as limited as those of the chronically mentally ill, if only because they may not even know how to comply. Although it is admittedly much more difficult to design, the program chronic patients will take to is one that considers their potential need to stay there forever: even if they do in fact move on, the important thing is that they can count on the program to be there to go back to when and if they need it. Not surprisingly, crazy people need a safe place, a family, to be able to turn to, and the odds are that they need it a lot more than the rest of us do.

What the Mentally Ill Typically Get

Many programs for chronic patients are not very well thought out. Much of what they provide in the way of activity is thinly disguised busywork, intended merely to fill time, even though it may bear a pompous name on the activity schedule, something like "Social Skills Training" or "Activities of Daily Living," "Poetry Group" or "Community Sing." Bored, patients and staff alike often get caught up in endless unspoken battles over who controls attendance, compliance, and patients' activity.

Constant Conflict, Petty Issues

An example of the kind of pointless struggle programs and their patients get themselves into over rules and their enforcement, not to mention the overarching question of who is in charge, comes from a large day program sponsored by (of all things) a psychoanalytic clinic, whose name and prestige attracted an unusual clientele to the day program. I worked in a supervisory job somewhat tangential to the program, which enabled me to watch the passing scene in a detached way.

The informal structure of this well-known day program included hundreds of exceptionally intelligent, well-educated chronic mental patients (called here "clients"), who reveled in the chance to match wits with a surprisingly pedestrian, much less well educated, unimaginative staff, trained not as psychotherapists but as vocational rehabilitation counselors. The counselors' mission was to prepare their clients for future work, albeit in nonexistent jobs; so the program's focus was kept strictly on the here and now and the minutiae of life on the job, with little if any interest shown in their clients' pasts or their psychodynamics, nor in much of anything *they* might be interested in. The core problem seemed to be that the clients had one set of interests and skills—they were verbal, articulate, and exceptionally creative, if somewhat bizarrely and flamboyantly so—while the staff were required to concentrate on things like punctuality, appropriateness of clothing, and regularity of attendance. The clients dismissed these concerns as "Mickey Mouse bullshit" and were obviously completely uninterested in the staff agenda. The staff, limited by their training and the terms of their funding, then dug deeper and deeper into what they could control as a means of exerting authority over a recalcitrant population they understood very poorly.

To illustrate the enormous disparity between clients and staff, I think of

Harold, an enormous black man who had spent most of his life in state mental hospitals for children. Harold had a prodigious memory, and he came up with an irrepressible stream of thoughts and ideas about religion and philosophy, which he chose to think about out loud, whether others were listening or not. Harold paced up and down in the hallway outside my office all day, spouting his intricate philosophical and theological formulations, many of which were very interesting, if largely useless. Harold was, in essence, a highly creative thinker, though one who had never learned how to shape and control the flow of his thoughts. Dismissed by most staff as "a babbling schizophrenic," Harold covered up his loneliness and isolation by becoming ever more bombastic and theatrical in his ravings. Finally, the program director elected to pick a fight with him over the length of his hair, which he had allowed to grow into a huge, bushy Afro because he believed for some complicated reason that he should only get one haircut per year. She threatened him with expulsion if he didn't cut it. This made no sense to Harold, who expostulated mightily about freedom of expression, to no avail. He got the haircut rather than lose the program, which he knew he needed; but he told me he never understood why: "What does it matter what's *on* my head? Why doesn't she care what's *in* my head?" I thought he had a point.

If helping the clients get better was the goal, the client–staff mix was disastrous, because the staff were so rigid and so needlessly authoritarian about limiting clients' attention to the task at hand that the clients were bound to wind up spending all their time dreaming up new and often quite creative ways to outwit the staff. In the long run, their rebelliousness only made the staff that much more doctrinaire (although I suspect everyone felt comfortable with the arrangement, which closely resembled many of the clients' home lives). So inflexible were the staff that in general, the client dropout rate was much lower than was the rate of patients thrown out for not fitting in or toeing the line. In this program, helping clients get better was not a goal; success was counted when a client made the transition to a dead-end job-training program.

Throughout my time there, I watched one battle rage unacknowledged between staff and clients. It lasted at least a year and began when the phony patient government committee, called the Action Committee by staff and the Passive Committee by clients, because it had no authority to do anything, surprised even itself by successfully obtaining money from the parent organization to buy a Ping-Pong table. The table was placed with great ceremony in a back room and naturally attracted much client attention at the outset, if only because of its novelty. A staff member whose office abutted on the Ping-Pong room deduced from the sounds that came her way that clients were using the table when they should have been attending her activity, a kind of required busywork with a grandiose vocational name that I have since forgotten; and she demanded at a staff meeting that access to the Ping-Pong table be limited to lunchtime and breaks. Her proposal was accepted, the new rules were announced, and clients responded by flocking to the room in large numbers to play Ping-Pong at all hours, defiantly closing the door behind them. The staff had the door removed from its hinges and confiscated the Ping-Pong paddles. Clients retaliated by abandoning use of the ashtrays throughout the building, grinding their cigarettes out on the carpeting instead; they also boycotted much of the program and spent the day sitting on the staircase in the lobby. I left the agency at about the point the clients were forming a "Liberation Group," which had already picketed the parent organization once, with plans for a return visit. For all I know, the battle rages to this day; it wouldn't surprise me.

Staff Concerns Must Always Come First

I chose the foregoing example of programmatic one-up-manship to illustrate a phenomenon I have witnessed repeatedly on the job: by and large, programs for the treatment of the chronically mentally ill are designed for the convenience of the staff rather than to address their patients' need to acquire more productive means of functioning in the world. Take the simple idea of outreach: we know beyond a doubt that chronically mentally ill patients will probably require an aggressive campaign of follow-up from the staff of an aftercare facility if they are to overcome their shyness, depression, and anxiety about coming to a new place, as well as their fabled negativism and resistance; yet it is the rare staff person who will cheerfully institute the admittedly time-consuming methods of follow-up, such as repeated phone calls and visits to the patients at home. Their excuses for not doing so are predictable and center on their self-perception, needs, professional image, and on-the-job comfort: I didn't have time. How do you expect me to see patients if I'm out in the field making home visits all the time? They live in a terrible neighborhood, and I didn't take the job so I could get killed. You're not paying me enough to take on these extra assignments. I didn't go to graduate school so I could become a policeman/desk clerk/drill sergeant. It is not difficult to rationalize such attitudes, as observers have noticed:

> The assumption is that what is good for the staff and the hospital is also good for the patient, for if he has been a good patient he will leave the hospital as a

well-adjusted member of society. This then, constitutes the ideal of a truly therapeutic—as well as a truly "total"—institution.[17]

It has been my experience that for most mental health professionals, even
very good, very caring ones, the ideal model of practice is the one derived from
medicine: one opens an office, and patients come to that office. Anything less
than that is somehow unprofessional and second-rate. It is easier by far to set
up a program that acknowledges professionals' need to feel first-rate by finessing the need for aggressive outreach in various ways than it is to get staff to
change.[18] However one does this—the usual way is to invent a new position
called, for example, "case aide," hire a paraprofessional, and stick that person
with all the outreach no one else wants to do, although I have worked in three
programs that used other patients to do it—the most frightened and/or angri-
est patients will not receive aftercare, because no one will come to them.
Programs can generally get away with what is, after all, an abdication of their
clinical responsibility to follow up on the most difficult patients, because it is
precisely those patients who are known to be most resistant to treatment. In
any case, the clinic's focus will typically be on its own internal maintenance;
it will most likely not be on advancing our collective understanding of the
special needs of the chronic population, nor on the design of special programs
to address those needs. And in this endeavor, all clinics get a big boost from
Medicaid.

How Funding Determines Programming

It is a fact that Medicaid, which supports most of the mental health programs that provide aftercare to the chronically mentally ill, pays the most for
the least care. A "clinic visit" lasting at least thirty minutes is worth more to
a program than a "full day visit" of at least five hours to a day hospital, because
the reimbursement rates are higher for the clinic visit, even though the expense
of providing the second is so much greater. Assuming they are aware of it and
care, Medicaid administrators' preference for clinic visits ignores the considerable volume of clinical and empirical evidence that has long since established
the superiority of day hospital treatment over individual therapy for the
chronically mentally ill.[19] Without debating the relative merits of the two
modalities for the chronic population, it is in any event striking that the more
comprehensive modality is reimbursed at a lower rate, even though it obviously
costs the provider more to administer.

Further, it is interesting that the home visit, that despised tool of aggressive outreach, is reimbursed at the clinic visit rate, even though it too costs more in staff time and travel expenses to provide; moreover, if the patient being visited is registered in a day program, any home visits would be considered part of that day program and would not be reimbursed separately at all. In short, by rewarding traditional office-based clinic practice, Medicaid has all but guaranteed that no program—even those already dedicated to working with the chronic population—will find it profitable to go to any great lengths to develop treatment strategies more likely to be effective with the chronic population than individual psychotherapy in an office.

Medicaid's approval notwithstanding, there are several reasons individual psychotherapy in an office is an inadequate prescription for chronic mental disorder. First, the problems of the schizophrenic (indeed, of any seriously disturbed mental patient) are *problems in living* much more than they are discrete and clearcut symptoms of illness, an insight we owe to the radical literature of the 1960s.[20] This notion is not in favor with the field's current experts on schizophrenia, who seek biological and genetic bases for mental illness to explain the phenomenon; but for those of us who still try to work with the people rather than with the illness, the problems-in-living idea has been a touchstone. It offers the therapist a rationale for dealing with problem behavior and its consequences, while we all wait for the genetic solution to the mystery of schizophrenia to be unraveled, or for the new drug to be synthesized, the one that will finally do the trick and cure mental illness. Regardless of the etiology of the condition, mentally ill people obviously need help in learning how to act like the rest of us. However, to view their erratic and bizarre activities as symptomatic, rather than as characteristic, behavior, as many people do, has been extraordinarily misleading and unproductive.

Consider that most *treatment* focuses on symptoms ("Do you hear any voices? What do they tell you?"), while most *problems* take place in the spaces and corners of the world that the patient tries to enter in the course of living his life. These problems do not necessarily manifest themselves in the course of the twenty minutes the patient might spend in the doctor's office in any given week, because that office is one of the few places where the mental patient's vast experience will almost certainly have taught him how to act. The patient's problems will take shape the minute he leaves, when he acts wrong in the waiting room or in the elevator or on the street or in the bus or at the drugstore where he gets his prescription filled or at the corner store where he buys his cigarettes or most especially in his room at an adult home, where he responds to the voices that tell him to stockpile every newspaper he can get his hands on to prevent some global catastrophe—which he dutifully does, only to get in big trouble for creating a fire hazard. This will be trouble he won't fully comprehend, of course, since to him, no fire hazard could be quite as threatening as the worldwide catastrophe he was trying to avert, but when he tells everyone this, they look at him as if he were crazy and start muttering about rehospitalization. *Those* are problems in living, and no clinician who only treats patients in an office will ever understand them, because he will never see them.

It is also the case that treatment of people whose problems are not necessarily the same as their symptoms has to be integrated into their daily lives to a much greater degree than traditional psychotherapy normally permits. In theory, the need for such integration is fully appreciated by the field, but in practice it almost never exists, for two reasons: (1) practitioners prefer and are encouraged to work out of offices to which their patients are expected to travel; and (2) in the world of public administration, treatment is medical, while residence is social, so the two are administered, funded, and regulated separately. As anyone who has ever tried to call a bureaucracy on the phone knows, what government separates, no man can ever hope to integrate. Unfortunately, this one distinction has probably stood more in the way of the creation of programming suitable for the chronic mentally ill than even the fabled stigma of mental illness has. Leona L. Bachrach views the lack of coordinated services for the chronic population as the result of the fact that planners have "failed to differentiate residential settings and treatment settings, even though the distinction is a crucial one. . . . They have often focused disproportionately on where patients *live* . . . and virtually overlooked their need for access to settings where treatment is provided."[21] In any case, the fact that treatment and housing are administered separately in most of government means that they are extremely unlikely ever to be coordinated, least of all at the case level.

Programs That Work

Fortunately, there are programs that function very well despite all of the roadblocks just described, doing all the right things even though they are neither fashionable nor endorsed by the bureaucracy. The best place to start is the last place it ever occurs to mental health programmers to go for program ideas: the patients themselves. (To quote one of my former supervisors: "But they're crazy! What could they know about treatment?") From a published account of what aftercare chronic mental patients feel they need, here are a few considerations:

> One of the most important things you first have to think about is where you're going to live when you leave the hospital . . . [after which] the greatest need is to have a place to go, where you are expected each day, a place where you can be with people like yourself and do things that mean something to yourself and others. . . . It's hard to explain, but I think everyone has to have something to do. No matter how much others may think we're ill or sick, even though we're on SSI or SSDI, or on welfare, and are looked at as disabled, that shouldn't mean we can't do anything that is needed or make sense to others. . . . We need, therefore, to be with others who believe that we are not at our best and that sufficient time will be given us to be at our best, maybe about as much time as the non–mentally ill have in order to achieve whatever their potential might be. . . . I don't mean to say that we're children, but I'm thinking about a family and what seems to go on there, at least I think so, and how this could really help a lot of chronic patients in the community.[22]

Obviously, these consumers have some definite preferences, if people would only ask.

Fountain House

The author of the foregoing passage has been involved in various capacities in New York City's Fountain House, a large and defiantly untraditional rehabilitation program (whose participants generally refer to it as a giant club). According to legend, Fountain House was started in the 1950s by three ex–state hospital patients who had nothing to do all day and who took to hanging out together at a soda fountain—hence the name. Once it dawned on them that there were no places for them to go to learn to become productive members of society, they formed a club and did it on their own. Much of their style of communication and programming is tinged with what I take to be the remnants of the founders' fury at the traditional mental health professions for abandoning them to the streets and their own supposedly inferior resources. The founders of Fountain House have certainly showed what mental patients are capable of, and by implication what mental health professionals were *not* capable of: in 1978, the club reported 10,000 client visits per month, or 400 per day on the average, aged anywhere from sixteen to seventy-eight; and the program also sponsored fifty-two apartments, a thrift shop, a snack bar, and had 130 clients placed in temporary paying jobs at forty-one businesses, where they learned how to function in the world of work.[23]

The Lodge

Another program, while not initiated by patients themselves, nonetheless was built on the idea of groups of mentally ill people taking care of one another. Lodge groups were formed while the patients were still in a hospital together, whereupon the patients were discharged en bloc to what the designers of this model called a "lodge"—a small, autonomous society, one in which "chronic mental patients could go to live and work in a supportive group situation."[24] The best-known exemplar of this idea, which flourished in California between 1963 and 1966, was designed as a controlled experiment. Its designers found that when compared with a control group, lodge residents showed little recidivism, high employment, high job satisfaction, and personal esteem.[25] The lodge program no longer exists, even though it cost half what hospitalization cost and one-third what it cost to care for the control group in more traditional community-based settings, and in spite of the fact that its researchers reported that the original lodge had eventually become self-supporting, which is to say, free to the taxpayer. Apparently, this very successful and money-saving program did not survive the experimental stage, nor has it ever been replicated to any lasting extent, perhaps, its founder says, because it was altogether *too* revolutionary:

> Even though an overwhelming amount of scientific evidence had been created to show the advantage of the lodge society, few mental hospitals were willing to accept it [because] to accept it demanded rather extensive social role and status changes among professional people. They had to become problem solvers and had in fact, in the final analysis, to become consultants rather than supervisors and, indirectly, to phase themselves out of the patients' society in order to give first-class citizenship to ex–mental patients.[26]

Evidently, although the lodge residents proved to be willing and flexible enough to alter their lifelong patterns of dependency and learned helplessness, the professional staff of the clinical facilities where they had first been treated were not willing or able to give up their authority and control over the patients' lives. It is hard not to notice the entrenched hypocrisy of the mental health professions, which are all for patient independence as long as the professionals get to call the shots. Still, it is nice to know the model worked.

PACT

A well-publicized program founded in the late 1960s in Madison, Wisconsin, is called PACT, or Program for Assertive Community Treatment.[27] PACT is predicated on the assumption that chronic mental patients can overcome a lifetime of defeat and psychotic experience culminating in repeated hospitalization by learning that they can, after all, survive in a community setting by mastering the tasks of daily living. This is harder to do than it may sound, for chronic patients are often helpless and dependent seemingly beyond reason, but the PACT people have managed quite well over the years. Their primary goal is to help free the chronic mental patient from what they term "pathological dependent relationships," which they accomplish by assertively helping patients acquire the material resources of independent life, helping them learn routine coping skills in real-life situations, and providing just as much support as is necessary to keep them in treatment. The principal recorders of the PACT program have identified two keys to their success: (1) they rehospitalize *only* when patients are imminently suicidal, homicidal, or very maniac, and then only very briefly, *never* in response to manipulative self-destructive behavior; and (2) the concept of "cure" is not a very useful one for the chronic population—they prefer "growth, stability and adequate quality of life, or even prevention of deterioration" as more realistic and worthwhile treatment goals.[28] Clearly, part of their success has to be credited to their willingness to rethink therapists' roles, tasks, and ways of working.

The Work Ward

Other interesting programs have reported success with the chronic population. One started with the assumption that hospitals were the worst possible place in which to learn how to live more productive lives, when what the patients needed to learn was how to work rather than how to stay in bed all day. The designers of this program turned a twenty-bed inpatient unit at the Los Angeles County–USC Medical Center Psychiatric Hospital into what became known as "the work ward," where newly admitted patients were put to work for pay at once, eventually graduating to work in the world combined with aggressive aftercare. Like PACT, the approach called for significant alterations in professional tasks: according to the authors, psychiatrists on the work ward had to go from "concentrating on insight and cure to getting the best possible adaptation;" each psychologist had to switch from being "one who furthers psychological understanding to one who evaluates ability to function"; social work on this ward "focuse[d] on the real and overwhelming problems the chronically disabled have in dealing with an urban environment;" occupational therapists taught work skills; recreational therapists taught the skills of daily life; and only nurses successfully avoided any change in their roles.[29]

Day Hospital

Another program that has tried to provide real services to the chronically mentally ill was sponsored by Massachusetts Mental Health Center, the community mental health center that serves the Boston area. The program encompassed a variety of aftercare and housing facilities, in keeping with their belief that a range of options are most useful for this varied population, including a quarterway house, five group homes, apartments, and the usual clinical settings. The truly unusual feature was that the program had shifted the locus of patient evaluation from its traditional setting, the inpatient unit, to the day hospital, around which the entire program was built. Patients in the process of being evaluated went home at night, were housed temporarily at the Inn, a kind of community residence sponsored by the center, or were hospitalized briefly for intensive care.

The program has reported no increase in either suicides or recidivism among its patients, and staff have noticed a decrease in their use of restraint and seclusion to control patients; moreover, they discovered that overall, the program could do well with less staff, a reduction that in and of itself saved the program about 13 percent of its direct-care costs. Unfortunately, insurance companies hate the day hospital modality and often will not reimburse for its services, on the grounds that hospitals use it merely to extend stays on the inpatient unit, that its existence merely adds to the overall demand for services, and that its use will not reduce the use of inpatient facilities. Consequently, the day hospital–centered model of treatment, while successful and cost-effective, is not feasible because it cannot be funded except by public money.[30]

Fort Logan CMHC

Another program that used its inpatient facility rarely and then only for brief periods was the Fort Logan Community Mental Health Center (CMHC) of Colorado, which did some 65 percent of its work with discharged mental patients by home visits. The program's aim was to intervene directly in "dysfunctional social systems" (i.e., families), rather than to isolate the identified patient in an environment that was both unnatural and cut off from the world, such as an inpatient unit. Whenever they found a patient who really needed to be removed from his home environment, they preferred to use special foster care–like settings of eight to ten patients each, which were located in the community not far from where the patient normally lived, rather than taking the more traditional route of having him admitted to a mental hospital. As much as possible, the Fort Logan people sought to make the social life of its treatment settings resemble real life so as to make the skills learned in treatment something the patients could continue to use when they left.[31]

A program with a similar emphasis helps families cope with their relatives who have been discharged from state facilities by considering the families to be the "primary caregivers." This program, which is sponsored by a community mental health center in Tucson, Arizona, known as La Frontera Center, Inc., offers encouragement and "support" (a ubiquitous concept now) to its clients as well as a structured educational program about the patients/relatives and their special needs.[32]

Self-Help

Quite recently, ex–mental patients have banded together into loose associations all their own. These groups hover somewhere in between political lobby and social club, striving both to expand their members' collective say in how they will be treated by the larger society in general and the helping professions in particular, and to provide acceptable places for ex-patients to "hang out" in, places where they will feel accepted and "be left alone, free to live their own lives."[33] In a number of cities, self-help groups have formed drop-in centers where former and current mental patients can go to make friends, feel accepted, and learn their rights to refuse treatment they feel is being unfairly forced upon them. Examples include the Ruby Rogers Center in Boston; the Alliance Center in Syracuse, New York; and the Oakland Independence Support Center in Oakland, California. Although the self-help movement is new, it is an interesting development and may well prove effective in promoting the notion that the mentally ill are not stupid people who should have no say in what happens to them.

* * *

Among the common threads that run through all successful programs is the focus they share on the transmission of social skills to promote patients' adaptation to the larger world—the one dire need of chronic mental patients that cannot be addressed chemically and cannot be met realistically in a hospital, self-contained and isolated from the larger world as it is. Although I do not believe most mental patients ever learn anything on an inpatient unit except how to live on that unit, I must acknowledge the possibility that in genuinely good hospitals, this is not the case. According to J. K. Wing, who is one of the most distinguished scholars of the treatment of schizophrenia, the principles of moral treatment can be and sometimes are applied in the hospital as well as out, and "social treatments" represent part of the "best aspects of the mental hospital tradition."[34]

Even so, the work of transmitting social skills has not changed much since the authors of moral treatment designed their "receptacles" 150 years ago, and whether we do the work or not, whether we call it "rehabilitation" or "social skills training" or "ADL" (for "activities of daily living"), it is the care the patients need the most. It is hard work to do well, if only because it is boring to communicate the same simple, low-level social skills over and over again to slow and resistant learners; and it is definitely far less glamorous than sitting in a professional office, rooting around in a patient's past to come up with useful and penetrating insights that will elucidate his present psychodynamics. The bottom line should be that this is the help the patients require, if they are ever to lead the kind of "normal" lives we say we want for them. Different programs reflect various ways of accomplishing the same thing, but they all pursue one aim: teaching the deranged how to act in the real world.

Why Programs Fail

One reason a lot of programs fail is that we have a long-standing tendency to idealize the pilot program. For one thing, it is far easier to get funding for a unique-sounding, experimental approach to the same old problems than it is to get funding to refine and improve some boring old day hospital, for example; and in a way it is safer to do the experimental pilot programs, because if you fail, you have the ready excuse that it was only an experiment anyway. The limitations of overreliance on pilot programs speak for themselves—no continuity, no coordination, constant reinvention of the wheel, not to mention unrealistic promises of cure, all come readily to mind—as do the several pitfalls implicit in too-rapid copying of pilot programs by others for use in areas for which they were not designed, following the cookie-cutter approach to social problems. To overinvest our limited resources in model programs is to discover over and over again that pilot programs by definition are meant to be short-term and limited in scope, so that they cannot help but fail to address the needs of the bulk of any given population; but this lesson we have so far avoided learning. To allow model programs to slip out of perspective and achieve the stature of established approaches to problems, instead of acknowledging them to be the experiments they really are, will only prolong the problems we already have even as new ones are, inevitably, created.[35]

Intensive Case Management

A good example of the overproduction of what is essentially a model program is the current vogue for case management, an idea that sounds great, that probably worked fairly well in its pilot form, and that is currently being hailed as *the* solution to the myriad problems "caused" by deinstitutionalization. In what seems to have been its earliest incarnation, the case manager was a worker indigenous to the community to which mental patients were discharged after lengthy stays in Philadelphia State Hospital. These workers had been specially trained as "social change agents," and were called "enablers;" their chief function was to keep track of their caseload for a full year after discharge, either by seeing them daily for two-hour visits, five days a week, or by having them live in their own house. For a year, the "enablers" helped the patients, who had been in the hospital an average of 13.2 years, master the skills they needed to get around and do whatever daily tasks they had to accomplish. It is important to note that in the pilot program, the enablers had begun their work while their patients were still in the hospital, during a twelve-week orientation period on a special hospital unit set up expressly for the careful, planned discharge of the long-stay patients. The entire program, as studied and reported, was tiny—a total of 263 patients were followed—and the results were mixed: using the standard measure of success, rehospitalization, fully 22 percent of the patients who got the two-hour visits were rehospitalized, although the rate for those who lived in the enablers' homes was only 4 percent.[36]

In a more recent incarnation, the "intensive case managers," or ICMs, as they are now called, have as their "targeted group" the *"severely* and *persistently mentally ill"* (inevitably, the SPMI), who are politely described as "our system's biggest challenge":

They are the most difficult to treat clients with indicators in their histories such as repeated hospitalizations, resistance to treatment, problems with medication compliance, frequent crises, absence of a social or constructive family network,

203

the display of severe psychiatric symptomatology when confronted with only mild to moderate degrees of stress, need for daily structure and/or difficulty in self monitoring.[37]

Case managers are now charged with the frankly impossible job of making the same system that has already failed the chronic patients work on their cases' behalf; and unlike their Philadelphia counterparts, today's case managers will not enjoy the advantage of preliminary work with their charges on a special hospital ward, nor the decided advantage of working with them just after discharge. To the contrary, the new case managers get to salvage their patients years after abandonment by mental health organizations and entitlement programs. They also get to be the *"single point of responsibility* helping the client to navigate through these diverse and often fragmented systems," establishing "linkages," utilizing an *"in vivo* approach"—home visits and "practical assistance"—always with the classic goal firmly in mind: *"to provide whatever services are necessary to meet their needs and to minimize the number of rehospitalizations."*[38]

Had this assistance been made available to the newly discharged mental patients ten, fifteen, or twenty years ago, it might have had a chance to succeed, but now, it is probably too late. After all, chronic patients have been shoved around by agencies that make no secret of the fact that they would rather work with other, more gratifying populations—and even the severely and persistently mentally ill aren't so crazed that they don't realize when they're not wanted. Now, sad to say, ex-patients are so angry and disgusted with a world that has treated them badly that it is next to impossible to form much of an alliance with them anymore, even though they need it so much.

If the System Won't Change, It Must Be the Patients' Fault

The main reason that intensive case management is likely to fail at this late date is that no simultaneous effort at change is being directed at the mental health system, the one that has so plainly failed to look after its own creation, the chronically dependent person who cannot function outside an institution, people the system has written off as CMI or, even worse, SPMI. Most likely, the ICM program will represent yet another funding stream to be mined and exploited by the usual agencies and hospitals. These facilities will sponsor programs with staff who will busily make linkages all over their community, "serving as the 'glue' connecting a complex and diverse psychiatric service system,"[39] even as the rest of the agency continues to refuse to treat schizophrenics on the grounds that they are too resistant, and even as the names of all the irritating chronics who regularly seek admission continue to be listed in the hospital's emergency room, so that admitting doctors can quickly turn them away.[40]

Problems can be addressed and recommendations can be made, but in the land of social programming, *plus ça change, plus c'est la même chose.* Consider the ultimate, if regrettable, fate of every pilot program, however excellent or promising of future usefulness:

> People get tired; they seek to regularize their work patterns; they desire to control the uncertainties and unpredictabilities in their environment. Thus they tend to push toward the bureaucratization of roles and the clear-cut definition of responsibilities and turfs; and they become smug about their own failures, less sensitive to the problems of their clients, and less committed to the jobs that have to be done.[41]

It is theoretically possible to design a new mental health system to take the place of the old one and make it live up to its promises and responsibilities, but it is unlikely such an entrenched bureaucracy as the one we have now will willingly change itself, any more than mental health professionals will suddenly decide on their own to make home visits to chronic mental patients. New York State recently tried, and failed, to do this. In September 1983, shortly after he took office, Governor Mario Cuomo established a commission to look into the problems of the mental health system, which was breaking down in an expensive way. Currently, it appears that nearly all of the commission's proposals have been ignored—especially the one that suggested that the state Office of Mental Health should stop pretending it could play an oversight role with regard to the network of psychiatric facilities it runs itself.[42] As the old saw goes, everyone is eager for change—for somebody else. People don't change readily, whether they're mentally ill or not—it's too hard.

We know perfectly well how to address the needs of the chronic mentally ill, and we have even had a blueprint for doing so since 1961, thanks to the report of the Joint Commission on Mental Illness and Health. As one critic of the system points out,

> There is no mystery about the nature of a more appropriate solution [to the problem of the chronic mentally ill homeless]. Essentially it would call for carrying out the aborted plans of the 1963 community mental health law by providing a spectrum of housing options and related health-care and social services for the mentally ill.[43]

There should be no mystery about why this doesn't happen, either, but we keep forgetting and looking only at the patients/clients for the solutions. Here is a great illustration of why things don't work the way we think they do or will or should: I heard the other day about a new program to get incarcerated drug addicts into drug-free therapeutic communities while they were still in jail. There was some dispute about whether the program would try to place its patients into (nonexistent) drug programs upon their discharge from jail. No! said the program's sponsoring bureaucrat. If we said we would do that, we'd fail and lose our funding! His solution: redefine the program's mission and goal to ignore the question of what happens to the addicts after they leave the jail and the program—never mind that once they leave, they'll probably go right back on drugs, because no simultaneous effort has been made to address the notorious gaps in the drug treatment program system. The important thing is that the jail-based program looks like a winner, and in the world of social policy, that's what counts.

PART III

1990
How the
Mental Health System
Works

It is better to understand how a mechanism operates than to endure its effects in ignorance.

—Robert Castel,
Françoise Castel, and Anne Lovell,
The Psychiatric Society (1982)

I'm sick of you mental health people, always making a buck off the back of my illness.

—Michelle H. (1984)

W HAT the mental health system is, basically, is big business. In 1981, the total spent by all fifty states on various mental health programs was $6,098,422,157, of which fully $168,760,149 was spent simply to run state offices of mental health.[1] That is a lot of money, and it has been assumed for some years that it is altogether too much money to trust to mental health professionals, who are widely viewed by the fiscally oriented as wild-eyed free-spenders who would cheerfully waste the entire gross national product on worthless programs for the mentally ill and so need constant oversight to curb and control their overzealous ambitions. Large portions of the public mental health system have long since been turned over to something called "the professional administrator," the chief qualification for which would appear to be computer skills.

Ironically, the people who run the system do not necessarily know how to do the work. Some of them may have, once upon a time, but the route to the higher echelons of our mental health regulatory and oversight system does not generally include extended exposure to the intricacies of practice, and it certainly does not require much more than a passing nod in that direction as the aspiring regulator zips along to the top. One exception to this rule, in some states, is the job of mental health commissioner, which often goes to a psychiatrist. The commissioner/doctor's presence at the top of the organization may be viewed as something of a sop to the professionals in the system: his or her presence reassures them that doctors really are in charge.

The bureaucracy is really in charge, no matter what the doctors think. The bureaucracy consists of all those monitoring and regulatory and oversight agencies, from the Joint Commission on the Accreditation of Health Care Organizations (JCAHO; see chapter 12) on down, through state departments of mental health and county or city offices of mental health, to local associations of mental health who sponsor citizens' committees to comment on the doings of mental health programs. An alcoholism specialist recently said to me that the regulatory bodies seemed to be proliferating. Not fifteen minutes after he said this, oddly enough, an auditor from a city agency, who was in our clinic to oversee the doings of another department, came up to me to say she was planning her next visit; she intended, she said, to bring along "a day care specialist," and they particularly wanted to talk to me. The auditor's interest in my views on day care puzzled me, for my job, indeed our whole program, had nothing to do with day care. But a rule of thumb one learns to follow early on is, Never Say No to an Auditor; so, of course, I said I would be delighted.

The trouble with the mental health bureaucracy, as seen from the field, is that it doesn't listen to practitioners, much less patients/consumers, so its spokesmen don't know what they're talking about. For just as mental health bureaucrats are openly contemptuous of the woolly-headed profligacy of mental health professionals, so too mental health professionals have no use for the outpourings of the bureaucracy, whether forms for the collection of trivial data or position papers that appear to have been written on Mars, for all the relevance they show to our actual work with real patients (a psychiatrist I know swears our local mental health department gets all its programs designed "by people who are on the last back ward" of a nearby state hospital). They think we're stupid, we think they're crazy; and never the twain shall meet.

The dangers inherent in this split, which so far as I can tell is entirely acceptable to both regulators and practitioners, should be obvious. If the people who design, implement, and oversee policy don't have a good source of information in the field, then they are truly working in a vacuum. If the people who do the actual work don't enjoy the confidence of the policymakers, then they will have no impact on the way the work is to be done across the board. Both groups need each other, both groups could clearly use each other's skills to advantage, and both groups play equally essential roles in the delivery of services to the mentally ill. Much as we hate to admit it, direct practitioners *need* the bureaucrats to get and distribute money to pay for programs, and then to keep that money coming, which means accounting for how it is spent; by the same token, the bureaucrats *need* practitioners to do the work they've dreamt up, funded, and programmed.

Now let us take a look at the bureaucracy: who is in it and what it does—as it appears to those of us who do the work of purveying mental health to the needy.

A Day in the Life of a Mental Health Bureaucrat (A True Story)

Help Wanted: Planning Analyst

Responsible for planning and budget, fiscal, service utilization and policy-oriented projects in mental hygiene system. Assists in the performance of certificate-of-needs (CON) application related administrative responsibilities, citywide project management functions. *Must have strong quantitative, analytical, verbal and written communicative skills, 5 years clerical-administrative experience, 1 year administrative/supervisory plus H.S. diploma.* Relevant planning, fiscal analysis and mental hygiene system experience preferred. MBA, MPA, MSW or other appropriate master's degree preferred.[2]

Once upon a time there was a twenty-four-year-old college graduate named George Spelvin. George had a B.A. in sociology, vague plans to go to business school someday, and a genuine interest in computer games. George got the job as planning analyst described in the ad, in part because of his computer skills and in large part because his father was a friend of the deputy commissioner. The job required him to oversee several programs intended to treat seriously mentally ill adults discharged from state mental hospitals. Paid for by the state, these program initiatives, as George soon learned to call them, were expressly designed to keep their patients out of state hospitals, by hook or by crook. George's job was to keep track of how well or how poorly they succeeded in this task. Mostly he did this by going to meetings with other people in his office.

One of the ways the patients were kept out of state hospitals was by being placed in board-and-care homes run for profit by independent owners who collected the patients' SSI checks. Although George's department had no oversight responsibility for the homes, it necessarily had to "interface" with those who did, namely, the state social services department senior staff. Because he was the newest consultant in the office, George had inherited the unpopular task of serving as his department's liaison with that part of social services—called "the SS" around the mental health department—in charge of regulating the homes. George's liaison work mostly took the form of attending a two-hour "task force" meeting every other week at SS headquarters.

One week, the SS meeting went beyond its usual agenda of endlessly recycled complaints about the food and anecdotes about hard-to-manage patients. George had had to report that the people who went into the homes to treat the mental illness of the patients who lived there were very concerned about the poor quality of the homes' ventilation; the air was bad, and the mental health workers were worried that it might be unhealthy both for the patients and for themselves. The SS people seemed terribly concerned about the situation and promised to look into it. One of them assured George that a report would be ready by the next meeting.

Two weeks later, George went as usual to the task force meeting. Somewhat to his surprise, he found the SS people all in a dither over The Ventilation Issue. It seems the home owners had screamed bloody murder at the suggestion that they should beef up their ventilation systems, an added expense that they predicted would certainly force each and every one of them into bankruptcy, not to mention compel them to demand a Rate Increase from the governor. The SS people knew George would understand how a Rate Increase was not possible in this, an election year. Besides, they pointed out, the home owners had identified the source of the problem: all the mental patients smoked too much.

At the next meeting, the SS were pleased to report that they had met on their own and come up with a really exciting plan for coping with The Ventilation Issue, one they knew would be acceptable to the home owners. The SS were fully prepared to help George design a psychoeducational program by which the mental health providers could help the patients stop smoking. To start, they intended to prepare a syllabus for the mental health workers to follow, utilizing as resources not only their counterparts in the state health department, but also calling upon experts from the American Cancer Society and consultants from the state education department. "We're going to go all out on this, George. We intend to have a model program here, one other states are going to want to follow. This is a great opportunity, George, and we know your people are going to get a lot out of it."

George quickly got caught up in their enthusiasm. Soon, he was busily involved in a committee charged with the job of implementing the SS plan, complete with visions of "maybe even a big conference, George!" The committee worked terribly hard and came up with a really great program, full of informative lectures and visual aids and videos and workshops and activity programs to help the mental health workers get the patients to stop smoking.

Unfortunately, George and the other people in his department didn't know very much about life in the homes where the mental patients lived, and they knew even less about the patients themselves. The social service people knew a little about the homes, most of it from the point of view of the owners, but they knew nothing at all about what chronic mental patients are really like. As a result, they designed an antismoking program with less than no chance of success. For as anyone who has ever worked in a custodial setting for the chronically mentally ill knows (and could have told George and Co., had they bothered to ask), chronic mental patients have two pleasures in life: smoking and coffee, with TV a distant third. They are about as ready to be "helped" to stop smoking as the APA is to renounce the *DSM-III-R*. [3]

Hired for their analytical, quantitative, and communication skills rather than because they had extensive clinical experience, George and his fellows have no way of knowing any of this, because their jobs do not require them to know anything about mental illness or to spend any time in the programs they monitor. If they had, they might have noticed that in the internal economy of the homes, the cigarette was the basic unit of exchange. That knowledge alone might have prevented the waste of weeks of public time on the design of a worthless plan—but then again, maybe it wouldn't have. For as we are about to see, there's not a whole lot about the workings of the mental health bureaucracy that makes a whole lot of sense.

CHAPTER 11

———◆———

The Mental Health Bureaucracy: Who's in Charge Here?

> Just as we are beginning to have a sense of the conse-
> quences of deinstitutionalization and a framework for de-
> veloping technologies for dealing with them, we are en-
> couraging severe—sometimes seemingly insuperable—
> barriers to the provision of care.
> —LEONA L. BACHRACH, "Asylum and Chronically Ill
> Psychiatric Patients" (1984)

I N 1972 the federal government got into the business of health care regulation, as had twenty states before it, beginning with New York in 1964. At both state and national levels, government's concern was the same: money. Medicaid, resisted strenuously at first by organized medicine, soon revealed itself to be a potential gold mine, and practitioners and institutions alike were quick to tap into the mother lode. Throughout the 1970s, government regulation of health care activity was confined chiefly to its mandate to approve large capital investments, such as construction projects, on the basis of need within the communities they were to serve; the process of review was called "certification of need."

Policy via Regulation: How It Got That Way

To avoid other forms of control of their costs and expenditures, hospitals themselves had proposed capital regulation as the best means for states to regulate health care costs, thinking, apparently, that limited construction could only cut down future competition for the health care dollar, and was therefore in hospitals' best interest. The precise target of cost controls turned out to be bed capacity: on the theory that hospitals would tend to fill all the beds they had, government regulators decided the best way to hold down costs was to limit the number of beds available to be filled.[1] The mechanism that performs this task is called the Health Systems Agency (HSA), a local authority required of each community under the terms of the National Health Planning and Resources Development Act of 1974. A local HSA is empowered to determine the number of hospital beds, the suitability of construction and/or improvement of existing facilities costing $100,000 or more, and the advisability of purchasing new equipment and/or services.[2]

The model for all health care regulation was implicit in the certificate-of-need program: costs could be contained by outside forces who looked at community need for service, though not at the work of treatment itself. For most practitioners in the mental health field, this was ideal regulation—leave us alone to do what we do, and you can plan and count beds all you want. To the practitioner, regulation is policy, and policy is boring, not to say irrelevant; these are irksome tasks best left to somebody else while we do what we know, which is treatment. Regulatory organizations thus were left to grow and develop entirely apart from the field they were to oversee and plan, a divergence that appears to have troubled no one.

How the System Works

Examination of the management of hospital costs by the regulation of bed supply shows that simply ignoring regulators, as mental health professionals generally prefer to do, does not make them go away. In fact, in the long run, ignoring them has aggravated problems that could have been avoided. It is very simple, really: cost-cutters in the 1970s eliminated beds in municipal psychiatric wards that in the following decade were desperately needed. Someone somewhere should have predicted this need, based on what mental health clinicians were seeing in the seventies: the first wave of never-institutionalized, as distinct from deinstitutionalized, mentally ill people.

Young Adult Chronic Patients

The 1970s saw the emergence of the first generation in a century never to have known long-term state hospitalization—the so-called young adult chronic patients. Born around the time when the state hospital census nationwide was at its peak, young adult chronic mental patients emerged as a distinct patient group in the late 1970s, presenting problems and issues for mental health treatment hitherto unknown. Never before, in living memory, had our society been asked to cope with schizophrenia, major affective disorders, and severe personality disorders—not to mention the various drug-induced or -related psychopathologies so common to this group—without the possibility of long-term hospitalization.[3]

In every way significant to a clinician, the young adult chronic patients were identical to those patients who previously had had access to long-term hospitals. They were (and are)

a generation of young adults in the age group eighteen to thirty-five who are now living in our communities, but who show persistent and severe impairment in their psychological and social functioning. They are young persons who, as they grow older, require services from mental health and other social agencies in a variety of ways and over a period of years . . . an emerging, uninstitutionalized generation; many of them are persons who in the past would have become long-stay patients in mental institutions, or at the least would have had one or several hospitalizations of one or more years' duration. . . . These young adults, then, are our first generation of chronic patients to grow up in community care and in the wake of the great wave of deinstitutionalization and its corollaries: admissions diversion, tightened involuntary admission criteria, and the limitation of hospital stays to the briefest possible time.[4]

We know all this now, and the authors of the preceding passage knew it in 1980, when they convened their first conference on the subject; but—and this is important—the *system* had no way of knowing it in time to provide services for a whole generation of patients. To the contrary, at roughly the moment clinicians were discovering young adult chronics to be the tremendous challenge to the field that they still are, the system was quietly cutting costs by eliminating hospital beds.

Here is another way to look at it. The system's planners and regulators insist on verifiable data; they like to have numbers and facts to work with, and they are not interested in projections, guesswork, or the kind of anecdotal material that clinicians tend to deal in. Even though we can appreciate their concerns—why spend money we don't have to, to develop services for a group that doesn't need them, for instance—their insistence on the demonstrated and the proven means that they "plan" things after the fact. When young adult chronic patients surfaced, it was inevitable that clinicians would spot them first and planners not until much later, if ever: the new population was not conveniently centralized anywhere long enough to be counted. Sometimes these patients came in for short hospitalizations and were counted by mental health bureaucrats, along with other mentally ill persons; sometimes they were arrested or jailed on drug charges and so were counted only by criminal justice bureaucrats, along with other offenders; but many times they were dropouts and street people (since renamed "the mentally ill homeless"), where for the longest time, they were not counted at all.[5] Even though clinicians *knew* there was a new breed of mental patient who kept returning to mental hospitals or psychiatric wards of general hospitals, generally staying a short time and often leaving abruptly with no intention of accepting follow-up care, this knowledge was not in verifiable statistical form and was therefore unavailable to planners until it was too late for them to do much about it.

The seeds of every current social problem we now blame on deinstitutionalization were evident in the presenting problems of the young adult chronic population, and these problems—homelessness, criminal activity, and serious drug abuse by mental patients—were documented in the literature of practice some ten years before the planning agencies caught on. Young adult chronic patients were known to include homeless street people as early as 1977;[6] their frequent brushes with the law had been noticed at least by 1980;[7] the profoundly significant interrelationship of their psychopathology with illicit drug use was well documented at least as early as 1979;[8] and the mental health system as then constituted was inadequate to care for these patients. Its general unwillingness to change in order to meet newly discovered needs can be inferred from the fact that it is still inadequate to care for those needs.[9]

Planning by Reacting

Once the needs of young adult chronic patients became impossible for planners to ignore, if only because practitioners were complaining too loudly, the system made its usual move: it created what it invariably calls "new program initiatives" to address needs it has just discovered, rather than adapt existing programs and services. It does this because the planning part of the mental health system is politically motivated and sensitive to exposure, rather than genuinely interested in addressing anyone's needs other than its own. The mental health system will create a program only if the need is so great it cannot be overlooked, which means it has attracted the attention of the media. In this way, the system has discovered mental patients who take drugs, dealing with the problem by funding special hospital wards called "dual diagnosis (for mental illness and substance abuse) programs." This is a worthy enterprise, to be sure, but one of dubious long-term value because so far it is exclusively hospital-based and includes no provision for aftercare—and we all know by now that the U.S. drug treatment network is far from adequate to meet the needs of addicts who are *not* mentally ill, let alone those who are. Similarly, the system has discovered the homeless mentally ill and funded special psychiatric services for them in shelters, just as it has discovered mental patients in jail and funded special institution-based services for them. In both instances, that is the extent of existing service provision; and since neither patient group is welcome in traditional aftercare settings, they will not be able to get any aftercare, either.

There are two great hazards implicit in taking such a piecemeal, after-the-fact approach to social problems: (1) the finished product is likely to be uncoordinated and fragmented; and (2) programs are going to be designed to fit funding requirements rather than to do the work. The latter problem is so endemic that one can see it in help-wanted advertisements for mental health administrators (not to be confused with program directors, who are usually clinicians); prime among the requirements for these jobs is familiarity with regulatory concerns. Here are excerpts from two typical advertisements, taken from the 28 March 1989 *New York Times:* "Candidate should be familiar with JCAHO, OSHA, and Department of Health requirements . . . " and "Responsibilities include protocol development, U.R., network development, credentialling, and Q.A."[10] It's the wise program that is run with its regulators in mind—especially when there is funding to be had.

Follow the Funding, Wherever It Goes

Mental health funding is a product of politics, expediency, and fads. It's a good idea to know what's "hot" at the moment, for that's where money for programs will be in the next fiscal year. For several years, extra money could be found for homeless mentally ill people, and before that, alcoholism was popular, as were programs for geriatric mental patients, briefly. In late 1989, mental health services for AIDS patients look like a good bet, and so do mental health programs for criminal offenders, if only because so much public money is being poured into corrections at the moment. Canny mental health administrators will want to keep their eyes on child abuse and substance abuse (especially crack), as well, in case the relevant agencies that normally deal with those problems are unequal to the task of addressing the mental health aspects thereof. In this fashion, the mental health industry keeps up to date, responding not so much to client need as to available funding.

Tailoring mental health programming to existing funds as they become

219

available to suit various political agendas has its strengths, clearly, in ensuring that some unmet or undetected needs get attention they might otherwise miss. Unfortunately, the process by which this is accomplished involves no planning, nor is it in all cases even necessary, since sometimes the problem thus addressed has vanished. In late 1985, a woman named Eleanor Bumpurs was shot and killed by New York City policemen fulfilling an order to evict her from her housing project apartment for nonpayment of rent. She allegedly lunged at them, and since she was very large and had a history of emotional disorder, the police felt justified in gunning her down. Embarrassed by this episode, the city raced to assure its citizens that steps were being taken to prevent any such future occurrence. Among those steps was the creation of a special unit within the city mental health department, whose task it would be to field all calls coming into the department to report dangerous behavior on the part of ex–mental patients; somehow this unit would detect which among the calls was significant and would alert other parts of the system to take care of it. (I know about this unit because in spring 1986, I was interviewed for the job of directing it.) The apparent purpose: to prevent future Eleanor Bumpurs cases. The real purpose: to enable the city to say, if challenged, that it was doing something to prevent future Eleanor Bumpurs cases. What we will never know is whether Eleanor Bumpurs's life could indeed have been saved by the existence of this unit, or whether her untimely death was part of an emerging trend, one that required the establishment of a whole departmental unit. In the way of bureaucracies everywhere, such a unit, once created, would naturally become a permanent fixture, needed or not.

Instant Program Designs

Some politically motivated programming arises in the eleventh hour of the appropriated funds: a governmental body has two months, say, before its fiscal year ends, and it has substantial funds allocated to address a politically hot problem but needs a way to spend them in a showy fashion, fast. This used to happen all the time in palmier days for mental health, such as the 1960s, when infusions of state and federal funds poured into localities in an effort to promote community-based services; a great many programs owe their current existence to such sudden funding. Of course, not every agency can literally come up with a program design overnight; large, established organizations with substantial support staff will clearly have the advantage. "I can remember getting calls from the city [department of mental health] saying, 'We have $200,000; can you come up with a program by tomorrow afternoon at three o'clock?' " recalls one head of such an agency. He believes good programs were inaugurated this way but agrees that the process did not reflect the best coordination or review: "It's a little hasty."[11] Anyone who doubts that this is one method by which government spends much of its money would do well not only to consider how the Department of Defense under the Reagan administration spent its money but also to watch spending by all levels of government on corrections over the next few years.

Flights of Fancy and Emotional Appeal

Finally, the system generates funding by the least scientific of methods: whim, prejudice, and fad. I have heard a wonderful story that perfectly illustrates this point, a story about how New York City's highly publicized program initiative geared to rescuing the mentally ill homeless, Project HELP (for Homeless Emergency Liaison Project), came to be. A few years ago, the story goes, a highly placed city bureaucrat took a walk with his eleven-year-old son, who wanted to know why there were crazy homeless people huddled on the street: "Why can't you help them?" the son asked his father. Stuck for an answer, the bureaucrat started Project HELP the next day. This turned out to be a move he later had cause to regret, incidentally, because the program is enormously expensive yet by no means successful in its stated mission, which is to get mentally ill homeless people off the streets into hospitals and shelters, since it turns out they do not always want to go.

Project staff drive around New York City in a van with a psychiatrist and a nurse or a social worker on board. The psychiatrist has the authority to order immediate hospitalization of dangerous people, but otherwise, the program is a lot like its less dramatic counterparts in other cities, which seek to befriend and advocate for the homeless. It costs a lot more because of its staffing (psychiatrists willing to ride around in vans visiting homeless people do not come cheap). Project HELP, however, is extremely showy and dramatic, as social programs go, a highly visible response to a highly visible social problem; so even though it is extraordinarily cost-inefficient, its future seems secure. As the story goes, its inventor now refers to it as "The Great White Whale."[12]

The Project HELP story also illustrates a little-appreciated fact about public policy in general: it is to a great extent fueled by unspoken, unrecognized social values and personal emotion. Much of our problem with welfare, which we provide in a grudging, even punitive, way, stems from our unacknowledged, but profound, devotion to the Protestant ethic: we believe that those who work deserve to be rewarded; whereas those who do not, do not. We have relatively little problem spending money to help those whose difficulties stem from circumstances they could not possibly control, like a natural disaster or a congenital birth defect; but we hate to give money to undeserving beggars, all of whom, we tell ourselves, are crooks or drunks or addicts, entirely, we assume, by their own choice. Our social policy reflects this attitude to a degree rarely recognized, because to a great extent the social welfare system is set up to act on the values it reflects, without ever looking at those values or the assumptions they generate: "We get fed back to us the solution to the issues that our values demand. . . . That does not contribute to rational or social scientific policy development, which is to say that policy develops at random."[13]

Our Notoriously Fragmented Mental Health System

The fact that the contemporary mental health system is uncoordinated, unplanned, chaotic, and fragmented is one of those things that everyone seems to know yet no one seems able to change. I have before me, for example, five written reports of large-scale surveys of the system, examined from different angles. One involved a nationwide study, done in 1988, of the mental health service system in place in each of the fifty states; private consumer advocate groups sponsored it.[14] Two were studies undertaken simultaneously in 1983 to 1984 in New York State, sponsored by the state.[15] The fourth was a study specifically of New York state mental hospital discharge practices and was performed in 1988 by a state-sponsored watchdog organization;[16] and the fifth was the product of a 1978 interagency task force charged with examining the particular problems of the chronically mentally ill in New York City, problems that had been attributed to deinstitutionalization.[17]

Even though ten years—a long time in government—had elapsed between the time the first one was written and the time the last one was completed, the results remained the same: as of 1978, "services are fragmented; responsibility is diffused"; and, as of 1988, "it is known that seriously mentally ill individuals living in the community need coordinated fiscal support, housing, education and rehabilitation yet these functions are often under separate state agencies which may have virtually no relationship to each other or to the state department of mental health."[18]

The Lure of Quick Fixes

In essence, fragmentation stems from the absence of any single organization to oversee the various efforts of governmental, voluntary, and private practitioners with an eye to their coherent unification and mutual interdependence in the name of better patient care. No one, in short, is in charge. Government at every level is trapped in the sorry conflict engendered by both administering and providing services; unfortunately, governments' ability to oversee service providers is often compromised by a built-in conflict of interest, since they, too, are providers. Ironically, one result of this dilemma has been the tendency of government agencies to seek short-term solutions to politically sensitive problems involving themselves as providers, rather than to fulfill their responsibility as planners and coordinators. A stunning example of this can be found in New York City's "Tripwire Agreement." Forged in 1981, the agreement stipulates that when psychiatric beds in city hospitals are full to an agreed-on capacity, the state must take some of the overflow patients upon notification.

The agreement does nothing, of course, to address underlying and much more serious problems, such as the inadequacy of services for the most vulnerable patients, or the strife that characterizes city–state hospital relations; if anything, mechanisms like the Tripwire Agreement obscure problems by falsely reassuring bureaucrats that they are accomplishing something, thus enabling them to tell us the same thing. If mental health departments were really controlling the mental health system, they would have no need for phony arrangements like the Tripwire Agreement; the problem would not arise. What we do have, illustrated neatly by the Tripwire, is a service network "operated primarily by the exigencies facing providers, rather than exclusively by the needs of the persons served."[19] (Recently, by the way, I attended a meeting along with the very bureaucrats who currently implement the Tripwire Agreement for New York City's hospitals. According to them, the agreement does not work because the state office staff never answer their phones, especially on Monday morning when the city hospital system is at its fullest.) What is discouraging is that so many people and organizations realize how deranged the system is, yet seem unable to exert the pressure needed to force change. When the results of the first nationwide survey ranking the fifty state mental health systems came out in 1986, an employee of Denver's Department of Social Services said openly, "If [Colorado is] the third best in the country, this country has a huge problem on its hands."[20]

The resulting difficulties are only too well known. There is wasteful duplication of some services—outpatient psychotherapy for the so-called worried well, for one—and very few services for some unpopular groups—the chronically mentally ill, for example. Competition for profitable services involving desirable populations is growing and is destructive in several ways: both fiscal and professional resources are siphoned off from the system as a whole, so the best practitioners wind up treating the least needy patients for the most money at the greatest expense to everyone.[21] Probably worse has been the fact that for all our talk about deinstitutionalization—which, as noted earlier, stems from such things as increasing clinical knowledge about how to care for seriously mentally ill persons outside institutions—all third-party reimbursement systems, whether public or private, have consistently favored institutional care. As one regular critic of the industry summed up, "While a quasi–free market has existed, the failure of mental health and government experts to manipulate it in noninstitutional directions has contributed to the perpetuation of what is widely known as our mental health 'nonsystem.' "[22]

Fragmentation for the Consumer

What all the task forces and the commissions and the study groups keep discovering is this: our mental health system grew out of a simple model of centralized, unified, comprehensive care—the state mental hospital—and it has yet to be reorganized, even though the old model clearly is obsolete. In the asylum's heyday, prior to 1955, publicly supported mental patients had all their needs met in one place, under one auspice. They were fed, clothed, housed, and given whatever form of clinical treatment was around at the time, all under one roof. If they got better and were discharged, they went home to their families and returned to a state hospital–sponsored aftercare clinic, where available; and if they became crazy again, back they went to the same state hospital. The system was simple, clear, and direct.

When the states maneuvered out from under the huge and growing burden of care for the mentally ill, however, they did so piecemeal, which probably was the only way to do it. For one thing, the most hopeful motivation behind deinstitutionalization was the idea that a deviant group might fare as well in normal surroundings as they had in the abnormal world of the total institution, if not better. Normal adult life is rarely as simple and clearcut as institutional life: normal adults do not have all their needs met for them by somebody else, under one roof and thanks to one funding source. For another thing, this move of large numbers of deviants from institutional care to the real world had never been tried by Americans before, and we had no way of knowing what would happen. Now we know, but we have yet to face the fact that we keep trying to find the old, simple model of the state hospital, somewhere in the community.

What we have in the community is a jumble of uncoordinated programs that may or may not add up to a total that includes all the services we require. There may or may not be suitable housing programs for people who cannot manage on their own. If there are, they may or may not be integrated with the treatment programs that may or may not serve chronic patients. These programs may be willing to accept the dually diagnosed (mental patients who also abuse substances or are mentally retarded), or they may not. Housing programs will be funded separately from treatment programs, and different monitoring agencies will oversee them. By the same token, patients' SSI will pay for their housing costs, but Medicaid will pay for their treatment; and although SSI staff will monitor only the recipients' ongoing eligibility, Medicaid staff will make sure that its money went to pay for the services as billed.

The system of bureaucracies that we have created to address public need and the commonweal *is* fragmented, diverse, diffuse, and hard to understand. But it is that way for all of us, not just for the mentally ill—mental patients simply point up its deficiencies particularly clearly, because they do not cope as well as the rest of us do. The service delivery system is full of holes one could drive a truck through: entire needy groups can and do get neglected because no one wants the responsibility for hard-to-treat, hard-to-place, hard-to-care-for people; not surprisingly, no caregiver wants to be seen failing. The most difficult groups always get the worst care, because it is so hard to provide. Think how hard it would be to design cost-effective programs to deal with the following needy groups: abandoned babies with AIDS (so-called boarder babies); adults who abuse their children; teenaged abandoned children; people whose mental illness has led them to commit violent crimes; and any group with two or three chronic disabilities, all at the same time. The chronically mentally ill, in other words, are not alone in being underserved.[23]

How the System Fails Everyone

I once got someone on Medicaid over the phone. I thought at the time that I had achieved a minor miracle, and I was terribly proud of having figured out at last how to "negotiate the system on behalf of the client," as the textbooks so cheerfully put it, as if doing so were the easiest thing in the world. Not until I was telling someone else of my triumph did I realize the truth: it was December 23rd, and I had called the Medicaid office in the middle of an exceptionally festive Christmas party; that, not superior skill, was the only reason I had gotten my patient's problem fixed so easily. For those who are lucky enough not to know, trying to get a person's Medicaid (or welfare or SSI or any other benefit) approved or adjusted is, as a general rule, a horrible experience. Comparable experiences might include—and I am not trying to be funny—having a root canal, a mortgage closing, or a tax audit. All three experiences induce a profound anxiety and dread in most of us, which is why we tend to joke about them so much; in all three cases we are forced to endure helplessness. Endodontists, bankers, and tax auditors, in turn, seem to cope with the anxiety and pain their jobs make them bring to others by trying to be as impersonal and detached as possible, as if to say, It's not me doing this to you; this is just how the system works.

Our welfare systems work in much the same way. Applying for a so-called entitlement is a mean, even cruel, process. Applicants are forced to endure humiliation and shame as they repeatedly reveal how little they have, which in our society means to reveal just how badly they have failed. No, they don't have a job. Yes, they have tried to find one. No, they don't have family to support them. Yes, they have used up all their savings. In most areas, the forms to be filled out are lengthy, repetitive, and couched in that terrible false language bureaucrats seem to love—it's the same stilted jargon used to write the instructions for filling out Form 1040 for income taxes. The interviewers are mean and unpleasant from the outset, and the atmosphere impersonal and indifferent, to the point of making it all too clear how much disdain and contempt the welfare system has for the applicant. It is this last trait that particularly characterizes entitlement systems, the one quality they do not necessarily share with other large, impersonal bureaucracies. I do not enjoy visiting the Department of Motor Vehicles, for instance, and my local office is an exceptionally ugly place in which to waste a few hours standing in line; but even there, the clerks are often cheerful and will occasionally joke with their hapless customers. Not so SSI or welfare—never. The client is treated with about as much respect as an army recruit or a first-time jail inmate.[24]

Back in the days when I had to get involved with patients' entitlements, mental health professionals held a fond belief that a patient's therapist could and would be able to help him get on welfare or get his Medicaid card or get him through his SSI hearing. The idea was that since we were not actually applying, the clerks would treat us better than they did the clients, and besides, all our education and verbal skills would enable us to zip to the head of the line and get through quickly. Some workers even studied relevant enabling legislation or administrative regulations on the principle that if one knew the law better than its enforcers, he could somehow get a better deal for his client (I never heard of anyone actually accomplishing this, but it sounded good). For the most part, it wasn't true—we were no more successful than our patients at negotiating the system, and in some ways our presence hindered the process, because the clerks resented us so much. Occasionally, an individual would hit it just right and get some help. For example, a secretary in a central Medicaid office once told me something genuinely useful: to approve a certain application, Medicaid's reviewers only looked at one line of a multipage form, and she even told me what they wanted it to say—but such help was given only to another worker, much in the spirit of "We're all in this together," and never to the client.

These are not systems that *anyone* can negotiate with ease. Mental health professionals who try, soon tell themselves they have "burned out" and find easier and more rewarding ways, such as private practice, to make a living. For deinstitutionalized mental patients, who do not have that option, trying to deal with a welfare bureaucracy is probably sheer torture, particularly if they are the least bit paranoid and given to suspecting other people of being out to get them (which would be entirely true at welfare, but the ex-patients would not necessarily know that). A few ex-patients, in my experience, have seemed to revel in the experience, perhaps because it gives them a legitimate opportunity to try to beat the system with no holds barred. One told me that her preferred practice was to wait until a sizable line had formed out on the street, ready to go in once the welfare office opened. At what my patient judged to be a few minutes before the doors were to open, she would fake a mild seizure, "coming out" of it to find herself the center of everybody's concern, whereupon she would reveal that her doctor had warned her this might happen if she were to stand out in the sun (or the rain or the snow or whatever the weather was that day); needless to say, she invariably went right to the head of the line and was first to be served. She probably was the exception and not the rule, but her achievement was nonetheless considerable, since it was more than most mental health professionals probably could muster in the same circumstance.[25]

Ex–mental patients not only have to come to terms with the bureaucracies of entitlement but also have to find ways to deal with whoever controls their housing arrangements, their clinics, their day programs, their pharmacists, and the people in their neighborhoods, who may look at them askance. In the face of real-world demands on people who are mentally ill, it seems irrelevant to worry about how fragmented the system is—*that* is a concern of a mental health practitioner looking for ways to make his job easier, not a paramount concern of handicapped individuals hoping to make their lives more bearable. Even if the system were as coordinated and unified as the Internal Revenue Service, it would still be a trial for its victims. Abandoning deinstitutionalized mental patients to struggle, alone and largely unaided, with the vagaries of the public social service system is something that *we,* the mental health professionals, did to them; it is not fair to blame that system for not being better coordinated on their behalf. This, by the way, is something the George Spelvins of the mental health world do not begin to understand.

The Onus Is on the Victim to Make the System Work

But that's real life, and reality is what we want our mentally ill to try to live in. It strikes me as entirely fair to expect a deinstitutionalized ex-patient to learn to cope with welfare, SSI, landlords, shopkeepers, and neighbors who stare at them: it's all part of learning to live in the real world and learning to act normal. What isn't fair, at all, is somehow convincing ourselves that giving someone a bed in an adult home or directions to welfare and/or a homeless shelter at the point of discharge constitutes adequate follow-up care—yet we still do this, every day; we *say* we don't, but it happens all the time. We have allowed ourselves to discharge patients to meager or worthless aftercare; we have given them minimal information and instructions about how to cope once they get there; we have actively or passively discouraged them from coming back for treatment once discharged; and we have gotten mad if they required rehospitalization, or became homeless, or committed crimes—any of which make it all too evident that the service delivery system we have created simply does not work as well as we have told ourselves it should.

Somehow it has become the patients' fault that the system has failed. Homelessness was easier to cope with if it resulted from mental illness, so we concentrated on a subgroup, the mentally ill homeless, and found that to be a convenient distraction from the certain evidence that the community-based mental health system had completely broken down in yet another area. Identifying the homeless mentally ill gave us something to quantify—which is more rewarding than acknowledging that our long-standing practice of discharging patients to welfare or shelters has contributed a great deal to creating such a subgroup. At the moment it is becoming fashionable to look at another subgroup, mentally ill criminals (sometimes called the dangerous mentally ill, or more benignly, the mentally ill in prison), which will doubtless prove equally distracting. Not only will we be able to attribute overcrowded jails to deinstitutionalization, but we will also be able to create all sorts of new program initiatives for the several subgroups likely to be identified by experts as they intensify their effort to quantify.[26] The mental health system will not work any better, but its experts will be so busy and productive that no one will notice.

Blaming chronic mental patients because they failed to make our mental health network function is blaming the victim—with a vengeance. It is as fair to blame patients for the weaknesses in the mental health system as it is to blame kindergarteners for the high dropout rate among high school students, and it makes as much sense. Yet that is precisely what we do—it is the patients' *chronicity* that makes them unable to use the psychoanalytic psychotherapy offered at one clinic, their *multiple diagnoses* that account for their poor performance in a day program, their *resistance* to treatment that makes them recidivists, or their *institutional transference* that explains their failure to get better in the community. We did everything we could, we tell ourselves, but they just didn't take advantage of what we had to offer.

When All Else Fails, Blame the System

Sometimes we blame the system for failing our patients, as if it were not our own creation. Take funding: after decades of exploiting each newly available funding stream in our zeal to create more and more new programs, it is now standard practice to express newfound dismay at the fact that mental health funding has become too complex and difficult to keep straight. Of course, that is perfectly true; but mental health professionals must accept a share of the responsibility for allowing it to happen. We could have demanded a "simplified" funding mechanism, one in which "decision-making [was] shifted back to what is best for patients,"[27] a long time ago; but we were too busy grabbing at federal funds to pay for model programs, or showing local mental health departments that we could implement a $200,000 demonstration project in under twenty-four hours, or figuring out how to fund a new clinic program using Medicaid. We wanted the money, so we didn't look too closely at the strings attached to it, and we certainly didn't stop to look at the total picture inevitably drawn by dependence on multiple funding sources to pay for services. Now, it turns out, it is not unusual to find that three separate reimbursements can be applied to one bill for service, a mind-boggling challenge to any program's billing procedures.[28]

Too late, mental health professionals have figured out that "the fiscal support of a state mental hospital, community mental health center or psychiatric outpatient clinic is so complex that a successful administrator must be equal parts certified public accountant, lawyer, and magician."[29] For the most part, mental health professionals prefer that somebody else worry about something as mundane as money. We do, however, want public funds to spend as we choose on programs of our own design, although we do not want anyone to tell us how to spend it, and we do not want to have to understand budgeting or finance enough to be able to account for its expenditure ourselves. Most mental health professionals do not see why they should have to understand Medicaid, for instance, even though it pays the bills for many publicly funded outpatient programs, and most professional schools do not bother to try to teach their students much about public policy in general, much less specifics of funding and budgeting, even though policy correlates pay the bills and control much of professional life. As one acknowledged expert on public policy put it at a recent conference of clinicians,

> It is remarkable the extent to which graduate programs don't teach the nuts and bolts of public policy—why programs work and don't work—neither the [political] right, to whom government programs are irrelevant and bad, or the left, to whom they are trivial. We are taught that policy doesn't matter.[30]

In my experience, most mental health professionals could not be less interested in public policy. Whether their disinterest is the result of faulty education or overinvestment in the minutiae of psychotherapeutic technique or their own anxiety in the face of the unknown, I don't know—probably it's a combination of all three. Every time I have tried to teach social policy or social theory to clinicians, I have encountered the same angry, stubborn resistance: "This is a waste of time. I came here to learn *clinical* material, not this policy stuff. It was a waste of time in my master's program, and it's a waste of time now," as one doctoral student put it.[31] What the student failed to realize, and what I clearly failed to teach, is that by dismissing "this policy stuff," mental health professionals are shooting themselves in the foot or cutting off their noses to spite their faces; for it is "this policy stuff"—and nothing else—that pays the bills, creates most of our jobs, and determines the conditions under which we're allowed to do them.

The High Cost of Divorcing Policy from Practice

The mental health system is run by "policymakers" like George Spelvin and by ex-practitioners-turned-bureaucrats who have long since switched allegiance from the individual case, the natural unit of study of the practitioner, to the big picture, the overview, the totality of the system. The difference in how practitioners and policymakers look at mental illness is profound, although it always sounds simple and routine: the one looks at the single case and extrapolates from that, whereas the other looks at "the numbers," as they like to call them, hoping to discern trends that can be addressed programmatically.

The gulf between those who look at individual cases for knowledge and insight and those who search for trends involving many cases is indeed great. Therapists, whose focus is on individuals, have no choice but to be reminded daily how different and unpredictable people are, even within the same diagnostic category; moreover, prolonged exposure to their individual differences makes therapists slow to generalize, quick to mistrust the generalizations of others, and well aware of just how faulty and speculative such guesswork is. On the other hand, those whose job it is to generalize have no patience with all our exceptions, our special cases, and our unique instances; they need to know the similarities, not the differences—the rule, not the exception. Put another way, the first group writes treatment plans for individuals, while the second writes treatment plans for enormous groups: the two tasks depend on very different findings on which formulations and plans will be based. In short, mental health practitioners and planners *must* look at things differently in order to do their quite different jobs.

Trouble crops up when one group, whether practitioners or policymakers/administrators, decides *its* view of mental health needs is the only correct one. This is something both groups do regularly, inevitably causing the conceptual gulf to widen into a chasm, across which the two cease to communicate, with dismal results. Policymakers lose touch with patients and start designing large-scale programmatic efforts that may be impossible to implement or are doomed to failure because patients and/or clinicians will have nothing to do with them, like George's stop-smoking initiative. Practitioners lose all respect for the people who design programs and award money and, instead, begin thinking up ways to distort clinical reality in order to tell bureaucrats what they clearly want to hear rather than what they need to know.

Accompanying this distorted relationship of convenience is a mutual disdain of sometimes entertaining, but always destructive, proportions. I attended one meeting in which seasoned practitioners amused themselves by dismissing all mental health administrators as callous and "cold-blooded," speculating that they had been promoted to their positions not so much because of superior skill as because of their need for refuge from positions that might expose their total lack of clinical knowledge and ability. The clinicians sneered at former colleagues so desperate for power, title, and a corner office that they had become blind to genuine human need. By the same token, I know that policymakers/administrators think practitioners are silly dimwits who talk in psychobabble, people who come up with ever more frivolous ideas for treatment programs, yet who cannot meet a deadline, write a clear and concise proposal, or guarantee a single result. To them, practitioners are not much better than a pack of airheads who rely exclusively on gossip and rumor to tell what is going on; who are devoted to the anecdote to communicate worthless, unverifiable data; and who are uniformly dedicated to the pursuit of unrealistic and, even worse, unscientific aims. The gulf is wide indeed, yet the real differences are very narrow, because in the end, the work is one and the same. This suggests a phenomenon Sigmund Freud called "the narcissism of minor differences." Said Freud, "It is precisely communities with adjoining territories, and related to each other in other ways as well, who are engaged in constant feuds and in ridiculing each other."[32]

Fragmentation at the Top

Whatever fragmentation the mental health system endures probably stems from the refusal of practitioners and policymakers to have anything to do with one another. I doubt that either group would readily concede that this is the case—practitioners, because of their total lack of interest in policy; policymakers, because many of them used to be practitioners and think they remember what it was like. It is much easier to sit on one's own side of the fence, among one's friends, and make snide jokes about the other side than it is to incorporate that other side's concerns into one's own thinking—how much more efficient simply to consult those who are certain to agree already! So practitioners talk to each other about how petty and irrelevant administrators' concerns are, while administrators hole up in an office somewhere and help each other devise empirically sound treatment strategies that are totally impractical or too late to do any good.

Through their separate literatures, both groups find it extremely easy to accuse one another of messing things up. Practice-oriented critics of the system sneer at the "driving force behind public mental health systems, the unspoken reason behind most reorganization decisions,"[33] which they suggest is nothing more than a crass and irresponsible desire to get some other funding source to pay for one's caseload. The remedy: simplify the funding maze and shift decision making back to what is best for patients. This sounds great, makes perfect sense to the clinician who prescribes it, and is of course naive and impossible to accomplish in reality, given that the system is run by people who have long since convinced themselves that only they know what is best for the patients, since they have the numbers and they know what works.

Compare these implicit accusations of bureaucratic incompetence with the following, written by David Mechanic, a scholar of public policy who is greatly respected in the field where policy is actually written. As Mechanic sees it,

> The first step in the revitalization of public mental health services is to understand the social and institutional processes of mental health care and how they have been shaped by historical factors and by our systems of government, law, and health and welfare entitlements. Mental health care is as much influenced by general social policy and culture as it is by policy decisions within the mental health specialty sector.[34]

The practice-oriented critic *knows* what is wrong with the system and *knows* what it needs to be fixed; the public policy scholar realizes just how complex and intricate contemporary social problems are, which implies that they will require lengthy scrutiny and careful study if they are to be changed at all. The one is intuitive, the other carefully rational; and the two comments might as well have been written in secret codes, given the gulf between their authors.

Mental Health: The Field That Doesn't Communicate

The secret is, of course, that both of the preceding views and both approaches are correct; their proponents simply see different things or look at the same things in very different ways. Fragmentation develops when they stop talking to each other, a move each justifies on the grounds that the other has nothing worthwhile to contribute, and that is what I think has happened in the mental health field. I work among clinicians every day, and the *only* things I ever hear my colleages say about policymakers, auditors, and administrators is how stupid, psychotic, and inept they are. All clinicians have their favorite stories to bolster their opinion, invariably calculated to reveal how clinically unaware policy-minded people are, which is another way of emphasizing how thoroughly unlike clinicians they are.[35]

As a rule, clinicians do not—and I think this is crucial—bother to share their opinions of policy or their insights into the realities of work with the mentally ill with the planners who come to visit programs. This is partly because the planners are not all that interested and partly because clinicians see an auditor's visit as a thing to be dreaded and got through as quickly as possible. Even practitioners who wanted to talk seriously to program evaluators might find it difficult, because more and more evaluators are hired expressly *because,* like George Spelvin, they have no clinical skills and bring what the bureaucracy likes to view as a differing perspective to an overly specialized enterprise.

So there you have it: a split in the system between those who do the work and those who plan it and control how it is to be done. It doesn't take too much imagination to see how devastating this division can be in terms of the services that actually get to the patients. (How easy it is to forget the patients when you're focusing on the nature and composition of the system itself—how irrelevant they seem.) The right hand doesn't know what the left hand is doing, but that's all right: the right hand doesn't *want* to know and the left hand would just as soon keep it to himself anyway. The mental health system is not coherent, nor is it highly suggestive of mental health—we tend to hospitalize people who think in such a distorted, rigidly compartmentalized way. Too bad we can't do the same for our poor, battered mental health system.

CHAPTER 12

The System in Action: Numbers, Not People

> Man's observation of the great astronomical regularities not only furnished him with a model for introducing order into his life, but gave him the first points of departure for doing so. Order is a kind of compulsion to repeat which, when a regulation has been laid down once and for all, decides when, where and how a thing shall be done, so that in every similar circumstance one is spared hesitation and indecision. . . . [But] human beings exhibit an inborn tendency to carelessness, irregularity and unreliability in their work, [so] that a laborious training is needed before they learn to follow the example of their celestial models.
> —SIGMUND FREUD, *Civilization and Its Discontents*
> (1930)

WHAT George Spelvin (who was introduced at the beginning of Part III) and his colleagues do all day, mostly, is count things, in or out of the perpetual meetings they all love to attend. They like to know how many patients there are in the system, how many beds are available in hospitals at any given moment, how many of other jurisdictions' patients are occupying their beds, how many "episodes of care" have taken place over a given period of time, and of course, how much it all cost the taxpayer. Almost all of this counting, like the meetings about counting, takes place in bureaucratic offices, but occasionally George and his colleagues check up on the data collection at its source. By so doing, they achieve the only point at which the mental health system's planners and its practitioners ordinarily intersect—the program review process, known variously as a program audit, evaluation, or outside assessment. Typically, a group of auditors (sometimes misleadingly called "consultants") from a relevant oversight organization makes a trip to "the field" to spend a day or a week visiting a program, seeing that it is run effectively, efficiently, and adequately, "based on systematic data collection and analysis."[1] I once was lucky enough to run a program whose relevant "consultant" actually *wanted* to see what we were doing with our patients, so she cheerfully participated in groups and chatted with the patients; but her approach was unusual. Most program auditors are content to visit a program's case records and file cabinets, although they do generally interview the person in charge, who invariably is most removed from the work.

This is not to say that there is no value in monitoring programs from the outside; there is. I am convinced that left to our own devices, mental health practitioners would pay as little attention as possible to some very crucial things, such as any of these "typical management tasks:"

- Determine unit costs of services
- Analyze cost per episode for specific groups or settings
- Compare patient demographics to census data to identify underserved groups
- Select the most cost-effective approach to serving a specific patient group
- Collaborate in integration of services for multiproblem patients
- Compare patient change from beginning to end of service with expected change[2]

Like most management tasks, these sound extremely boring to a committed clinician and would no doubt be exhausting to perform—the sort of thing one would put off until the last possible second, welcoming any excuse to do something else.

The value of the information sought through evaluative instruments is unquestioned. As two enthusiasts put it,

Without the "eyes and ears" of appropriate and timely information about the program, mental health managers risk struggling and stumbling from one crisis to another, experiencing increasing demands on their limited time and attention, and may progressively lose confidence in their capacity to manage effectively.[3]

No mental health program director would disagree with the need to avoid management-by-crisis; we know as well as anyone why it is probably the least effective way to make decisions. I suspect many of us would take exception, however, to two things prominent in most evaluative thinking: (1) the idea that quantifiable data *ever* tells the whole story about any clinical enterprise; and

(2) the assumption that only evaluators get to ask the questions and set the agenda, because only evaluators know what "appropriate and timely information" is.

The Tyranny of the Statistic

I used to run a day program for chronic schizophrenics. Despite our parent agency's participation at several levels in what passed in that community for interagency planning, it was housed in the same building as another, very similar program targeted to exactly the same population. No, this made no sense; yes, it was wasteful duplication; no, it didn't work out very well; yes, it was confusing to disoriented patients; and yes, the building's owner "knew someone" (so much for community planning via interagency collaboration). The two programs were funded differently and had different oversight agencies with somewhat different goals for program outcome, which naturally affected the way the two were designed. Ours was state-funded, through what was then a new mechanism designed to get services to deinstitutionalized chronic mental patients in the settings where they had wound up subsequent to their discharge from state hospitals.[4] Its goal, a worthy one even though it had been formulated some years after the fact of discharge, was to help eligible patients adjust to community life and guide them into the mainstream of American society.

The other program was also state-funded, by a slightly older funding mechanism that was targeted to a relatively small group of patients discharged after very long stays in state facilities.[5] The agency with whom the state had contracted for this program had previously specialized in the vocational training of largely dependent populations; this particular program, however, was in no way vocationally oriented. To the contrary, it very much resembled an inpatient ward's activity program, complete with low-stress arts and crafts, sing-alongs, and every summer, a weekly barbecue in the parking lot. The point of the program seemed to be to get the patients out of the adult homes they lived in, by hook or by crook. To this end, the program sent buses to pick up the patients every morning, and "paid" each participant one dollar for each day he or she attended the program; furthermore, as one of the program's directors told me once, "We're big on food. We figure they love to eat, so a lot of our groups are food-oriented." The result was a low-demand, high-reward program for dependent chronic patients, all with psychiatric histories and many with documented mental retardation as well, a program whose goal was maximum attendance, presumably forever. Patients were brought in by bus, kept indoors most of the time, entertained or given childish things to do, and fed all day. To this day, I am hard pressed to see any real difference between such a program and life in a state hospital.

By contrast, and, I suspect, rather naively, our rival program was designed to undo some of the effects years of inactivity in state hospitals had had on patients. We too sought to get patients out of the adult homes they had been placed in, but we preferred that participants take enough of the responsibility for their treatment to travel there on their own; moreover, as much of our programming as possible was future-oriented if not vocational in nature, an approach chosen to reinforce the idea that our patients really *had* a future. We did not "pay" patients to attend, and we did not feed them all day; our goal was to move as many patients as possible into workshops or larger vocational training programs, where they might find a role in life other than professional mental patient. This is difficult programming to maintain, for the pressures on patients to lapse into chronicity are very great; but we felt strongly that it was worth a try, even with our *very* low-functioning state hospital patients.

Without a doubt, the first program looked better on paper. It had a far greater daily attendance, an extremely low dropout rate, and probably a nonexistent rehospitalization rate. It was also probably relatively inexpensive to run, because the staff would not have needed much advanced training, if any, to lead sing-alongs, arts and crafts groups, or barbecues. Our program had spotty attendance, which is bad enough; but because we were pushing patients to learn new skills, they tended to get anxious a lot of the time, which resulted, inevitably, in the occasional dropout and/or rehospitalization. The work of teaching chronic mental patients that there is life after the state hospital is extraordinarily difficult, and to do it well, staff need some skills and training to be effective in the long run. Paraprofessionals can do the work, and do it very well, but only with intensive supervision from people who have a clear idea of the nature of the patients' condition and who can interpret and explain some of their more worrisome symptoms and behavior for the paraprofessional staff. Our staffing was therefore considerably more expensive than the other program's, especially considering that they posted a greater daily attendance, which lowered their "unit cost" even more.[6] Statistically speaking, their program looked great, whereas ours looked shaky; moreover, since theirs sought to maximize patients' comfort, relapse into psychosis was rare, while ours expected periodic outbursts of symptomatic behavior in response to what we knew to be stressful demands on patients to abandon old ways and learn new skills.

In every other way, however, our program was a better clinical vehicle for what all programs claim to provide for the chronically mentally ill—the opportunity to learn new ways of coping with real life in the community. Their program directors apparently were content to re-create life on the ward of a state hospital in the community, a life that was familiar and easy for the patients to adjust to, with the result that they needed to acquire no new skills.[7] Unfortunately for patient care, such a program precisely fits the needs and requirements of its funding sources rather than those of its patients, and this one was probably designed in just that way. The method is simple and straightforward: find out what the funding body wants and design a program to deliver it—never mind whether what the funding body wants is suitable or desirable for the target population, or even feasible. Such is the tyranny of audits-by-statistical-analysis that thoughtful and creative treatment has long since moved to the back of the bus.

Program Audits Are a One-Way Process

I do not know how oversight agencies decide what to look for when they audit a treatment program, or how they choose their indices of success and failure. I do not, for example, know how they all decided that rehospitalization was the single best indicator of treatment failure among a population for whom it is a periodic inevitability. What I do know is that for the most part, auditors do not listen when they come to "the field" to talk to program administrators, who are themselves removed from the work. Here is a good example, from the audit I participated in most recently.

The program was an on-site evaluation and treatment service for mentally ill inmates of a city jail, run by a voluntary hospital on a city contract paid for by one municipal department (corrections), administered by a second (health), with the collaboration of yet a third (mental health). At least three separate overseers were thus involved in keeping a regulatory eye on the program at all times (not to mention the Joint Commission on the Accreditation of Health Care Organizations, which did not play a direct role in this story). Not surprisingly, each group had vastly different interests and looked at entirely different things during their "site visits." Fortunately, site visits are generally announced well in advance, so it is usually easy to keep the different agendas straight. On this occasion, a long-planned visit from the mental health people, the agenda was to center on the treatment plan, by which they meant the document in a patient's chart. To establish how we arrived at our treatment plans, the auditors and I reviewed the mechanics of our program from the point of intake. Discussion was limited to the auditors' asking me questions from a prepared form, and at one point, the subject of our waiting list came up: "And how big is your waiting list?" I was frankly stumped by the question:

by definition, our population was made up of any and all inmates housed in the jail on any given day, any of whom could theoretically be referred to us at any time, and of whom a fairly regular percentage were so referred. Did that leave us with anything that could conceivably qualify as a waiting list? The truth was that we had no waiting list at all, but the auditors seemed to have no way of putting that answer on their form, and I felt under some pressure to come up with one.

What followed was the kind of discussion that I associate with auditors and program analysts exclusively. First, I tried to suggest that they were barking up the wrong tree, that the concept of "waiting list" did not apply, that in fact the concept "clinic" did not apply, that even "treatment," as mental health professionals generally understand it, did not apply. Next, I tried to engage them in a discussion of what *did* apply: I described how referrals came in, from whom, how I sorted them out, how we tried to make sure they all got followed up—how, in short, the program worked within the rather unusual limits imposed by the host setting. I tried humor, making the admittedly farfetched suggestion that perhaps we should estimate the number of criminals who do not get caught on any given day and call them a hypothetical waiting list. Nothing seemed to help. Here were three decent people, with clipboards full of prepared questions, who could not imagine what to do with answers that would not fit. As I have before, I finally chose to tell them the truth as I saw it and let them struggle to fit it into their matrix or protocol or whatever they call it. What I later decided was that the city mental health department had undertaken to oversee and monitor jail-based programs but had not designed a relevant format for themselves to follow while doing so. Instead, they were— and for all I know, still are—trying to shoehorn jail-based mental health programs into their all-purpose outpatient clinic format, regardless of any and all glaring inconsistencies and anomalies thus exposed. The fact that the programs under review utterly failed to fit the protocol was somehow, in the auditors' minds, the program's fault, not theirs.[8]

I say this with some regret, for audits have always struck me as opportunities to send some information back to program planners about what "the field" is really like, information I strongly suspect they do not have but could use. For caseloads do change, not dramatically or suddenly, but fairly constantly; every now and again, one realizes there is a pattern to the work or to the referrals— more of the patients are homeless, or addicted, or retarded, or schizophrenic, or have college degrees—that represents a change in the population coming in for help. The type of help sought changes, too: for weeks people will come in wanting counseling to help them lead happier lives, for instance; then, gradually, one realizes that more and more people are coming in for help with external problems over which they have no control, say, things like housing, welfare, or unemployment. Rarely is a single mental health worker or program by itself able to detect a really big trend like homelessness, but we all get our share and may be in a position to alert planners early on to what is coming up—but not if they don't want to hear what isn't already on their form.

Everyone Plays the Game

Among the various bits of practice-based wisdom I have heard about auditors is that they will never address a serious problem for fear they will get in trouble for not having spotted it before. I first heard this from a woman whose job it was to handle all matters involving outside accrediting and audits in an agency that was accountable to at least five oversight bodies, an agency that had been in trouble with Medicaid in the past and was determined to stay out of trouble forever. Years before it became standard practice in the field, the agency in question had hired a special accreditation/licensing specialist to anticipate audits and keep it in compliance with regulations; and according to her, auditors only ask what they have decided in advance to find out and are not at all interested in unpleasant surprises. Her explanation for the phenomenon was that if something untoward were to show up, the overseers would then have to do something about it and run the risk of being blamed for having let it happen in the first place—"it" might be Medicaid fraud or patient abuse or, worst of all, anything that might attract the interest of the media. There are two results of this reluctance to find anything seriously wrong in the agencies one is reviewing: (1) program directors and their auditors can and do collude to keep potentially damaging problems covered up as long as possible; and (2) auditors give so much advance warning of their visits that an agency's administration would have to be truly incompetent to fail to clean up its act in time. The audit is thus not intended to be a fact-finding operation but rather a routine check to make sure things are running as they should. As I see it, we are all the poorer for this exercise—they don't learn anything about what we really do, and we don't learn anything new about our operation.

Another piece of practice-based wisdom is a paradoxical inversion of the foregoing: auditors must find something wrong, to prove they have done the review at all; what is more, they must leave a program with something to fix, a deficiency to address, so that the solution will be there for them to follow up on next time. All this is very well—no program is perfect, to say the least, and we can all stand to improve—but I am troubled by what strikes me as a particularly dishonest arrangement. Auditors (who, by the way, always claim to be there to *help,* a phony claim in and of itself, since they are there to judge and report, and everyone knows it) ask prepared questions, do not want any surprises, cannot or will not fit the truth into their questionnaires, and know in advance that they will find something deficient. Yet this is the only place in the whole system at which policy and practice intersect, the one moment where practice can inform policy and policy can reflect practice—but no one wants the information. Instead, they want to fill in their prepared questionnaire, read a few charts, find something wrong, and leave. (I know of only one exception to this pattern, one that has a very limited application: the New York State Commission on Quality of Care for the Mentally Disabled apparently makes it a point to visit the state's mental hospitals without warning, at 2:00 A.M. if necessary, in order to learn what is really going on.)[9]

For our part, we are just as glad to see the auditors go and will carefully prepare a highly selective display of our work for their benefit, one that in no way reflects "business as usual." They get to see the best charts, the cleanest offices, the cheeriest waiting rooms. They get the freshest coffee and the nicest chairs. The policy manual, normally lost, reappears for the occasion. Everyone smiles and is abnormally polite while inspectors are around—in short, they see a picture of facility life that is in no way representative and may well be deceptive. They see precisely what we want them to see, and we cannot wait to get rid of them.

As I was writing this, I heard a real-life story that is the single most dramatic example I have heard of how far a facility will go to look good on an audit. I called a nearby inpatient unit to seek admission for a patient and talked to the chief psychiatrist, bringing her up to date on the patient, whom she had treated before. At the moment of referral, my staff felt the patient was out of control and in need of the kind of diagnostic evaluation and rapid intervention that everyone agrees is very difficult to accomplish outside of a hospital. The psychiatrist listened, paused awkwardly, and said, rather sheepishly, "Do you suppose you could send her on Wednesday?" [It was Friday.] "Well," I said, "she kind of needs help now." "Yes, I know," the psychiatrist replied. "It's just that I have state inspectors coming for a site visit on Monday through Wednesday, and I want to put our best foot forward. You know how it is: the last thing I need is *her* acting up all over the place and making us look bad." Think about it. She felt she had to hide her *patients* from the auditors to make sure her facility looked good.

Program Review: A Missed Opportunity

The net result—a system characterized by policy made on one level, practice conducted on another, with any and all communication between the two forced, artificial, and self-serving—is probably not what we want, although it certainly is what we deserve. There is obviously a need for regulation and monitoring of the vast complex of treatment facilities; occasional exposure of instances of substantial Medicaid fraud proves that by itself. Following the medical model, though, the field of practice is extraordinarily jealous of what it sees as its right to control itself from within, on the traditional grounds that only a doctor/mental health professional can truly know and therefore accurately judge the quality of another's work. Left to its own devices, however, the field of mental health does not police itself any better than has the medical profession, of which it is a sort of appendage. Therein lies a policymaker's dilemma: we know the field needs regulating, but we know it will not accept regulation willingly, so what do we do?

To get around this dilemma, it looks as if regulators have decided to oversee that which is most neutral, the nuts and bolts of the business—physical plant, case records, finances, staff credentials, and policy and procedure manuals. In the process of designing methods and procedures for doing this, regulators have created an intimidating, incomprehensible, and elaborate bureaucratic system of their own, which now requires the presence in most large facilities of an expert whose sole job is to understand and interpret the overlapping regulations and requirements of the several organizations to whom the facility is accountable. One has only to read the health care job ads in the Sunday *New York Times* every week to know that quality assurance coordinator jobs are regularly available (which says something about the satisfying nature of the jobs themselves), and even smaller facilities on the periphery of the mental health field now seek in-house help with regulations. One ad, for executive director of a relatively small child welfare agency, listed the usual "strong administrative skills" as required for the job, followed by the inevitable: "Familiarity with regulatory agency requirements is mandatory."[10]

What Regulators Look At

The business of regulating health care providers is the legacy of multiple failed efforts at self-control, dating back to the First World War, when the American College of Surgeons first tried to standardize hospital practices. The model for most regulatory enterprise is the Joint Commission on Accreditation of Hospitals (usually known as JCAH, although in the late 1980s, the "H" was changed to "HO," for Health Care Organizations), formed in 1951 by the American College of Surgeons, the American College of Physicians, the American Hospital Association, and the American and Canadian Medical Associations. Notice that the American Psychiatric Association (APA) is not listed among the founding members of the JCAH: resisting outside control to the last, the APA members chose to write their own standards for practice even as the JCAH members were writing theirs, but since it had no legal authority over facilities, the APA could only come up with "guidelines."[11] Outside control of psychiatric facilities took over in earnest with the creation of Medicare and Medicaid in the 1960s, since the federal government made it a requirement for reimbursement that a hospital be JCAH-accredited, and some states made accreditation a requirement for licensure. Even though accreditation by JCAHO is theoretically voluntary, the fact that accreditation is tied to reimbursement makes the term *voluntary* somewhat less than apt.

In keeping with the fact that the psychiatric establishment did not get into the regulation industry on the ground floor, it has not sat still since for any set of standards others wish to impose on it. When JCAH came up with its *1972 Accreditation Manual for Psychiatric Facilities,* a project of no fewer than ten psychiatric and mental health organizations, many psychiatric organizations found the standards unsuitable as proposed and came up with their own alternatives, specifically tied to their particular specialty. This led to the composition of separate manuals for both alcoholism and drug abuse facilities, as well as separate guidelines for child and adolescent programs. JCAH published these in their next manual, the *1979 JCAH Consolidated Standards for Child, Adolescent and Adult Psychiatric, Alcoholism and Drug Abuse Programs,* which does not cover community mental health centers and has since been criticized for being overspecific, redundant, plagued with omissions, and given to setting controversial standards. An ongoing source of conflict, one that has paralyzed organized psychiatry before, is the question of who should be in charge: the APA, for example, holds that if a facility is to be labeled "psychiatric," as opposed to "multidisciplinary," then only psychiatrists can and should be accountable and responsible for overall patient care.[12] It is on such crucial questions of power and control that organized psychiatry tends to focus its efforts at self-regulation.

Into the chaos created by professional infighting and resistance to controls of any kind, on the one hand, and funding bodies' demand for accountability, on the other, have come a confusing collection of overlapping standards for, generally, the minutiae of practice. JCAH strongly criticized one program I worked for because, among other things, a closet on its premises had a burned-out light bulb in it. Another program, a community mental health center, reported that three surveyors from JCAH made three separate recommendations designed to solve the problem of what to keep in their walk-in refrigerator in case someone got locked in—one surveyor proposed keeping a fire axe inside, another preferred a ball-peen hammer, and the third specified the installation of "a threaded, U-shaped bolt, equipped with wing nuts, for opening the latch from inside."[13] The need to resolve these three opinions led the program to find out about standard refrigerator safety devices, available, as it turned out, for years. In our jail-based medical clinic, the nurses had tried to make the area look less like a jail and more like a clinic by taping up cheerful posters, some with useful medical advice, some with irrelevant but pretty pictures. In advance of the JCAH site visit, someone made them take all the posters down, citing the JCAH rule that all pictures on walls be framed behind glass. Since breakable glass is, for obvious reasons, not allowed in jail, the clinic went back to looking like a jail.

What Clinicians Care About

JCAH is famous among practitioners for its emphasis on physical plant, what it calls "life safety issues," and administrative detail, including timeliness of record keeping, minutes and notes of meetings, and up-to-date policies and procedures. Of course these concerns are important, and of course they must be attended to. Imagine how terrible it would be if someone, a patient, say, had got locked into that refrigerator—but a fire axe? Is that an implement anyone wants lying around loose in a psychiatric facility? In my experience, it is the extremely specific nature of the JCAH recommendations for physical plant and administrative deficiencies that is so irritating to those whose job involves treatment and its very different concerns for patient safety and well-being. I understand perfectly, for example, the frustration of the physician in charge of the jail-based medical clinic mentioned earlier, normally a very quiet man, who erupted in fury at a pre-JCAH planning meeting focused on the number, location, and size of his clinic's wastebaskets: "I've got a building full of TB [tuberculosis] I can't treat and syphilitics I can't find, both of which constitute a serious public health crisis, and you want me to care about *wastebaskets!*"

I suppose someone does have to care about those wastebaskets, and I suppose we should be glad JCAH has taken on the task of monitoring them. My objection to the approach taken by surveyors in general is that in their zeal to come up with highly objective, empirically valid standards that can be applied nationwide and across the board, they may have lost sight of what is important besides what they survey. Why weren't they as concerned as the physician surveyed about untreated TB and syphilis in an overcrowded, short-stay, municipal jail? Why did the subject never come up? Why did none of the surveyors ask him, as clinic director, what *his* concerns were? How did the number and location of clinic wastebaskets become more important to official guardians of the public health than untreated communicable disease? I suspect the answer is simply that it is possible to set measurable guidelines and standards for wastebasket provision, but it is difficult to do so for clinical practice across a wide variety of host settings, ranging from traditional hospitals to such untraditional health care settings as homeless shelters and municipal jails (not to mention the fact that people in charge of wastebaskets are rarely as touchy about their autonomy as doctors are). I think about this every month as I prepare the latest ridiculous case record review in the name of quality assurance. I carefully count, for example, how many cases out of my assigned total were seen within forty-eight hours of their being referred, or how many were seen weekly thereafter or how many were seen by a psychiatrist within seventy-two hours or how many were born in the month of May—whatever the thing being measured for that particular month is. And I think, why do they call this *quality* assurance when the sole concern is the timing of treatment—never the treatment itself, much less its quality?

The answer is, of course, that both timeliness and appropriateness of treatment are important components of its quality—I know that. What I regret is the fact that since it is so much easier to measure timeliness, that is what empiricists and program monitors have come increasingly to focus on and study, even to the exclusion of other key components of treatment quality, its nature and implementation. Yet it is the latter—exclusively, by the way—that interests good clinicians, to whom each case is a unique individual phenomenon, generalizable only insofar as that informs diagnostic or prognostic thinking, which in turn is of interest only if it helps one treat one's patients more effectively.

The trouble is, none of the things just mentioned is measurable (though not for lack of trying), and indeed should not be measurable, since each makes up a piece of the ineffable—the art, as opposed to the science, of clinical practice. No one who has ever been part of or witness to a skillful psychotherapeutic interview will have any trouble understanding what I am talking about: sometimes a therapist's ability to relate to *that* patient at *that* moment can do wonders, can establish a working therapeutic alliance in a split second, can pinpoint precisely the patient's resistance and address it, can offer hope where there was none before. When the therapeutic alliance works, it is something very special; and good, responsible clinicians are always striving to expand their abilities to be ready to take advantage of those rare moments when the patient–therapist fit is just right, when the magic of exactly right psychotherapy is possible. But work like that will certainly never be measured, predicted, audited, or controlled.

So we count those wastebaskets and we make sure referrals get seen in forty-eight hours and we document, document, document, because our jobs and our programs depend on it. A psychiatrist–turned–JCAH surveyor has observed that in all the programs she has visited, professionals and nonprofessionals involved in direct care of patients invariably cared about the quality of that care above all else; she found their devotion "impressive." By contrast, she noticed, administration and upper management were chiefly interested in "getting accredited"; and physicians and psychiatrists alike were hostile or indifferent to the whole process. Somewhat weakly, she suggests that these disparate groups can use the accreditation process as a learning tool for developing better care; and she dismisses psychiatrists' resistance to regulation as tantamount to shielding their autonomy in the face of what she defends as *"professionally defined* standards" supposed to enhance that care.[14] She may be right, but I think it is time regulators faced the fact that their standards may be not only professionally defined but also irrelevant and extraneous to most of the practice they are so eager to control.

Patients Pay the Price

Somewhere in the midst of all this are the patients, ranging from the so-called worried well to the ever-neglected chronics. No one ever asks them what they think of the system or of the care it provides, of course, and even if someone were to ask, any criticisms they might come up with could readily be dismissed on the grounds that their illness interferes with their understanding of the question. What we have is a system made up of two competing aggregates of professionals—those who treat and those who administer, both of whom *know* what the mentally ill person "really needs" in the way of services. What we also have is a system that paradoxically is less influenced by its consumers than it is by any and everyone else who takes an interest in its structure or functioning. With rare exceptions, the people most responsible for running the mental health business in any of its aspects have, like George in my earlier example, the least access to patients. By the same token, the people who do see patients have neither the interest nor the opportunity to divulge what they know about patients' needs and wants. Worst of all, neither group seems particularly interested in knowing what the patients they are there to serve think of that service.

It is not a particularly healthy enterprise that fails to solicit its customers' views as to its effectiveness, and we are unquestionably the poorer for our failure to do so in this instance. On 14 April 1989, I was privileged to attend an unusual conference called "Mental Health Alternatives—The Perspective of Veterans and Users of Service."[15] The speakers I heard were all ex–mental patients (they preferred to use the term *veterans*), who had become active in the fledgling self-help movement, an attempt to develop patient-driven alternatives to traditional mental health programs and one that is modestly successful in some areas of the country—California, New York, Vermont, Massachusetts, and Pennsylvania were all represented.

I was struck by three things at this conference. First, there was more genuine energy and excitement among participants and auditors than at any other conference I have ever attended; most people were there because they *cared* about the proceedings. Second, the veterans were far more tolerant of mental illness, both in theory and in practice, than any other group I have seen cope with symptomatic behavior; confronted with agitation and disorganization on the part of one of the participants, the other speakers calmly accepted her behavior and generously allowed her to find her own way out of what was almost certainly a painful humiliation. And third, I was struck by the makeup of the audience: by far, the bulk of those present were patients from Bronx Psychiatric Center, the New York state hospital hosting the conference. Scattered among them was only a handful of mental health professionals, beginners, for the most part, and a grand total of only three mental health administrators, one from the state, one from the city, and a third whom I didn't recognize.

Too bad. What practitioners and administrators would have learned at this very entertaining conference is that veterans of the system see it as almost totally a tool of social control. They dismiss medication as a particularly oppressive method of that control and are uniformly hostile to the idea that forced treatment of any sort is in patients' best interests. One of the biggest laughs any speaker got came in response to one young woman's comment that she had flatly refused to take part in any activity groups while in a mental hospital, because, as she put it, "I already *went* to kindergarten."[16] Critical though these veterans of the mental health system were of its failures, they were uniformly polite and surprisingly tolerant in their perceptions of its efforts on their behalf, much more so than mental health professionals tend to be when meeting to discuss why patients do not get better. The veteran patients gave us, in absentia, credit for having tried, at least, which is something we do not always give them. They seemed able to see that ineffective or unhelpful treatment may well be a product of therapists' incomplete knowledge rather than an artifact of malevolence or oppression, although they were uniformly and consistently hostile to the idea of forced administration of *any* form of treatment.

The mental health system is not currently able to utilize criticism like theirs; it is far too caught up in its devotion to empiricism and the lure of science in the form of measurable therapeutic interventions like medications and technological devices—"tests" of all kinds, beloved of practitioners, and "research," the more rigorous the better, beloved of administrators. There seems to be no room in the empiricists' vision of treatment for the human voice, the lone individual who is brave or desperate enough to speak out and say, "This is not what we need; this is not working." As one student of the system has observed,

> It is a paradox that the most important person in the health services covenant has consistently the least direct influence on the structure and process of care. Yet, it is the recipient of that care for whom the health care system is supposedly established and who will ultimately express his or her needs, either directly and appropriately or in some misdirected or pathological manner. *When the expression of distress or disease is negatively influenced by the structure or process of the health care system, then the system must be considered inefficient or incompetent.* [17]

Our system—whose rejects and discards stumble miserably through city streets on their forced odyssey to nowhere, live out their unhappy days in grudging, inhospitable shelters for the homeless, or wait to die in indifferently run adult homes where they serve only as a profit center—can make no claims to be otherwise. Ironically, it was in the name of fiscal efficiency that the whole community-based movement started, a move that has been corrupted time and again, always in the name of cost cutting and compliance with third-party payers' demands.

The System That Makes No Sense

The mental health system has had its eye on the bottom line for so long that it has apparently forgotten there are other parts to the equation. Knowing, as it certainly does, that there are big gaps in its community-based service network, the system continues to plow money into its inpatient facilities instead, adding beds wherever and whenever it can to try to relieve the overflow from municipal emergency rooms. Never mind that the emergency rooms are full because so many patients are discharged with no follow-up plan from inpatient wards to housing that probably will not meet their ongoing treatment needs; never mind that we know thousands of patients need supportive housing in community residences that simply do not exist; never mind that we are now frittering away money on intensive case management, not to improve a system that does not work but to pay professionals to try to make it work on a case-by-case basis; and never mind that all aftercare services for the sickest patients begin and end with the provision of medications, even though we must know by now medication by itself is nowhere adequate to the task, and despite the fact that many patients resist taking it. Never mind all this—we *know* what they need: what our third-party payers are willing to reimburse us for providing.

Consider the following: Everyone knows the United States desperately needs community residences for chronic mentally ill patients to live in.[18] Not long ago, the *New York Times* pointed out something many of us have known for years: New York State, for all its talk about how building new community residences is its top mental health priority, maintains two separate pay scales, one for state hospital employees, the other for community residence staff; and the pay scale for hospital-based employees is nearly twice that of community-based workers. According to the *Times,* the 1989 state budget provided a 5 percent raise for hospital workers, and none at all for most community staff. Lamely, a spokesman for the state Office of Mental Hygiene agreed with the *Times* reporter that "it's a real problem."[19] The spokesman went on to apologize for the commissioner, whose response to community residence directors' request for additional financial support from the state in order to raise salaries had been that maybe they should hold bake sales. If this is an example of a commissioner's thinking on a subject his department claims is a priority, if bake sales can seriously be suggested as the solution to the problem of a discrepant salary differential that discriminates against the state's avowed priority service, then the system is in worse trouble than we think.

Desperate to prove they are in control of things, mental health departments like New York State's spend much of their time chasing the holy grail of quality assurance in statistical form. The trouble with selecting a business-oriented index to measure program success is that cost-efficient and cost-effective service models invariably reward cost cutting over service provision, as indeed they are designed to do. While this may make sense in the competitive world of consumer products, where buyer choice is a given, it is decidedly out of place as a measure of success in public psychiatry, where consumer choice is not a real variable—if the state or the city governments are not providing the best care for the money, where else can we go? The whole idea behind quality assurance is irrelevant to the chronic caseload, for whom the cost of care is invariably high and the chances for success, measured as no longer needing that care, are nonexistent. Yet for years now we have tried to apply these extraneous measures of success to our chronic caseload, and what has happened is what always happens when a product fails to come up a winner: it is taken off the market. Public psychiatry, in a market-driven, competitive environment, is a clear loser; winners, on the other hand, are programs that serve the kind of patients who quietly generate uncontested income from reimbursement by third-party payers, require low overhead by not needing intensive staffing, and do not disrupt the system by, say, attracting media attention.[20] The seriously mentally ill will *never* fill that bill, which is why no one wants to work with them.

That is also why the system is driven not by patient need but by what reimbursement schemes will pay for. Because of the way hospital reimbursement rates are calculated, it may well pay a hospital to keep its beds full rather than risk lowering current unit cost and jeopardize its future rates accordingly.[21] With each new mechanism for controlling health care costs, alert bureaucrats detect loopholes that permit maximum exploitation of the available public funding, exploitation that often has little to do with patients' treatment needs. In the reimbursement model known as "diagnostic-related groups," or DRGs, for example, hospitals are reimbursed according to disease category rather than by costs, which affects psychiatry in several ways. Even though psychiatric care in a hospital is the cheapest for the hospital to provide, we know from experience that it leads to relatively lengthy stays, so the DRG price tag will be rather high despite the relatively low costs. "The short-run incentive, then, will be to increase census and maximize revenue by shortening the length of stay. This will inevitably lead to a lower 'price tag,' which will require even greater velocity, and the downward spiral will grow," predicts one mental health businessman.[22] In this case, certainly, increased census may maximize revenue, but it will do so regardless of whether patient need increases, decreases, or remains the same. The need to maximize revenue is what drives the system; and this is why it is naive, even if correct, to call for a return to public policy made on the basis of what patients need.

Fragmentation Revisited

Any way you look at it, the mental health system is huge, diffuse, and uncoordinated. No single agency oversees it; no single governmental body regulates it. Run by its need to maintain a certain level of reimbursement, its directors plan its services to do just that. If it is easiest to get reimbursed for treating people in an outpatient clinic, then that is what most programs—95 percent in New York State, for one[23]—will provide. If it takes two years to get all the necessary bureaucratic approval to open a community residence for the mentally ill or the addicted, which is about what it takes, then it is not likely that too many agencies will venture into that part of the field, however great the overall need among the chronic caseload, if only because they will not be reimbursed during those two years. If financially beleaguered hospitals can survive a little longer by keeping their relatively inexpensive to operate psychiatric beds full, then they will certainly find reasons to do so, no matter what the occupants of those beds want or need. If the system chooses to regulate some aspects of practice closely while leaving others pretty much alone, it will almost certainly invite unscrupulous speculators who are by no means above turning a tidy profit on misallocated public funds; the regulatory system has not, by its mere existence, "proved to be a reliable deterrent to mismanagement and wrongdoing."[24]

Unquestionably, the mental health system is terribly fragmented. It is also overly responsive to the whims, fantasies, and fads of remote, detached, and faceless bureaucrats who may or may not know what they are talking about, but who wield incalculable power over our system of patient care, simply because they hold the purse strings. It is, however, full of decent and responsible clinicians who care only about helping patients get better, and it is equally full of crooks who care only about screwing the system out of every dime they can get their hands on. It is given to overreacting to the news that someone, somewhere, has a new program idea that he or she thinks works, rushing to clone the successful program, whether it makes sense to do so or not. It is also given to overreacting to bad press, rushing to plug whatever gaps in the system the press have uncovered, whether the gap still exists or not, whether it can be filled or not. Mostly, it is an anxious and insecure system, made up of people and agencies uncertain of their ability to perform their assigned task; vulnerable because it is in confusion, the system is, above all else, an easy target for its many critics.

Defensively, mental health professionals have tried to protect the system from criticism and limit outside control by proving things through the magic of numbers. Unfortunately, not everything can or should be measured statistically; what's more, some things simply have to be done in spite of the fact that they are neither profitable nor likely to be successful. If we are to have a fully accountable, completely cost-efficient system of mental health care, then we must abandon all the chronic, dependent, hopeless cases to whatever fate they can muster for themselves. If we are going to provide for those hopeless cases what we know they need in the way of service and treatment, then we must spend public money for a long time with no assurance of measurable results. The fact of incurable mental illness is no more the mental health system's fault than it is deinstitutionalization's fault or the patients' fault: it simply *is*, and we are stuck with it, whether it fits the questions on our clipboard or not.

A Twentieth-Century Ship of Fools

> No society can tolerate the thought that those who choose to desert it may be acting in a rational manner. Society's deviants, like doctors' mistakes, have to be explained away, and the assumption that "the insane are not responsible for their actions" provides the proper and indeed the perfect explanation. Obviously, only someone who is quite mad (or "not in his right mind," "duped," "misguided") could commit such a treasonable act. . . . By providing a reassuring interpretation of society's deviants, psychiatry not only justifies its own existence but also unwittingly insures the perpetuation of a scandalous double hypocrisy: "the myth of mental illness" continues to be foisted, enabling a complacent society to misconceive utterly the nature of its most essential reforms.
>
> —Benjamin Braginsky,
> Dorothea Braginsky, and Kenneth Ring,
> *Methods of Madness: The Mental Hospital as a Last Resort* (1969)

ANYONE who writes a book like this one is bound by tradition to make suggestions and recommendations for the future. Although I certainly have thoughts on the subject, I sometimes think the mental health field has altogether too many people with too many ideas about fixing it and not enough people willing to do the actual work. Sometimes these thoughtful individuals are called "consultants," sometimes they are "experts," but always they are full of ideas about changes that are easy to propose because their implementation will certainly fall to someone else. I do not want to add to their number.

I do want to defend the idea of deinstitutionalization, which has gotten the same kind of bum rap that the mentally ill get when they fail to improve despite all our help: it is somehow their fault that we did not do a good enough job. In this instance, we have been quick to pin the blame on deinstitutionalization for the fact that we implemented it in a very hypocritical way. Of course it is better for people with disabilities to live in the real world with the rest of us; it is better for them and for us. Of course incarceration is not something that will promote adaptation to the outside world; people who still think it is are lying to themselves. Forced incarceration, be it involuntary hospitalization or frank imprisonment, can in no way be conceived of as doing its victims a favor; it is done for the good of society exclusively, and any benefit the inmate gets along the way is purely serendipitous. We are a bit more honest with ourselves about this in the case of corrections than we are in the psychiatric field, although I don't see much difference between forcing someone into a cell and forcing him or her into a hospital bed, and neither do the mentally ill.

Consider the following, which is taken from the "Goals and Philosophy Statement" of the National Alliance of Mental Patients, a group based in South Dakota:

> To work towards the end of involuntary psychiatric intervention, including civil commitment and forced procedures such as electroshock, psychosurgery, forced drugging, restraint and seclusion, holding that such intervention against one's will is not a form of treatment, but a violation of liberty and the right to control one's own body and mind. We emphasize freedom of choice for people wanting to receive psychiatric services through true informed consent to treatment, which includes the right to refuse any unwanted treatments.[1]

Any therapeutic intervention that is good and effective will be welcomed by those who are in pain, but why would something that has to be forced on people against their will be viewed as anything but "a violation of liberty," as indeed it is? For whether we call it "civil commitment" or "involuntary hospitalization" or "asylum," the fact is that the recipients of institutional care are not uniformly grateful for the service. Deinstitutionalization was a great step forward, and we are right to keep trying to make it work.

Our mistake was in thinking that to initiate the process was to complete it. Simply discharging patients to community life was not, as we have seen, the whole of the exercise. First we had to find out what they would need to survive—who knew? We had never done anything like this before—and *now* we have to supply it. To the extent that they think about the seriously mentally ill at all, most clinical practitioners, except those in love with the out-of-date idea that hospitals are the only suitable venue for the seriously mentally ill, realize that merely to have discharged someone from a hospital does not constitute adequate care.

What killed deinstitutionalization was that it saved public money. This instantly attracted the attention of bureaucrats in charge of the bottom line, and rightly so—nothing is quite so draining of society's resources as the expenses of maintaining large institutions, something we will soon face anew in the wake of our current fad for building prisons. It is relatively easy to get political and public support for the one-time allocation of money to build an institution, and quite another to muster the same kind of enthusiasm for keeping it staffed, repaired, and heated for the indefinite future. The great lie of institutional care is that it works, which it does not; but we think it will because we want it to so much that we cheerfully tell ourselves, again and again, that *this* time will be different—the inmates/patients will emerge from the institutional cocoon, refreshed and restored, ready to join the rest of us as fully functioning members of polite society. Meanwhile, it costs us an arm and a leg to keep institutions going, and no institution, once opened, will ever voluntarily empty itself to save someone else money.

The point that deinstitutionalization makes so clearly but that is missed by so many is that it is possible to be seriously and chronically mentally ill outside a total institution and survive; it is even possible, under certain circumstances, to do very well indeed. But just as different patients adjust differently to life in a hospital, so they have been adjusting differently to life outside. Yet mental health professionals, instead of noting these differences and taking them into account for future planning, shift anxiously and look for someone or something to blame for what might look like a mistake. Stupidly, we allowed ourselves to think we had done the work by emptying out the back wards and dreaming up new entitlements like SSI, forgetting for a moment that the same mentally ill people who went into those back wards were the ones who were going to come out, complete with the hallmark symptoms of the condition itself *plus* the regrettable mannerisms and behaviors of the caged animal.

So now we're angry, because all those mental patients didn't become normal and act like responsible citizens from the day of their discharge on. We feel tricked, because they're still crazy, and we don't want to continue to spend money on taking care of them. What's worse, we have inflexible models for spending the money we do spend on mental illness: we have hospitals, we have shelters, we have jails, we have clinics that don't want to treat them; we have the idleness of unemployment and we have the dole. And we don't see why we—society at large and the mental health system in particular—should have to change our ways of doing business: we think the mentally ill should have to change, so they'll fit into our models better. The most we seem willing to do at the moment in order to adapt to the realities of life after deinstitutionalization is to consider augmenting our supply of models of care with a resuscitated version of the state hospital, which we propose to rename "asylum." So far, we haven't even done that.

That is the state of the art of care for the seriously mentally ill in the wake of deinstitutionalization, and I see no reason to think it will change significantly unless the system itself changes, which, centered as the system is in entrenched government bureaucracies, is most unlikely. If we could change the system, the most effective intervention in its operation would be to heal the artificial split that has been created over the years between practitioners and administrators, a split that permeates the system.

How the split occurs is no secret: the more administrative and supervisory responsibility people have, the less access they have to their program's patients. Since in most facilities the only way to be promoted is to take on administrative and supervisory responsibilities, the best workers, by and large, will be rewarded by jobs that reduce their opportunities to do the work they do well. Increasingly, they will spend their days talking to other people in like positions, who also see few, if any, patients firsthand. As one goes up the promotional ladder, one sees fewer and fewer vestiges of the real work of the program, with correspondingly expanding responsibility for and influence over it. This remove from the work, incidentally, is sometimes touted as a benefit of administration: recently, a young internist told me that her boss had encouraged her to take a promotion to chief physician in her clinic on the grounds that she would "get to see a lot fewer patients."

For some of us, reduced access to patients is no benefit; we will manage to keep a hand in, no matter what. For many others, however, for whom the work of treating patients is too difficult or too tedious or not personally gratifying enough, administration can be a refuge, a chance to dictate and control without having to expose the limits of one's own skills and abilities. These ubiquitous people are a great danger to the field, because they do not always know what they are talking about yet are in positions that authorize them to wield profound influence over the work of others. They are the ones who can say to a group of supervisors, with a straight face, things like, "I *know* there are profoundly disturbed people being treated here; you're not diagnosing them correctly," even though they themselves have interviewed none of the patients treated by the program.

The only remedy for this is to stop designing jobs that take people away from the work. For example, every program administrator ought to see patients in the course of each administrative day—doing intakes or running a group, for instance—to know what the staff are talking about and whom the program is treating. Such a realignment would benefit workers and administrators alike; and it would enable the system as a whole to have readier information about the caseload, by giving those who set and/or implement policy better and more accurate information on which to base their policy-making. Private practice does not count, by the way: in my scheme, administrators would have to see the patients served by the programs they run. I thought for a long time I was alone in being convinced that this simple remedy could cure a lot of programmatic and systemic ills; but recently I heard of a social worker who claims to have made a lot of money as a consultant to social agencies, to all of which he makes the same recommendation over and over again: he tells administrators to see clients.

One other crucial thing is to figure out a way to replace our regulators with practicing clinicians. The regulators I have seen who claim to be psychiatrists and social workers and psychologists need to go back to the field and work again; their aging memories are not serving them well. By the same token, it would not hurt some of our more naive practitioners to have to look at "that policy stuff" firsthand, perhaps by having to write policy and procedure manuals or doing outcome studies in programs they consider suitably clinical. Some way, in short, should exist that would enable each of these groups to understand better what it is the other does, what problems the other faces. As it is, the split we have created between those who do the work and those who oversee it is unnatural, forced, and deceptive, for it encourages each group to ignore the other's reality. We would not view such an artificial situation as healthy were we treating it in a dysfunctional family or couple, so why maintain it among ourselves?

That is what I would change, if I had a magic wand and the power to use it. What I would hope for as a result would be a system that was somewhat more invested in treating mentally ill *people* than it was in cases, diagnoses, or statistical data. When one looks at cases as individual human beings, it is a lot harder to maintain silly distinctions beloved by those to whom patients only exist on paper, distinctions such as the one that tries to keep separate the mentally ill and the mentally retarded, the alcoholics and the drug addicts, the mental patients and the addicts, the clinical treatment and the social service. These distinctions are all very well on paper and in theory, but in the real world of practice the separated conditions sometimes show up all together in a real person who needs all the services we can come up with—remember Aida Sanchez?—and then all the flaws in our overly specialized system are exposed.

The system itself is immune to such exposure, as nearly as I can tell, but individual patients are not, because the flaws prevent them from getting any help. Surely it is bad enough to be mentally ill, without having to worry about whether your condition fits the criteria of the program to which you have gone, with your hurts and your pain, for help. As things are now, what patients like Aida Sanchez get when they come to us for help is the added burden of knowing they do not fit in, even among the dregs of society served by public

258

psychiatry. While it may increase program efficiency to be careful and precise on paper about who it is you will serve and what it is you will do for them, and while it may be satisfying to specify in high-sounding clinical jargon why your program is not for everyone, it is not fair to expect seriously mentally ill people to understand our fine distinctions as well as we do in order to know better than to come to us for help. If there are gaps in the system, that is our problem. Their problem is that they are mentally ill, and that should be enough of a burden for anyone.

NOTES

———◆———

Chapter 1

1. David J. Rothman, *The Discovery of the Asylum: Social Order and Disorder in the New Republic* (Boston: Little, Brown, 1971), p. 42.
2. Michel Foucault, *Madness and Civilization: A History of Insanity in the Age of Reason,* trans. Richard Howard (New York: Mentor, 1965), p. 18.
3. Albert Deutsch, *The Mentally Ill in America,* 2d ed. (New York: Columbia University Press, 1949), p. 209.
4. Gerald Grob, *Mental Institutions in America: Social Policy to 1875* (New York: Free Press, 1973), p. 68.
5. New York State Senate, *Report of the Select Committee on Report and Memorial of County Superintendents of the Poor, on Lunacy and Its Relation to Pauperism,* document no. 71 (Albany, N.Y.: 5 March 1856), pp. 22–23.
6. Pliny Earle, Superintendent of Northampton State (Mass.) Lunatic Hospital, for example, accused Samuel Woodward, Superintendent of Worcester State (Mass.) Lunatic Hospital and first president of what is now the APA, of listing readmissions as new admissions, counting each discharge as a separate cure, even when the same person was counted over and over. See Grob, *Mental Institutions,* pp. 182–83.
7. Ibid., p. 188.
8. Ibid., p. 343.
9. Deutsch, *Mentally Ill,* p. 254.

10. Gerald N. Grob, *Mental Illness and American Society, 1875–1940* (Princeton, N.J.: Princeton University Press, 1983), p. 92.

11. David J. Rothman, *Conscience and Convenience: The Asylum and Its Alternatives in Progressive America* (Boston: Little, Brown, 1980), p. 12.

12. Not the least of Meyer's contributions was his brilliant and prescient strategy of allying the psychopathic hospitals with medical schools, for as Starr has made abundantly clear, the ultimate power base of organized medicine has been the medical schools, with their ties to universities and their control of hospitals. See Paul Starr, *The Social Transformation of American Medicine* (New York: Basic Books, 1982), especially pp. 116, 360–63.

13. Grob, *Mental Illness,* p. 143.

14. Rothman, *Conscience and Convenience,* pp. 363–64. He points out that in 1939, New York State reported a total of only 9 percent of its patient population on parole status, a figure that was very likely inflated by the inclusion of escapees, who were usually counted as being on parole.

15. Grob, *Mental Illness,* p. 151.

16. Deutsch, *Mentally Ill,* p. 317.

17. See Grob, *Mental Illness,* p. 168, or Deutsch, *Mentally Ill,* p. 372.

18. Franz J. Kallmann, "Review of Psychiatric Progress 1947: Heredity and Eugenics," *American Journal of Psychiatry* 104 (January 1948): 450–51.

19. Nicholas N. Kittrie, *The Right to Be Different: Deviance and Enforced Therapy* (Baltimore: Penguin Books, 1973), pp. 325–31.

20. Grob, *Mental Illness,* pp. 180–83.

21. Rothman, *Conscience and Convenience,* p. 375.

22. John Maurice Grimes, *Institutional Care of Mental Patients in the United States* (Chicago: J. M. Grimes, 1934; reprint, New York: Arno, 1980), pp. viii–xii.

23. Ibid., p. 8.

24. Ibid., p. 110.

25. Ibid., pp. 113–17. Grimes's use of the term *de-institutionalization* can be found on p. 113 and is doubtless the first use of the term.

26. Ibid., pp. 96–97.

27. Grimes's perception of public psychiatry as actively countertherapeutic is confirmed by a recent study of the North Carolina mental hospital system, where political forces, not clinical considerations, were found to have been the most powerful factor in determining the course of the hospitals' history. In North Carolina, state hospital superintendents have historically hidden their problems from the state legislature, providing inspectors with a falsely optimistic view of the facilities and cutting off all avenues to assistance with the very real problems facing the institutions. "In fact," says Cahow, "the traditional notions and fears concerning mental illness were reinforced through lack of information and public contact with the hospitals' administrators and patients." See Clark R. Cahow, *People, Patients and Politics: The History of the North Carolina Mental Hospitals 1848–1960*

(New York: Arno, 1980), p. 54. Another historian, Norman Dain, reported much the same steady undermining of therapeutic principles by political accommodation in the state hospitals of nineteenth-century Virginia, in *Disordered Minds: The First Century of Eastern State Hospital in Williamsburg, Virginia, 1766–1866* (Williamsburg, Va.: Colonial Williamsburg Foundation, 1971).

28. Briefly, fever therapy involved the deliberate inculcation of malaria or rat-bite fever in mental patients to eliminate psychosis, theoretically by overwhelming it with delirium; as late as 1937, adherents of the practice held an international conference in New York City. Insulin shock therapy was first developed in 1928 by Manfred Sakel, who established that following the induction of hypoglycemia or coma, mental patients seemed to have an improved mental status, although no one really knew why; notwithstanding this gap in the knowledge base, insulin coma therapy is still in use in several countries. Similarly, Ladislas von Meduna observed that epileptics rarely have schizophrenia as well, which gave him the idea of inducing epileptoid seizures to eliminate schizophrenic symptoms; originally he used Metrazol to induce the seizures, although by 1940 ECT had supplanted the drug. Approximately 90,000 Americans receive ECT each year, according to a study cited in Richard D. Weiner, "Convulsive Therapies," from Harold I. Kaplan and Benjamin Sadock, *Comprehensive Textbook of Psychiatry/IV*, 4th ed., vol. 2 (Baltimore: Williams & Wilkins, 1985), p. 1559. A surgical procedure, lobotomy was first performed in Lisbon in 1935 by Dr. Egas Moniz, who wanted to eliminate violent behavior in deranged patients; Moniz received the Nobel Prize in medicine in 1949. See the section on "Organic Therapies" in Kaplan and Sadock, *Comprehensive Textbook*, pp. 1481–1575.

29. Lewis B. Hershey, quoted in Deutsch, *Mentally Ill*, p. 464. Hershey was director of the Selective Service System.

30. Ibid., pp. 466–67.

31. Actually, 17 percent is very close to what we now believe to be the prevalence of mental illness in the public at large; modern epidemiologists have established the prevalence rate as 15 percent and are not including the mentally retarded, as the army was in the 1940s. See Morton Kramer, "The Increasing Prevalence of Mental Disorders: A Pandemic Threat," *Psychiatric Quarterly* 55 (1983): 117.

32. Ernest Gruenberg, "The Deinstitutionalization Movement," in *Public Mental Health: Perspectives and Prospects*, ed. Morton O. Wagenfeld, Paul V. Lemkau, and Blair Justice (Beverly Hills, Calif.: Sage, 1982), p. 268.

33. David F. Musto, "Whatever Happened to 'Community Mental Health?'" *Public Interest* 39 (Spring 1975): 61. The role of the conscientious objectors in refocusing federal attention on the state hospitals is also mentioned by Philip K. Armour in *The Cycle of Social Reform: Mental Health Policy Making in the United States, England, and Sweden* (Washington, D.C.: University Press of America, 1981), p. 168.

34. Harry C. Solomon, "The American Psychiatric Association in Relation to American Psychiatry," *American Journal of Psychiatry* 115 (July 1958): 1–9.

Chapter 2

1. Paul Starr, *The Social Transformation of American Medicine* (New York: Basic Books, 1982), p. 347.
2. Council of State Governments, *The Mental Health Programs of the Forty-eight States* (Chicago, Ill.: The Council, 1950), pp. 4–13.
3. Ibid., p. 29. Emphasis in the original.
4. Ibid., pp. 33–34.
5. Ibid., p. 5. Emphasis in the original.
6. Ibid., p. 227.
7. Howard A. Rusk, "States Map a New Attack to Combat Mental Illness," *New York Times,* 21 February 1954, p. 46.
8. R. H. Felix and Morton Kramer, "Extent of the Problem of Mental Disorders," *Annals of the American Academy of Political and Social Science* 286 (March 1953): 14.
9. Harry C. Solomon, "The American Psychiatric Association in Relation to American Psychiatry," *American Journal of Psychiatry* 115 (July 1958): 7.
10. Ibid., p. 8.
11. Daniel P. Moynihan, *Coping: Essays on the Practice of Government* (New York: Random House, 1973), p. 22.
12. *New York Times,* 10 March 1955, p. 28.
13. *New York Times,* 10 March 1955, p. 28; 11 March 1955, p. 27; and 27 March 1955, p. 64.
14. *New York Times,* 24 March 1961, p. 1.
15. Joint Commission on Mental Illness and Health, *Action for Mental Health* (New York: Basic Books, 1961; reprint, New York: Arno, 1980), p. 58. Emphasis in the original.
16. Ibid., p. 72.
17. Ibid., p. 122.
18. Ibid., pp. 268–70.
19. David J. Vail, *Dehumanization and the Institutional Career* (Springfield, Ill.: Thomas, 1966), p. 205.
20. Robert H. Felix, *Mental Health and Social Welfare* (New York: Columbia University Press, 1961), p. 18.
21. *New York Times,* 26 March 1962, p. 33.
22. Karl Menninger, *The Vital Balance: The Life Process in Mental Health and Mental Illness* (New York: Viking, 1963), p. 8.
23. *New York Times,* 7 May 1963, p. 19.
24. Joint Commission, *Action for Mental Health,* p. 70.
25. Ibid., pp. 52–55.
26. Starr, *The Social Transformation,* p. 361.
27. Albert Deutsch, *The Shame of the States* (New York: Harcourt, Brace, 1948), pp. 138–39.
28. Starr, *The Social Transformation,* p. 346.

Chapter 3

1. Phenothiazines are one class of the psychotropic medications—drugs that affect psychic function, behavior, or experience. These medications are subdivided into six classes: (1) *neuroleptics or phenothiazines,* also known as antipsychotics or major tranquilizers, for their antipsychotic and sedating effects (Thorazine, Haldol, Mellaril); (2) *anxiolytics,* or minor tranquilizers, the antianxiety agents (Valium, Librium, etc.); (3) *antimanic agents,* or Lithium; (4) *antidepressants* (Elavil, Tofranil); (5) *psychostimulants* (caffeine, amphetamines); and (6) *psychedelics* (LSD, mescaline, cannabis). Robert J. Campbell, *Psychiatric Dictionary,* 6th ed. (New York: Oxford University Press, 1989), pp. 604-5.
2. Henry Brill, "State Hospitals Should Be Kept—For How Long?" in *State Mental Hospitals: Problems and Potentials,* ed. John A. Talbott (New York: Human Sciences, 1980), p. 151.
3. Sue E. Estroff, *Making It Crazy* (Berkeley, Calif.: University of California Press, 1981), p. 70.
4. Elliot S. Valenstein, *Great and Desperate Cures: The Rise and Decline of Psychosurgery and Other Radical Treatments for Mental Illness* (New York: Basic Books, 1986), pp. 154–61.
5. Quoted in Judith P. Swazey, *Chlorpromazine in Psychiatry: A Study in Therapeutic Innovation* (Cambridge, Mass.: MIT Press, 1974), p. 105. This wonderful book recounts the surprisingly fascinating history of the synthesis and marketing of chlorpromazine, a drug that has had a profound impact on the practice of psychiatry in a very short time.
6. Ross J. Baldessarini, *Chemotherapy in Psychiatry: Principles and Practice,* rev. ed. (Cambridge, Mass.: Harvard University Press, 1985), p. 15.
7. See the standard library index, *Quarterly Cumulative Index Medicus,* 1954–1957, under *chlorpromazine* and *phenothiazine.*
8. Charles Bolling and Frazier Cheston, interviewed in January 1971 by Swazey and quoted by her at length; see Swazey, *Chlorpromazine in Psychiatry,* pp. 202–7.
9. Ibid., p. 203.
10. Ibid.
11. Henry Brill and Robert E. Patton, "Analysis of 1955–1956 Population Fall in New York State Mental Hospitals in the First Year of Large-Scale Use of Tranquilizing Drugs," *American Journal of Psychiatry* 114 (December 1957): 509–17; "Analysis of Population Reduction in New York State Hospitals during the First Four Years of Large-Scale Therapy with Psychotropic Drugs," *American Journal of Psychiatry* 116 (December 1959): 495–509; and "Clinical-Statistical Analysis of Population Changes in New York State Mental Hospitals since the Introduction of Psychotropic Drugs," *American Journal of Psychiatry* 119 (July 1962): 20–35.
12. Swazey, *Chlorpromazine in Psychiatry,* p. 204.
13. Ibid., p. 199.
14. N. William Winkelman, Jr., "Chlorpromazine in the Treatment of Neuropsychiat-

ric Disorders," *Journal of the American Medical Association,* 155 (May 1954), pp. 8–21.

15. Winkelman quoted in Swazey, *Chlorpromazine in Psychiatry,* pp. 197–98.

16. John Vernon Kinross-Wright quoted, ibid., p. 199.

17. The study was done in Montreal by Heinz E. Lehmann and T. E. Hanrahan, who gave what were then considered large doses of up to 800 milligrams of CPZ to seventy-one patients aged eighteen to eighty-two over a four-month period. They found the drug to be most effective with manic patients and least effective, ironically enough, with "chronic patients showing considerable deterioration." Ibid., pp. 152–58.

18. See especially Baldessarini, *Chemotherapy in Psychiatry,* pp. 4–10. Baldessarini, a psychiatrist who does research in psychopharmacology, sees the oversale of drugs as leading to the lack of solid clinical findings to support the premise that so appealed to medicine and psychiatry at the time: that psychopathology has a biological basis. See also Andrew Scull, *Decarceration,* 2d ed. (New Brunswick, N.J.: Rutgers University Press, 1984), pp. 80–89. John M. Davis's section on psychopharmacology in the standard psychiatry text pays particular attention to the confusing results of the early studies, attributing much of this to the early researchers' failure to use the now-standard practice of the double-blind study, in which neither the patient nor the person administering the test drug knows whether the drug or a placebo is being given; see Davis, "Antipsychotic Drugs," in *Comprehensive Textbook of Psychiatry,* 3d ed., ed. Harold I. Kaplan, Alfred M. Freedman, and Benjamin J. Sadock (Baltimore: Williams & Wilkins, 1980), pp. 2257–89.

19. See Baldessarini, *Chemotherapy in Psychiatry,* p. 12; and Gerald N. Klerman, "Psychopharmacology Deserves Better," *Contemporary Psychology* 17 (1972): 685.

20. Swazey, *Chlorpromazine in Psychiatry,* p. 160.

21. John Kinross-Wright quoted, ibid., p. 200. See also Valenstein, *Great and Desperate Cures,* p. 296.

22. Brill and Patton, "Analysis of 1955–1956 Population Fall," p. 517.

23. Brill and Patton, "Analysis of Population Reduction," p. 509.

24. Brill and Patton, "Clinical-Statistical Analysis," p. 33.

25. Morton M. Hunt, "Pilgrim's Progress," *The New Yorker,* 30 September 1961, p. 71.

26. Joint Commission, *Action for Mental Health,* p. 39.

27. Winfred Overholser quoted in Swazey, *Chlorpromazine in Psychiatry,* p. 209; comment from Washington, D.C., 1956.

28. Martin Fleishman, quoted, ibid., p. 201; comment from California, 1968.

29. Maryland Department of Mental Hygiene, quoted, ibid., p. 209; comment from Maryland, 1955/56.

30. Hirsch L. Gordon, "Introduction," in *The New Chemotherapy in Mental Illness,* ed. Hirsch L. Gordon (New York: Philosophical Library, 1958), p. xvi.

31. Probably the best single description of the course of treatment open to many, and maybe to most, chronic schizophrenics after deinstitutionalization is that found in

Susan Sheehan's *Is There No Place on Earth for Me?* (Boston: Houghton Mifflin, 1982).

32. Swazey, *Chlorpromazine in Psychiatry,* chart on pp. 210–13. The figure of 551,400 patients in all U.S. mental hospitals in 1956 is taken from Morton Kramer, *Psychiatric Services and the Changing Institutional Scene, 1950–1985* (Rockville, Md.: National Institute of Mental Health, 1977), p. 78.
33. William Gronfein, "Psychotropic Drugs and the Origins of Deinstitutionalization," *Social Problems* 32 (June 1985), p. 453.
34. Swazey, *Chlorpromazine in Psychiatry,* pp. 210–13; see chart.
35. Ibid., p. 160.
36. See George E. Crane, "Clinical Psychopharmacology in Its 20th Year," *Science,* 13 July 1973, pp. 126–28.
37. Robert Castel, Françoise Castel, and Anne Lovell, *The Psychiatric Society,* trans. Arthur Goldhammer (New York: Columbia University Press, 1982), p. 112. The authors, one of whom is a French psychiatrist, seem somewhat shocked by what they perceive as an American psychiatric indifference to the question of whether heavy use of neuroleptics is wise, nor did they encounter much professional criticism of the use of "chemical straitjackets."
38. Michael J. Goldstein, "Premorbid Adjustment, Paranoid Status, and Patterns of Response to Phenothiazine in Acute Schizophrenia," *Schizophrenia Bulletin* 3 (1970): 36.
39. See Baldessarini, *Chemotherapy in Psychiatry,* p. 3; Lawson and Cooperrider, *Clinical Psychopharmacology: A Practical Reference for Nonmedical Psychotherapists* (Rockville, Md.: Aspen, 1988), pp. 83–84, or any of the many handbooks on psychopharmacology.
40. Alfred M. Freedman, "Drugs and Society: An Ecological Approach," in *Psychopathology and Psychopharmacology,* ed. Jonathan O. Cole, Alfred M. Freedman, and Arnold J. Friedhoff (Baltimore: Johns Hopkins University Press, 1973), p. 278.
41. John M. Davis, "Antipsychotic Drugs," in Kaplan, Freedman, and Sadock, *Comprehensive Textbook,* p. 2270.
42. See Baldessarini, *Chemotherapy in Psychiatry* (1985), p. 2, for but one reference to the fabled 10,000 papers.
43. John M. Davis, "Antipsychotic Drugs," in Kaplan, Freedman, and Sadock, *Comprehensive Textbook,* p. 2257. See also Martin E. Lickey and Barbara Gordon, who say, "The effectiveness of the new drugs can be illustrated by examining the number of patients in U.S. mental hospitals between 1900 and 1975." *Drugs for Mental Illness: A Revolution in Psychiatry* (New York: Freeman, 1983), p. 4.
44. Peter Stastny, personal communication, 1989.
45. See Nancy Scheper-Hughes and Anne M. Lovell, eds., *Psychiatry Inside Out: Selected Writings of Franco Basaglia,* trans. Anne M. Lovell and Teresa Shtob (New York: Columbia University Press, 1987).
46. See Claire Selltiz, Marie Jahoda, Morton Deutsch, and Stuart W. Cook, *Research*

Methods in Social Relations, rev. ed. (New York: Holt, Rinehart & Winston, 1959), p. 497, for a description of the Hawthorne studies.

47. John S. Strauss and Hisham Hafez, "Clinical Questions and 'Real' Research," *American Journal of Psychiatry* 138 (1981): 1593.

Chapter 4

1. Paul Watzlawick, John H. Weakland, and Richard Fisch, *Change: Principles of Problem Formation and Problem Resolution* (New York: W. W. Norton, 1974), p. 95.
2. R. D. Laing, *The Divided Self* (Baltimore: Penguin, 1960), p. 36.
3. A famous (or infamous, depending on one's point of view) article by psychologist David L. Rosenhan takes this criticism of psychiatric diagnosis and runs with it. Rosenhan had eight officially sane adults feign vaguely schizophrenic symptoms— each claimed to hear unclear voices saying the words *empty, hollow,* and *thud*—in order to get admitted to mental hospitals; once admitted, they were to cease acting crazy and revert to normal behavior. Unhappily, the patients' "normal" behavior looked crazy to hospital staff because they expected it to do so, no matter how innocuous it was—one pseudopatient's hospital chart revealed that the "patient engages in writing behavior," for example. All of this led Rosenhan to conclude that the diagnostic process is anything but scientific. See Rosenhan, "On Being Sane in Insane Places," *Science,* 19 January 1973, pp. 150–58.
4. Ibid., p. 33.
5. Peter Sedgwick, *Psycho Politics* (New York: Harper & Row, 1982), p. 122.
6. Thomas S. Szasz, *The Myth of Mental Illness,* rev. ed. (New York: Perennial Library, 1974), pp. x–xi. Susan Sontag made a similar observation in her discussion of the pervasive and misleading use of cancer as a metaphor for anything awful; her concern is that the overuse of the metaphor prevents realistic understanding of the genuine illness. See Sontag, *Illness as Metaphor* (New York: Vintage Books, 1979), pp. 84–85.
7. Szasz, *The Myth,* p. 267.
8. Ibid., p. 268.
9. E. Fuller Torrey, *The Death of Psychiatry* (New York: Penguin Books, 1974), pp. 153–54. It is interesting to note that Torrey felt compelled to include a most unusual disclaimer to the effect that the book reflected his own opinions, not those of the National Institute of Mental Health or the U.S. Public Health Service.
10. Robert Perrucci, *Circle of Madness: On Being Insane and Being Institutionalized in America* (Englewood Cliffs, N.J.: Prentice-Hall, 1974), pp. 161–62.
11. Benjamin M. Braginsky, Dorothy D. Braginsky, and Kenneth Ring, *Methods of Madness: The Mental Hospital as a Last Resort* (New York: Holt, Rinehart & Winston, 1969), pp. 39–45.

12. Thomas J. Scheff, *Being Mentally Ill: A Sociological Theory* (Chicago: Aldine, 1966), p. 82.
13. Erving Goffman, "The Moral Career of the Mental Patient," in *The Making of a Mental Patient,* ed. Richard H. Price and Bruce Denner (New York: Holt, Rinehart & Winston, 1973), p. 153.
14. Ibid., pp. 148–49. Emphasis in the original.
15. M. Harvey Brenner, *Mental Illness and the Economy* (Cambridge, Mass.: Harvard University Press, 1973), p. 10.
16. Ibid., p. 201.
17. August B. Hollingshead and Frederick C. Redlich, *Social Class and Mental Illness: A Community Study* (New York: Wiley, 1958), p. 217.
18. Alfred H. Stanton and Morris S. Schwartz, *The Mental Hospital* (New York: Basic Books, 1954). Other well-known studies from the pre-Goffman years include Ivan Belknap's *Human Problems of a State Mental Hospital* (New York: McGraw-Hill, 1956; reprint, New York: Arno, 1980), and William Caudill's *The Psychiatric Hospital as a Small Society* (Cambridge, Mass.: Harvard University Press, 1958).
19. Erving Goffman, *Asylums* (Garden City, N.Y.: Anchor Books, 1961), p. 74.
20. David K. Reynolds and Norman L. Farberow, *Endangered Hope: Experiences in Psychiatric Aftercare Facilities* (Berkeley, Calif.: University of California Press, 1977), p. 8.
21. Charles Steir, *Blue Jolts: True Stories from the Cuckoo's Nest* (Washington, D.C.: New Republic Books, 1978), pp. 223–26.
22. J. K. Wing, "Institutionalism in Mental Hospitals," in *Mental Illness and Social Processes,* ed. Thomas J. Scheff (New York: Harper & Row, 1967), p. 223.
23. Werner M. Mendel, *Supportive Care: Theory and Technique* (Los Angeles, Calif.: Mara Books, 1975), p. 201.
24. David J. Vail, *Dehumanization and the Institutional Career* (Springfield, Ill.: Thomas, 1966), p. 140.
25. Ibid., p. 184.
26. Kai T. Erikson, "Notes on the Sociology of Deviance," in *Mental Illness and Social Processes,* ed. Thomas J. Scheff (New York: Harper & Row, 1967), p. 300.
27. Belknap, *Human Problems,* p. 36.
28. William Ryan, *Blaming the Victim,* rev. ed. (New York: Vintage Books, 1976), p. 155.
29. Leona L. Bachrach, "A Conceptual Approach to Deinstitutionalization," *Hospital & Community Psychiatry* 29 (September 1978): 576.
30. Nicholas N. Kittrie, *The Right to Be Different: Deviance and Enforced Therapy* (Baltimore, Md.: Penguin Books, 1973), p. 371.
31. Perrucci, *Circle of Madness,* pp. 155–59.
32. Steir, *Blue Jolts,* p. 47.
33. Quoted in Andrew T. Scull, *Decarceration: Community Treatment and the Deviant:*

A Radical View (Englewood Cliffs, N.J.: Prentice-Hall, 1977), p. 109. Emphasis in the original.

Chapter 5

1. Joint Commission on Mental Illness and Health, *Action for Mental Health* (New York: Basic Books, 1961; reprint, New York: Arno, 1980), p. v.
2. Morton Kramer and Earl S. Pollack, "Problems in the Interpretation of Trends in the Population Movement of the Public Mental Hospitals," *American Journal of Public Health* 48 (August 1958): 1019.
3. Joint Commission, *Action for Mental Health*, p. 175. The quotation is from an extended passage taken by them from a report then being prepared for the commission by Morris S. Schwartz et al., called *New Perspectives on Mental Patient Care.*
4. Joint Commission, *Action for Mental Health*, p. 174.
5. Ibid., p. 85.
6. Ibid., pp. 262–64.
7. See Howard E. Freeman and Ozzie G. Smith, *The Mental Patient Comes Home* (New York: Wiley, 1963); William W. Michaux et al., *The First Year Out: Mental Patients after Hospitalization* (Baltimore, Md.: Johns Hopkins University Press, 1969); Ann E. Davis, Simon Dinitz, and Benjamin Pasamanick, *Schizophrenics in the New Custodial Community: Five Years after the Experiment* (Columbus, Ohio: Ohio State University Press, 1974); and Nina R. Schooler et al., "One Year after Discharge: Community Adjustment of Schizophrenic Patients," *American Journal of Psychiatry* 123 (February 1967): 986–95.
8. Kenneth Minkoff, "A Map of Chronic Mental Patients," in *The Chronic Mental Patient: Problems, Solutions, and Recommendations for a Public Policy*, ed. John A. Talbott (Washington, D.C.: American Psychiatric Association, 1978), p. 18.
9. Ibid.
10. Ibid.
11. Joint Commission, *Action for Mental Health*, p. 175.
12. Minkoff, "A Map," p. 18.
13. F. Ross Woolley and Robert L. Kane, "Community Aftercare of Patients Discharged from Utah State Hospital: A Follow-up Study," *Hospital & Community Psychiatry* 28 (February 1977): 116.
14. Minkoff, "A Map," p. 19.
15. Ibid., p. 21.
16. Kenneth J. Neubeck, "Capitalism as Therapy?" *Social Policy* 8 (May/June 1977): 41–45. This is an odd article, and it is hard to know how the author viewed the events he recorded; his tone is somewhat ironical and sardonic, but he never actually criticizes the practices of the unidentified state bureaucracy.

17. Joint Commission, *Action for Mental Health,* p. 179.
18. Harry Schnibbe quoted in Franklin D. Chu and Sharland Trotter, *The Madness Establishment: Ralph Nader's Study Group Report on the National Institute of Mental Health* (New York: Grossman, 1974), p. 18; Schnibbe was executive director of the National Association of State Mental Health Program Directors.
19. Joint Commission, *Action for Mental Health,* p. 179.
20. Ibid., p. 49.
21. Ibid., p. 263.
22. See Chu and Trotter for a revealing discussion of the catchment area in theory and practice. The community mental health center planners decided on the official size of the areas for "no real reason," according to one of the experts involved; the actual numbers were selected arbitrarily because "we felt that 75,000–200,000 was about right." *The Madness Establishment,* pp. 71–76.
23. Joint Commission, *Action for Mental Health,* p. 51. The study is described on pp. 49–52.
24. Of the 1,294 clinics found in 1955, 330 were in New York, 102 in Massachusetts, 71 in Illinois, 65 each in New Jersey and Pennsylvania, 64 in California, 51 in Michigan, 44 in Ohio, 35 in Connecticut, 26 in New Hampshire, 24 in Virginia, 22 in Wisconsin, and 21 each in Florida, Kansas, and Texas. Ibid., p. 50.
25. Hazel Farkas, "Aftercare in Community Mental Health Centers," *Hospital & Community Psychiatry* 21 (September 1970): 304–5.
26. Beverly Winston, personal communication, July 1988.
27. Stuart A. Kirk and Mark E. Thierren, "Community Mental Health Myths and the Fate of Former Hospitalized Patients," *Psychiatry* 38 (1975): 212.
28. For one example of the party line see Aaron S. Mason and Robert P. Granacher, *Clinical Handbook of Antipsychotic Drug Therapy* (New York: Brunner/Mazel, 1980), p. 88.
29. See ibid., pp. 88–93; Patrick T. Donlon et al., *A Manual of Psychotropic Drugs: A Mental Health Resource* (Bowie, Md.: Brady, 1983), pp. 7–8; or Gary W. Lawson and Craig A. Cooperrider, *Clinical Psychopharmacology: A Practical Reference for Nonmedical Psychotherapists* (Rockville, Md.: Aspen, 1988), p. 76.
30. Stephen R. Marder et al., "A Study of Medication Refusal by Involuntary Psychiatric Patients," *Hospital & Community Psychiatry* 35 (July 1984): 724–26.
31. Internal memorandum dated 19 October 1988.
32. Sue E. Estroff, *Making It Crazy: An Ethnography of Psychiatric Clients in an American Community* (Berkeley, Calif.: University of California Press, 1981), pp. 89–97.
33. Ibid., p. 98.
34. Ibid., pp. 100–106.
35. Ibid., p. 105.
36. Ibid., p. 106.
37. New York State Assembly, S. 3804, "Outpatient Commitment." (Pending legislation as of fall 1989.) (photocopy.)

38. Francis J. Braceland, appendix VII, in Joint Commission, *Action for Mental Health,* p. 330.

Chapter 6

1. I am indebted to Willie Martin, Jr. for his invaluable insights into the true nature of "the game."
2. Gerald Grob, *Mental Institutions in America: Social Policy to 1875* (New York: Free Press, 1973), pp. 196–201.
3. *New York Times,* 2 February 1954, pp. 15–16.
4. Ernest Gruenberg, "The Deinstitutionalization Movement," in *Public Mental Health: Perspectives and Prospects,* ed. Morton O. Wagenfeld, Paul V. Lemkau, and Blair Justice (Beverly Hills, Calif.: Sage, 1982), p. 271.
5. See Gruenberg, "The Deinstitutionalization Movement," p. 270; and Paul H. Hoch, "State Care," *Atlantic Monthly,* July 1964, p. 82. Gruenberg was one of the authors of the CMHSA legislation and Hoch was commissioner of New York State's Department of Mental Hygiene in the early 1960s.
6. *New York Times,* 2, 3, 14 February; 22 April; and 6 June 1954.
7. Council of State Governments, *The Mental Health Programs of the Forty-eight States* (Chicago, Ill.: The Council, 1950), p. 107.
8. Ibid., p. 117.
9. Ibid.
10. Ibid., p. 227. See also pp. 4–13.
11. Ibid., p. 105.
12. See Robert Castel, Françoise Castel, and Anne Lovell, *The Psychiatric Society,* trans. Arthur Goldhammer (New York: Columbia University Press, 1982), p. 27, for a good description of the psychopathic hospitals.
13. Walter E. Barton, "Services for the Mentally Ill," *Annals of the American Academy of Political and Social Sciences* 286 (March 1953): 111–12.
14. See Lewis Thomas, *The Lives of a Cell: Notes of a Biology Watcher* (New York: Bantam Books, 1974), p. 37.
15. Paul H. Hoch, "State Care," *Atlantic Monthly,* July 1964, p. 85.
16. New York State Commission on Quality of Care for the Mentally Disabled, *A Review of Living Conditions in New York State Psychiatric Centers, May, 1984* (Albany, N.Y.: The Commission, 1984), p. xviii.
17. Council of State Governments, p. 5. Emphasis in the original.
18. U.S. General Accounting Office, *Returning the Mentally Disabled to the Community: Government Needs to Do More* (Washington, D.C.: U.S. Government Printing Office, 1977), p. 81.
19. Ibid., pp. 90–92.

20. Paul Lerman, *Deinstitutionalization and the Welfare State* (New Brunswick, N.J.: Rutgers University Press, 1982), p. 100.
21. Gruenberg, "The Deinstitutionalization Movement," p. 277.
22. U.S. Bureau of the Census. *1970 Census of Population. Vol. I: Characteristics of the Population* (Washington, D.C.: U.S. Government Printing Office, 1973).
23. Jonathan O. Cole, George Gardos, and Michael Nelson, "Alternatives to Chronic Hospitalization—The Boston State Hospital Experience," in *Alternatives to Mental Hospital Treatment,* ed. Leonard I. Stein and Mary Ann Test (New York: Plenum, 1978), p. 219. The authors point out that the census of their particular state hospital went from 3,000 patients in the late 1940s to 2,000 in 1963 to between 230 and 350 in 1978. Fully *1,200* of the 1963 population went to nursing homes (pp. 209–21).
24. Good overviews of SSI legislation are available in several handbooks, such as Robert J. Myers, *Social Security,* 3d ed. (Bryn Mawr, Pa.: McCahan Foundation, 1985), pp. 713–20. There are a few articles about SSI specifically as it affects the mentally ill: see Martha N. Ozawa, "SSI: Progress or Retreat?" *Public Welfare* 32 (Spring 1974): 33–40; or Duncan Lindsey and Martha N. Ozawa, "Schizophrenia and SSI: Implications and Problems," *Social Work* 24 (March 1979): 120–26.
25. I have yet to come across anyone able and/or willing to speculate as to the dollar value of these savings.
26. Lindsey and Ozawa, "Schizophrenia and SSI," p. 120.
27. U.S. General Accounting Office, *Returning the Mentally Disabled,* p. 124.
28. Lerman, *Deinstitutionalization,* p. 94.
29. Howard H. Goldman and Antoinette A. Gattozzi, "Murder in the Cathedral Revisited: President Reagan and the Mentally Disabled," *Hospital & Community Psychiatry* 39 (1988): 505–9.
30. In late 1988, the New York State Commission on Quality of Care for the Mentally Disabled released a report of a study in which they followed sixty patients for six months after discharge from five New York City inpatient facilities, two of which were state facilities, and three of which were part of general hospitals. The commission found that in only 2 percent of cases did the inpatient facilities follow up to see that the patients actually got the aftercare they had recommended. See *Newsletter of the NYS Commission on Quality of Care* 37 (August–September 1988): 1.
31. Castel, Castel, and Lovell, *The Psychiatric Society,* p. 90. For a comprehensive view of the fate of the L-P-S Act, see Eugene Bardach, *The Implementation Game: What Happens after a Bill Becomes Law* (Cambridge, Mass.: MIT Press, 1977). See also Gary E. Miller, "The Public Sector: The State Mental Health Agency," in *The New Economics and Psychiatric Care,* ed. Steven S. Sharfstein and Allan Beigel (Washington, D.C.: American Psychiatric Association, 1985), pp. 178–79, for a brief description not only of California's "incentive-based funding models," as Miller calls them, but of similar ones currently operating in Texas, Wisconsin, and Pennsylvania.
32. Ironically, the same Congress that legislated a mandate that community mental health centers seek third-party payment for their services also wrote the statutory

language that prevented any significant federal insurance reimbursement for the treatment of the mentally ill. Two critics of the reimbursement system contend that "the limitations were intended, and have succeeded, to provide strong disincentives for the integration of the mentally ill elderly and disabled into the Medicare program." Jay B. Cutler and Theodora Fine, "Federal Health Care Financing of Mental Illness: A Failure of Public Policy," in *The New Economics and Psychiatric Care,* ed. Sharfstein and Beigel, p. 20.

33. Gary E. Miller, "The Public Sector," p. 171. Miller warns that the federal government is now trying to have nursing homes declared IMDs and therefore ineligible for Medicaid payments, a decision currently in litigation in several states (p. 172).

34. In 1985, SSI paid $325 per month to a single person living alone, less if he or she lived with relatives, according to the Social Security Administration's Publication no. 05–11015, *A Guide to Supplementary Security Income* (March 1985), p. 14. As of 1 January 1985, SSI paid $649.86 per month to house someone in an adult home. This is known as "SSI, level two" and is available only to proprietors of such facilities; the recipient actually receives something like $30 allowance to spend personally. New York City Department of Mental Health, Mental Retardation, and Alcoholism Services, personal communication, 24 March 1986.

35. Studies that look strictly at the comparative costs of treating mental patients outside the hospital include these: Gary R. Bond, "An Economic Analysis of Psychosocial Rehabilitation," *Hospital & Community Psychiatry* 35 (April 1984): 356–62; Jane G. Murphy and William E. Datel, "A Cost–Benefit Analysis of Community versus Institutional Living," *Hospital & Community Psychiatry* 27 (March 1976): 165–70; and Jonathan O. Cole, George Gardos, and Michael Nelson, "Alternatives to Chronic Hospitalization: The Boston State Hospital Experience," in *Alternatives to Mental Hospital Treatment,* ed. Leonard I. Stein and Mary Ann Test (New York: Plenum, 1978), pp. 209–23. Steven S. Sharfstein and Harry W. Clark, on the other hand, have written about the importance and the difficulty of accurately compiling data reflecting *all* the costs of caring for patients in the community: see "Economics and the Chronic Mental Patient," *Schizophrenia Bulletin* 4 (1978): 399–414. Working with a variety of coauthors, Sharfstein has written a large body of articles on the subject of the economics of mental health, sensing early on the need for clinicians to appreciate how critically important money and funding sources have become to the field.

36. Darrel A. Regier, Irving D. Goldberg, and Carl A. Taube, "The De Facto U.S. Mental Health Services System," *Archives of General Psychiatry* 35 (June 1978): 685–93.

37. Robert F. Drinan, "Who Will Fend for the Chronically Mentally Ill in the Community?" *Psychiatric Quarterly* 55 (1983): 209–10.

38. Ann E. Moran, Ruth I. Freedman, and Steven S. Sharfstein, "The Journey of Sylvia Frumkin: A Case Study for Policymakers," *Hospital & Community Psychiatry* 35 (September 1984): 887–93. For the Sylvia Frumkin story, see Susan Sheehan, *Is There No Place on Earth for Me?* (Boston: Houghton Mifflin, 1982).

39. Irvin L. Muszynski, Jr., "Prospective Pricing: The Common Denominator in a Changing Health Care Market and Its Implications for Psychiatric Care," in *The New Economics and Psychiatric Care,* ed. Sharfstein and Beigel, p. 15.

40. John G. Gunderson and Loren B. Mosher, "The Cost of Schizophrenia," *American Journal of Psychiatry* 132 (September 1975): 902. They arrive at a figure of $1 to $1.4 billion for schizophrenics in hospitals and $7.5 to $10 billion for those in the community as best representing the loss to society of the productive work of schizophrenics.

41. Jeanne Mueller and Michael Hopp, "A Demonstration of the Cost Benefits of Case Management Services for Discharged Mental Patients," *Psychiatric Quarterly* 55 (1983): 17–24. The authors do not provide precise cost figures for case management services but do show their calculations of the benefit-to-cost ratio to be 2.03 or 2.72, depending on the size of the case manager's caseload. Their index of benefit appears to have been the number of days the patients were not readmitted to the state hospital, at a cost of $102 per day per patient.

42. Russell Long, chairman of the U.S. Senate Finance Committee, said this during debates about future mental health funding that took place during the late 1960s and early 1970s, at a time when the Senate was getting nervous about the spiraling costs of the community mental health center system. See Cutler and Fine, "Federal Health Care Financing," pp. 27–28.

Chapter 7

1. This example comes from Steven S. Sharfstein, Richard G. Frank, and Larry G. Kessler, "State Medicaid Limitations for Mental Health Services," *Hospital & Community Psychiatry* 35 (March 1984): 213. However, the observation is so ubiquitous that I was able to find it in the top three journals on a chaotic pile in my study.

2. Gerald N. Grob, *Mental Illness and American Society, 1875–1940* (Princeton, N.J.: Princeton University Press, 1983), p. 182.

3. New York State Department of Mental Hygiene memorandum no. 68-27, quoted in Sarah Connell, "Current Issues in Law and Psychiatry: The Homeless and Deinstitutionalization" (Paper presented at the Association of the Bar of the City of New York, N.Y., 23 May 1983), p. 2. Connell was New York City regional director, New York State Office of Mental Health, at the time.

4. Hugh G. Lafave, Alex Stewart, and Frederic Grunberg, "Community Care of the Mentally Ill: Implementation of the Saskatchewan Plan," *Community Mental Health Journal* 4 (February 1968): 39.

5. Alvin M. Mesnikoff, personal interview, 28 April 1986. In the 1970s, Mesnikoff was Sarah Connell's predecessor as New York City regional director, New York State Office of Mental Health.

6. Alvin M. Mesnikoff, "From Restraint to Community Care: An Intersection of

Historical Trends" (Revised version of a paper presented at APA New York State District Branches Annual Meeting, New York, N.Y., 21 November 1969).

7. Robert Stevens and Rosemary Stevens, *Welfare Medicine in America: A Case Study of Medicaid* (New York: Free Press, 1974), p. 51.

8. Jonathan O. Cole, George Gardos, and Michael Nelson, "Alternatives to Chronic Hospitalization—The Boston State Hospital Experience," in *Alternatives to Mental Hospital Treatment,* ed. Leonard I. Stein and Mary Ann Test (New York: Plenum, 1978), p. 209.

9. Ibid., p. 221. The authors acknowledge that their numbers are vague and imprecise.

10. Cited by Carol A. B. Warren, "New Forms of Social Control: The Myth of Deinstitutionalization," *American Behavioral Scientist* 24 (1981): 727.

11. Elizabeth W. Markson, "After Deinstitutionalization, What?" *Journal of Geriatric Psychiatry* 18 (1985): 43–44.

12. William R. Shadish, Jr., and Richard R. Bootzin, "Nursing Homes and Chronic Mental Patients," *Schizophrenia Bulletin* 7 (1981): 489–90.

13. Earl S. Pollack and Carl A. Taube, "Trends and Projections in State Hospital Use," in *The Future Role of the State Hospital,* ed. Jack Zusman and Elmer F. Bertsch (Lexington, Mass.: Lexington Books, 1975), pp. 50–53.

14. U.S. General Accounting Office, *Returning the Mentally Disabled to the Community: Government Needs to Do More* (Washington, D.C.: U.S. Government Printing Office, 1977), pp. 10–11.

15. Ibid., p. 16.

16. Robert Castel, Françoise Castel, and Anne Lovell, *The Psychiatric Society,* trans. Arthur Goldhammer (New York: Columbia University Press, 1982), p. 95.

17. Andrew Scull, "Deinstitutionalization and Public Policy," *Social Science and Medicine* 20 (1985): 548.

18. Andrew Scull, "A New Trade in Lunacy: The Recommodification of the Mental Patient," *American Behavioral Scientist* 24 (1981): 745. Scull used the 1977 GAO report *Returning the Mentally Disabled to the Community: Government Needs to Do More* as his source for these reports.

19. Castel, Castel, and Lovell, *The Psychiatric Society,* p. 91.

20. A senior consultant, New York City Department of Mental Health, Mental Retardation, and Alcoholism Services, personal communication, 24 March 1986. I am not the first person who has tried and failed to find out how many patients are housed in adult homes. Kenneth Minkoff tried but found no counts had been taken, according to his otherwise comprehensive study, "A Map of Chronic Mental Patients," in *The Chronic Mental Patient,* ed. John A. Talbott (Washington, D.C.: American Psychiatric Association, 1978), p. 19. I wonder if this is not at least part of the explanation for the fact that according to E. Fuller Torrey, NIMH cannot account for the whereabouts of some 58 percent of adult schizophrenics in the United States. See Torrey, *Nowhere to Go: The Tragic Odyssey of the Homeless Mentally Ill* (New York: Harper & Row, 1988), pp. 34–35.

21. Howard H. Goldman, Antoinette Gattozzi, and Carl A. Taube, "Defining and

Counting the Chronically Mentally Ill," *Hospital & Community Psychiatry* 32 (January 1981): 24–26.

22. Robert M. Emerson, E. Burke, Jr., and Linda L. Shaw, "Economics and Enterprise in Board and Care Homes for the Mentally Ill," *American Behavioral Scientist* 24 (1981): 776–84.

23. Scull, "Deinstitutionalization and Public Policy," p. 548.

24. *New York Times,* 28 August 1979, p. II, 3; 21 October 1982, p. 21; 15 July 1985, p. II, 3.

25. New York City Council Subcommittee on Adult Homes, "The Adult Home Industry: A Preliminary Report" (New York, n.d., Unpublished); this report was probably written in 1975. In *The Psychiatric Society,* Castel, Castel, and Lovell report that the gigantic national chain of nursing homes known as Beverly Enterprises opened thirty-eight board-and-care homes in a single year and saw profits of 550 percent almost immediately (p. 91). Recently, the *New York Times* (7 January 1989, p. I, 37) reported that Beverly Enterprises had overextended itself and was in considerable financial trouble.

26. Stevens and Stevens, *Welfare Medicine in America,* p. 139.

27. Bruce C. Vladeck, *Unloving Care: The Nursing Home Tragedy* (New York: Basic Books, 1980), p. 87.

28. Mary Adelaide Mendelson, *Tender Loving Greed* (New York: Vintage, 1975), p. 37.

29. Ibid., pp. 30–31. Also, U.S. Congress, House, Committee on Interstate and Foreign Commerce, *Nursing Home Abuses, Hearings before the Congressional Subcommittee on Oversight and Investigations,* 95th Cong., 1st sess., 1977, pp. 122–26, 133–40.

30. Mendelson, *Tender Loving Greed,* p. 7. See also Vladeck, *Unloving Care,* p. 87; and Claire Townsend, *Old Age: The Last Segregation* (New York: Grossman, 1971), pp. 218–19.

31. Mendelson, *Tender Loving Greed,* pp. 37–38. The political battles waged over Medicare and Medicaid were chronicled by Richard Harris in *A Sacred Trust* (New York: New American Library, 1966).

32. Vladeck, *Unloving Care,* pp. 176–80; Mendelson, *Tender Loving Greed,* pp. 43–52; Townsend, *Old Age,* pp. 55–132; and U.S. Congress, *Nursing Home Abuses,* especially pp. 115, 133.

33. Mendelson, *Tender Loving Greed,* pp. 177–79; U.S. Congress, *Nursing Home Abuses,* p. 140.

34. Vladeck, *Unloving Care,* p. 18.

35. Cole, Gardos, and Nelson, "Alternatives to Chronic Hospitalization," p. 219.

36. Nancy Scheper-Hughes, " 'Mental' in 'Southie': Individual, Family, and Community Responses to Psychosis in South Boston," *Culture, Medicine, and Psychiatry* 11 (1987): 74.

37. U.S. Congress, Senate Special Committee on Aging, "Medicine and Aging: An Assessment of Opportunities and Neglect." Report of a hearing before the Special Committee on Aging, U.S. Senate, 94th Cong., 2d sess., Washington, D.C., 13 October 1976.

38. Warren, "New Forms of Social Control," p. 726. Warren points out that Andrew Scull has also made this point, in his book *Decarceration* (Englewood Cliffs, N.J.: Prentice-Hall, 1977), p. 120; and he has expanded on it in his 1981 article, "A New Trade in Lunacy." See also Castel, Castel, and Lovell, *The Psychiatric Society*, p. 89.

39. A good example of this debate can be found in a series of articles published in *Schizophrenia Bulletin* in 1981. William R. Shadish, Jr., and Richard R. Bootzin published "Nursing Homes and Chronic Mental Patients" (7: 488–98), which was challenged in the next issue by Paul J. Carling, in an article called "Nursing Homes and Chronic Mental Patients: A Second Opinion" (7: 574–79). Shadish and Bootzin followed this with a rebuttal, "Long-term Community Care: Mental Health Policy in the Face of Reality" (7: 580–85). The argument centered on the question of whether we should use the nursing home as part of creative policy initiatives, since the patients are already there (Shadish and Bootzin), or whether to do so is to capitulate to an unacceptable status quo caused by the indiscriminate dumping of unwanted individuals (Carling). It is perhaps of interest that the former are academics and the latter a state mental health official.

40. For an extensive discussion of the problems inherent in the attempt to make substantial political change in psychiatric systems, see *Psychiatry Inside Out: Selected Writings of Franco Basaglia*, ed. Nancy Scheper-Hughes and Anne M. Lovell, trans. Anne M. Lovell and Teresa Shtob (New York: Columbia University Press, 1987).

41. Castel, Castel, and Lovell, *The Psychiatric Society*, p. 21. Another dramatic example of employee resistance to the perceived threat of deinstitutionalization can be found in a short book commissioned from a journalist by American Federation of State, County and Municipal Employees (AFSCME), the enormous union that represents the bulk of public sector civil servants. This book has enjoyed considerable circulation, judging from the number of bibliographies it shows up on: Henry Santiestevan, *Deinstitutionalization: Out of Their Beds and into the Streets* (Washington, D.C.: AFSCME, 1979).

42. Robert Reich and Lloyd Siegel, "Psychiatry under Siege: The Chronically Mentally Ill Shuffle to Oblivion," *Psychiatric Annals* 3 (1973): 55. The use of readmission statistics as an index of a program's success is ubiquitous. The top two articles on a random pile in my office both referred to admission rates in their first paragraphs: see Stuart A. Kirk, "Effectiveness of Community Services for Discharged Mental Hospital Patients," *American Journal of Orthopsychiatry* 46 (1974): 646; and William Kohen and Gordon L. Paul, "Current Trends and Recommended Changes in Extended-Care Placement of Mental Patients: The Illinois System as a Case in Point," *Schizophrenia Bulletin* 2 (1976): 575.

43. The figures come from an NIMH Statistical Note and were cited in Castel, Castel, and Lovell, *The Psychiatric Society*, pp. 107–8.

44. Ernest Gruenberg, speaking at an international conference in 1976, quoted in Alan D. Miller, "Deinstitutionalization in Retrospect," *Psychiatric Quarterly* 57 (1985): 161.

277

45. Stein and Test, "Introduction," *Alternatives to Mental Hospital Treatment,* ed. Stein and Test, p. vi.

46. David K. Reynolds and Norman L. Farberow, *Endangered Hope: Experiences in Psychiatric Aftercare Facilities* (Berkeley, Calif.: University of California Press, 1977), p. 67.

47. Priscilla Allen, "A Consumer's View of California's Mental Health Care System," *Psychiatric Quarterly* 48 (1974): pp. 5–6.

48. The point that merely to leave the institution does not constitute deinstitutionaliza-tion is made in at least two comments on the phenomenon: one was written by Leopold Bellak, in his introduction to a book he edited, *A Concise Handbook of Community Psychiatry and Community Mental Health* (New York: Grune & Strat-ton, 1974), p. 6; and the other was by Paul R. Dokecki, Barbara J. Anderson, and Philip S. Strain, "Stigmatization and Labeling," in *Deinstitutionalization: Program and Policy Development,* ed. James L. Paul, Donald J. Stedman, and G. Ronald Neufeld (Syracuse, N.Y.: Syracuse University Press, 1977), p. 48. The second book concerns deinstitutionalization specifically of the mentally retarded.

49. Benjamin M. Braginsky, Dorothea D. Braginsky, and Kenneth Ring, *Methods of Madness: The Mental Hospital as a Last Resort* (New York: Holt, Rinehart & Winston, 1969), p. 170.

50. Accountants for the Public Interest, *The Transfer of People Versus Dollars: Intergov-ernmental Financing for Mental Health Services in the State of New York* (New York: API, 1983), pp. 38–39.

51. Alvin M. Mesnikoff, quoted in "A Seminar Report: The Lost Chronic Mental Patient: A Positive Approach to Community Care," *Hospital & Community Psychi-atry* 26 (1975): 28.

Chapter 8

1. *New York Times,* 21 December 1988, p. B1.

2. Two similar studies of homelessness in nine and eight U.S. cities, respectively, were conducted at roughly the same time, and report similar, and even some identical, findings: National Coalition for the Homeless, *The Homeless and the Economic Recovery* (New York: NCH, November 1983); and Dan Salerno, Kim Hopper, and Ellen Baxter, *Hardship in the Heartland: Homelessness in Eight U.S. Cities* (New York: Community Service Society, 1984). Four cities (Denver, Chicago, Cleveland, and Detroit) were surveyed by both.

3. Marjorie Hope and James Young, "The Politics of Displacement: Sinking into Homelessness," in Jon Erickson and Charles Wilhelm, eds., *Housing the Homeless* (New Brunswick, N.J.: Center for Urban Policy, 1986), p. 107. This article also appeared in *Commonweal,* 15 June 1984, pp. 368–71.

4. *New York Times,* 19 December 1988, p. A1.
5. Ibid.
6. Raymond J. Struyk, John A. Tuccillo, and James P. Zais, "Housing and Community Development," in *The Reagan Experiment,* ed. John L. Palmer and Isabel V. Sawhill (Washington, D.C.: Urban Institute Press, 1982), p. 414 and chart on p. 415.
7. Ibid., p. 406.
8. Ibid., p. 417.
9. Chester Hartman, "The Housing Part of the Homeless Problem," in *The Mental Health Needs of Homeless Persons,* ed. Ellen L. Bassuk (San Francisco, Calif.: Jossey-Bass, 1986), p. 76.
10. Ibid. He points out that 70 percent of this deduction goes to people earning over $30,000 per year.
11. Struyk, Tuccillo, and Zais, "Housing and Community Development," p. 403. The authors comment that "one must also include various tax expenditures to get an accurate picture of federal budget outlays . . . even if all outlays for housing assistance and community development were directed to lower-income households, federal housing policy—as reflected in expenditures—would have to be labeled as one predominantly benefiting middle- and higher-income families" (p. 403). The total of all mortgage interest deducted in 1981 by homeowners who occupied their own homes was $20,145,000,000; and property taxes deducted in the same way totaled $9,125,000,000. The total outlay for all subsidized housing programs for fiscal year 1981 was $5,746,000,000 (statistics taken from chart, p. 402).
12. Salerno, Hopper, and Baxter, *Hardship in the Heartland,* p. 7.
13. Women's City Club of New York, *"With Love and Affection": A Study of Building Abandonment* (New York, 1977), p. 1.
14. Ibid., p. 2.
15. Ibid.
16. Joan Hatch Shapiro, *Communities of the Alone* (New York: Association Press, 1971), pp. 41–42.
17. U.S. Senate, Special Committee on Aging, *Single Room Occupancy: A Need for National Concern. An Information Paper* (Washington, D.C.: U.S. Government Printing Office, 1978), pp. 2–3.
18. Ibid.
19. Ibid., p. 4.
20. Ibid.
21. Ibid., pp. iv–v.
22. Shapiro, *Communities,* p. 136.
23. City of New York, Human Resources Administration, *The Changing Face of New York City's SRO's: A Profile of Residents and Housing* (New York: The Administration, October 1987), pp. 12–15.
24. Ibid.
25. *New York Times,* 25 July 1982, sec. 4, p. 6.

26. U.S. Senate, Special Committee on Aging, *Single Room Occupancy*, p. 4.

27. Shapiro, *Communities*, p. 137.

28. Howard M. Bahr, *Skid Row: An Introduction to Disaffiliation* (New York: Oxford University Press, 1973), pp. 37–38.

29. National Coalition for the Homeless, *The Homeless and the Economic Recovery*, and Salerno, Hopper, and Baxter, *Hardship in the Heartland*, both provide these statistics.

30. Manhattan Borough President's Task Force on Housing for Homeless Families, *A Shelter Is Not a Home* (New York: The Task Force, March 1987), p. 38.

31. Hope and Young, "The Politics of Displacement," p. 109.

32. Ibid. Similar observations are made in many sources, including National Coalition for the Homeless, *The Homeless and the Economic Recovery*, and Manhattan Borough President's Task Force, *A Shelter Is Not a Home*, p. 38.

33. Manhattan Borough President's Task Force, *A Shelter Is Not a Home*, pp. 41–43.

34. Ibid., pp. 31–32.

35. Salerno, Hopper, and Baxter, *Hardship in the Heartland*, p. 24. Ironically, one of the most public critics of the people who are alarmed about doubled-up families has been New York City's former mayor Edward Koch, who apparently spent many years of his own youth in a doubled-up family after his father's business failed during the Great Depression. See Jack Newfield and Wayne Barrett, *City for Sale: Ed Koch and the Betrayal of New York* (New York: Harper & Row, 1988), p. 105.

36. Ibid., pp. 91–94 (Cleveland) and pp. 111–17 (Detroit). See also National Coalition for the Homeless, *The Homeless and the Economic Recovery*, which details similar findings.

37. Salerno, Hopper, and Baxter, *Hardship in the Heartland*, pp. 71–81. See also National Coalition for the Homeless, *The Homeless and the Economic Recovery*, p. 2.

38. Salerno, Hopper, and Baxter, p. 146 (Tulsa), p. 157 (Milwaukee), and pp. 134–39 (Denver). National Coalition for the Homeless, p. 2, also looked at Denver.

39. Salerno, Hopper, and Baxter, p. ii.

40. *New York Times*, 29 January 1989, sec. 4, p. 5. The poll was conducted nationwide by the *Times* and CBS News.

41. Manhattan Borough President's Task Force, *A Shelter Is Not a Home*, p. 6.

42. Salerno, Hopper, and Baxter, *Hardship in the Heartland*, p. 176.

43. U.S. Department of Housing and Urban Development, *A Report to the Secretary on the Homeless and Emergency Shelters* (May 1, 1984), reprinted in *Housing the Homeless*, ed. Erickson and Wilhelm, p. 139.

44. This point is made quite openly by a staunch supporter of the HUD report. See S. Anna Kondratas, "A Strategy for Helping America's Homeless," in *Helping the Homeless*, ed. Erickson and Wilhelm, p. 148. This article also appeared in *The Heritage Foundation Backgrounder* 431 (6 May 1985): 3–6.

45. Hartman, "The Housing Part," p. 77.

46. Quoted in Kondratas, "A Strategy for Helping America's Homeless," in *Helping the Homeless*, ed. Erickson and Wilhelm, p. 146.

47. National Coalition for the Homeless, *The Homeless and the Economic Recovery,* p. 2.

48. This account was taken from an interview I did on 16 January 1986 with a social worker who has since asked, with some regret, to remain anonymous. He believes that his current work as an advocate on the policymaking level would be impossible if he were to be exposed as someone who talks about what he knows of the mental health system. "You're either one of them or they won't return your calls and you become ineffective," he points out. I try to work in the same system, so I know he is correct; but still, it seems a sad comment on the *mental health* system, of all things, if it cannot tolerate even this much exposure of the ways it conducts its business. Apparently, all systems are, first and foremost, essentially political.

49. Ibid.

50. Mark J. Stern, "The Emergence of the Homeless as a Public Problem," in *Housing the Homeless,* ed. Erickson and Wilhelm, p. 116. This article can also be found in *Social Service Review* 58 (1984): 291–301.

51. Marvin W. Kahn et al., "Psychopathology of the Streets: Psychological Assessment of the Homeless," *Professional Psychology: Research and Practice* 18 (1987): 581; see table 1, summarizing the twelve major studies, all of which were done between 1978 and 1985. The low percentage was obtained in a 1985 study done in Ohio by Dee Roth, Gerald J. Bean, Jr., and Pamela S. Hyde, "Homelessness and Mental Health Policy: Developing an Appropriate Role for the 1980s," *Community Mental Health Journal* 22 (1986): 203–14; the high one comes from New York City, and was reported in a study done in 1983 by Frank R. Lipton, Albert Sabatini, and Steven E. Katz, "Down and Out in the City: The Homeless Mentally Ill," *Hospital & Community Psychiatry* 34 (1983): 817–21.

52. See Marjorie Hope and James Young, *The Faces of Homelessness* (Lexington, Mass.: Lexington Books, 1986), p. 20. The authors report their telephone discussion with Ellen L. Bassuk, whose 1983 study found 40 percent of a shelter's clients to be psychotic, 29 percent chronically alcoholic, and 21 percent with personality disorders. The article in the popular press added these percentages and came up with a total of 90 percent, claiming that to be the rate at which shelter clients were found to have mental illness. As Bassuk pointed out to Hope and Young, while it is probable that a majority of shelter clients are mentally ill, definitional problems abound that cannot be buried in a sweeping total that equates psychosis with personality disorder. The original article in question is Ellen L. Bassuk, Lenore Rubin, and Alison Lauriat, "Is Homelessness a Mental Health Problem?" *American Journal of Psychiatry* 141 (1984): 1546–50.

53. For an anecdotal study, see Robert Reich and Lloyd Siegel, "The Emergence of the Bowery as a Psychiatric Dumping Ground," *Psychiatric Quarterly* 50 (1978): 191–201. A recent study tries hard to examine all the other studies and outdo them for precision; this study is highly critical of others' overdependence on the shelters and gets caught up in the question of how researchers define *psychiatric hospitalization.* See Lillian Gelberg, Lawrence S. Linn, and Barbara D. Leake, "Mental

Health, Alcohol and Drug Use, and Criminal History among Homeless Adults," *American Journal of Psychiatry* 145 (1988): 191–96.

54. Leona L. Bachrach et al., "The Homeless Mentally Ill in Tucson: Implications of Early Findings," *American Journal of Psychiatry* 145 (1988): 112–13.

55. Marjorie J. Robertson, "Mental Disorder among Homeless Persons in the United States: An Overview of Recent Empirical Literature," *Administration in Mental Health* 14 (1986): 14–27.

56. David A. Snow et al., "The Myth of Pervasive Mental Illness among the Homeless," *Social Problems* 33 (1986): 407–23.

57. The actual results of the Ohio study are found in Roth, Bean, and Hyde, "Homelessness and Mental Health Policy," pp. 203–14. The article that looks specifically at the relationship between mental illness and homelessness is Gerald J. Bean, Jr., Mary E. Stefl, and Steven R. Howe, "Mental Health and Homelessness: Issues and Findings," *Social Work* 32 (1987): 411–16.

58. F. Stevens Redburn and Terry F. Buss, *Responding to America's Homeless: Public Policy Alternatives* (New York: Praeger, 1986), p. 81. The authors were, respectively, a senior analyst at HUD and director of the Center for Urban Studies at Youngstown State University.

59. See Brian Kates, *The Murder of a Shopping Bag Lady* (New York: Harcourt Brace Jovanovich, 1985).

60. Roth, Bean, and Hyde, "Homelessness and Mental Health Policy." This study, which identified what the researchers termed a "relatively low" prevalence of mental illness among the homeless, was sponsored by the Ohio Department of Mental Health, which specifically wanted to know if the mentally ill homeless were being served.

61. Reich and Siegel, "The Emergence of the Bowery," p. 192. This article was written in 1978 and cites an empirical study, "Report on Men Housed for One Night on the Bowery," done in 1976 by the Men's Shelter Study Group in New York City. The study found that 8 percent of the city shelter clients had been discharged there by state hospitals. Ellen Baxter and Kim Hopper's highly-publicized study was *Private Lives/Public Spaces: Homeless Adults on the Streets of New York City* (New York: Community Service Society, 1981).

62. Paul S. Appelbaum, "The Disability System in Disarray," *Hospital & Community Psychiatry* 34 (1983): 783.

63. Ibid. See also Ellen Baxter and Kim Hopper, "Shelter and Housing for the Homeless Mentally Ill," in *The Homeless Mentally Ill*, ed. H. Richard Lamb (Washington, D.C.: American Psychiatric Association, 1984), p. 132. Salerno, Hopper, and Baxter, in *Hardship in the Heartland*, report that by the end of 1983 the federal government had thrown over half a million disabled people off Social Security (p. 11).

64. Paul S. Appelbaum, "Housing for the Mentally Ill: An Unexpected Outcome of a Class-Action Suit against SSA," *Hospital & Community Psychiatry* 39 (1988): 479–80. The case is known as *City of New York v. Heckler.*

65. Madeleine R. Stoner, "The Plight of Homeless Women," in *Housing the Homeless,* ed. Erickson and Wilhelm, p. 279.
66. Baxter and Hopper, "Shelter and Housing," p. 117.
67. Ibid., p. 116.
68. Salerno, Hopper, and Baxter, *Hardship in the Heartland,* p. 54.
69. See Baxter and Hopper, "Shelter and Housing," p. 117. I have corrected their calculation of the percentage of patients found to be in need of involuntary hospitalization.
70. Pamela J. Fischer et al., "Mental Health and Social Characteristics of the Homeless: A Survey of Mission Users," *American Journal of Public Health* 76 (1986): 519. This epidemiological study of the homeless is more responsible and informative than most.
71. Patricia Cayo Sexton, "The Life of the Homeless," in *Housing the Homeless,* ed. Erickson and Wilhelm, pp. 78–81. This article also appeared in *Dissent* 30 (1983): 79–84.
72. *New York Times,* 10 December 1983.
73. Thomas J. Main, "The Homeless of New York," *Public Interest* 72 (1983): 24.

Chapter 9

1. Judith Godwin Rabkin, "Criminal Behavior of Discharged Mental Patients: A Critical Appraisal of the Research," *Psychological Bulletin* 86 (1979): 2.
2. H. Richard Lamb, "Keeping the Mentally Ill Out of Jail," *Hospital & Community Psychiatry* 35 (1984): 529.
3. Ibid.
4. Rabkin, "Criminal Behavior," p. 2.
5. For example, "It is said that many of the mentally ill who would formerly have been treated in mental hospitals are being forced into the jail and prison system by changes in commitment laws, shortages of hospital beds, deinstitutionalization." H. Richard Lamb and Robert W. Grant, "The Mentally Ill in an Urban County Jail," *Archives of General Psychiatry* 39 (1982): 21.
6. The percentage of Americans in prison has more than doubled since 1970, even though the crime rate has periodically fallen since then, and the U.S. Justice Department continues to report substantial increases in the prisoner population nationwide—6.7 percent, for example, between April 1987 and April 1988 alone. *New York Times,* 25 April 1988, p. A1.
7. *New York Times,* 23 December 1954, p. 26.
8. John Maurice Grimes, *Institutional Care of Mental Patients in the United States* (Chicago: J. M. Grimes, 1934; reprint, New York: Arno, 1980), p. 96. Emphasis added.

9. Jails are used to hold "detainees," people charged with crimes and awaiting either trial or sentencing; prisons are used for the serving of sentences. The distinction is more significant than one might suspect, if only because we know a lot more in general about prisons than we do about jails, yet it is jails that are assumed to contain large numbers of disaffiliated people, including the mentally ill.

10. Karl Menninger, *The Crime of Punishment* (New York: Viking, 1968), p. 45. Emphasis in the original.

11. This condition is called erotomania. The 1971 Clint Eastwood movie *Play Misty for Me* is about just such a relationship, one in which a man is unwittingly the object of a deluded woman's obsessive interest.

12. Robert Liss and Allen Frances, "Court-Mandated Treatment: Dilemmas for Hospital Psychiatry," *American Journal of Psychiatry* 132 (1975): 924.

13. Ibid., pp. 925–26.

14. Ibid., pp. 924–25. The authors particularly point to the presence of homosexual threats and temptations, which are extraordinarily common in jail, as especially disorganizing for this group.

15. Freda Adler, "Jails as a Repository for Former Mental Patients," *International Journal of Offender Therapy and Comparative Criminology* 30 (1986): 228.

16. This material is reviewed most comprehensively by Judith Godwin Rabkin in "Criminal Behavior of Discharged Mental Patients: A Critical Appraisal of the Research," *Psychological Bulletin* 86 (1979): 9–10.

17. Carl I. Cohen, "Crime among Mental Patients—A Critical Analysis," *Psychiatric Quarterly* 52 (1980): 104. The rule of thumb is also mentioned by Henry J. Steadman et al., in "The Impact of State Mental Hospitalization on United States Prison Populations, 1968–1978," *Journal of Criminal Law and Criminology* 75 (1984): 474. Steadman et al. are among the many scholars who mourn the lost opportunity to count the number of mentally ill offenders before deinstitutionalization (p. 477).

18. Richard Smith, "How Many Mentally Abnormal Prisoners?" *British Medical Journal* 288 (28 January 1984): 309.

19. Cohen, "Crime among Mental Patients," p. 103.

20. Ibid., p. 106.

21. The consensus seems to be that the three early studies are these: Ashley (1922), Pollock (1938), and Cohen and Freeman (1945). The middle group includes Brill and Malzberg (1962), Rappeport and Lassen (1965, 1966), Giovannoni and Gurel (1967); and the late group includes Zitrin et al. (1976), Durbin et al. (1977), Steadman et al. (1977), and Sosowsky (1978). For more complete bibliographic information and a detailed review of the studies and their findings, see Rabkin, "Criminal Behavior."

22. Rabkin, "Criminal Behavior," p. 25.

23. Frederic Grunberg, Burton I. Klinger, and Barbara Grumet, "Homicide and Deinstitutionalization of the Mentally Ill," *American Journal of Psychiatry* 134 (1977): 687.

24. Henry J. Steadman, Joseph J. Cocozza, and Mary Evans Melick, "Explaining the

Arrest Rate among Mental Patients: The Changing Clientele of State Hospitals," *American Journal of Psychiatry* 135 (1978): 819.

25. Richard Smith, "How Many," p. 309, alludes to this problem.

26. Henry J. Steadman et al., "A Survey of Mental Disability among State Prison Inmates," *Hospital & Community Psychiatry* 38 (1987): 1088; see table 1.

27. Ibid., p. 1089, table 2.

28. Lamb and Grant, "Urban County Jail," p. 19.

29. Ibid., p. 18. Another widely read study offered similarly distracting conclusions by emphasizing that 22 percent of the 545 inmates evaluated in Denver County Jail over one year were diagnosed as psychotic. This sounds alarming until one realizes the psychotic inmates made up only .94 percent of the whole jail population for that year. See Glenn E. Swank and Darryl Winer, "Occurrence of Psychiatric Disorder in a County Jail Population," *American Journal of Psychiatry* 133 (1976): 1331–33.

30. Lamb and Grant, "Urban County Jail," p. 21.

31. Susan Seidman and I completed this study, with the help of Philip Alcabes, at that time our staff epidemiologist. Although we tried to be scientific about it, Rikers is so huge and such an enormous undertaking is involved in keeping track of things that our sample may not have been complete: we reviewed 78 cases that had been evaluated during one week in July 1988, as well as the medical records of 25 inmates who had not been referred for mental health evaluation. In the final tally, we discarded eight cases from consideration because both Susan Seidman and I disagreed with the recorded diagnosis, based on our reading of the record. This study was carried out under the auspices of Montefiore Medical Center Rikers Island Health Service, a component of Correctional Health Services, New York City Department of Health.

32. For the Cook County report, I used a preliminary unpublished report, dated June 1986, titled "The Prevalence of Mental Illness for Jail Detainees at the Cook County Correctional Facility." No name appears on the report, and although the last paragraph mentions an upcoming final report, I have not come across one. For the national data see the section on epidemiology in the *Comprehensive Textbook of Psychiatry*, 4th ed., vol. 1, ed. Harold I. Kaplan and Benjamin J. Sadock (Baltimore: Williams & Wilkins, 1985), pp. 309–11.

33. These findings are amply supported by two studies, one done in Louisiana and the other in St. Louis, Missouri. The first is presented by Patricia B. Sutker and Charles E. Moan in "A Psychosocial Description of Penitentiary Inmates," *Archives of General Psychiatry* 29 (1973): 663–67; and the second is described in several articles, one of which is Samuel B. Guze, Robert A. Woodruff, Jr., and Paula J. Clayton, "Psychiatric Disorders and Criminality," *Journal of the American Medical Association* 227 (11 February 1974): 641–42.

34. Arthur J. Lurigio and Dan A. Lewis, "The Criminal Mental Patient: A Descriptive Analysis and Suggestions for Future Research," *Criminal Justice and Behavior* 14 (1987): 282.

35. I am grateful, as always, to Willie Martin for his matchless and insightful observations. Personal communication, 22 March 1989.

36. Robert Brennan, personal communication, 27 March 1989. Brennan is warden of Rose M. Singer Center, Rikers Island, New York. Although I may not have conveyed it adequately in the text, Warden Brennan is one of many corrections personnel I have met whose intelligence, keen observation, and psychological sophistication belie all the stereotypes of uniformed corrections personnel as dumb and uneducated.

37. Judith Godwin Rabkin and Arthur Zitrin, "Antisocial Behavior of Discharged Mental Patients: Research Findings and Policy Implications," in *Psychiatric Patient Rights and Patient Advocacy,* ed. Bernard L. Bloom and Shirley J. Asher (New York: Human Sciences Press, 1982), p. 166.

38. No one knows the origin of the term, although creative speculation abounds; for example, that centuries ago, a mean judge named Bing doled out extremely harsh sentences and is memorialized accordingly. Another explanation: the inmates thought it up.

39. Norval Morris, *Madness and the Criminal Law* (Chicago: University of Chicago Press, 1982), p. 31.

40. Darold A. Treffert, "Dying with Their Rights On," *American Journal of Psychiatry* 130 (1973): 1041.

41. Stephen J. Morse, "A Preference for Liberty: The Case against Involuntary Commitment of the Mentally Ill Disordered," in *The Court of Last Resort,* ed. Carol A. B. Warren (Chicago: University of Chicago Press, 1982), p. 70.

42. Ibid., p. 71. Emphasis in the original.

43. Marc F. Abramson, "The Criminalization of Mentally Disordered Behavior: Possible Side-Effect of a New Mental Health Law," *Hospital & Community Psychiatry* 23 (1972): 103. This article has been widely quoted since it first appeared.

44. Ibid.

45. For two examples, see Lamb and Grant, "Urban County Jail," p. 21; or Bernadette M. M. Pelissier, "Mental Health Research in the Federal Bureau of Prisons: Current Trends and Future Developments," *Psychiatric Annals* 18 (1988): 703.

46. Jack Zusman, "The Need for Intervention: The Reason for State Control of the Mentally Disordered," in *The Court of Last Resort,* ed. Warren, p. 133.

Chapter 10

1. David Mechanic, "Editor's Notes," in *Improving Mental Health Services: What the Social Sciences Can Tell Us,* ed. David Mechanic, *New Directions for Mental Health Services* no. 36 (San Francisco: Jossey-Bass, 1987), p. 1.

2. William Buchan, *Domestic Medicine* (Philadelphia: Printed by John Dunlap for R. Aitken, 1772), quoted in Norman Dain, *Concepts of Insanity in the United States, 1789–1865* (New Brunswick, N.J.: Rutgers University Press, 1964), p. 39.

3. See Albert Deutsch, *The Mentally Ill in America,* 2d ed., rev. (New York: Columbia

University Press, 1949), p. 209, for Kirkbride's twenty-six rules governing the capital construction of a moral treatment facility.

4. Isaac Ray, *A Treatise on the Medical Jurisprudence of Insanity* (Boston: 1838; reprint, Cambridge, Mass.: Belknap Press of Harvard University Press, 1962), p. 11.

5. Gerald Grob, *Mental Institutions in America: Social Policy to 1875* (New York: Free Press, 1973), p. 68.

6. Constance M. McGovern, *Masters of Madness: Social Origins of the American Psychiatric Profession* (Hanover, N.H.: University Press of New England, 1985), p. 171.

7. Donald J. Dellario and William A. Anthony, "On the Relative Effectiveness of Institutional and Alternative Placement for the Psychiatrically Disabled," *Journal of Social Issues* 37 (1981): 21–33.

8. The idea that high dropout rates suggest the target population is not being reached, rather than the more usual explanation that the population is resistant, is mentioned by Leonard I. Stein and Mary Ann Test in "The Clinical Rationale for Community Treatment: A Review of the Literature," in *Alternatives to Mental Hospital Treatment,* ed. Leonard I. Stein and Mary Ann Test (New York: Plenum, 1978), p. 17.

9. Abbott S. Weinstein, "The Mythical Readmissions Explosion," *American Journal of Psychiatry* 140 (1983): 332–35. In another example, Carol L. M. Caton et al. studied 119 chronic patients over time and found that regardless of where they were living, 14 percent had been rehospitalized within one month, 26 percent within 120 days, and 58 percent within one year. See Caton et al., "Rehospitalization in Chronic Schizophrenia," *Journal of Nervous and Mental Disease* 173 (1985): 139–48.

10. *"No* hospitalization experiments have demonstrated that severely ill patients can be maintained in the community." Stein and Test, "Clinical Rationale," p. 17. Emphasis in the original.

11. See, for example, Alan S. Bellack and Kim T. Mueser, "A Comprehensive Treatment Program for Schizophrenia and Chronic Mental Illness," *Community Mental Health Journal* 22 (1986), especially pp. 179–85, where the authors list all the elements they view as vital for such a program.

12. R. Jay Turner, "Jobs and Schizophrenia," *Social Policy* 8 (1977): 39.

13. I am indebted to Catherine Donnell for this information, which she obtained on a visit to Cuba in the early 1980s.

14. I used to work with a very talented psychiatrist who said of schizophrenics that what they need is "cigarettes, coffee, and Thorazine—in that order." Someone once told me they had seen a journal article in which another psychiatrist speculated that caffeine and nicotine somehow counteract the sedative effects of psychotropic medications, and that is why the patients partake of both as much as they do. This makes sense to me, so I looked for the article, but I have not found it.

15. Susan Sheehan, *Is There No Place on Earth for Me?* (Boston: Houghton Mifflin, 1982); see pp. 185–92. Sylvia's reminiscences about her favorite therapist appear on pp. 219 and 333.

16. Joint Commission on Mental Illness and Health, *Action for Mental Health* (New York: Basic Books, 1961; reprint, New York: Arno, 1980), p. 53. Emphasis in the original.

17. Robert Castel, Françoise Castel, and Anne Lovell, *The Psychiatric Society,* trans. Arthur Goldhammer (New York: Columbia University Press, 1982), p. 115.

18. Mary Ann Test mentioned this problem and the need for the field to promote "philosophical and behavioral departures by clinicians" in her article, "Effective Community Treatment of the Chronically Mentally Ill: What Is Necessary?" *Journal of Social Issues* 37 (1981): 83.

19. Empirical studies of the day hospital modality include the well-known work of Marvin I. Herz, Jean Endicott, and Robert L. Spitzer, described in "Brief Hospitalization: A Two-Year Follow-Up," *American Journal of Psychiatry* 134 (1977): 502–7. See also Greg Wilkinson, "Day Care for Patients with Psychiatric Disorders," *British Medical Journal* 288 (1984): 1710–12; and J. K. Wing and Rolf Olsen, eds., *Community Care for the Mentally Disabled* (New York: Oxford University Press, 1979), for their accounts of Britain's success with the day treatment modalities.

20. I refer, of course, to the collected works of Thomas Szasz, as well as to those that followed *The Myth of Mental Illness: Foundations of a Theory of Personal Conduct,* rev. ed. (New York: Perennial Library, 1974), including books like Benjamin M. Braginsky, Dorothea D. Braginsky, and Kenneth Ring, *Methods of Madness: The Mental Hospital as a Last Resort* (New York: Holt, Rinehart & Winston, 1969), and E. Fuller Torrey, *The Death of Psychiatry* (New York: Penguin Books, 1974)—even though this last book seems to have been disowned by its author, who subsequently wrote another book in which he disdains what he labels "the myth of mental health" and calls for all mental *health* facilities to change their names to mental *illness* facilities. The author fails to note this about-face in the later book. See E. Fuller Torrey, *Nowhere to Go: The Tragic Odyssey of the Homeless Mentally Ill* (New York: Harper & Row, 1988), especially p. 206.

21. Leona L. Bachrach, "The Challenge to Service Planning for Chronic Mental Patients," *Community Mental Health Journal* 22 (Fall 1986): 172.

22. Ronald Peterson, "What Are the Needs of Chronic Mental Patients?" in *The Chronic Mental Patient,* ed. John A. Talbott (Washington, D.C.: American Psychiatric Association, 1978), especially pp. 40–44.

23. John H. Beard, "The Rehabilitation Services of Fountain House," in *Alternatives to Mental Hospital Treatment,* ed. Stein and Test, pp. 201–8.

24. George W. Fairweather et al., *Community Life for the Mentally Ill: An Alternative to Institutional Care* (Chicago: Aldine, 1969), p. 4.

25. George W. Fairweather, "The Development, Evaluation, and Diffusion of Rehabilitative Programs: A Social Change Process," in *Alternatives to Mental Hospital Treatment,* ed. Stein and Test, pp. 299–300.

26. Ibid., p. 300.

27. For a unique look at this program, see Sue E. Estroff, *Making It Crazy: An*

Ethnography of Psychiatric Clients in an American Community (Berkeley, Calif.: University of California Press, 1981). Estroff is a cultural anthropologist who lived for two years among the staff and clients of PACT, applying the techniques of the cultural anthropologist to the special culture of the psychiatric client, as she calls them. It is a wonderful book.

28. Stein and Test, "Clinical Rationale," pp. 52–54.

29. Werner M. Mendel and Robert E. Allen, "Rescue and Rehabilitation," in *Alternatives to Mental Hospital Treatment,* ed. Stein and Test, p. 190. The authors acknowledge the limitations of the choice of an inpatient unit for their experiment but explain that the site was chosen "because the ward [was] there and available while other facilities [were] not." They also point out that their unit was expensive to run, which is not surprising, considering the richness of the professional staff; see p. 197.

30. The program is described by John E. Gudeman and Miles F. Shore, "Public Care for the Chronically Mentally Ill: A New Model," in *The New Economics and Psychiatric Care,* ed. Steven S. Sharfstein and Allan Beigel (Washington, D.C.: American Psychiatric Association Press, 1985); see especially pp. 195–200. Their observation of the distrust insurance companies have for the day hospital as a treatment modality is confirmed by William Guillette et al. in "Day Hospitalization as a Cost-Effective Alternative to Inpatient Care: A Pilot Study," *Hospital & Community Psychiatry* 29 (1978): 525–27. Guillette's article reports an effort by one insurance company and two private day hospitals to establish whether money could be saved by using day hospital, rather than inpatient, services; they found that for thirty-one patients placed in a day hospital rather than on an inpatient ward, a total of $255,000 was saved. They conclude the article by noting that since the study, the private day hospitals have closed, proving the authors' point that inadequate reimbursement of day hospitals only promotes use of inpatient facilities, which are of questionable clinical value for the chronic population and are certainly far more expensive.

31. See Paul R. Polak, "A Comprehensive System of Alternatives to Psychiatric Hospitalization," in *Alternatives to Mental Hospital Treatment,* ed. Stein and Test, pp. 115–37. I have heard that this promising program, and maybe even the whole center that sponsored it, has bit the dust since the article was written, but I cannot cite a specific source for this rumor.

32. Patricia A. Ferris and Catherine A. Marshall, "A Model Project for Families of the Chronically Mentally Ill," *Social Work* 32 (1987): 110–14.

33. National Alliance of Mental Patients pamphlet "Our Purpose, Our People, Our Promise" (Sioux Falls, n.d.).

34. J. K. Wing and G. W. Brown, *Institutionalism and Schizophrenia: A Comparative Study of Three Mental Hospitals, 1960–1968* (Cambridge, England: Cambridge University Press, 1970), pp. 192–94.

35. Leona L. Bachrach, "Overview: Model Programs for Chronic Mental Patients," *American Journal of Psychiatry* 137 (1980): 1023–31.

36. Bernard Weinman and Robert J. Kleiner, "The Impact of Community Living and Community Member Intervention on the Adjustment of the Chronic Psychotic Patient," in *Alternatives to Mental Hospital Treatment,* ed. Stein and Test, pp. 139–59.

37. New York City Department of Mental Health, Mental Retardation and Alcoholism Services, "Intensive Case Management in New York City: An Overview" (New York: The Department, August 1988, photocopied), p. 2.

38. Ibid., p. 6. Emphasis in the original.

39. Ibid.

40. This is standard practice and one of those things that everyone knows but will not admit openly—except for Vernon D. Patch, who years ago wrote an article called "Blacklisting Mental Hospital Patients," *Hospital & Community Psychiatry* 21 (1970): 269–71. Nothing has changed.

41. David Mechanic, "Alternatives to Mental Hospital Treatment: A Sociological Perspective," in *Alternatives to Mental Hospital Treatment,* ed. Stein and Test, p. 316.

42. See New York State Governor's Select Commission on the Future of the State–Local Mental Health System, *Final Report* (Albany, N.Y.: The Commission, 1984).

43. Ellen L. Bassuk, "The Homelessness Problem," *Scientific American* 251 (1984): 44.

Part III Introduction

1. Carl A. Taube and Sally A. Barrett, eds. *Mental Health, United States 1985* (Rockville, Md.: National Institute of Mental Health, 1985), p. 106.

2. *New York Times,* 5 March 1989, sec. 4, p. 20. This advertisement was placed by the New York City Department of Mental Health, Mental Retardation and Alcoholism Services. Emphasis added.

3. The American Psychiatric Association publishes a standard manual of psychiatric diagnoses: *Diagnostic and Statistical Manual of Mental Disorders,* 3d ed., rev. (Washington, D.C.: American Psychiatric Association Press, 1980), known as *DSM-III-R.* It is followed by everyone, at least on paper, if only because the regulatory bodies and certain funding sources require its use.

Chapter 11

1. Paul Starr, *The Social Transformation of American Medicine* (NY: Basic Books, 1982), pp. 398–99.

2. H. Robert Cathcart, "Issues Facing American Hospitals," *Hospital & Community Psychiatry* 30 (1979): 194.

3. Two excellent sources for information about the young adult chronic patient

population, both prepared at the time this group first became prominent in practice settings, are in the July 1981 issue of *Hospital & Community Psychiatry* (vol. 32), which included a special section devoted to the young adult chronic mental patient in the community, and Bert Pepper and Hilary Ryglewicz, eds., *New Directions for Mental Health Services: The Young Adult Chronic Patient*, no. 14 (San Francisco, Calif.: Jossey-Bass, 1982).

4. Bert Pepper, Hilary Ryglewicz, and Michael C. Kirshner, "The Uninstitutionalized Generation: A New Breed of Psychiatric Patient," in *The Young Adult Chronic Patient*, ed. Pepper and Ryglewicz, pp. 3–4.

5. Leona L. Bachrach, "Program Planning for Young Adult Chronic Patients," in *The Young Adult Chronic Patient*, ed. Pepper and Ryglewicz, p. 100. Bachrach despairs, not for the first time and always to little apparent effect, of our ever giving up our romance with the "model program," in which, she says, "we persevere with little questions and keep looking for new and better models" even as we "fail to ask big questions, on a systems level" (p. 107).

6. Steven P. Segal, Jim Baumohl, and Elsie Johnson, "Falling through the Cracks: Mental Disorder and Social Margin in a Young Vagrant Population," *Social Problems* 24 (1977): 387–400.

7. Pepper, Ryglewicz, and Kirshner, "The Uninstitutionalized Generation," p. 7. The authors found 24 percent of their 300 patients to have known criminal backgrounds.

8. Ibid. The researchers found 37 percent of their patients had a known history of marijuana use, 28 percent a known history of other drug abuse, and 37 percent a known history of alcohol abuse—with some overlap, clearly. See also John L. Sheets, James A. Prevost, and Jacqueline Reihman, "The Young Adult Chronic Patient: Three Hypothesized Subgroups," in *The Young Adult Chronic Patient*, ed. Pepper and Ryglewicz, pp. 16–17. The authors surveyed 369 young adult chronics in 1979 and found 25 percent reported drug and/or alcohol abuse, as compared to 11 percent of their control group, the middle-aged chronic patients treated at the same facility. We are just now, in 1990, developing specialized services to this group of patients, who are now known as MICA (mentally ill chemical abusers).

9. The systemic failure to address the needs of the chronically mentally ill is so widely deplored in the literature that documenting it is superfluous—read any article with the term *deinstitutionalization* or *chronically mentally ill* in the title. Two recent examples, however, include Howard H. Goldman and Joseph P. Morrissey, "The Alchemy of Mental Health Policy: Homelessness and the Fourth Cycle of Reform," *American Journal of Public Health* 75 (1985): 727–31; and Leona L. Bachrach and H. Richard Lamb, "What Have We Learned from Deinstitutionalization?" *Psychiatric Annals* 19 (1989): 12–21.

10. To translate: JCAHO is the Joint Commission on the Accreditation of Health Care Organizations. U.R. is Utilization Review, a required system of internal checks to determine if a program's services are both necessary and provided in a cost-efficient manner; U.R. is supposed to prevent abuse by guaranteeing that those who get

served actually need it. Q.A. stands for Quality Assurance, a required system of internal checks on the adequacy of a program's work. "Quality assurance" is a misnomer, in my experience—*quantity* assurance would be more accurate, since what usually happens is that "episodes" of service get counted to make sure they are taking place "in a timely fashion" or at all; for all anyone knows, the quality of the service could be the worst in the world, but at least we know, and can *prove,* that it is taking place. Credentialing and the development of both networks and protocols are regulation-inspired tasks designed to ensure that a program's staff is documented to have the required training and that its services will follow certain guidelines in set situations. Here, too, the staff can be totally inept and unable to speak the language of their patients, say, but at least the program can *prove* it has X number of licensed physicians or social workers. It is entirely possible that the staff never actually follows its protocols (who, in an emergency, takes the time to thumb through a fifty-pound policy and procedure manual?), but the important thing is to *have* them when the auditors come around.

11. Jerome M. Goldsmith, personal interview, 14 February 1986. Goldsmith was the executive vice-president of the Jewish Board of Family and Children's Services, New York, N.Y.

12. I promised not to reveal my source, but this story is true; my source was present at the creation.

13. Alvin L. Schorr, "Public Policy and Private Interest," in *The Use and Abuse of Social Science,* 2d ed., ed. Irving Louis Horowitz (New Brunswick, N.J.: Transaction Books, 1975), p. 32.

14. E. Fuller Torrey, Sidney M. Wolfe, and Laurie M. Flynn, *Care of the Seriously Mentally Ill: A Rating of State Programs,* 2d ed. (n.p.: Public Citizen Health Research Group and the National Alliance for the Mentally Ill, 1988). "Public Citizen" is the name of Ralph Nader's consumer-lobby organization, and the National Alliance for the Mentally Ill (NAMI) is a self-help organization made up of the families and friends of the mentally ill.

15. Governor's Health Advisory Council, *Alternative Futures for Mental Health Services in New York: 2000 and Beyond* (Albany, N.Y.: New York State Health Planning Commission, 1984); Governor's Select Commission on the Future of the State–Local Mental Health System, *Final Report* (Albany, N.Y.: The Commission, November 1984).

16. New York State Commission on Quality of Care for the Mentally Disabled, *Discharge Practices of Inpatient Psychiatric Facilities* (New York: The Commission, August 1988).

17. Advisory Board to the New York City Department of Mental Health, Mental Retardation, and Alcoholism Services, *Deinstitutionalization and the Community: Final Report of the Interagency Task Force on Problems of Deinstitutionalization and the Chronically Mentally Ill* (New York: The Board, July 1978).

18. Ibid., p. 10; and Torrey, Wolfe, and Flynn, *Care of the Seriously Mentally Ill,* p. 96.

19. Governor's Select Commission, *Final Report,* pp. 15–16.
20. Torrey, Wolfe, and Flynn, *Care of the Seriously Mentally Ill,* p. 2.
21. See John A. Talbott, "Editor's Notes," in *Unified Mental Health Systems: Utopia Unrealized,* ed. John A. Talbott (San Francisco, Calif.: Jossey-Bass, 1983), p. 2. See also Torrey, Wolfe, and Flynn, *Care of the Seriously Mentally Ill,* p. 11.
22. Talbott, "Editor's Notes," p. 3.
23. For a book on the subject, see Lonnie R. Snowden, ed., *Reaching the Underserved: Mental Health Needs of Neglected Populations* (Beverly Hills, Calif.: Sage, 1982).
24. For an unforgettable look at what life is like for a career welfare recipient, see Susan Sheehan, *A Welfare Mother* (New York: Mentor, 1977). The material first appeared in *The New Yorker* 51, 29 September 1975, 42–99.
25. Compare the various strategies employed by "Mrs. Santana" in *A Welfare Mother* to cope with welfare in the early 1970s, when it was supposedly easier to get assistance than it is now, in the wake of Reaganomics; see Sheehan, *A Welfare Mother,* pp. 80–88.
26. Articles about this population are beginning to appear more and more regularly in journals read by clinicians and administrators. See, for example, Ron Jemelka, Eric Trupin, and John A. Chiles, "The Mentally Ill in Prisons: A Review," *Hospital & Community Psychiatry* 40 (1989): 481–91.
27. Torrey, Wolfe, and Flynn, *Care of the Seriously Mentally Ill,* p. 13. Theirs is just one example; everyone who looks at the system and its funding says roughly the same thing, including me. For another example, see Governor's Select Commission, *Final Report,* pp. 13–15. Jeffrey Rubin takes a similar position but, as befits an economist writing for clinicians, is much more understanding of the fiscal realities of mental health funding. See Rubin, "Financing Care for the Seriously Mentally Ill," in *Improving Mental Health Services: What the Social Sciences Can Tell Us,* ed. David Mechanic (San Francisco, Calif.: Jossey-Bass, 1987), pp. 112–15, for his suggested reforms.
28. Haroutan M. Babigian, "Budgeting," in *Psychiatric Administration,* ed. John A. Talbott and Seymour R. Kaplan (New York: Grune & Stratton, 1983), p. 341.
29. Torrey, Wolfe, and Flynn, *Care of the Seriously Mentally Ill,* p. 12.
30. Bruce Vladeck, extemporaneous remarks made at the Annual Meeting of the American Orthopsychiatric Association, New York, N.Y., 4 April 1989, when he presented his paper "The Scandal of Homelessness." Vladeck is president of the United Hospital Fund of New York and chairman of the National Academy of Science, Committee on Health Care for Homeless People. He is also the author of an excellent book on nursing homes, *Unloving Care: The Nursing Home Tragedy* (New York: Basic Books, 1980).
31. This discouraging comment came to me from an anonymous student's written evaluation of a course I taught on social theory in a doctoral program for clinical social workers. It was fairly representative of the attitude held by much of the class, I am sorry to say.
32. Sigmund Freud, "The Future of an Illusion, Civilization and Its Discontents,"

The Standard Edition, vol. 21, trans. James Strachey (London: Hogarth, 1961), p. 114.

33. Torrey, Wolfe, and Flynn, "Care of the Seriously Mentally Ill," p. 13.
34. David Mechanic, "Editor's Notes," *Improving Mental Health Services*, ed. Mechanic, p. 1.
35. Recently I heard an unusually detailed fantasy about auditors and planners. The author had worked out a particularly intricate theory about how old WASP families had found they each had a son left over after sending one to Wall Street, one to the army, and one to the church; but the fourth son had no particular capabilities to speak of. In desperation, the families turned to old private charities and arranged for their inept sons to become planners of social services. A variant of this theory involved the notion that some years ago, Harvard and Stanford found they did not have enough students to fill up their business schools, so they gladly accepted the same inept WASP sons, made them M.B.A.'s, and placed them in public policy jobs where they could do the least harm. This fantasy was told by a psychologist as a joke (but not really), to explain why mental health programs have to keep certain statistical records.

Chapter 12

1. William A. Hargreaves and C. Clifford Attkisson, "Program Evaluation," in *Psychiatric Administration*, ed. John A. Talbott and Seymour R. Kaplan (New York: Grune & Stratton, 1983), p. 287.
2. Ibid., pp. 290–91; all these examples are from table 20–1.
3. Ibid., p. 288.
4. Community Support Services (CSS) was introduced by New York State in 1977 as "a mechanism for building comprehensive and integrated mental health services for a chronically mentally ill population . . . intended to forge a partnership among service agencies whose common goal is meeting the community living needs of the target clientele," in the words of the New York State Office of Mental Health. New York State Governor's Select Commission on the Future of the State–Local Mental Health System, *Final Report* (Albany, N.Y.: The Commission, 1984), p. 14.
5. Ibid. Known as "620," this rather specialized service was introduced in 1974 under chapter 620 of the Mental Hygiene Law. "Local governments or voluntary agencies having a contract to provide services to persons who were patients in a state facility for a period of five or more years following January 1, 1969" were given 100 percent funding for "approved net operating costs."
6. All of publicly funded programming sooner or later involves the figuring of the unit cost. Very simply, it represents the amount of money it costs a program to provide a unit of service to one patient—"unit" being one clinic visit, for example, or one day in a day hospital. To arrive at it, one adds up all relevant costs and divides

by the average daily attendance. Unit cost is one example of something called "prospective reimbursement." For a more technical explanation of how a relatively simple concept is made incredibly complicated through implementation, see Robert C. Brice, "Financing of Psychiatric Services," in *Psychiatric Administration*, ed. Talbott and Kaplan, pp. 360–62.

7. In 1964, the Joint Commission on Mental Illness and Health formed a study group to recommend new approaches to patient care in line with the new-found interest in community-based care for the mentally ill. In a discouragingly prescient, even prophetic, report, the authors pointed out that there was no aftercare system or network in place to discharge patients to, merely "a service in name only. . . . Much of what is available is nominal, rendered in compliance with the law or the policy attending the release of patients from state mental hospitals" (p. 207). They suggested that the best one could hope for in the way of community-based care for the seriously mentally ill might well be programs that were content to foster overdependency and something they called "psychiatric hypochondriasis" among patients whose only role in life was to be mentally ill, wherever they were. Morris R. Schwartz and Charlotte Green Schwartz, *Social Approaches to Mental Patient Care* (New York: Columbia University Press, 1964), pp. 207–12.

8. Some program administrators are like this, too. I once worked for one who was convinced on the basis of conjecture that all the staff were "underdiagnosing" patients: he had decided there "had to be" more schizophrenics and manic-depressives among our patients than was the case, according to those who actually worked with them; and he was forever berating middle management to "make sure patients were being diagnosed correctly" (that is, his way). So much for the science of clinical diagnosis.

9. See New York State Commission on Quality of Care for the Mentally Disabled, *A Review of Living Conditions in Nine New York State Psychiatric Centers* (Albany, N.Y.: The Commission, December 1984). The commission's reports are unusual for the breed in that they are full of anecdotes about and case histories of real patients. I have never been involved in one of their audits, so I have no idea whether they are as interested in the realities of practice as their reports suggest.

10. *New York Times,* 11 June 1989, sec. 4, p. 23.

11. Ethel M. Bonn, "Accreditation and Regulation of Psychiatric Facilities," in *Psychiatric Administration,* ed. Talbott and Kaplan, p. 299.

12. Ibid., pp. 300–301.

13. Ibid., p. 305.

14. Ibid., pp. 304–5. Emphasis in the original.

15. The conference was sponsored jointly by Mental Health Association in New York State, Inc., and the Rehabilitation Research and Training Center for Psychiatrically Disabled Individuals at Albert Einstein College of Medicine, Bronx, N.Y.

16. Laura Ziegler, "Survivor's Rights," at the same conference cited in note 15 above. Ziegler represented a group called Project Release, which is based in New York City.

17. Alex R. Rodriguez, "An Introduction to Quality Assurance in Mental Health," in *Handbook of Quality Assurance in Mental Health,* ed. George Stricker and Alex R. Rodriguez (New York: Plenum, 1988), p. 15. Emphasis added.
18. See E. Fuller Torrey, Sidney M. Wolfe, and Laurie M. Flynn, *Care of the Seriously Mentally Ill: A Rating of State Programs,* 2d ed. (n.p.: Public Citizen Research Group and the National Alliance for the Mentally Ill, 1988), for a state-by-state breakdown of rehabilitation and housing services available to the seriously mentally ill. According to them, only a handful of the very smallest states—Rhode Island, New Hampshire, Maine, and Wisconsin—are doing well in actually providing what they all have claimed to believe in for thirty years. See also New York State Commission on Quality of Care for the Mentally Disabled, *Discharge Practices of Inpatient Psychiatric Facilities* (New York: The Commission, August 1988), which points out that New York State still has only about 6,000 supervised community beds in its system, even though for years documentation has shown the need to be much greater.
19. *New York Times,* 13 June 1989, p. B1.
20. Rodriguez, "Quality Assurance," p. 26.
21. Robert C. Brice, "Financing of Psychiatric Services," in *Psychiatric Administration,* ed. Talbott and Kaplan, p. 362.
22. Ibid., p. 365.
23. New York State Commission on Quality of Care for the Mentally Disabled, *Annual Report, 1987–1988* (New York: The Commission, 1988), p. 56.
24. Ibid., p. 44.

Epilogue

1. "Goals and Philosophy Statement," National Alliance of Mental Patients, Sioux Falls, S.D. (n.d.). Photocopy.

INDEX